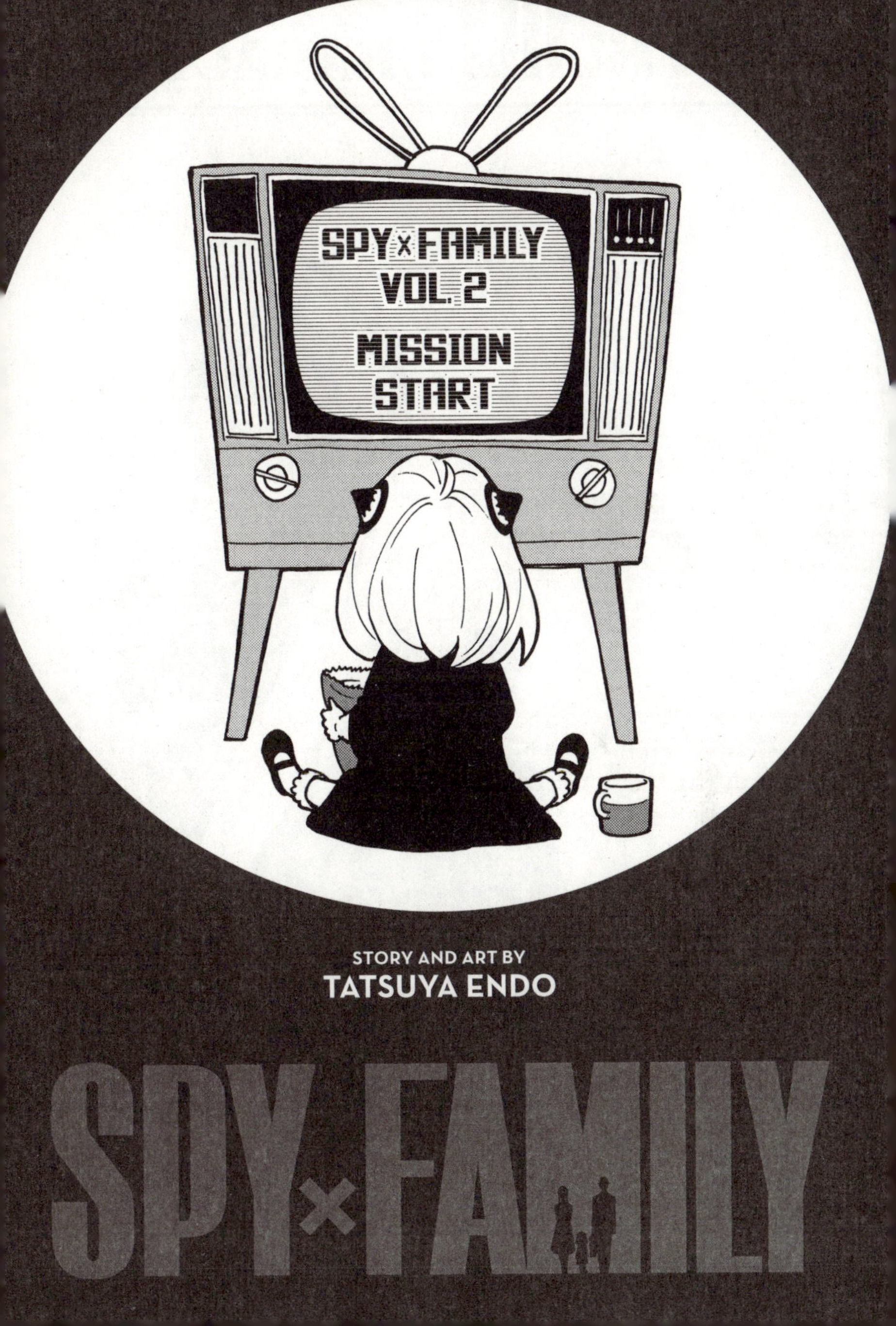
SPY×FAMILY
VOL. 2
MISSION
START

STORY AND ART BY

TATSUYA ENDO

SPY×FAMILY

SPY×FAMILY CHARACTERS

LOID FORGER

ROLE: **Husband**
OCCUPATION:
Psychiatrist

A spy and master of disguise covertly serving the nation of Westalis. His code name is "Twilight."

ANYA FORGER

ROLE: **Daughter**

A telepath whose abilities were created in an experiment conducted by a certain organization. She can read the minds of others.

YOR FORGER

ROLE: **Wife**
OCCUPATION:
City Hall Clerk

Lives a secret life as an assassin. Her code name is "Thorn Princess."

MISSION

OPERATION STRIX

Spy on Donovan Desmond, a dangerous figure who threatens to disrupt peace between the East and West. Must gain entry into the prestigious Eden Academy to breach the target's inner circle.

TARGET

DONOVAN DESMOND

The focus of Operation Strix. Chairman of Ostania's National Unity Party.

KEY PEOPLE

FRANKY

Intelligence asset who works with Twilight.

HENRY HENDERSON

Housemaster at Eden Academy.

STORY

Westalis secret agent Twilight receives orders to uncover the plans of Donovan Desmond, the warmongering chairman of Ostania's National Unity Party. To do so, Twilight must pose as Loid Forger, create a fake family and enroll his child at the prestigious Eden Academy. However, by sheer coincidence, the daughter he selects from an orphanage is secretly a telepath! Also, the woman who agrees to be in a sham marriage with him is secretly an assassin!

While concealing their true identities from one another, the three set about gaining Anya's admission to Eden Academy. An animal stampede disrupts things on the day of the admissions interview, but disaster is averted thanks to Loid's cool composure, Anya's telepathy and Yor's physical prowess. Their efforts earn the Forgers the admiration of Housemaster Henderson. But when a faculty member poses a cruel question to Anya, Loid smashes a table in anger! Will that ruin Anya's chances of being offered a spot at Eden? The fate of the world hangs in the balance!

CONTENTS

SPY×FAMILY ②

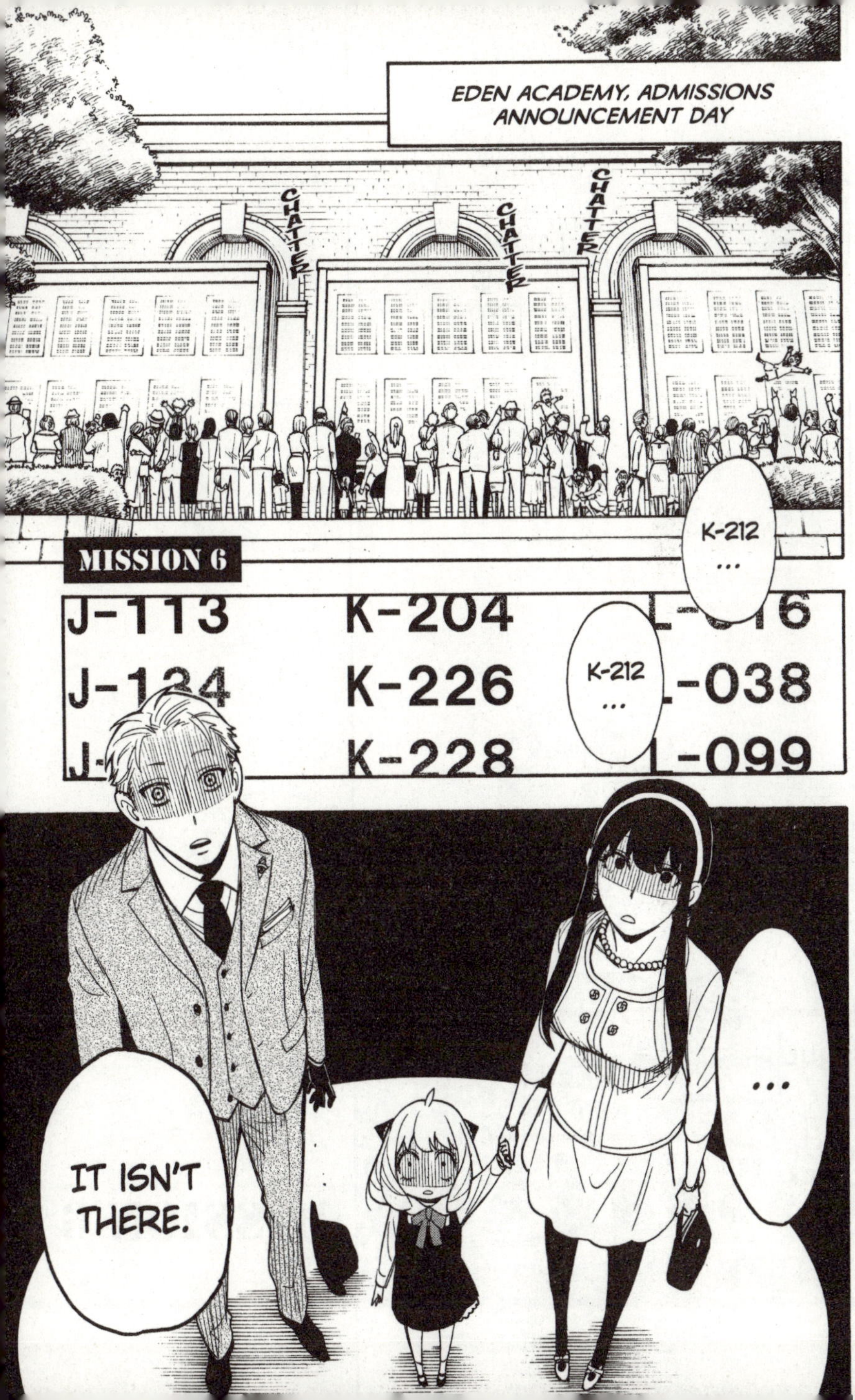
EDEN ACADEMY, ADMISSIONS ANNOUNCEMENT DAY
CHATTER
CHATTER
CHATTER
K-212 ...
MISSION 6
J-113
K-204
K-226
K-228
L-038
L-099
K-212 ...
...
IT ISN'T THERE.

TODAY'S THE DAY!

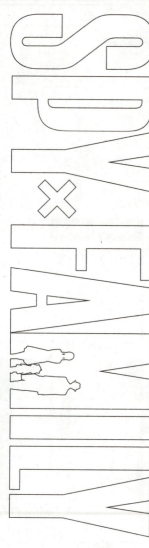

SPY×FAMILY

MISSION 6

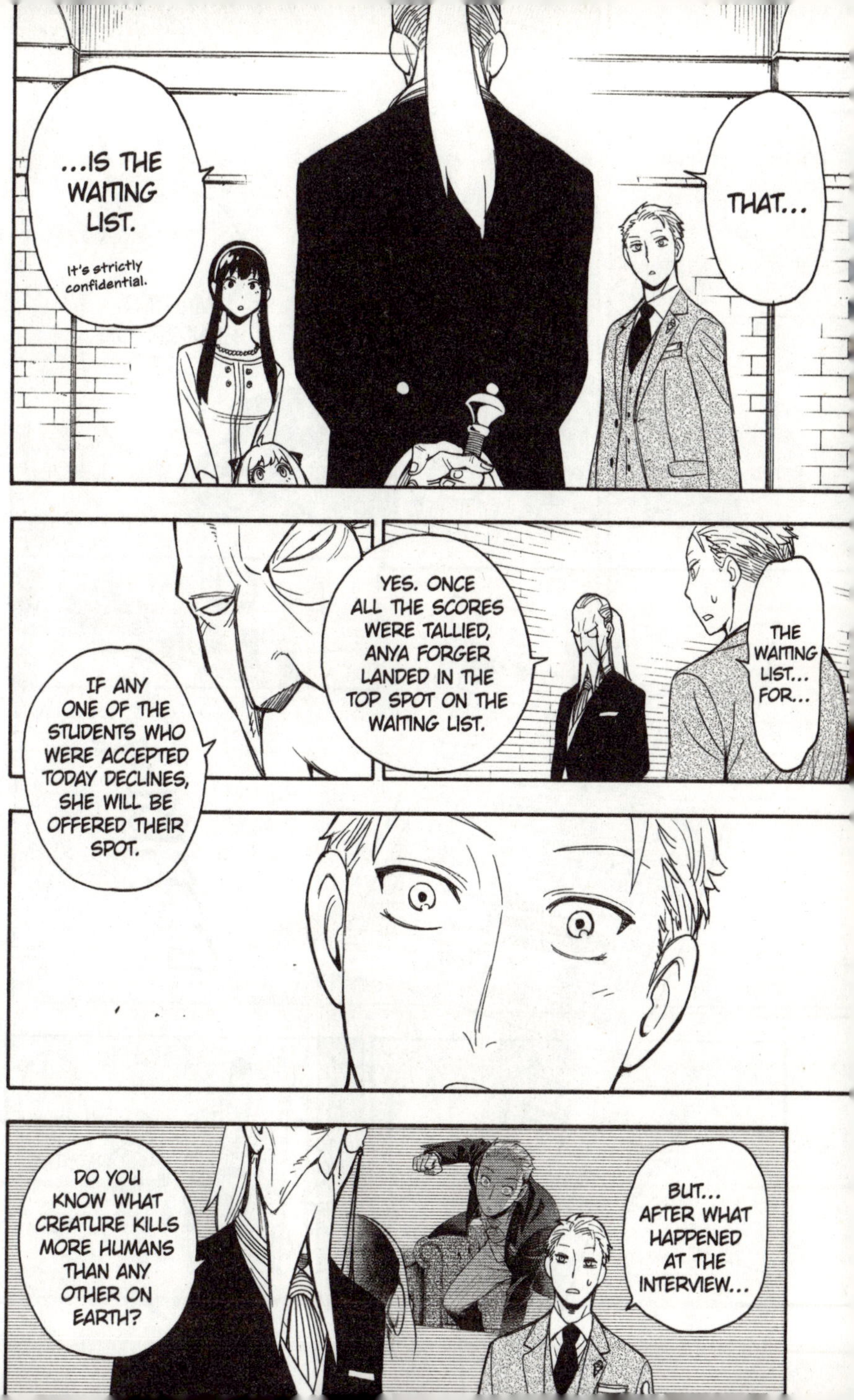
THAT...
...IS THE WAITING LIST.
It's strictly confidential.
THE WAITING LIST... FOR...
YES. ONCE ALL THE SCORES WERE TALLIED, ANYA FORGER LANDED IN THE TOP SPOT ON THE WAITING LIST.
IF ANY ONE OF THE STUDENTS WHO WERE ACCEPTED TODAY DECLINES, SHE WILL BE OFFERED THEIR SPOT.
BUT... AFTER WHAT HAPPENED AT THE INTERVIEW...
DO YOU KNOW WHAT CREATURE KILLS MORE HUMANS THAN ANY OTHER ON EARTH?

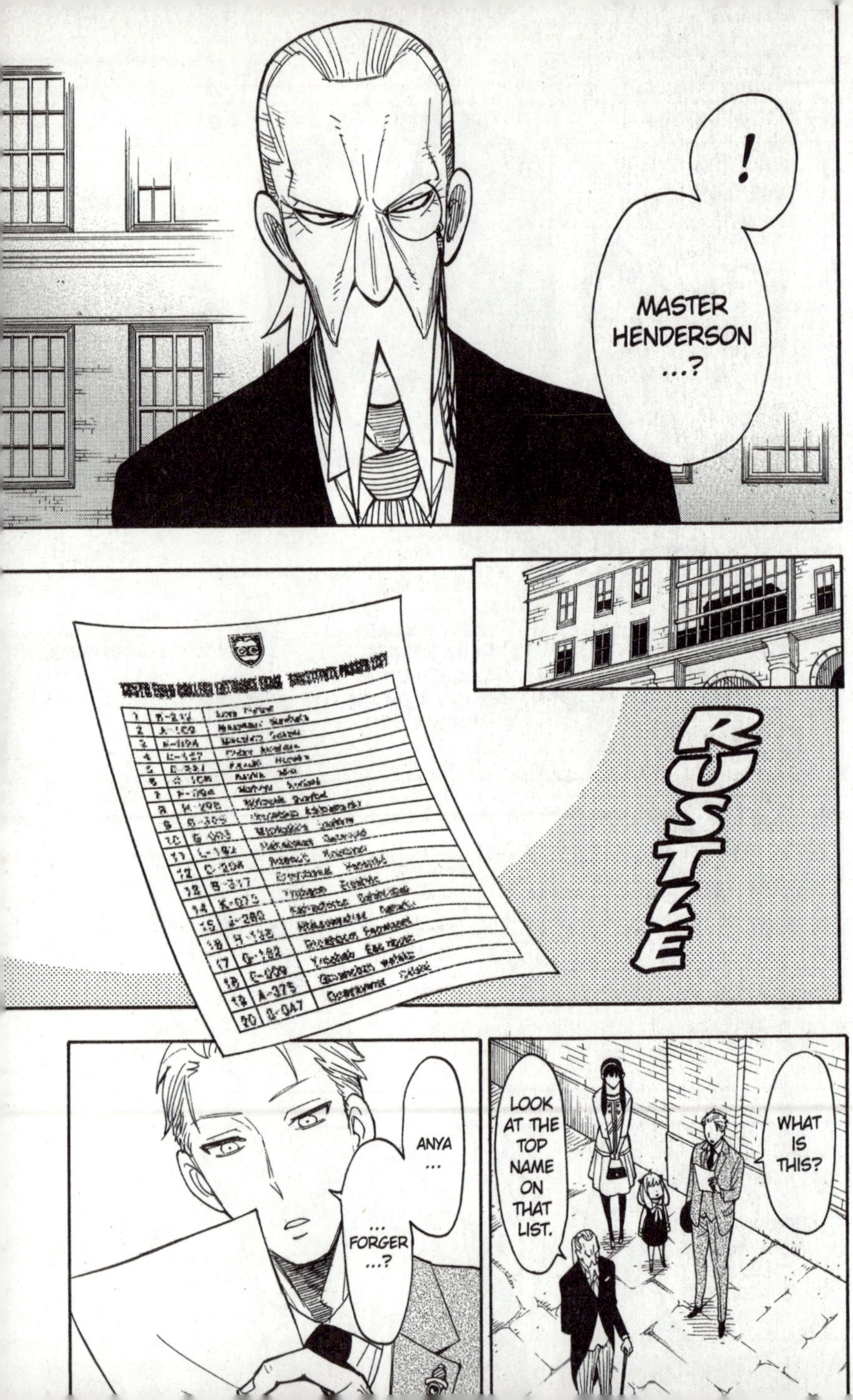
!
MASTER HENDERSON ...?
RUSTLE
WHAT IS THIS?
LOOK AT THE TOP NAME ON THAT LIST.
ANYA ...
... FORGER ...?

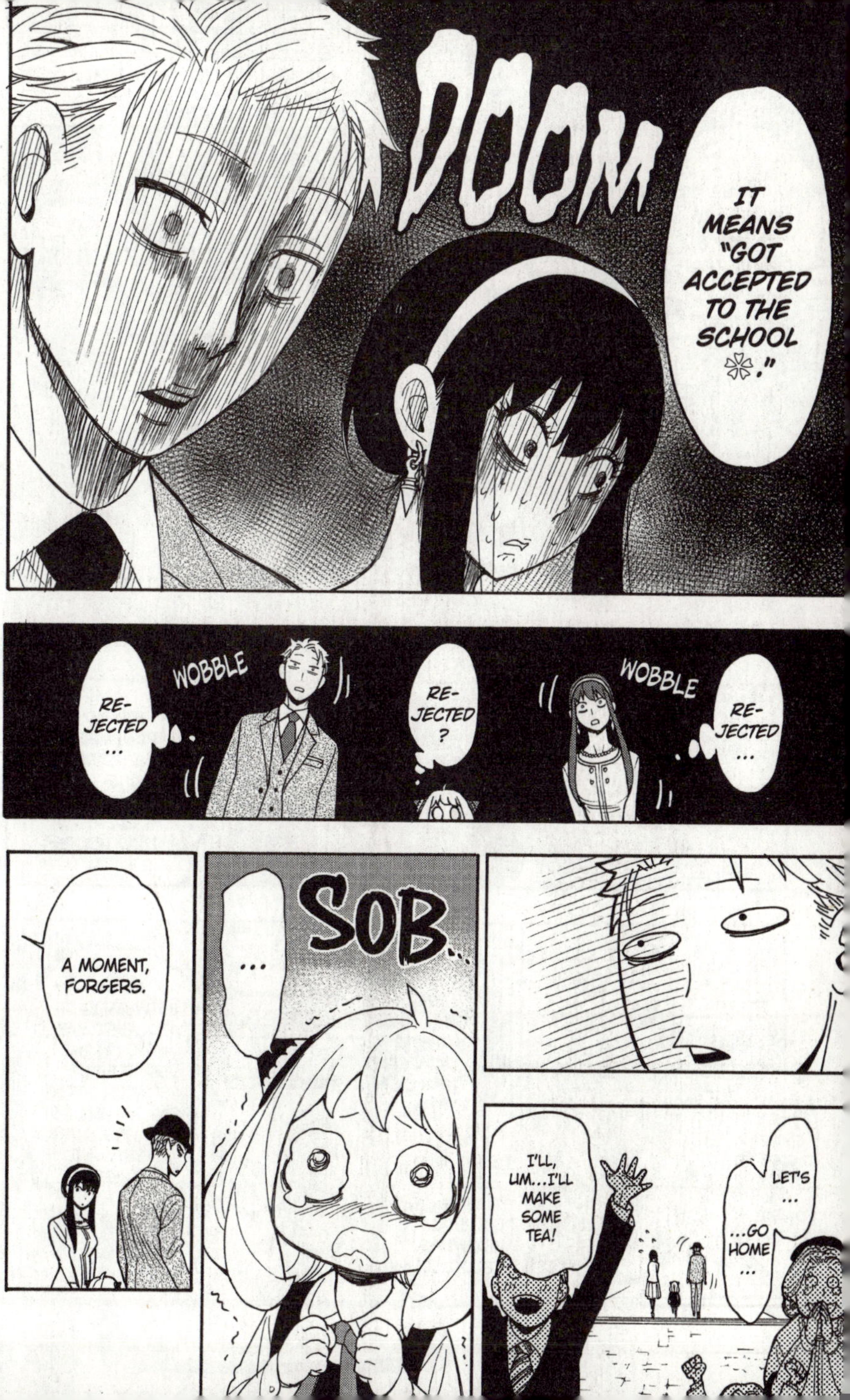
IT MEANS "GOT ACCEPTED TO THE SCHOOL ✿."
DOOM
RE-JECTED ...
WOBBLE
RE-JECTED ?
WOBBLE
RE-JECTED ...
LET'S ... ...GO HOME ...
I'LL, UM...I'LL MAKE SOME TEA!
SOB...
...
A MOMENT, FORGERS.

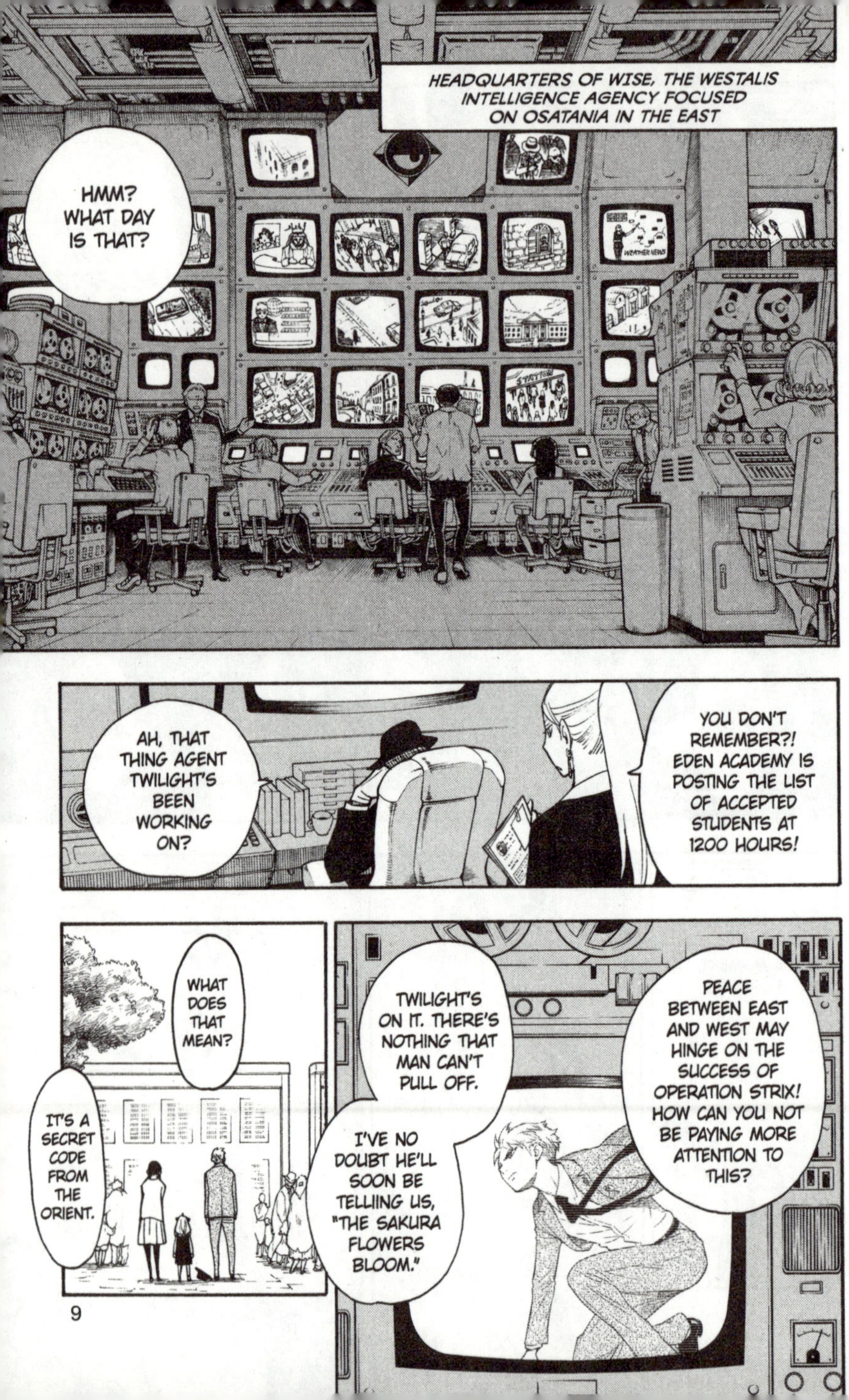
HEADQUARTERS OF WISE, THE WESTALIS INTELLIGENCE AGENCY FOCUSED ON OSATANIA IN THE EAST
HMM? WHAT DAY IS THAT?
YOU DON'T REMEMBER?! EDEN ACADEMY IS POSTING THE LIST OF ACCEPTED STUDENTS AT 1200 HOURS!
AH, THAT THING AGENT TWILIGHT'S BEEN WORKING ON?
PEACE BETWEEN EAST AND WEST MAY HINGE ON THE SUCCESS OF OPERATION STRIX! HOW CAN YOU NOT BE PAYING MORE ATTENTION TO THIS?
TWILIGHT'S ON IT. THERE'S NOTHING THAT MAN CAN'T PULL OFF.
I'VE NO DOUBT HE'LL SOON BE TELLIING US, "THE SAKURA FLOWERS BLOOM."
WHAT DOES THAT MEAN?
IT'S A SECRET CODE FROM THE ORIENT.

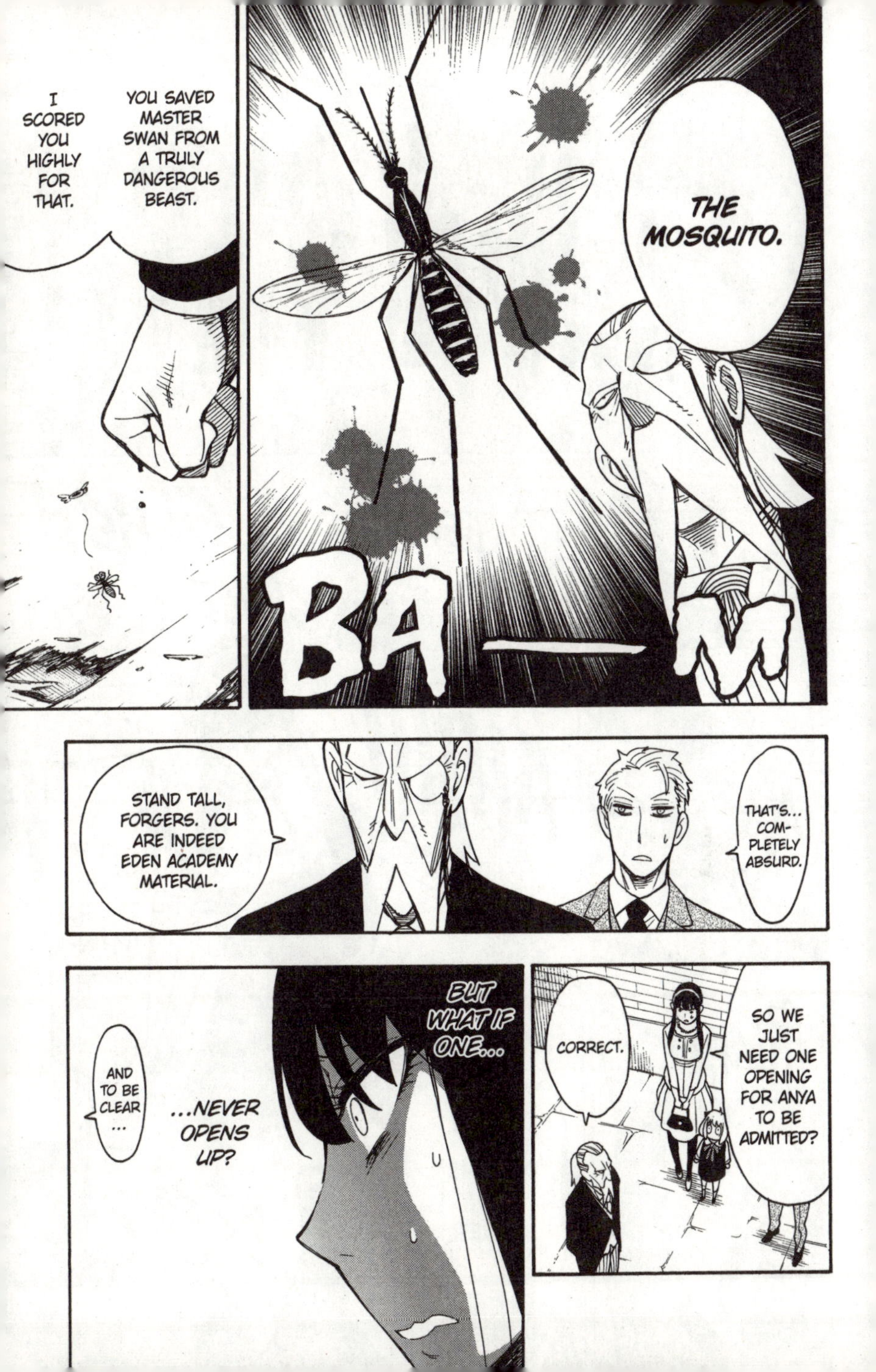
THE MOSQUITO.
BA—M
YOU SAVED MASTER SWAN FROM A TRULY DANGEROUS BEAST.
I SCORED YOU HIGHLY FOR THAT.
THAT'S... COMPLETELY ABSURD.
STAND TALL, FORGERS. YOU ARE INDEED EDEN ACADEMY MATERIAL.
SO WE JUST NEED ONE OPENING FOR ANYA TO BE ADMITTED?
CORRECT.
BUT WHAT IF ONE...
...NEVER OPENS UP?
AND TO BE CLEAR...

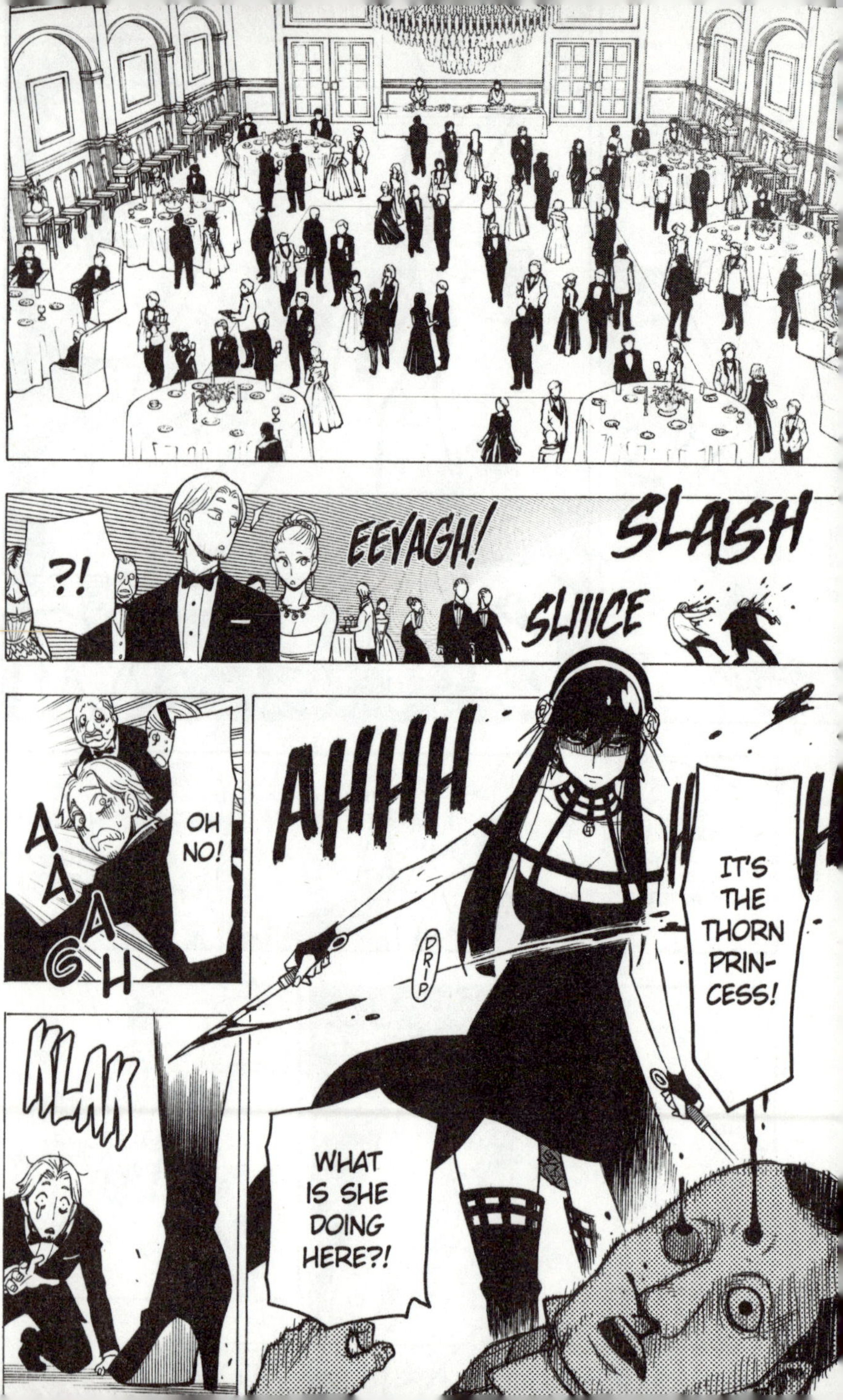
SLASH
SLIIICE
EEYAGH!
?!
IT'S THE THORN PRIN-CESS!
AHHHH
DRIP
WHAT IS SHE DOING HERE?!
OH NO!
AAAGAH
KLAK

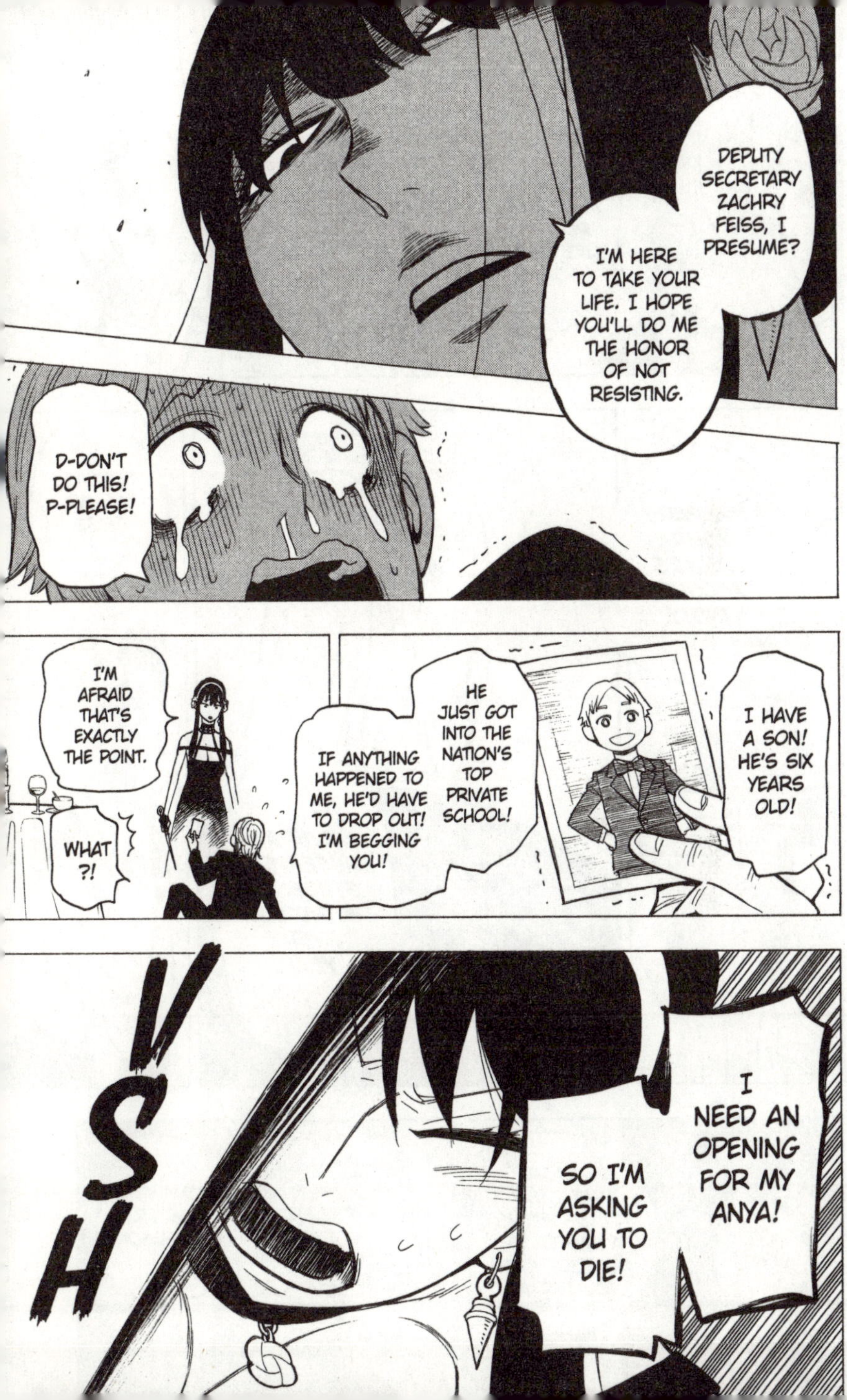
DEPUTY SECRETARY ZACHRY FEISS, I PRESUME?
I'M HERE TO TAKE YOUR LIFE. I HOPE YOU'LL DO ME THE HONOR OF NOT RESISTING.
D-DON'T DO THIS! P-PLEASE!
I HAVE A SON! HE'S SIX YEARS OLD!
HE JUST GOT INTO THE NATION'S TOP PRIVATE SCHOOL!
IF ANYTHING HAPPENED TO ME, HE'D HAVE TO DROP OUT! I'M BEGGING YOU!
I'M AFRAID THAT'S EXACTLY THE POINT.
WHAT?!
I NEED AN OPENING FOR MY ANYA!
SO I'M ASKING YOU TO DIE!
VSH

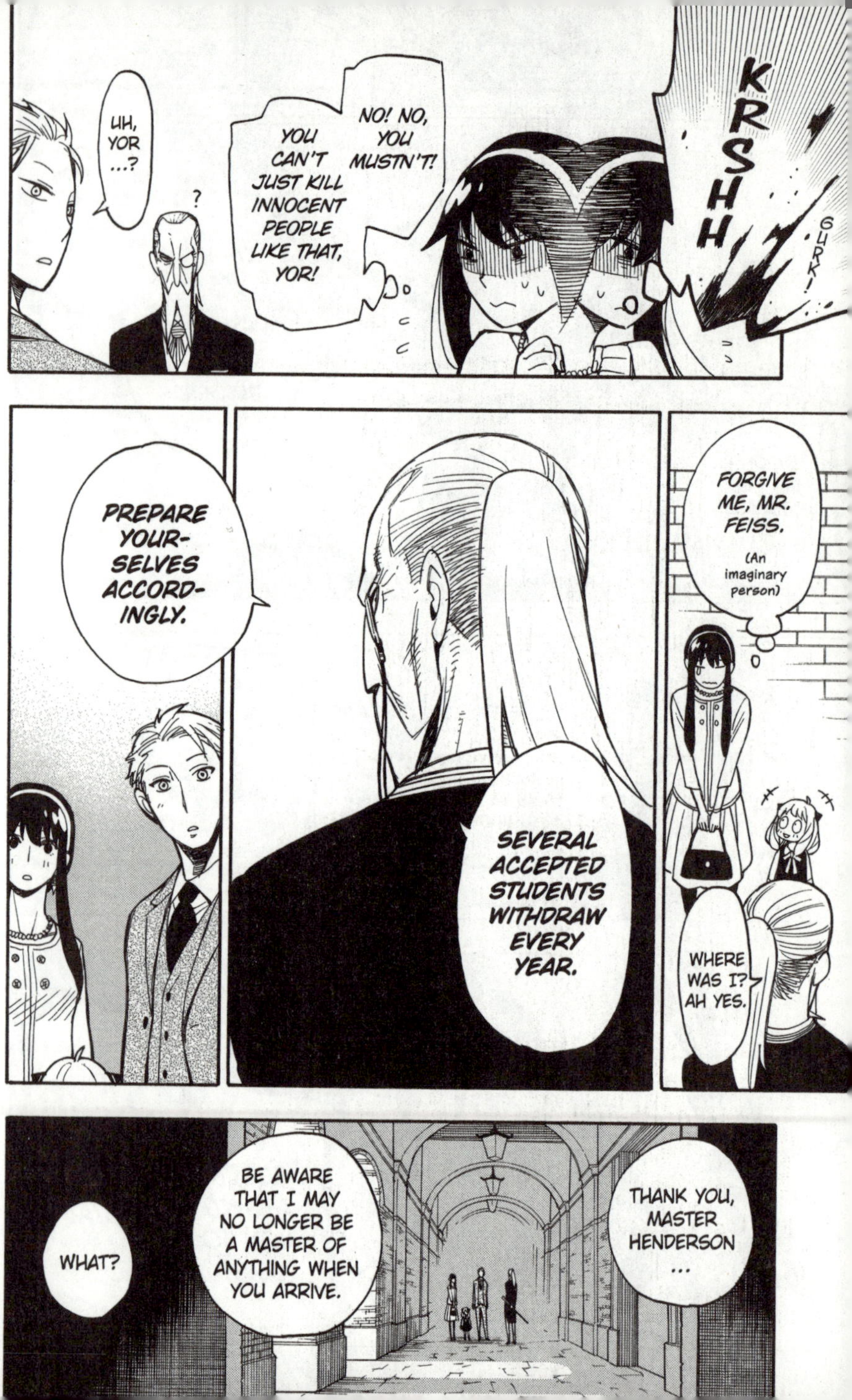
KRSHH
GURK!
NO! NO, YOU MUSTN'T! YOU CAN'T JUST KILL INNOCENT PEOPLE LIKE THAT, YOR!
?
UH, YOR ...?
FORGIVE ME, MR. FEISS.
(An imaginary person)
WHERE WAS I? AH YES.
SEVERAL ACCEPTED STUDENTS WITHDRAW EVERY YEAR.
PREPARE YOUR-SELVES ACCORD-INGLY.
THANK YOU, MASTER HENDERSON ...
BE AWARE THAT I MAY NO LONGER BE A MASTER OF ANYTHING WHEN YOU ARRIVE.
WHAT?

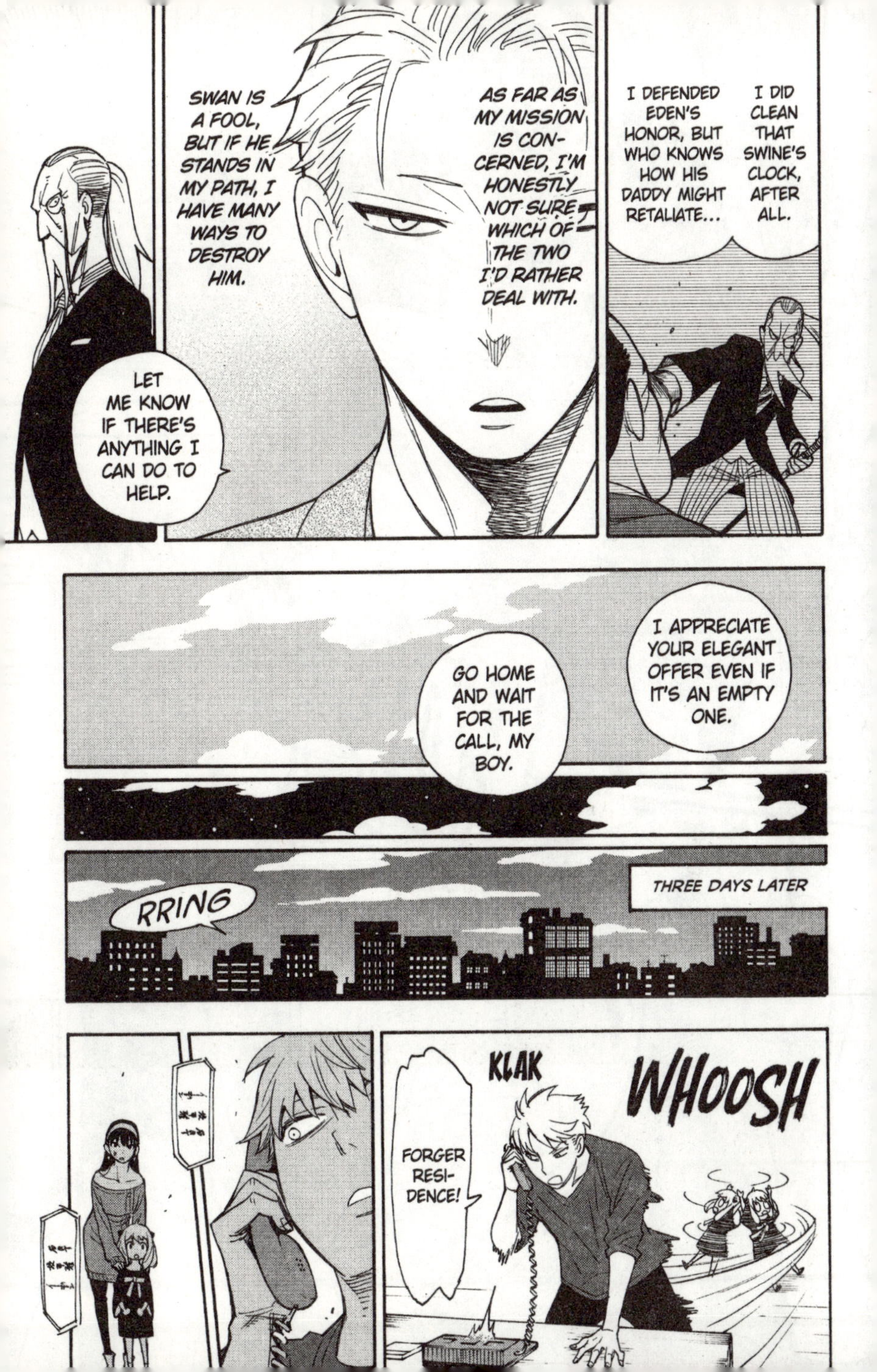
I DID CLEAN THAT SWINE'S CLOCK, AFTER ALL.
I DEFENDED EDEN'S HONOR, BUT WHO KNOWS HOW HIS DADDY MIGHT RETALIATE...
AS FAR AS MY MISSION IS CONCERNED, I'M HONESTLY NOT SURE WHICH OF THE TWO I'D RATHER DEAL WITH.
SWAN IS A FOOL, BUT IF HE STANDS IN MY PATH, I HAVE MANY WAYS TO DESTROY HIM.
LET ME KNOW IF THERE'S ANYTHING I CAN DO TO HELP.
I APPRECIATE YOUR ELEGANT OFFER EVEN IF IT'S AN EMPTY ONE.
GO HOME AND WAIT FOR THE CALL, MY BOY.
THREE DAYS LATER
RRING
WHOOSH
KLAK
FORGER RESIDENCE!

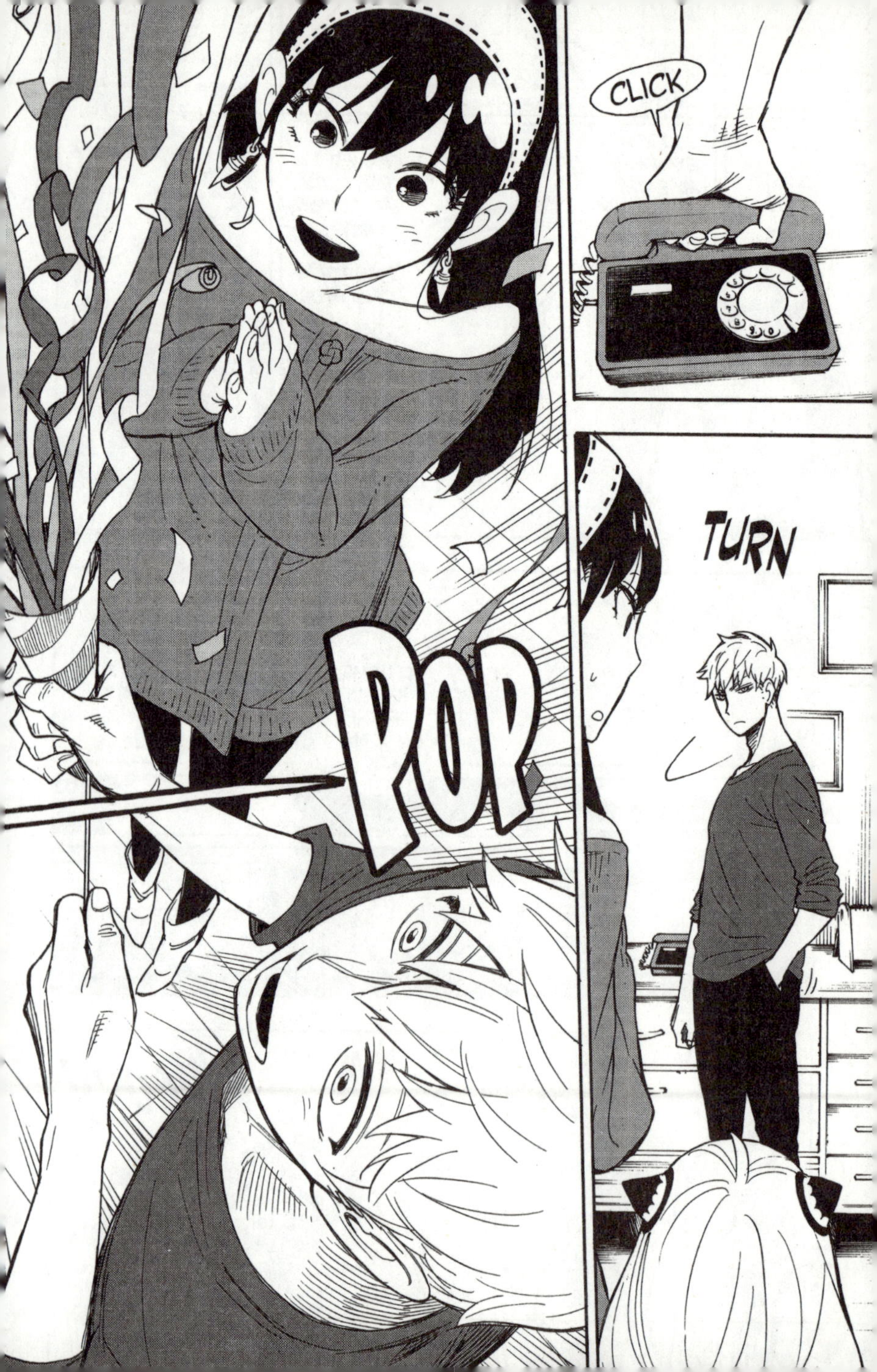
CLICK
TURN
POP

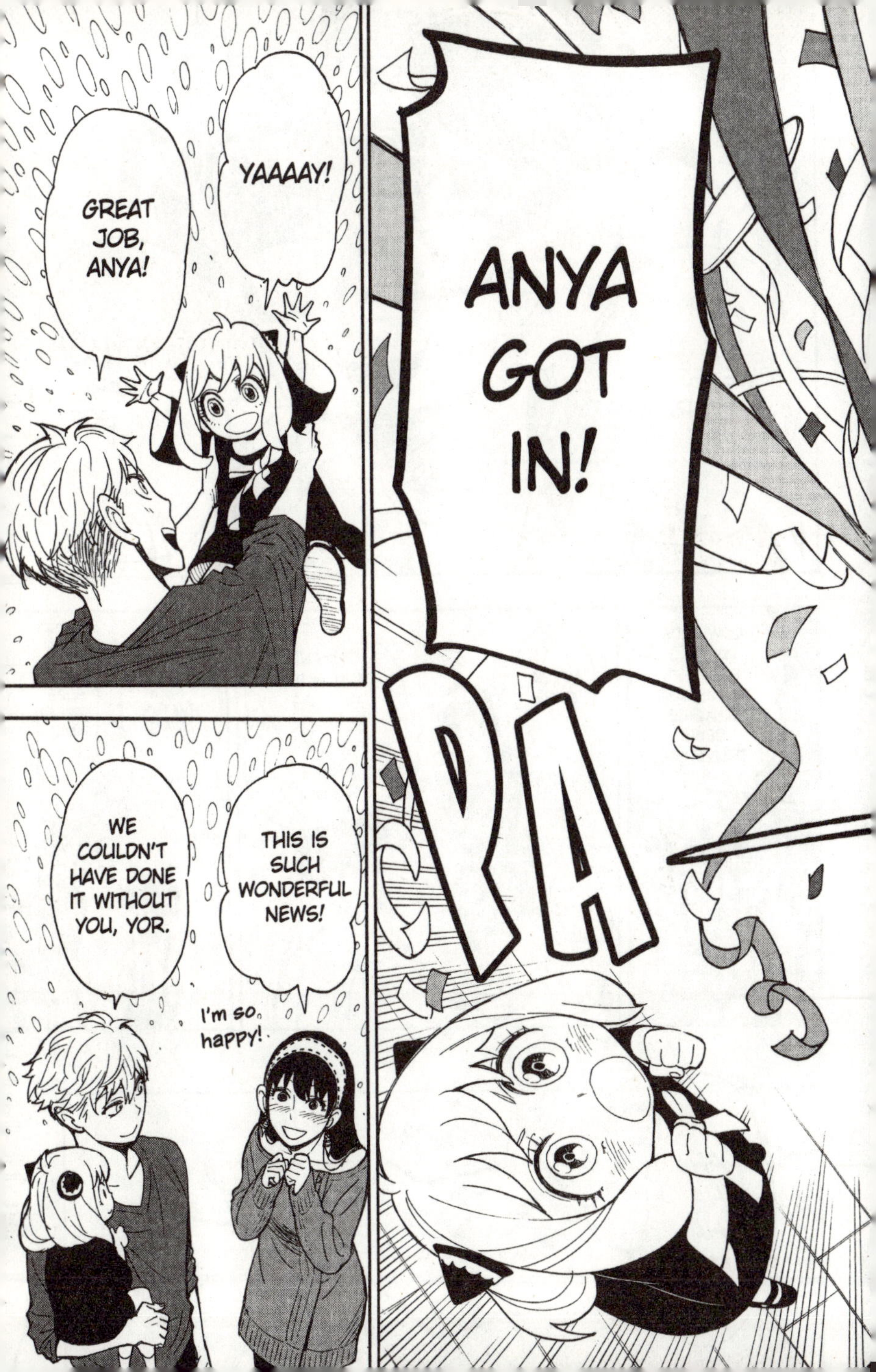
ANYA GOT IN!
PA
YAAAAY!
GREAT JOB, ANYA!
THIS IS SUCH WONDERFUL NEWS!
WE COULDN'T HAVE DONE IT WITHOUT YOU, YOR.
I'm so happy!

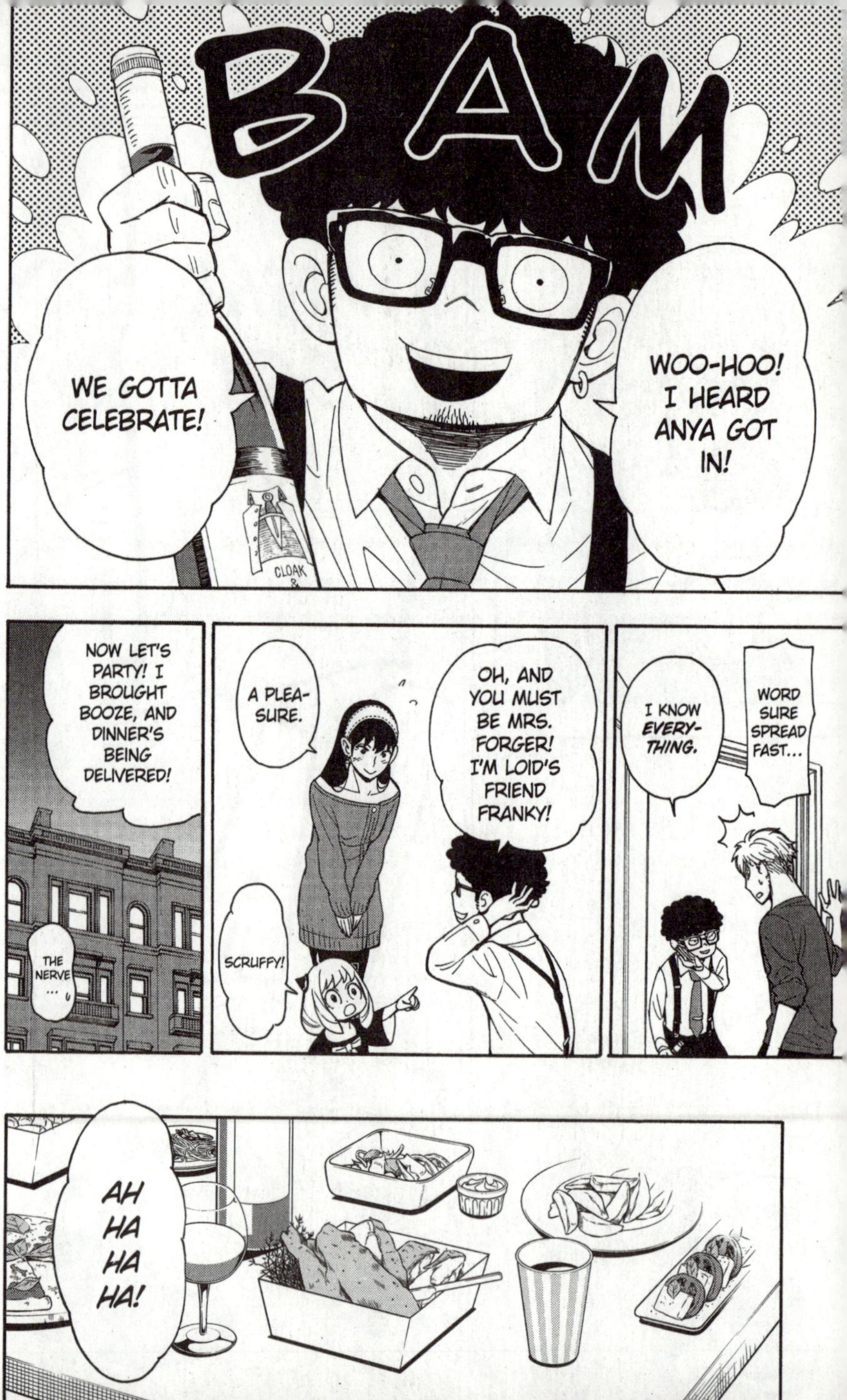
BAM
WOO-HOO! I HEARD ANYA GOT IN!
WE GOTTA CELEBRATE!
CLOAK &
WORD SURE SPREAD FAST...
I KNOW *EVERYTHING.*
OH, AND YOU MUST BE MRS. FORGER! I'M LOID'S FRIEND FRANKY!
A PLEASURE.
SCRUFFY!
NOW LET'S PARTY! I BROUGHT BOOZE, AND DINNER'S BEING DELIVERED!
THE NERVE...
AH HA HA HA!

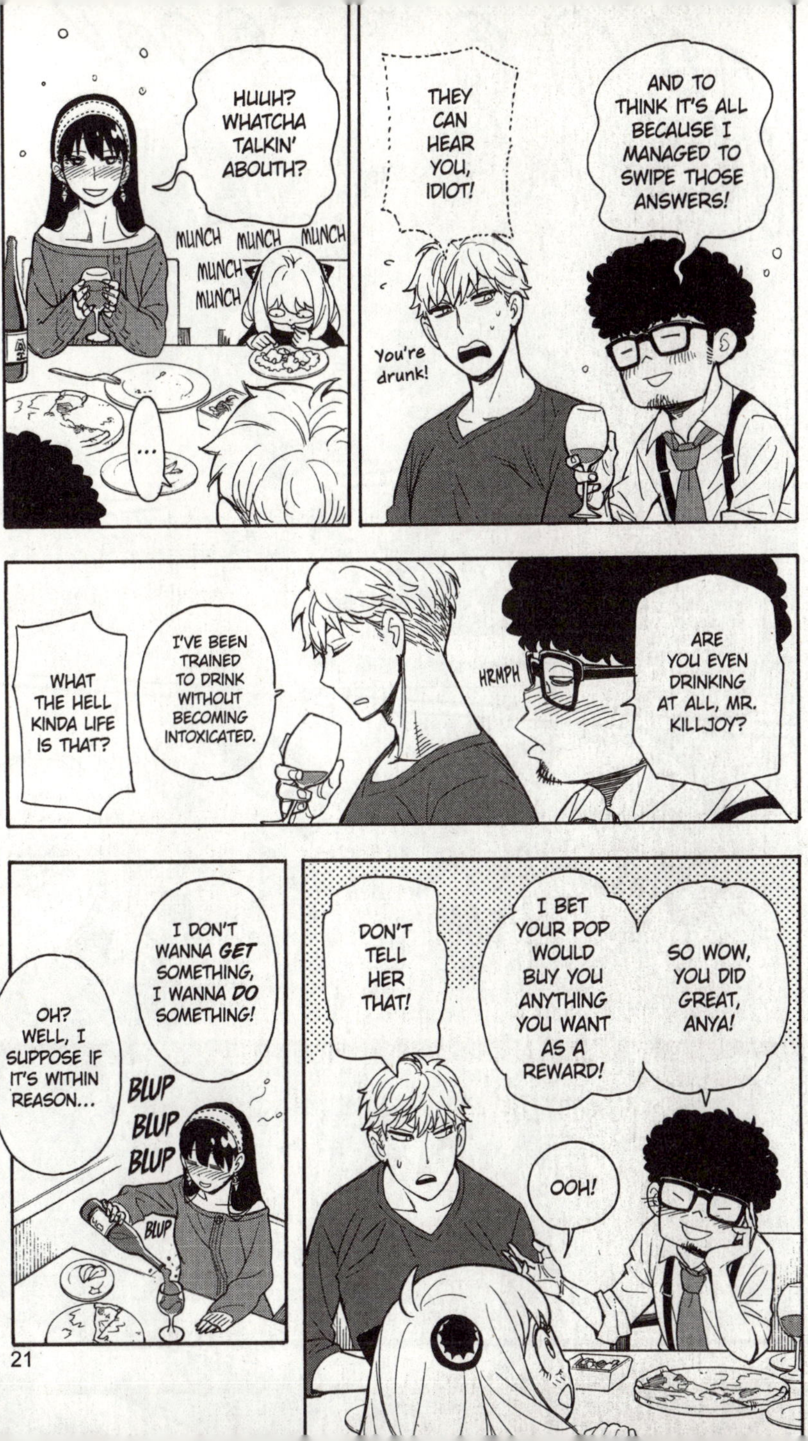
AND TO THINK IT'S ALL BECAUSE I MANAGED TO SWIPE THOSE ANSWERS!
THEY CAN HEAR YOU, IDIOT!
You're drunk!
HUUH? WHATCHA TALKIN' ABOUTH?
MUNCH MUNCH MUNCH MUNCH MUNCH
...
ARE YOU EVEN DRINKING AT ALL, MR. KILLJOY?
HRMPH
I'VE BEEN TRAINED TO DRINK WITHOUT BECOMING INTOXICATED.
WHAT THE HELL KINDA LIFE IS THAT?
SO WOW, YOU DID GREAT, ANYA!
I BET YOUR POP WOULD BUY YOU ANYTHING YOU WANT AS A REWARD!
DON'T TELL HER THAT!
OOH!
I DON'T WANNA GET SOMETHING, I WANNA DO SOMETHING!
OH? WELL, I SUPPOSE IF IT'S WITHIN REASON...
BLUP BLUP BLUP
BLUP

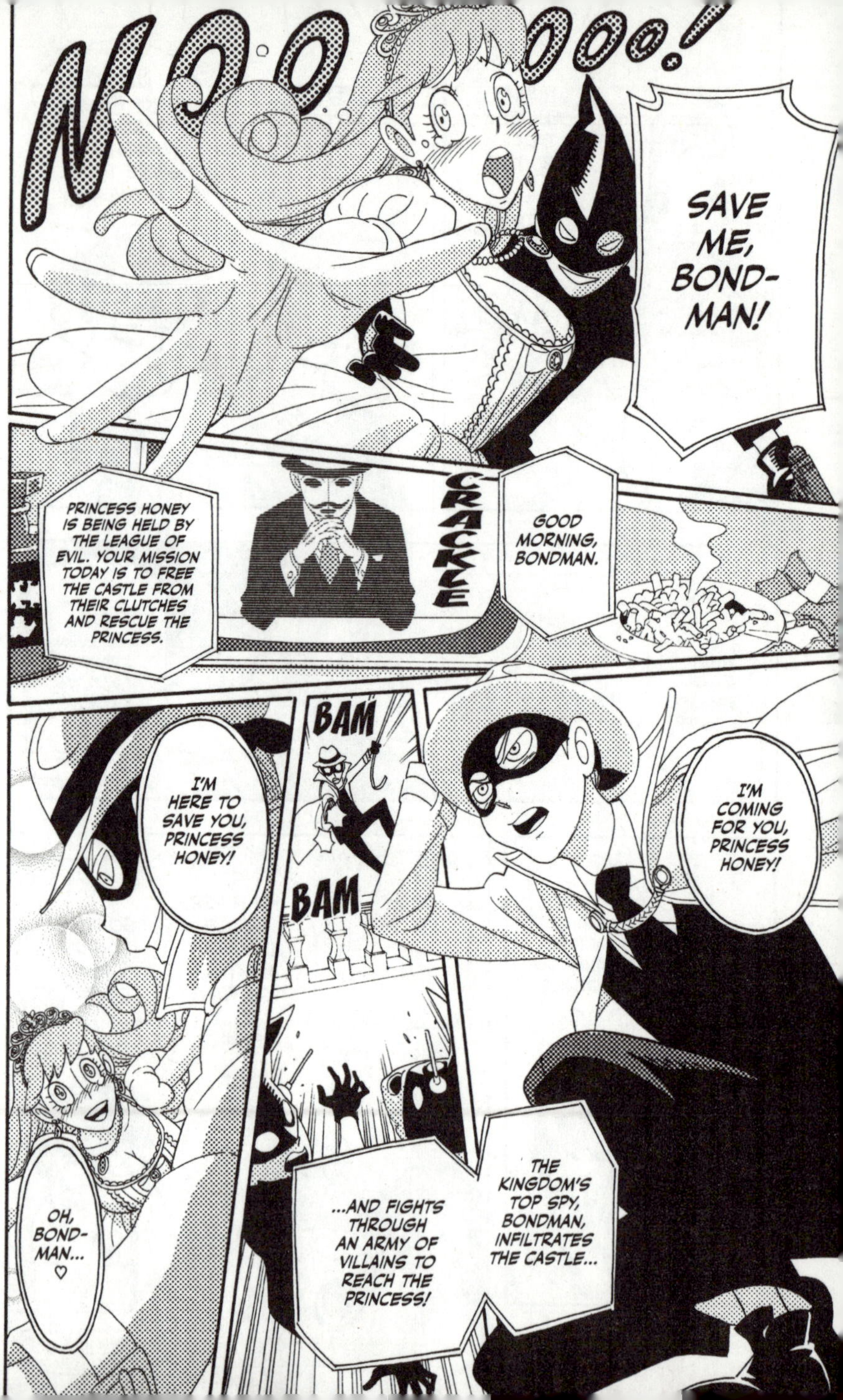
NOOOoooo!
SAVE ME, BOND-MAN!
GOOD MORNING, BONDMAN.
CRACKLE
PRINCESS HONEY IS BEING HELD BY THE LEAGUE OF EVIL. YOUR MISSION TODAY IS TO FREE THE CASTLE FROM THEIR CLUTCHES AND RESCUE THE PRINCESS.
I'M COMING FOR YOU, PRINCESS HONEY!
THE KINGDOM'S TOP SPY, BONDMAN, INFILTRATES THE CASTLE...
...AND FIGHTS THROUGH AN ARMY OF VILLAINS TO REACH THE PRINCESS!
BAM
BAM
I'M HERE TO SAVE YOU, PRINCESS HONEY!
OH, BOND-MAN... ♡

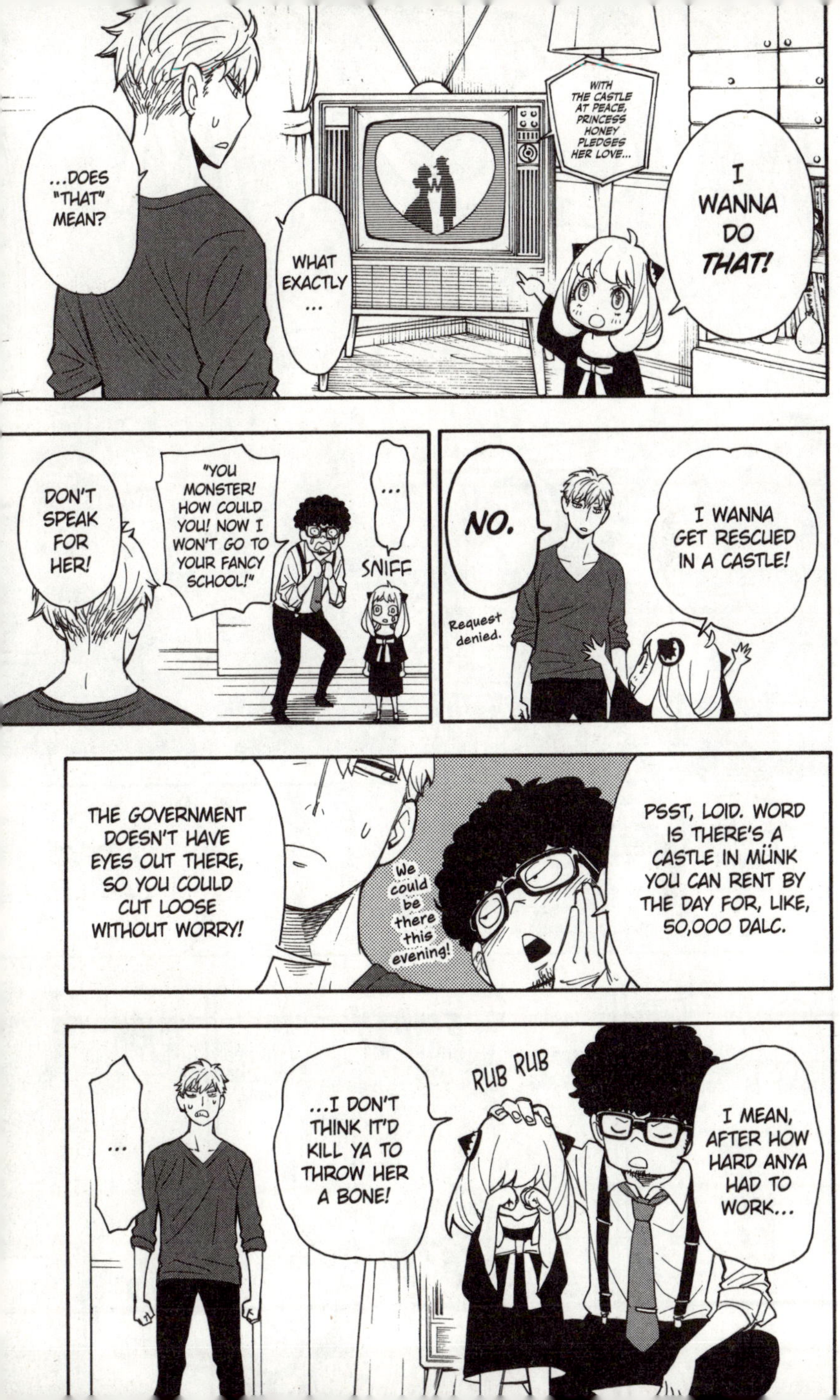

WITH THE CASTLE AT PEACE, PRINCESS HONEY PLEDGES HER LOVE...
I WANNA DO *THAT!*
WHAT EXACTLY ...
...DOES "THAT" MEAN?
I WANNA GET RESCUED IN A CASTLE!
NO.
Request denied.
...
SNIFF
"YOU MONSTER! HOW COULD YOU! NOW I WON'T GO TO YOUR FANCY SCHOOL!"
DON'T SPEAK FOR HER!
PSST, LOID. WORD IS THERE'S A CASTLE IN MÜNK YOU CAN RENT BY THE DAY FOR, LIKE, 50,000 DALC.
We could be there this evening!
THE GOVERNMENT DOESN'T HAVE EYES OUT THERE, SO YOU COULD CUT LOOSE WITHOUT WORRY!
I MEAN, AFTER HOW HARD ANYA HAD TO WORK...
RUB RUB
...I DON'T THINK IT'D KILL YA TO THROW HER A BONE!
...

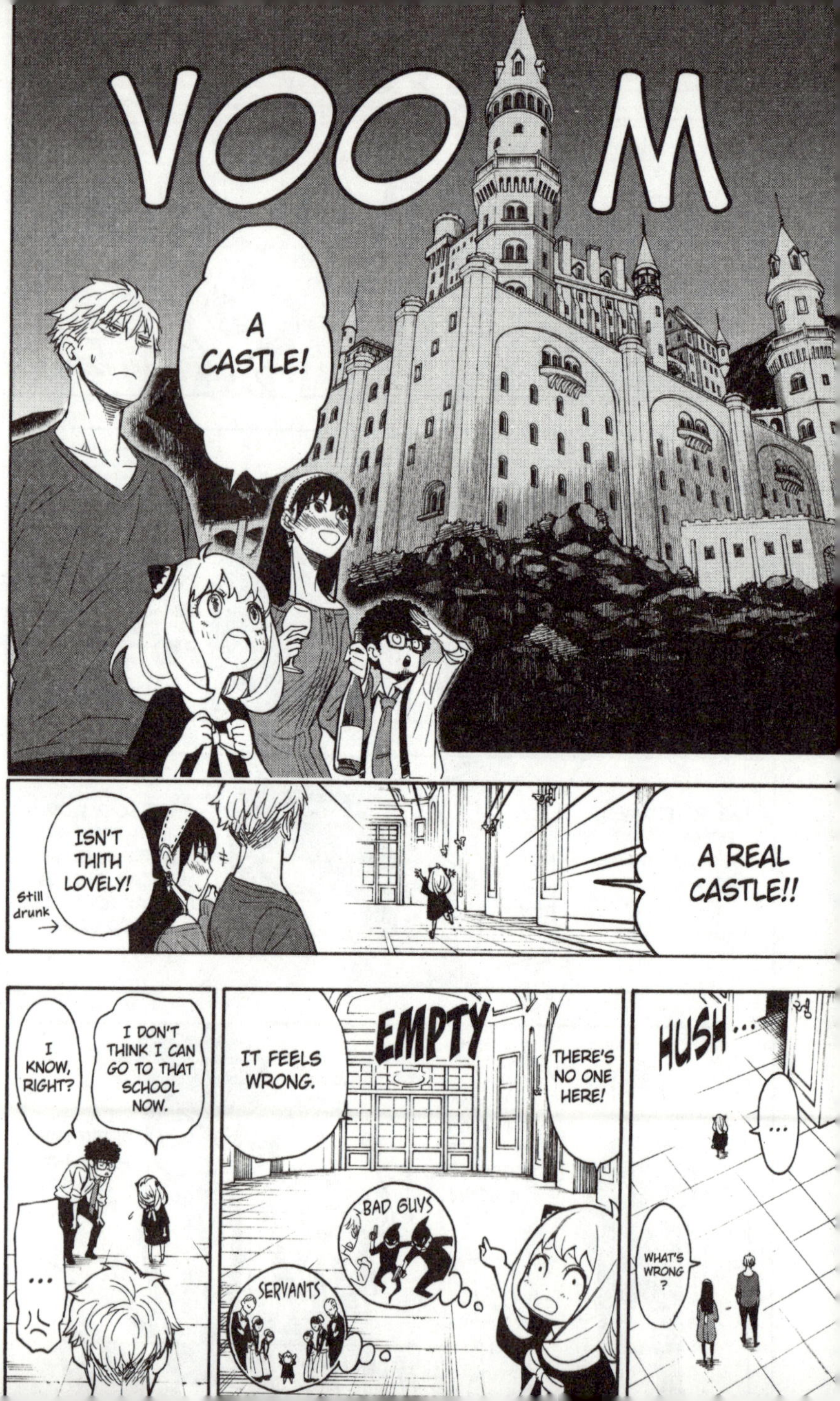
VOOM
A CASTLE!
A REAL CASTLE!!
ISN'T THITH LOVELY!
Still drunk →
HUSH...
...
WHAT'S WRONG ?
EMPTY
THERE'S NO ONE HERE!
IT FEELS WRONG.
BAD GUYS
SERVANTS
I DON'T THINK I CAN GO TO THAT SCHOOL NOW.
I KNOW, RIGHT?
...

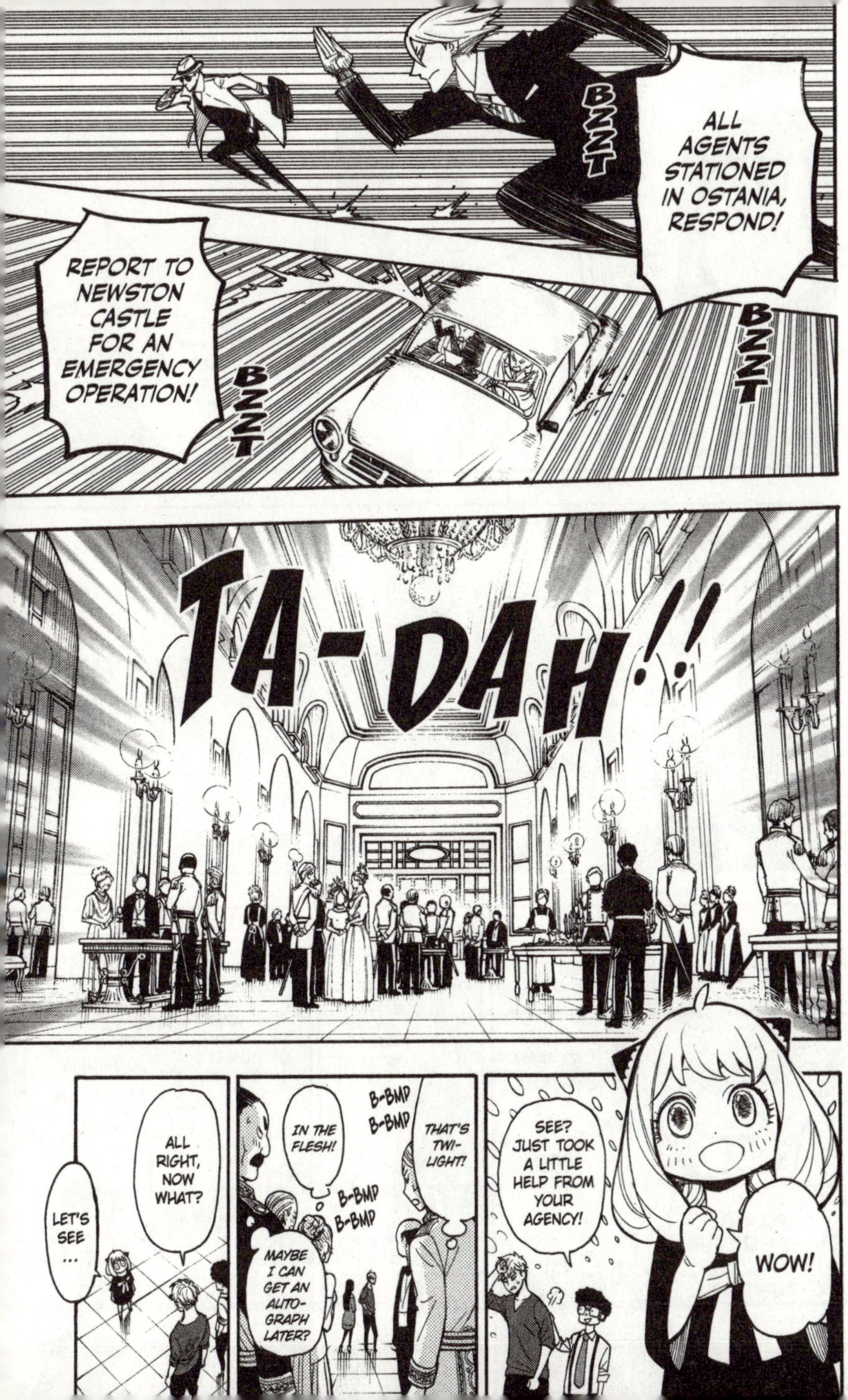
ALL AGENTS STATIONED IN OSTANIA, RESPOND!
BZZT
BZZT
REPORT TO NEWSTON CASTLE FOR AN EMERGENCY OPERATION!
BZZT
TA-DAH!!
WOW!
SEE? JUST TOOK A LITTLE HELP FROM YOUR AGENCY!
THAT'S TWI-LIGHT!
B-BMP B-BMP
IN THE FLESH!
B-BMP B-BMP
MAYBE I CAN GET AN AUTO-GRAPH LATER?
ALL RIGHT, NOW WHAT?
LET'S SEE ...

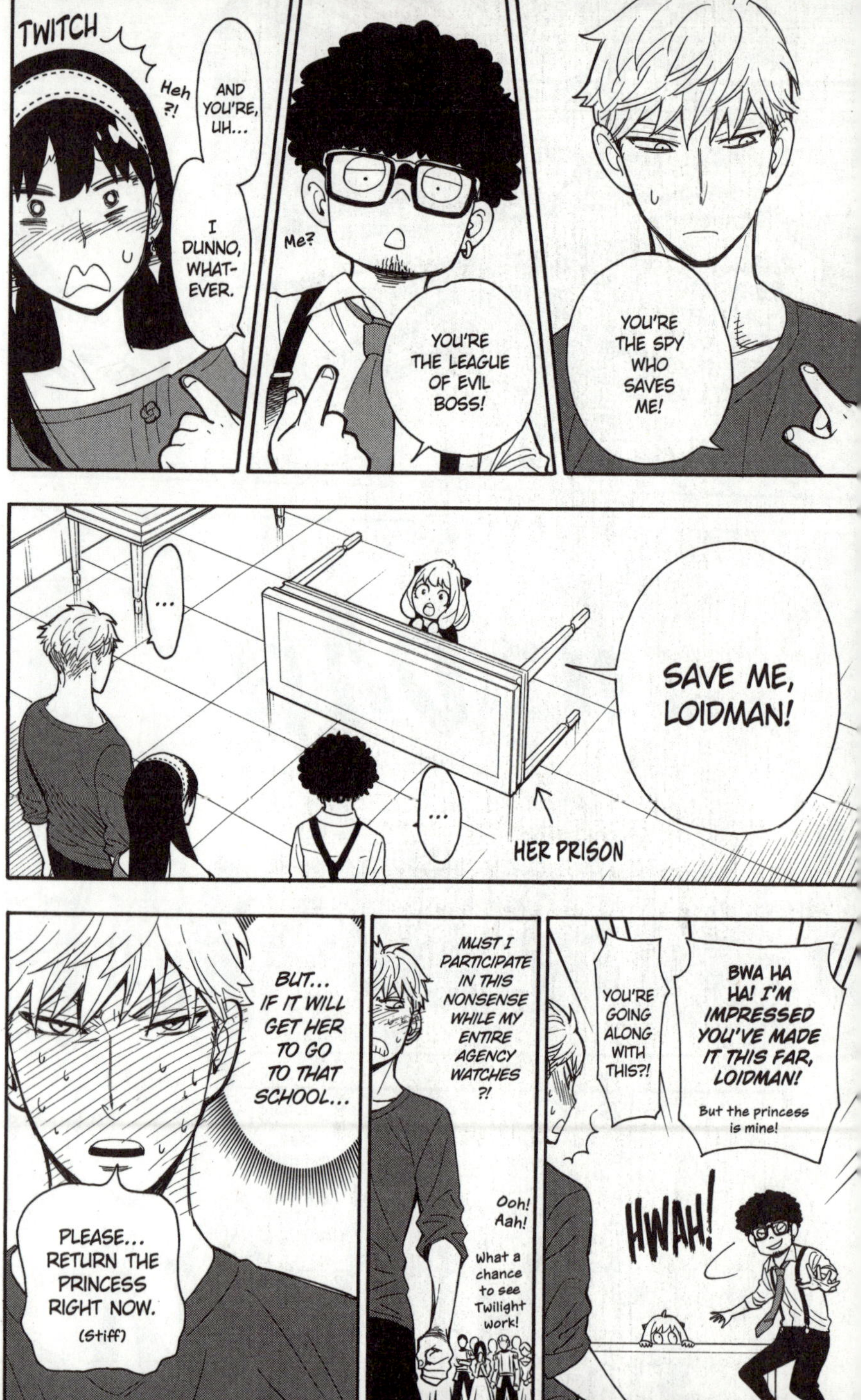
YOU'RE THE SPY WHO SAVES ME!
Me?
YOU'RE THE LEAGUE OF EVIL BOSS!
AND YOU'RE, UH...
I DUNNO, WHATEVER.
TWITCH
Heh ?!
SAVE ME, LOIDMAN!
HER PRISON
...
...
BWA HA HA! I'M IMPRESSED YOU'VE MADE IT THIS FAR, LOIDMAN!
But the princess is mine!
HWAH!
YOU'RE GOING ALONG WITH THIS?!
MUST I PARTICIPATE IN THIS NONSENSE WHILE MY ENTIRE AGENCY WATCHES ?!
Ooh! Aah!
What a chance to see Twilight work!
BUT... IF IT WILL GET HER TO GO TO THAT SCHOOL...
PLEASE... RETURN THE PRINCESS RIGHT NOW.
(Stiff)

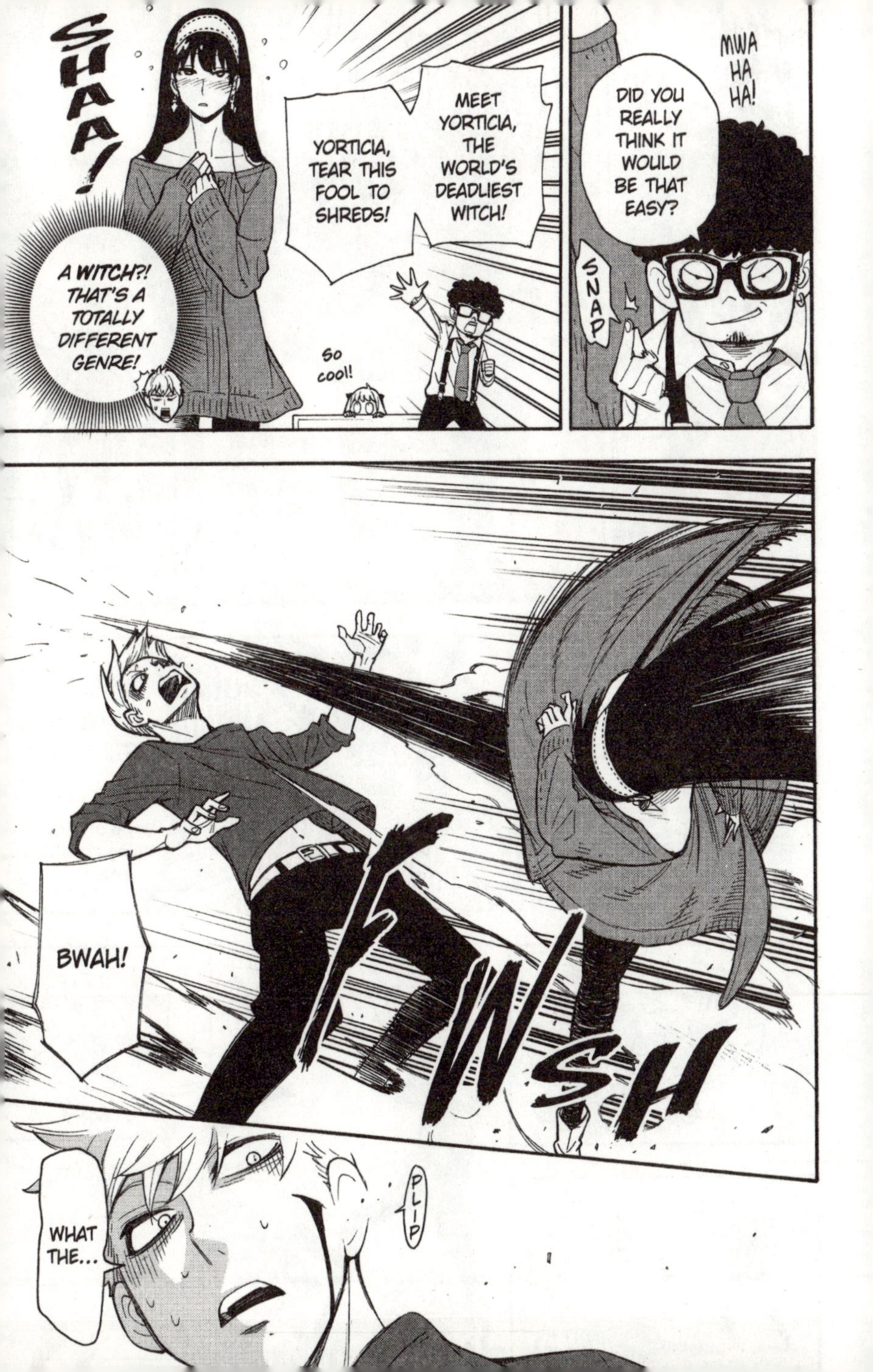
MWA HA HA!
DID YOU REALLY THINK IT WOULD BE THAT EASY?
SNAP
MEET YORTICIA, THE WORLD'S DEADLIEST WITCH!
YORTICIA, TEAR THIS FOOL TO SHREDS!
SHAA!
So cool!
A WITCH?! THAT'S A TOTALLY DIFFERENT GENRE!
FWSH
BWAH!
PLIP
WHAT THE...

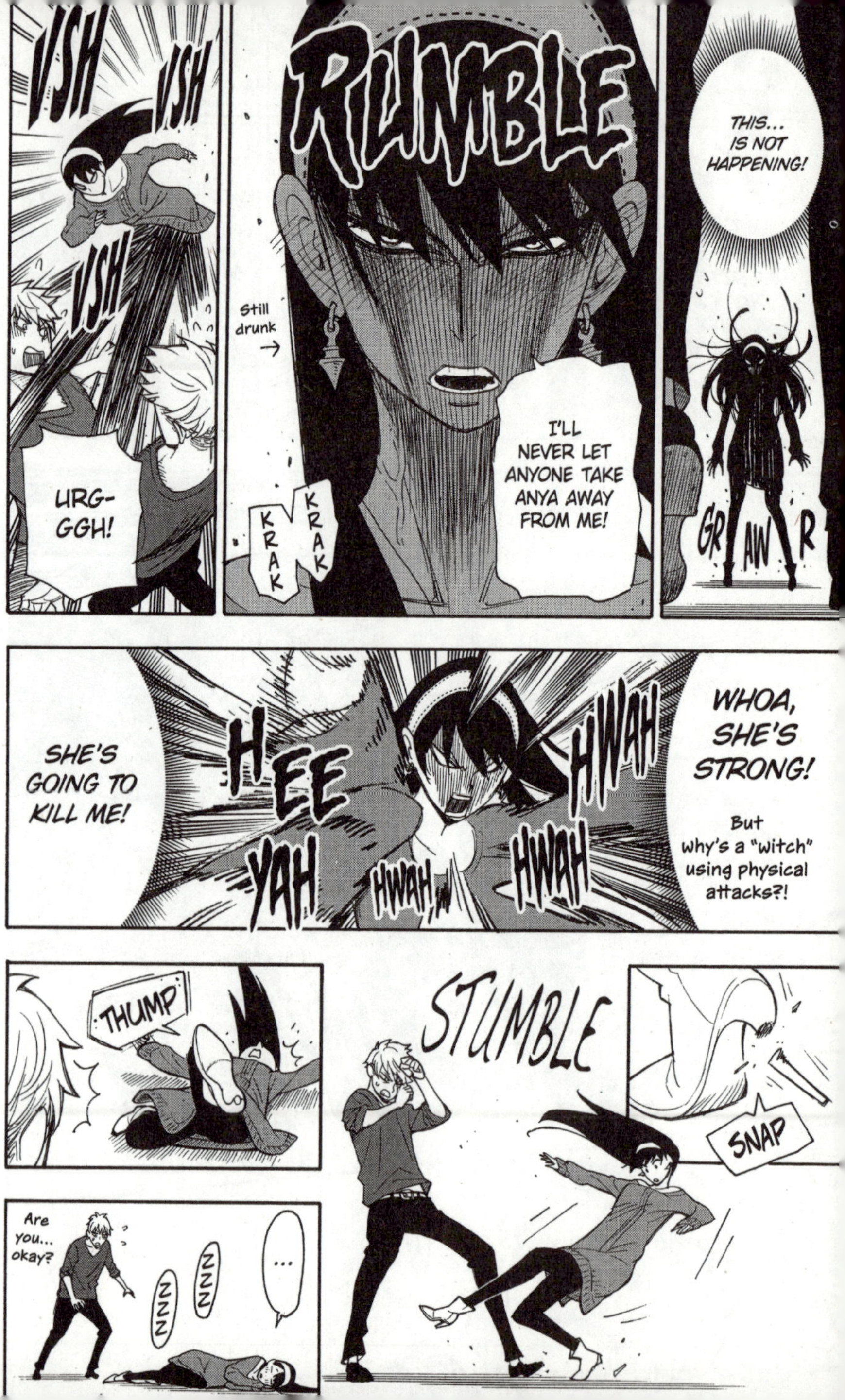
THIS... IS NOT HAPPENING!
GRAWR
RUMBLE
I'LL NEVER LET ANYONE TAKE ANYA AWAY FROM ME!
Still drunk →
KRAK
KRAK
VSH
VSH
VSH
URG-GGH!
WHOA, SHE'S STRONG!
But why's a "witch" using physical attacks?!
HWAH
HWAH
HWAH
HEE YAH
SHE'S GOING TO KILL ME!
SNAP
STUMBLE
THUMP
...
ZZZ
ZZZ
Are you... okay?

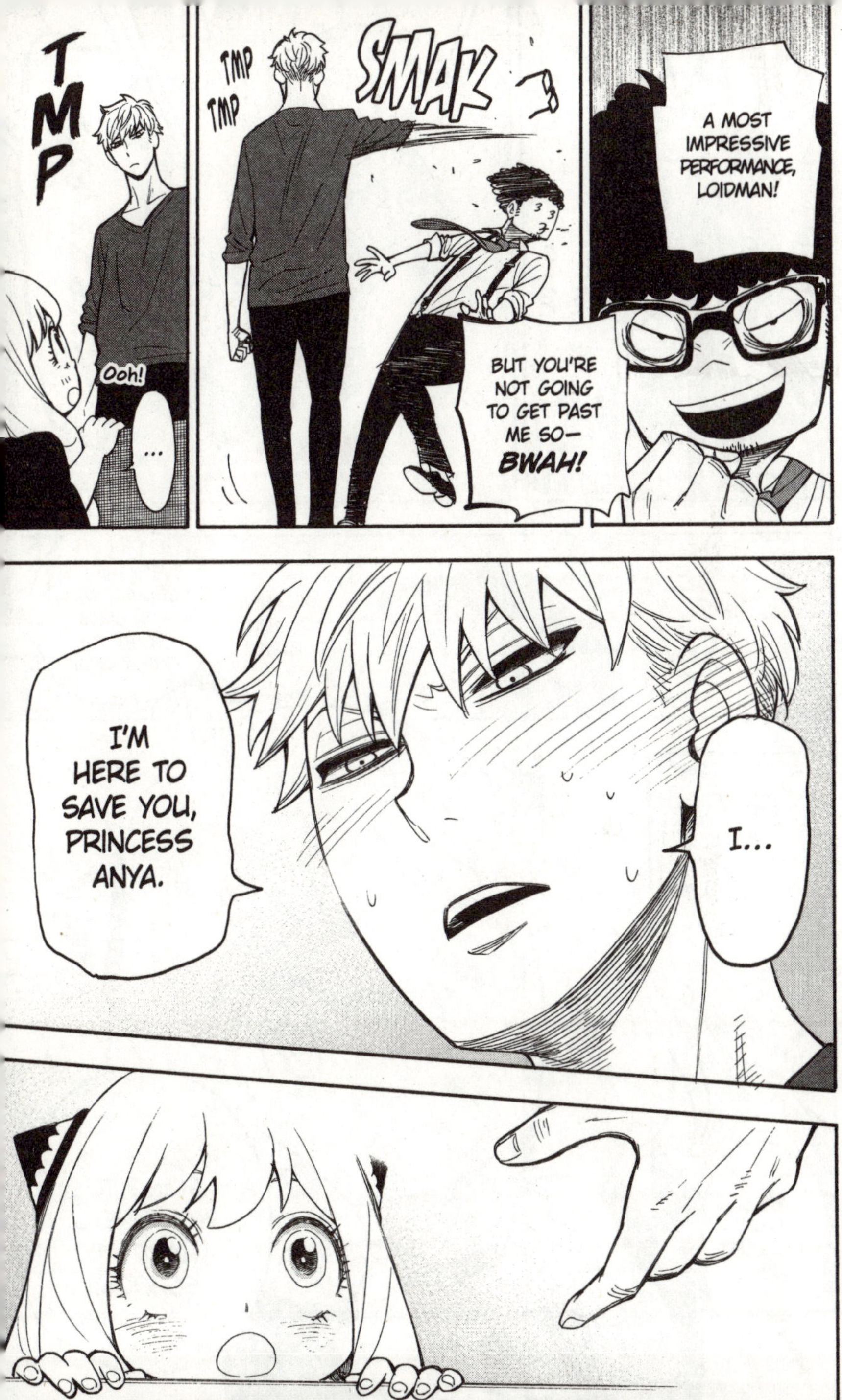
A MOST IMPRESSIVE PERFORMANCE, LOIDMAN!
BUT YOU'RE NOT GOING TO GET PAST ME SO— BWAH!
SMAK
TMP TMP
TMP
Ooh!
...
I...
I'M HERE TO SAVE YOU, PRINCESS ANYA.

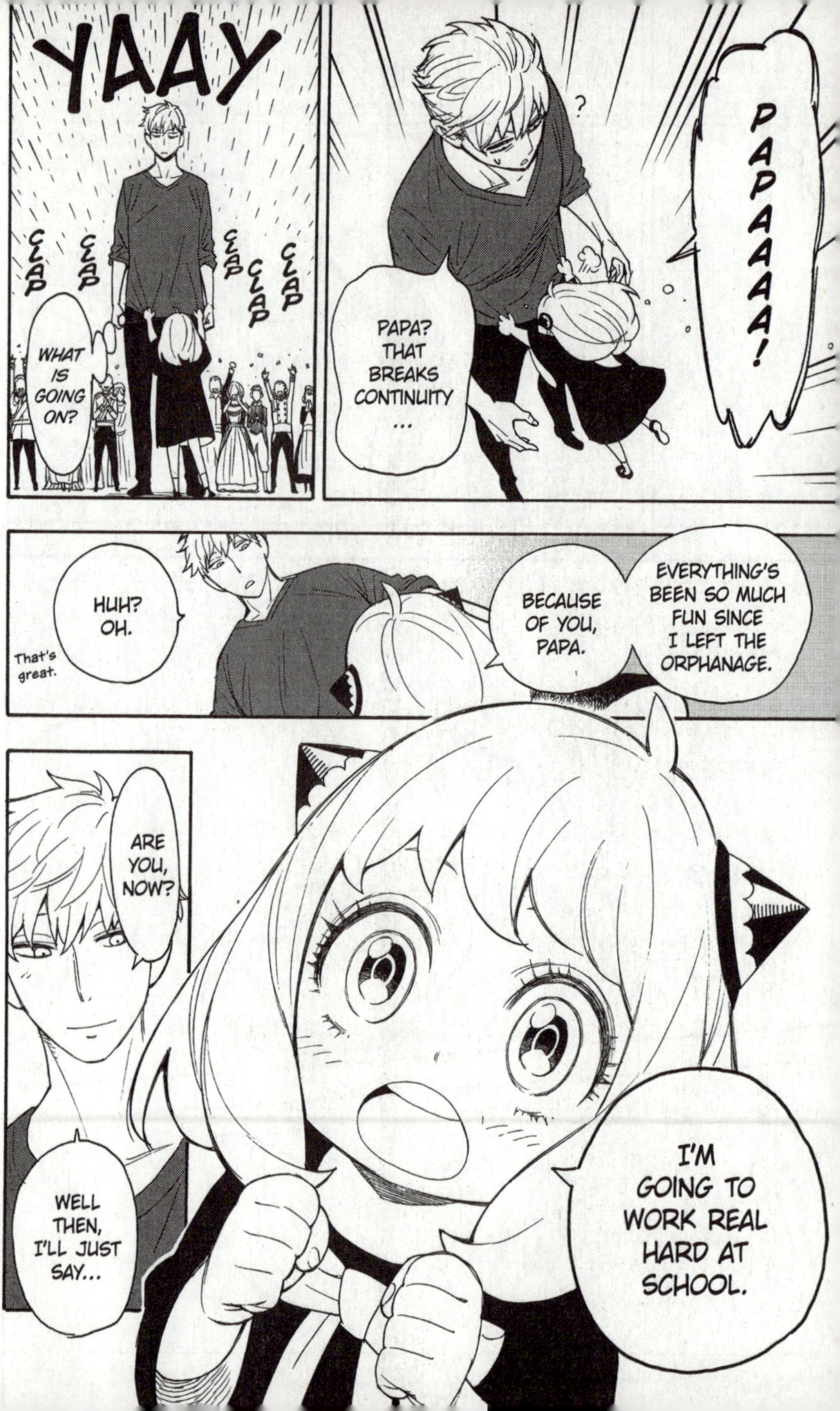
PAPAAAAA!
?
PAPA? THAT BREAKS CONTINUITY ...
YAAY
CLAP
CLAP
CLAP
CLAP
CLAP
WHAT IS GOING ON?
EVERYTHING'S BEEN SO MUCH FUN SINCE I LEFT THE ORPHANAGE.
BECAUSE OF YOU, PAPA.
HUH? OH.
That's great.
I'M GOING TO WORK REAL HARD AT SCHOOL.
ARE YOU, NOW?
WELL THEN, I'LL JUST SAY...

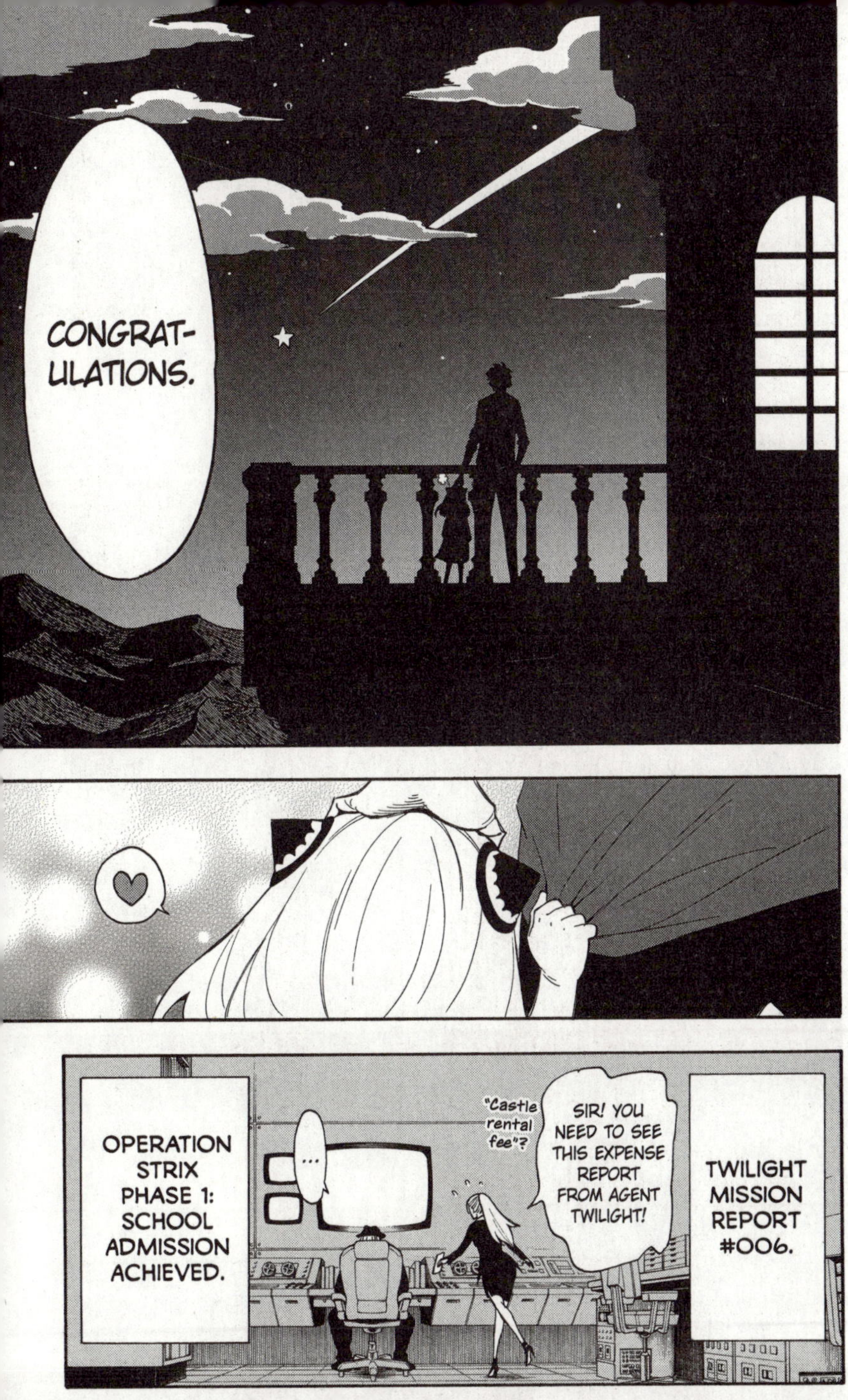
CONGRAT-ULATIONS.
TWILIGHT MISSION REPORT #006.
SIR! YOU NEED TO SEE THIS EXPENSE REPORT FROM AGENT TWILIGHT!
"Castle rental fee"?
...
OPERATION STRIX PHASE 1: SCHOOL ADMISSION ACHIEVED.

SPY×FAMILY

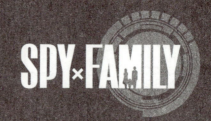

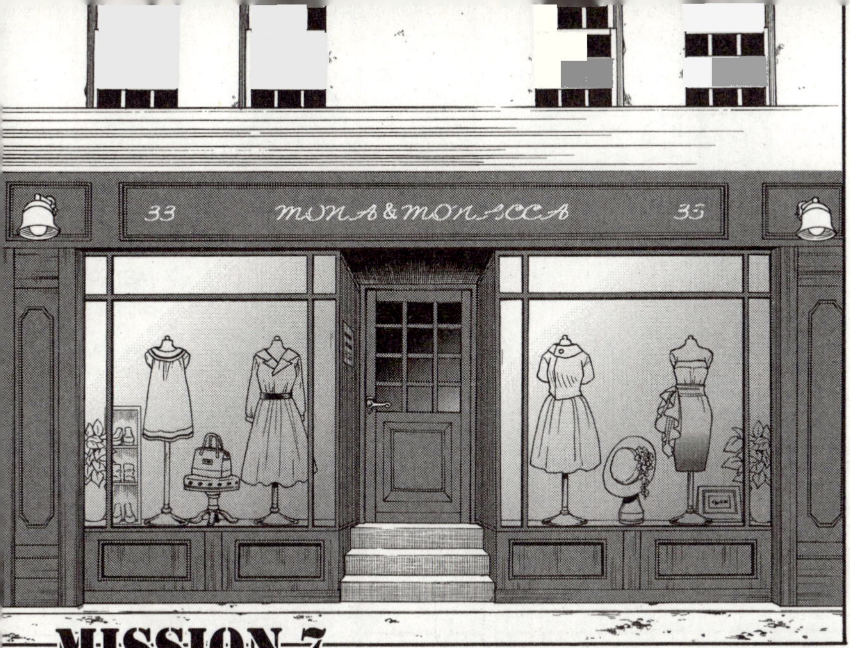
33
MONA & MONACCA
35

MISSION 7

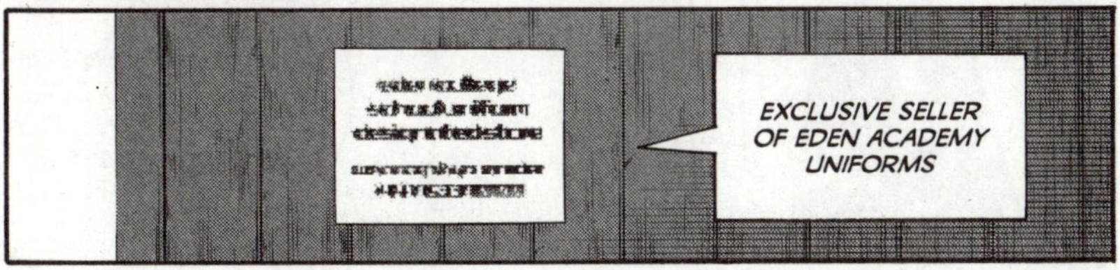
EXCLUSIVE SELLER OF EDEN ACADEMY UNIFORMS

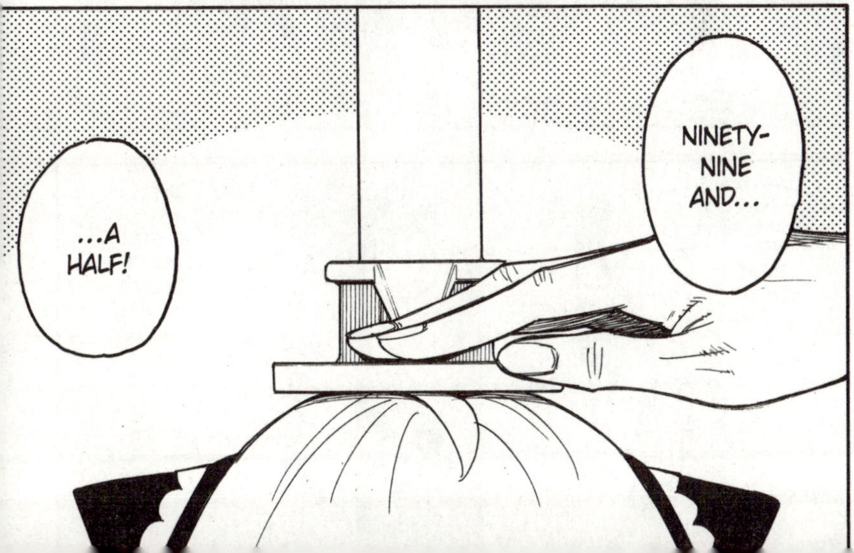
NINETY-NINE AND...
...A HALF!

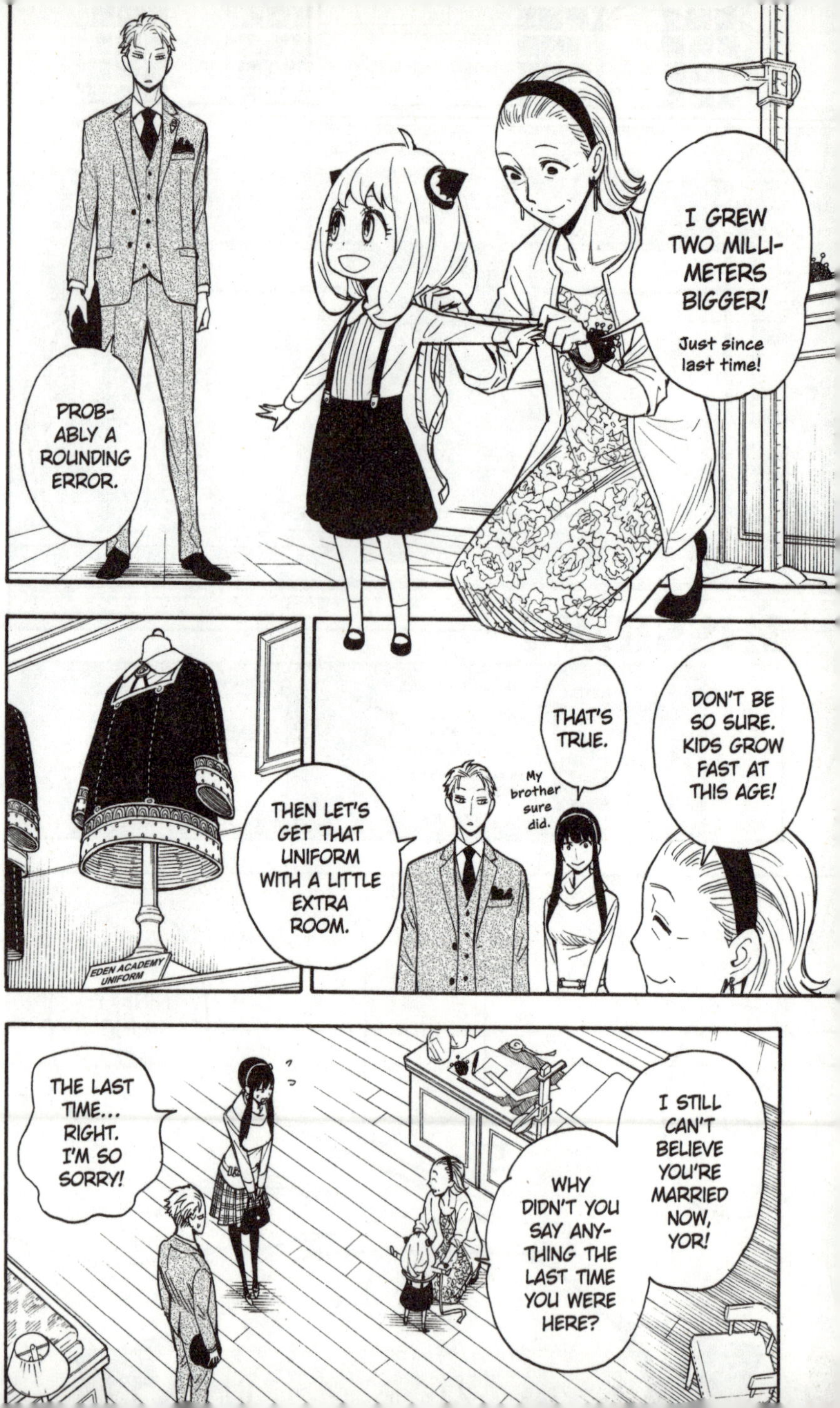
I GREW TWO MILLI-METERS BIGGER!
Just since last time!
PROB-ABLY A ROUNDING ERROR.
DON'T BE SO SURE. KIDS GROW FAST AT THIS AGE!
THAT'S TRUE.
My brother sure did.
THEN LET'S GET THAT UNIFORM WITH A LITTLE EXTRA ROOM.
EDEN ACADEMY UNIFORM
I STILL CAN'T BELIEVE YOU'RE MARRIED NOW, YOR!
WHY DIDN'T YOU SAY ANY-THING THE LAST TIME YOU WERE HERE?
THE LAST TIME... RIGHT. I'M SO SORRY!

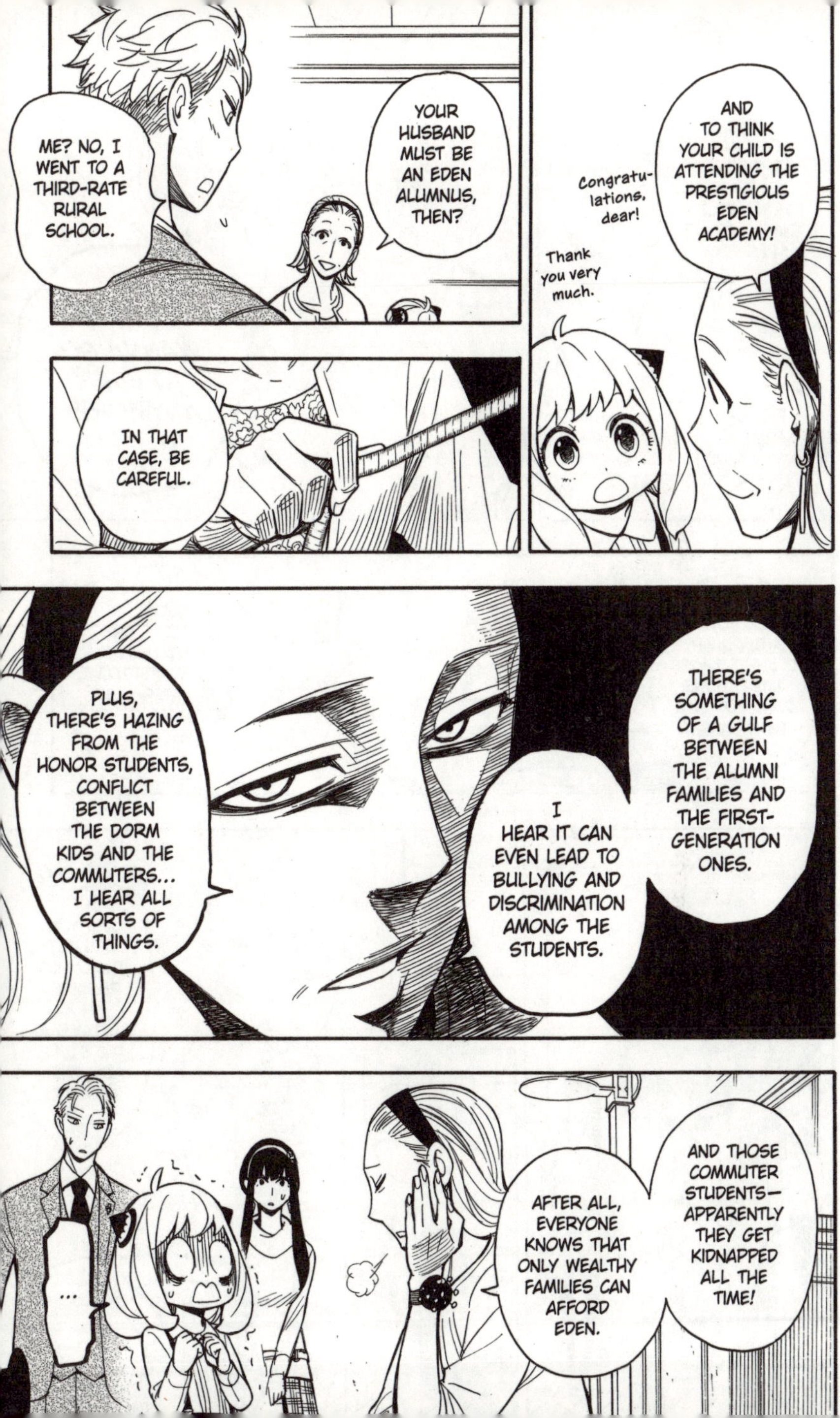
AND TO THINK YOUR CHILD IS ATTENDING THE PRESTIGIOUS EDEN ACADEMY!
Congratu-lations, dear!
Thank you very much.
YOUR HUSBAND MUST BE AN EDEN ALUMNUS, THEN?
ME? NO, I WENT TO A THIRD-RATE RURAL SCHOOL.
IN THAT CASE, BE CAREFUL.
THERE'S SOMETHING OF A GULF BETWEEN THE ALUMNI FAMILIES AND THE FIRST-GENERATION ONES.
I HEAR IT CAN EVEN LEAD TO BULLYING AND DISCRIMINATION AMONG THE STUDENTS.
PLUS, THERE'S HAZING FROM THE HONOR STUDENTS, CONFLICT BETWEEN THE DORM KIDS AND THE COMMUTERS... I HEAR ALL SORTS OF THINGS.
AND THOSE COMMUTER STUDENTS—APPARENTLY THEY GET KIDNAPPED ALL THE TIME!
AFTER ALL, EVERYONE KNOWS THAT ONLY WEALTHY FAMILIES CAN AFFORD EDEN.
...

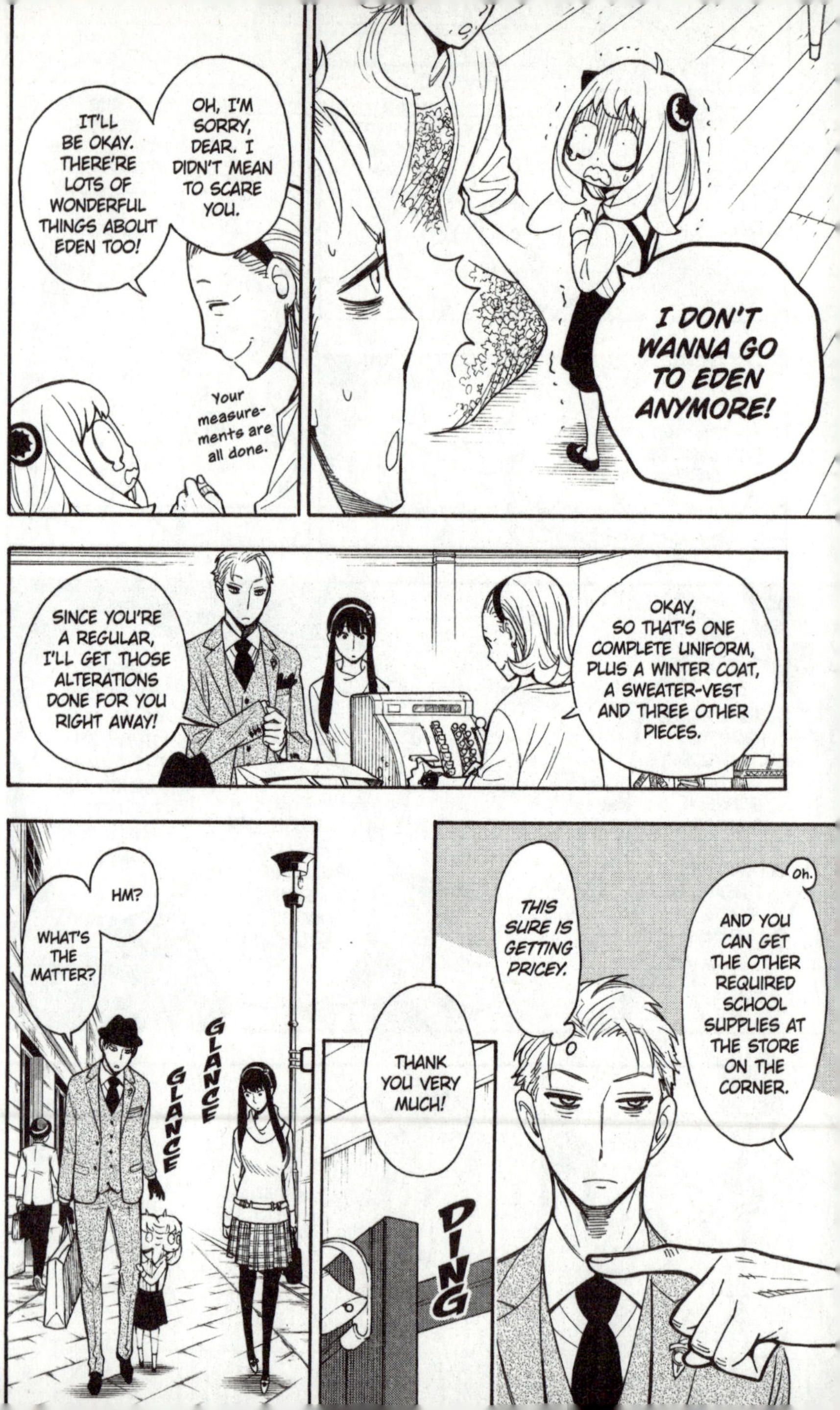
I DON'T WANNA GO TO EDEN ANYMORE!
OH, I'M SORRY, DEAR. I DIDN'T MEAN TO SCARE YOU.
IT'LL BE OKAY. THERE'RE LOTS OF WONDERFUL THINGS ABOUT EDEN TOO!
Your measurements are all done.
OKAY, SO THAT'S ONE COMPLETE UNIFORM, PLUS A WINTER COAT, A SWEATER-VEST AND THREE OTHER PIECES.
SINCE YOU'RE A REGULAR, I'LL GET THOSE ALTERATIONS DONE FOR YOU RIGHT AWAY!
Oh.
AND YOU CAN GET THE OTHER REQUIRED SCHOOL SUPPLIES AT THE STORE ON THE CORNER.
THIS SURE IS GETTING PRICEY.
THANK YOU VERY MUCH!
DING
GLANCE
GLANCE
HM?
WHAT'S THE MATTER?

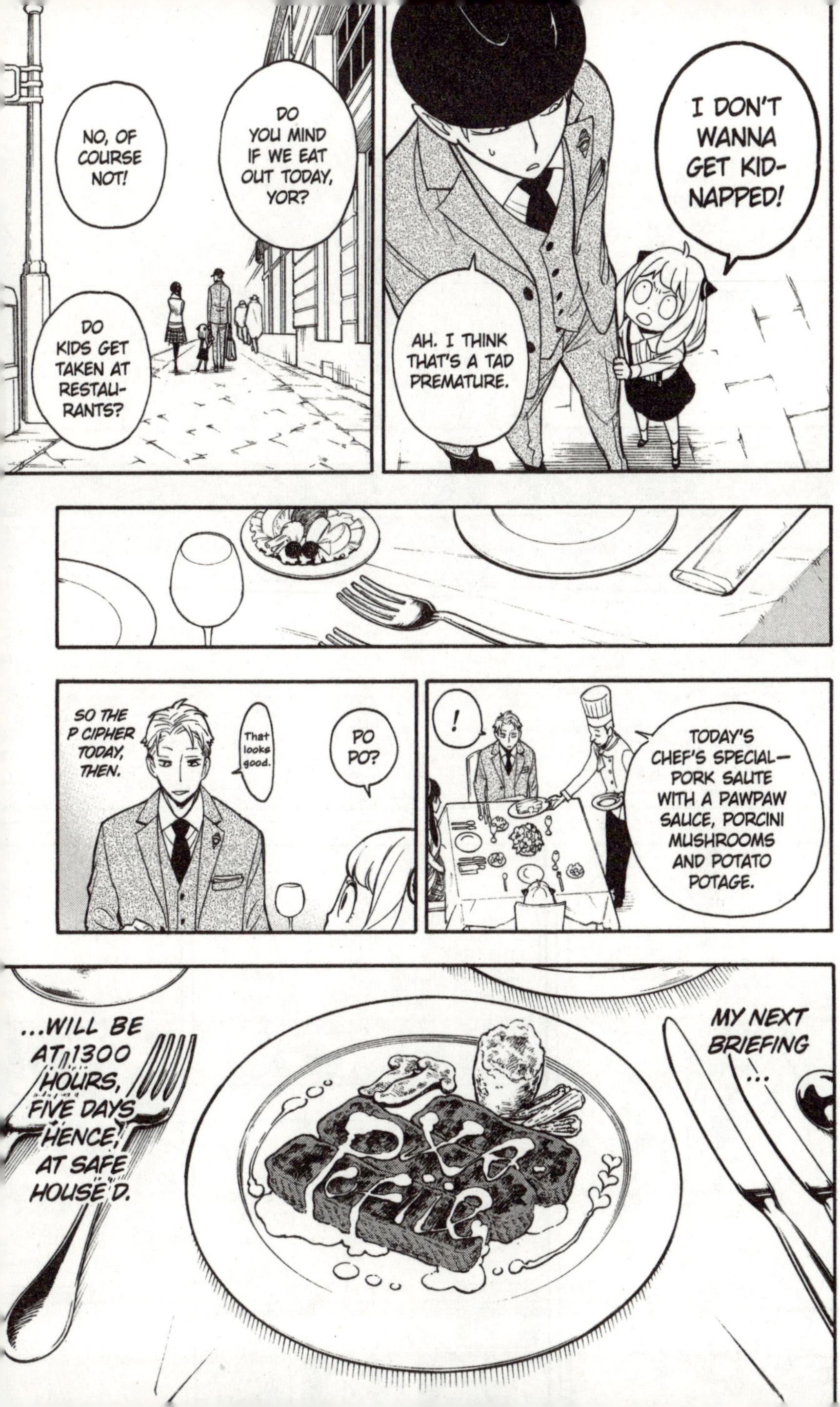
I DON'T WANNA GET KID-NAPPED!
AH. I THINK THAT'S A TAD PREMATURE.
DO YOU MIND IF WE EAT OUT TODAY, YOR?
NO, OF COURSE NOT!
DO KIDS GET TAKEN AT RESTAURANTS?
!
TODAY'S CHEF'S SPECIAL—PORK SAUTE WITH A PAWPAW SAUCE, PORCINI MUSHROOMS AND POTATO POTAGE.
PO PO?
That looks good.
SO THE P CIPHER TODAY, THEN.
MY NEXT BRIEFING ...
...WILL BE AT 1300 HOURS, FIVE DAYS HENCE, AT SAFE HOUSE D.

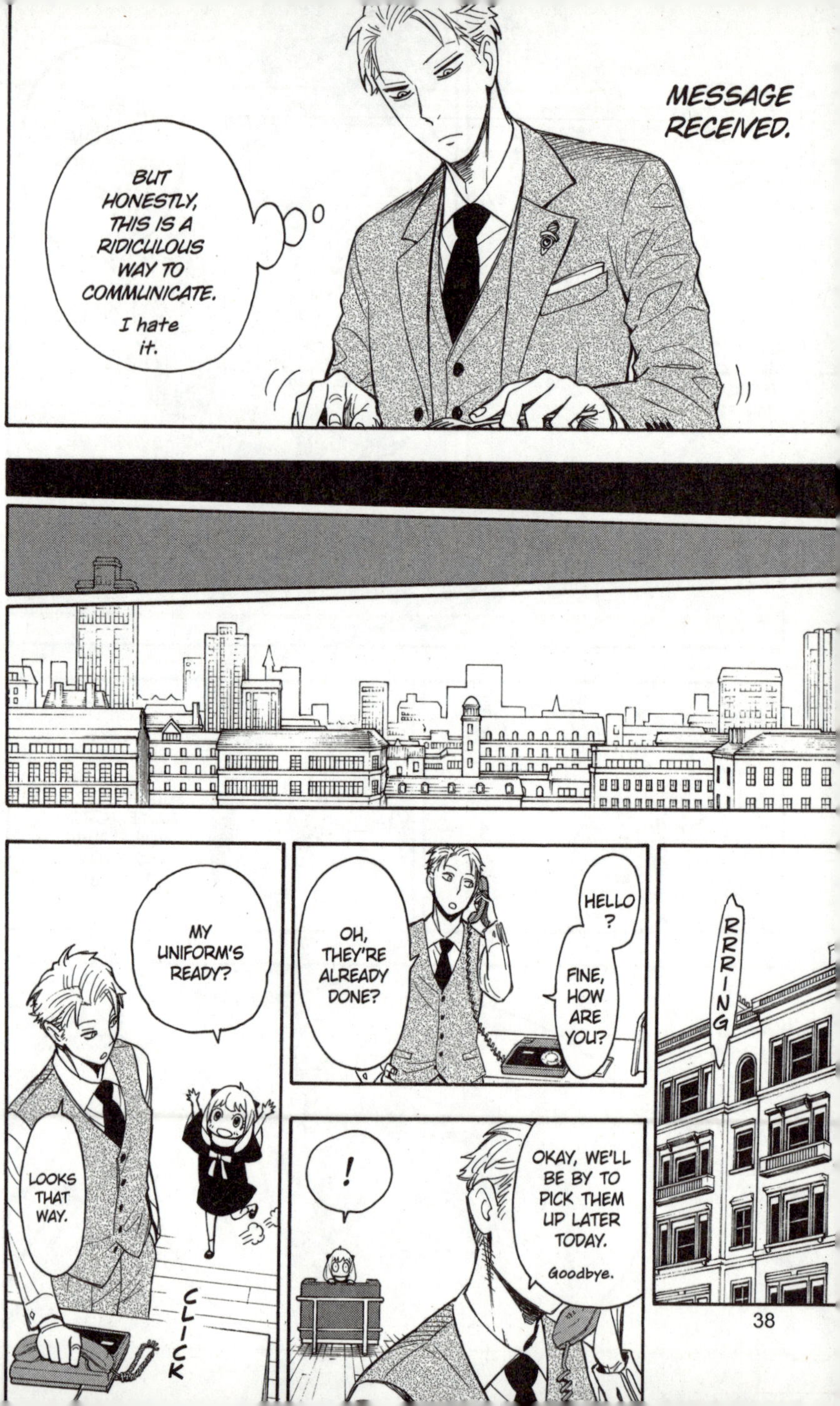
MESSAGE RECEIVED.
BUT HONESTLY, THIS IS A RIDICULOUS WAY TO COMMUNICATE.
I hate it.
RRRING
HELLO?
FINE, HOW ARE YOU?
OH, THEY'RE ALREADY DONE?
OKAY, WE'LL BE BY TO PICK THEM UP LATER TODAY.
Goodbye.
!
MY UNIFORM'S READY?
LOOKS THAT WAY.
CLICK

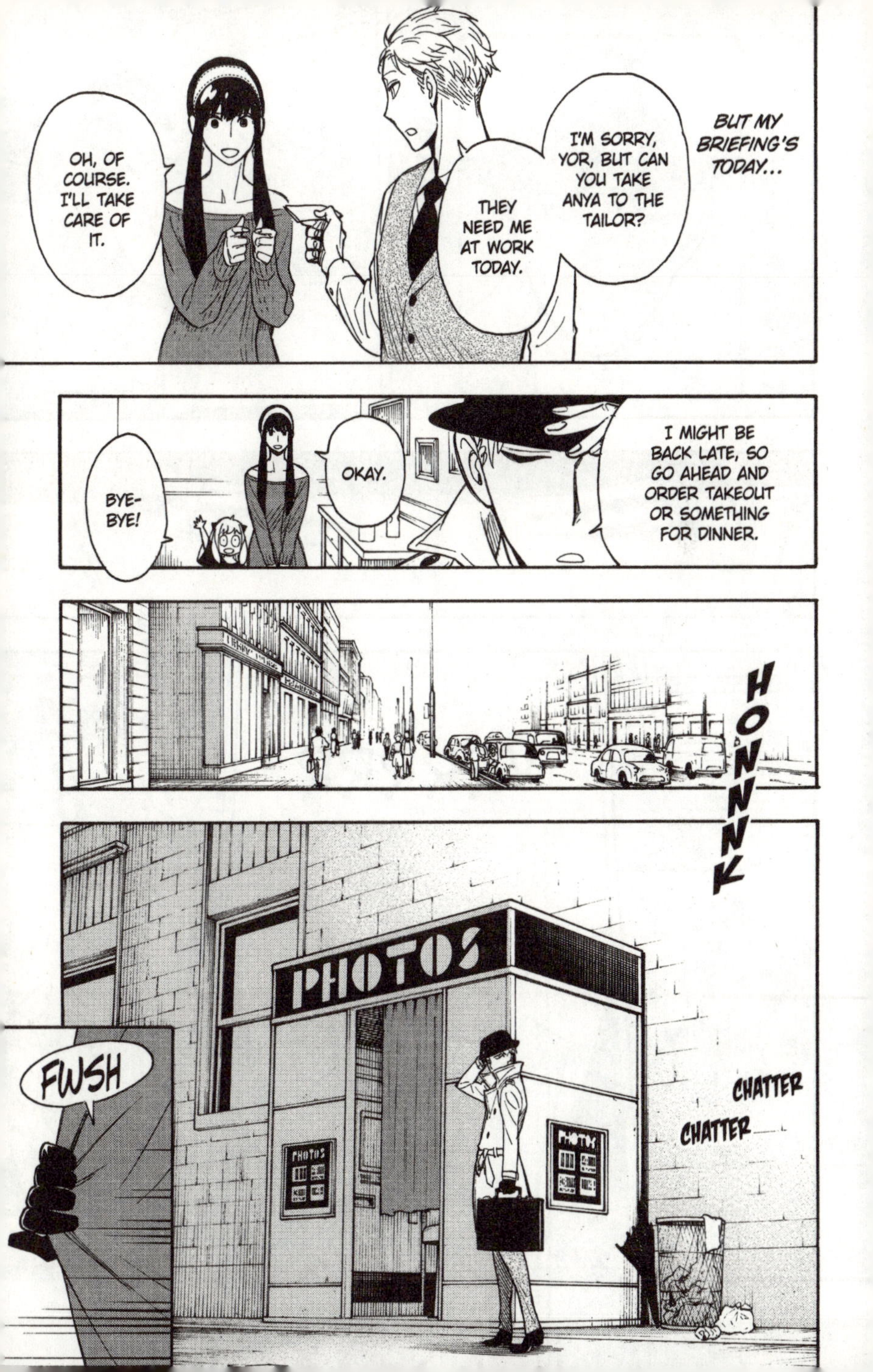
BUT MY BRIEFING'S TODAY...
I'M SORRY, YOR, BUT CAN YOU TAKE ANYA TO THE TAILOR?
THEY NEED ME AT WORK TODAY.
OH, OF COURSE. I'LL TAKE CARE OF IT.
I MIGHT BE BACK LATE, SO GO AHEAD AND ORDER TAKEOUT OR SOMETHING FOR DINNER.
OKAY.
BYE-BYE!
HONNNK
PHOTOS
CHATTER
CHATTER
FWSH

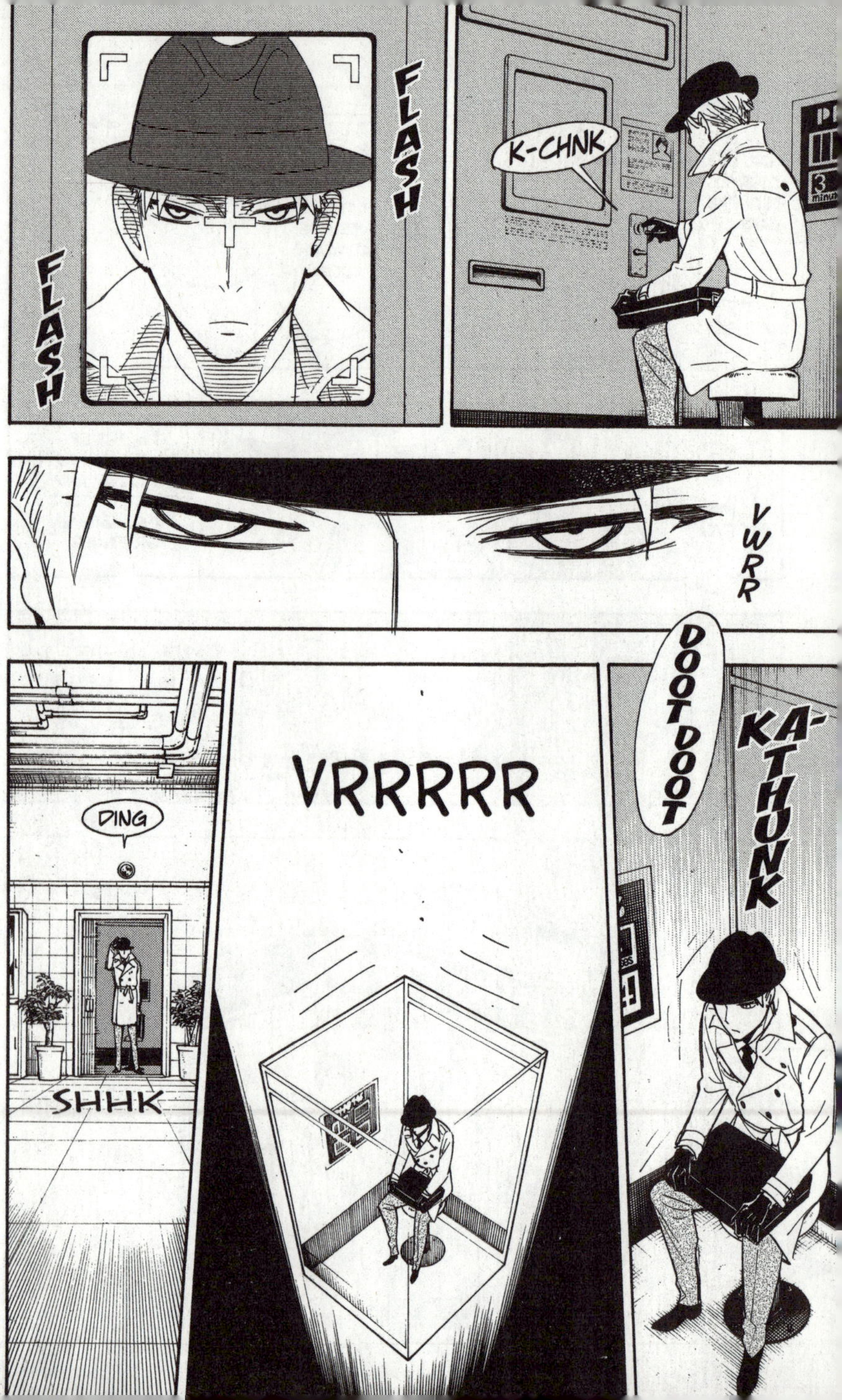
K-CHNK
FLASH
FLASH
VWRR
DOOT DOOT
KA-THUNK
VRRRRR
DING
SHHK

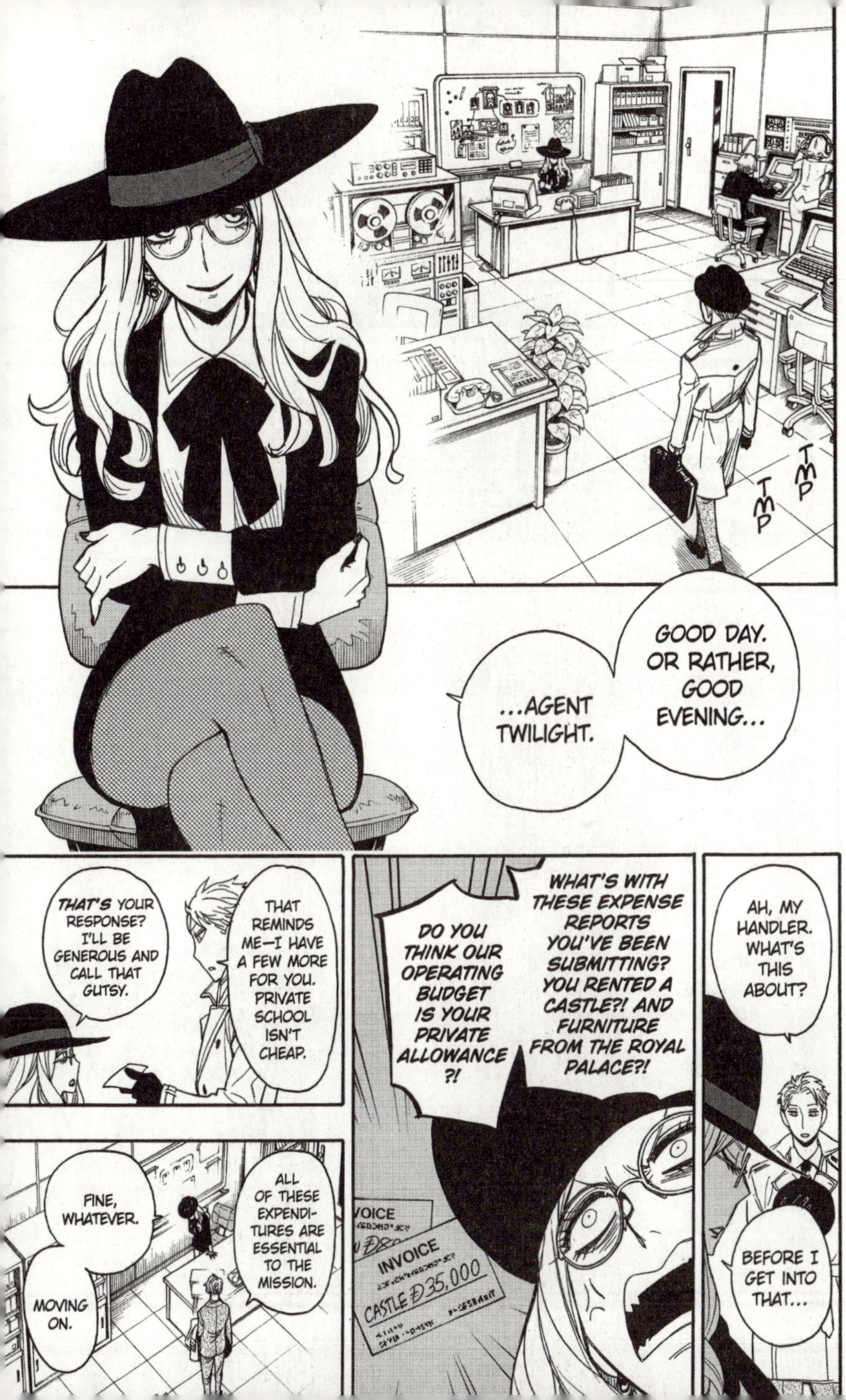
TMP
TMP
GOOD DAY. OR RATHER, GOOD EVENING...
...AGENT TWILIGHT.
AH, MY HANDLER. WHAT'S THIS ABOUT?
BEFORE I GET INTO THAT...
WHAT'S WITH THESE EXPENSE REPORTS YOU'VE BEEN SUBMITTING? YOU RENTED A CASTLE?! AND FURNITURE FROM THE ROYAL PALACE?!
DO YOU THINK OUR OPERATING BUDGET IS YOUR PRIVATE ALLOWANCE?!
INVOICE
CASTLE Đ35,000
THAT REMINDS ME—I HAVE A FEW MORE FOR YOU. PRIVATE SCHOOL ISN'T CHEAP.
THAT'S YOUR RESPONSE? I'LL BE GENEROUS AND CALL THAT GUTSY.
ALL OF THESE EXPENDITURES ARE ESSENTIAL TO THE MISSION.
FINE, WHATEVER.
MOVING ON.

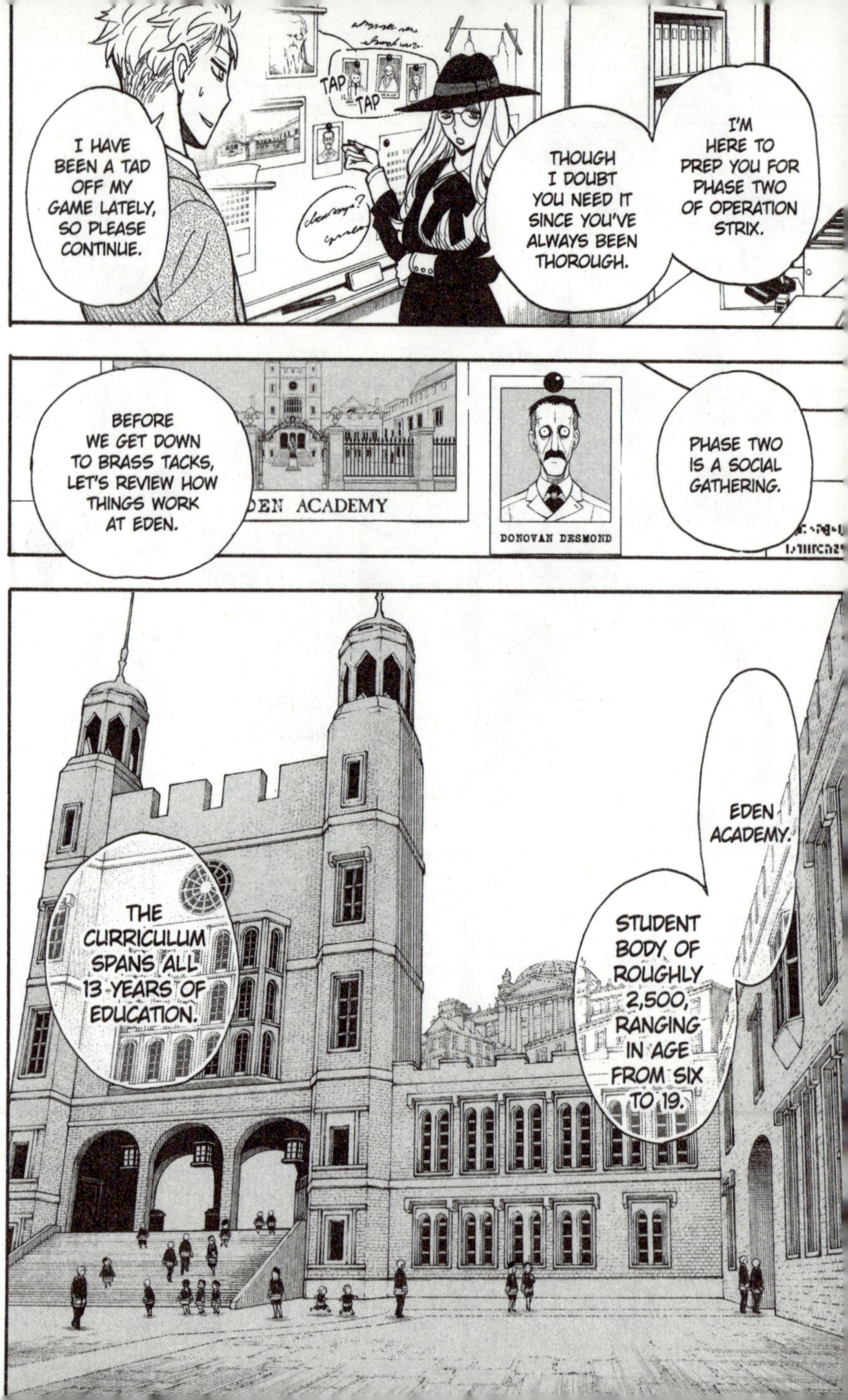
I'M HERE TO PREP YOU FOR PHASE TWO OF OPERATION STRIX.
THOUGH I DOUBT YOU NEED IT SINCE YOU'VE ALWAYS BEEN THOROUGH.
TAP TAP
I HAVE BEEN A TAD OFF MY GAME LATELY, SO PLEASE CONTINUE.
PHASE TWO IS A SOCIAL GATHERING.
DONOVAN DESMOND
DEN ACADEMY
BEFORE WE GET DOWN TO BRASS TACKS, LET'S REVIEW HOW THINGS WORK AT EDEN.
EDEN ACADEMY.
STUDENT BODY OF ROUGHLY 2,500, RANGING IN AGE FROM SIX TO 19.
THE CURRICULUM SPANS ALL 13 YEARS OF EDUCATION.

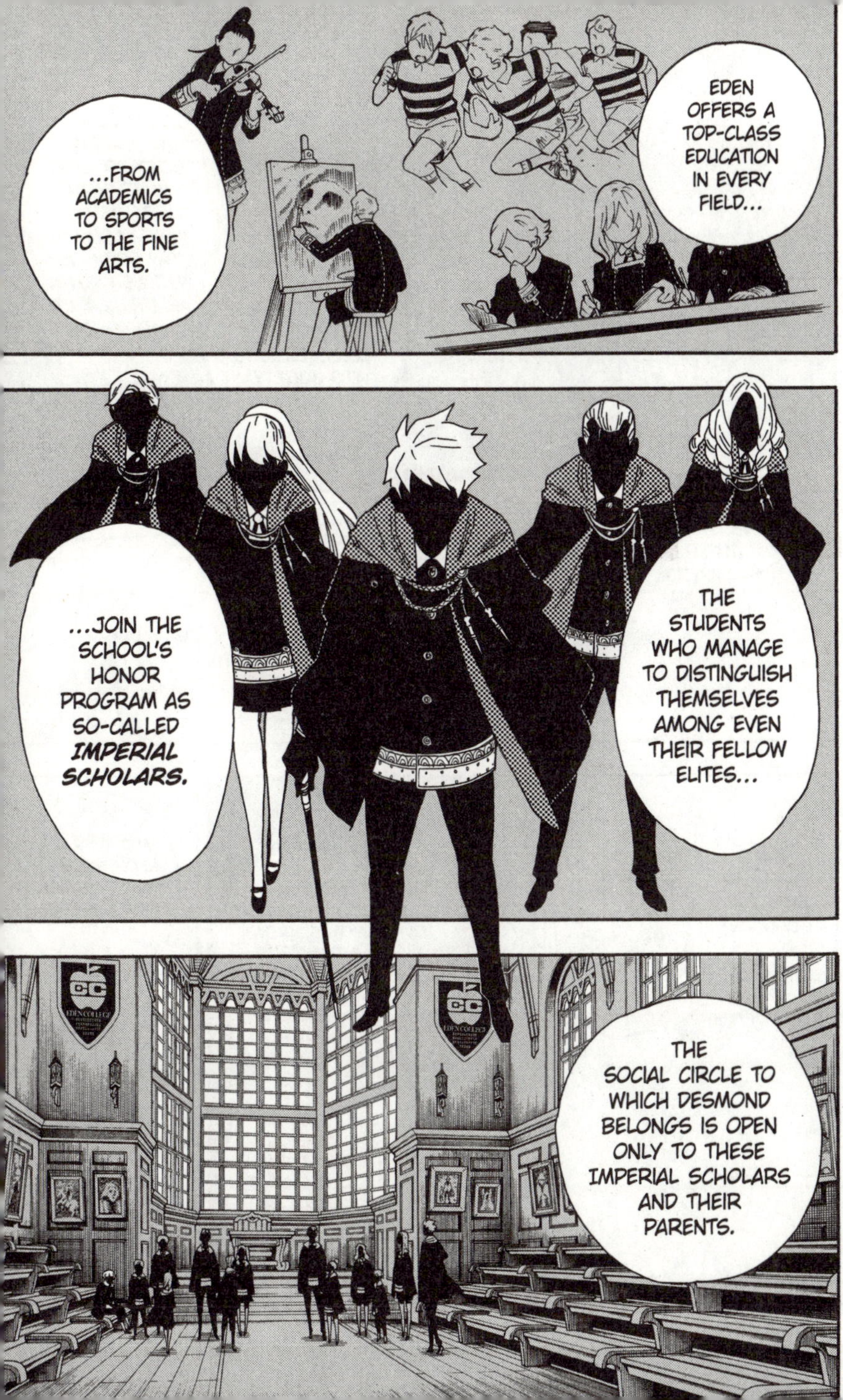
EDEN OFFERS A TOP-CLASS EDUCATION IN EVERY FIELD...
...FROM ACADEMICS TO SPORTS TO THE FINE ARTS.
THE STUDENTS WHO MANAGE TO DISTINGUISH THEMSELVES AMONG EVEN THEIR FELLOW ELITES...
...JOIN THE SCHOOL'S HONOR PROGRAM AS SO-CALLED ***IMPERIAL SCHOLARS.***
EDEN COLLEGE
THE SOCIAL CIRCLE TO WHICH DESMOND BELONGS IS OPEN ONLY TO THESE IMPERIAL SCHOLARS AND THEIR PARENTS.

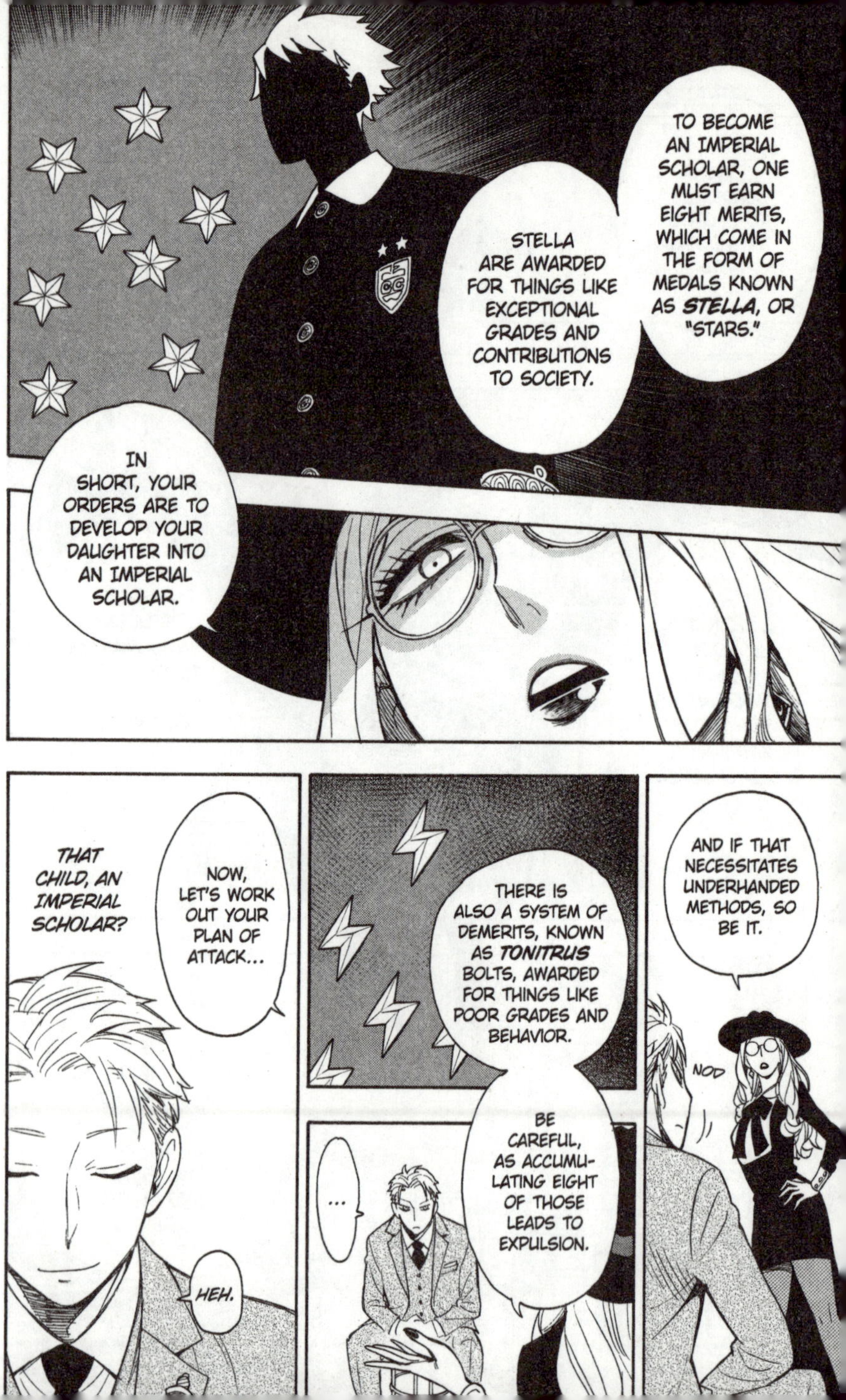
TO BECOME AN IMPERIAL SCHOLAR, ONE MUST EARN EIGHT MERITS, WHICH COME IN THE FORM OF MEDALS KNOWN AS *STELLA*, OR "STARS."
STELLA ARE AWARDED FOR THINGS LIKE EXCEPTIONAL GRADES AND CONTRIBUTIONS TO SOCIETY.
IN SHORT, YOUR ORDERS ARE TO DEVELOP YOUR DAUGHTER INTO AN IMPERIAL SCHOLAR.
AND IF THAT NECESSITATES UNDERHANDED METHODS, SO BE IT.
NOD
THERE IS ALSO A SYSTEM OF DEMERITS, KNOWN AS *TONITRUS* BOLTS, AWARDED FOR THINGS LIKE POOR GRADES AND BEHAVIOR.
BE CAREFUL, AS ACCUMU-LATING EIGHT OF THOSE LEADS TO EXPULSION.
...
NOW, LET'S WORK OUT YOUR PLAN OF ATTACK...
THAT CHILD, AN IMPERIAL SCHOLAR?
HEH.

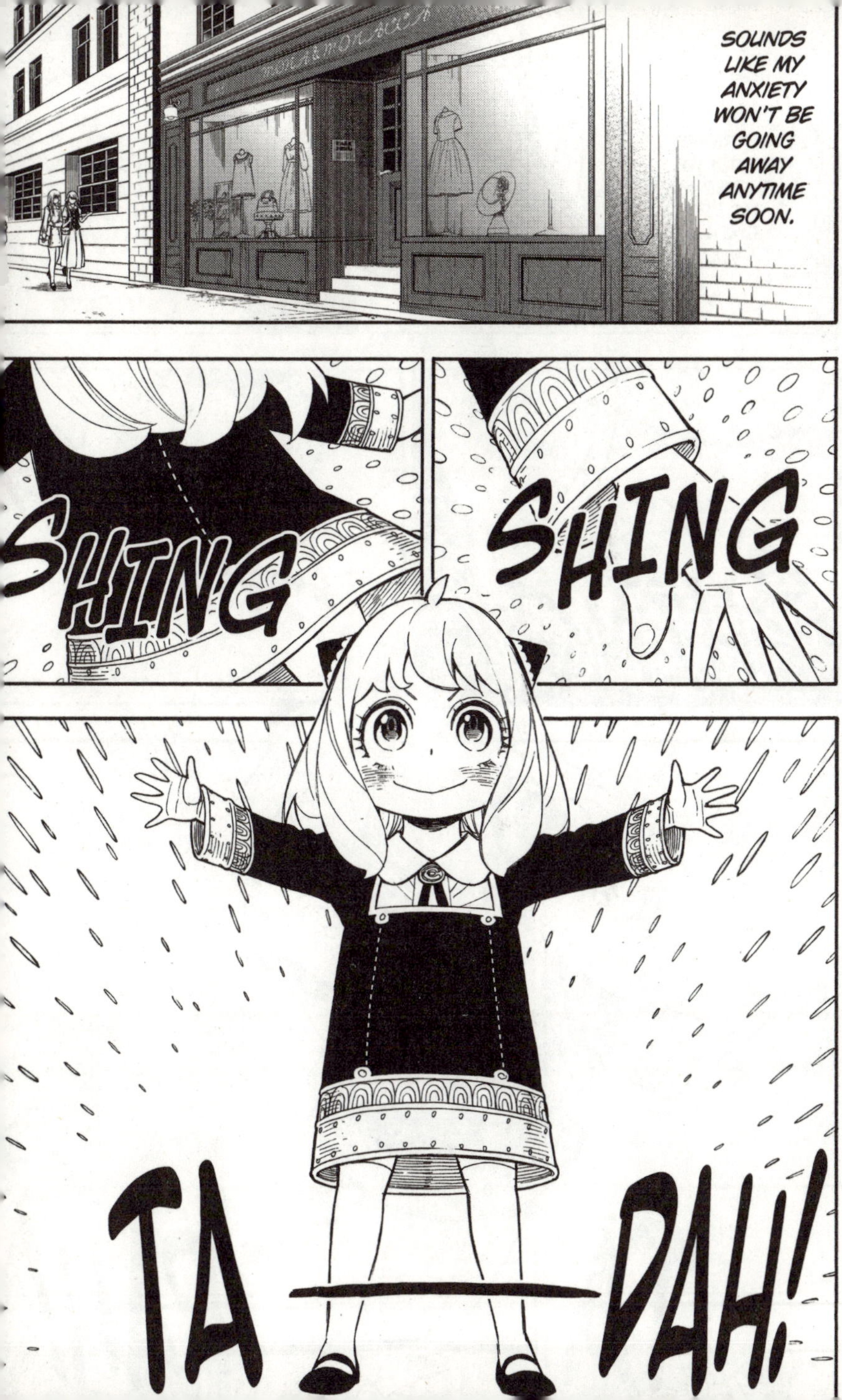
SOUNDS LIKE MY ANXIETY WON'T BE GOING AWAY ANYTIME SOON.
SHING
SHING
TA——DAH!

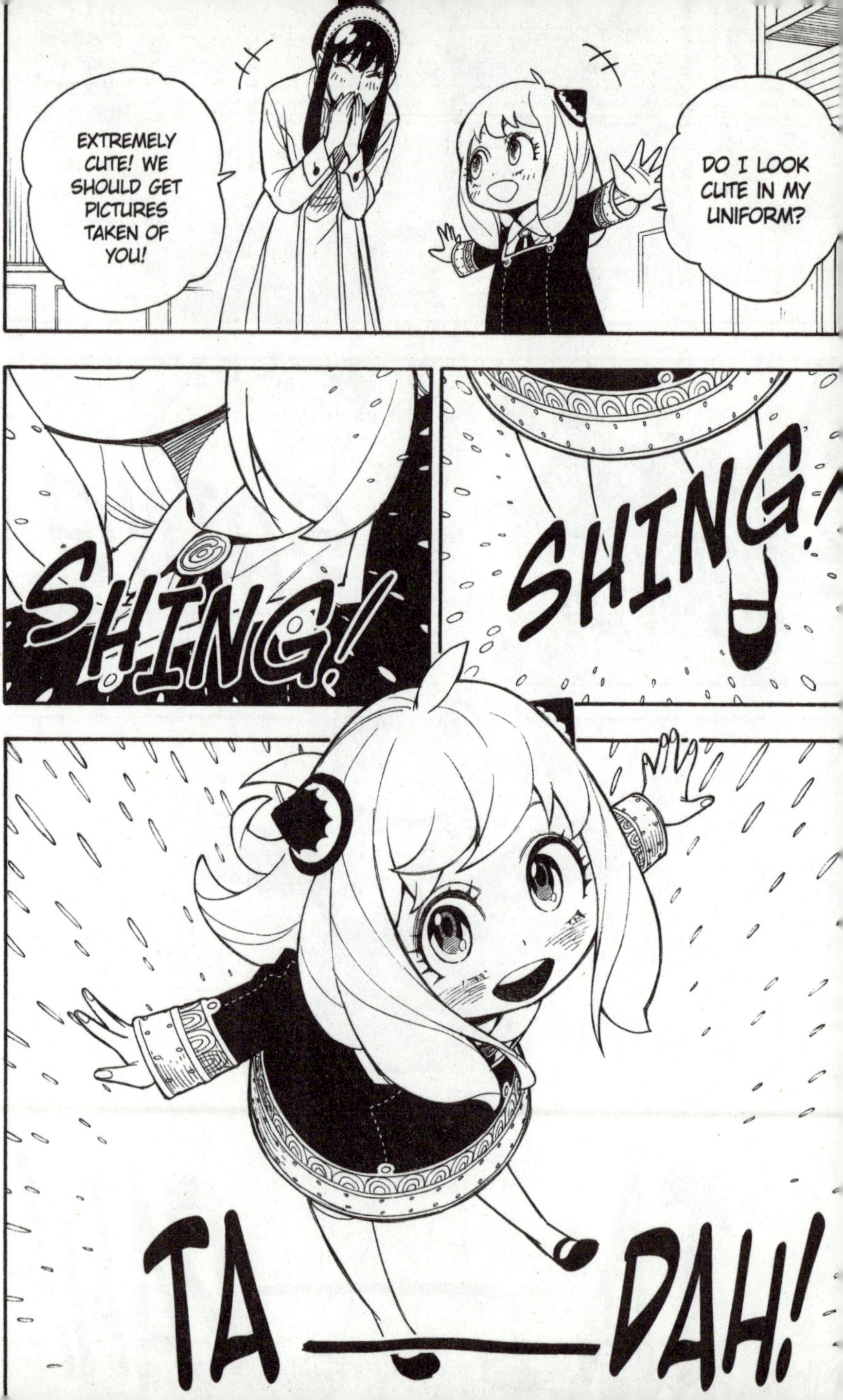
DO I LOOK CUTE IN MY UNIFORM?
EXTREMELY CUTE! WE SHOULD GET PICTURES TAKEN OF YOU!
SHING!
SHING!
TA——DAH!

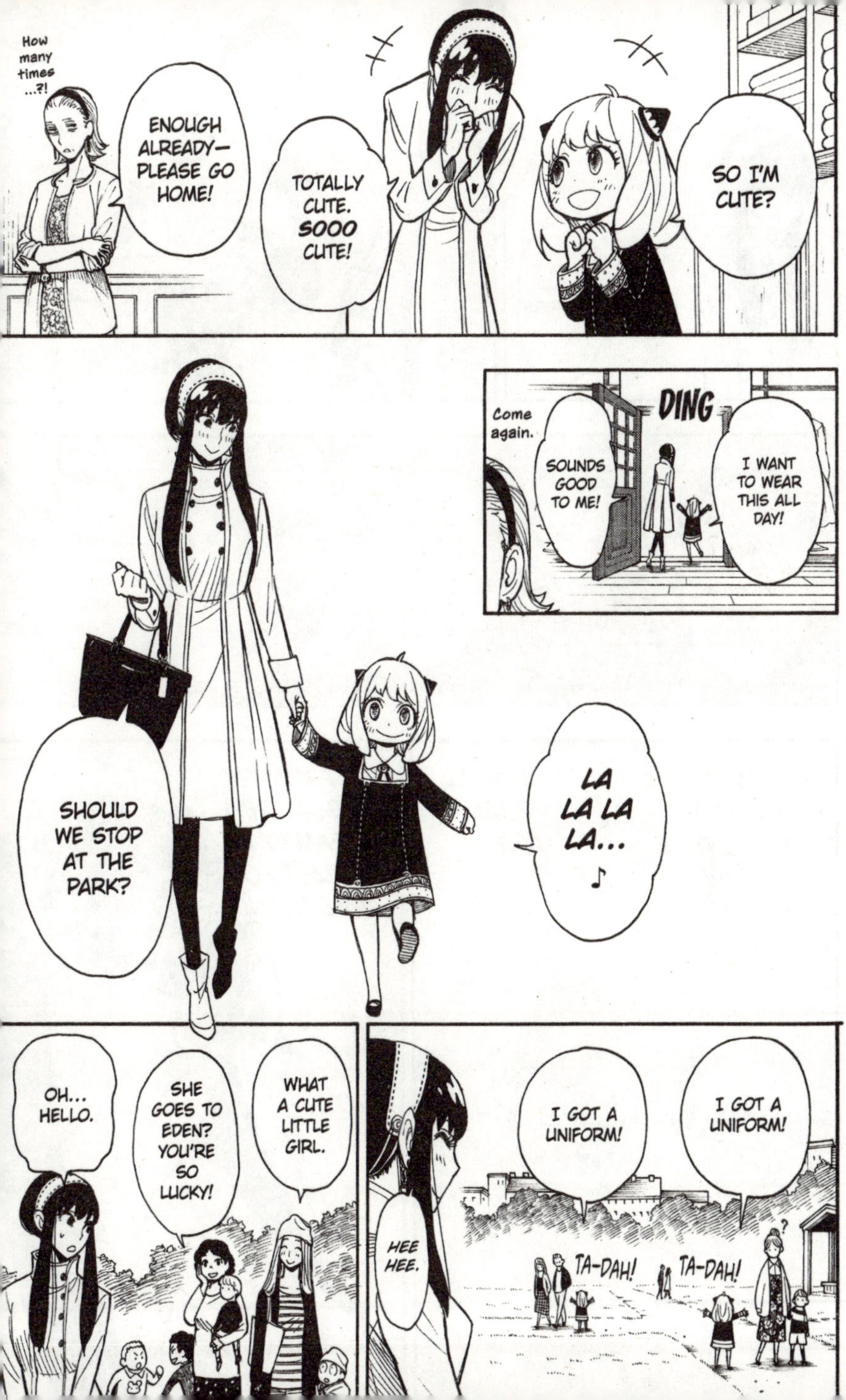
SO I'M CUTE?
TOTALLY CUTE. SOOO CUTE!
ENOUGH ALREADY—PLEASE GO HOME!
How many times ...?!
I WANT TO WEAR THIS ALL DAY!
DING
SOUNDS GOOD TO ME!
Come again.
LA LA LA LA... ♪
SHOULD WE STOP AT THE PARK?
I GOT A UNIFORM!
I GOT A UNIFORM!
TA-DAH!
TA-DAH!
HEE HEE.
WHAT A CUTE LITTLE GIRL.
SHE GOES TO EDEN? YOU'RE SO LUCKY!
OH... HELLO.

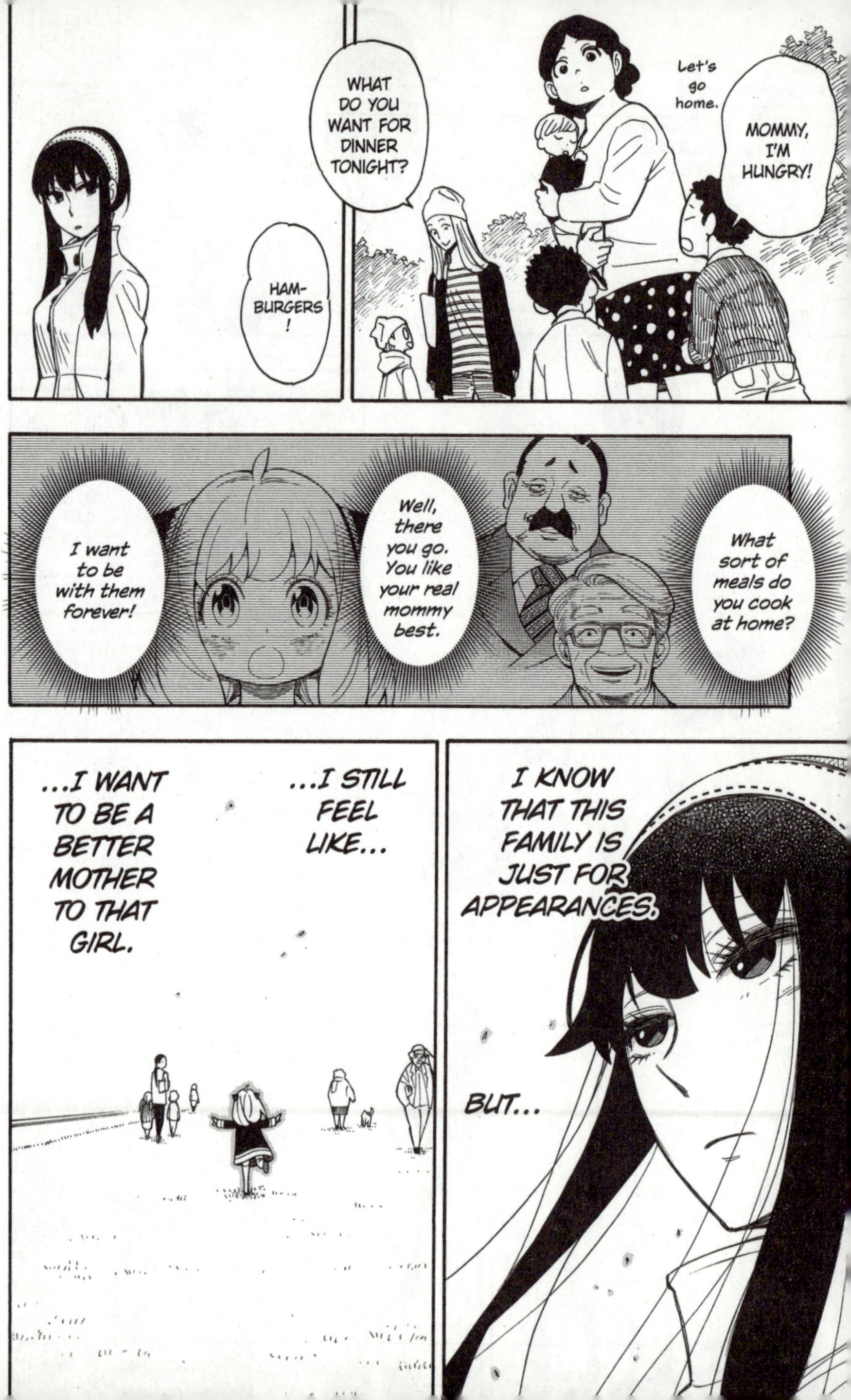
MOMMY, I'M HUNGRY!
Let's go home.
WHAT DO YOU WANT FOR DINNER TONIGHT?
HAM-BURGERS!
What sort of meals do you cook at home?
Well, there you go. You like your real mommy best.
I want to be with them forever!
I KNOW THAT THIS FAMILY IS JUST FOR APPEARANCES.
BUT...
...I STILL FEEL LIKE...
...I WANT TO BE A BETTER MOTHER TO THAT GIRL.

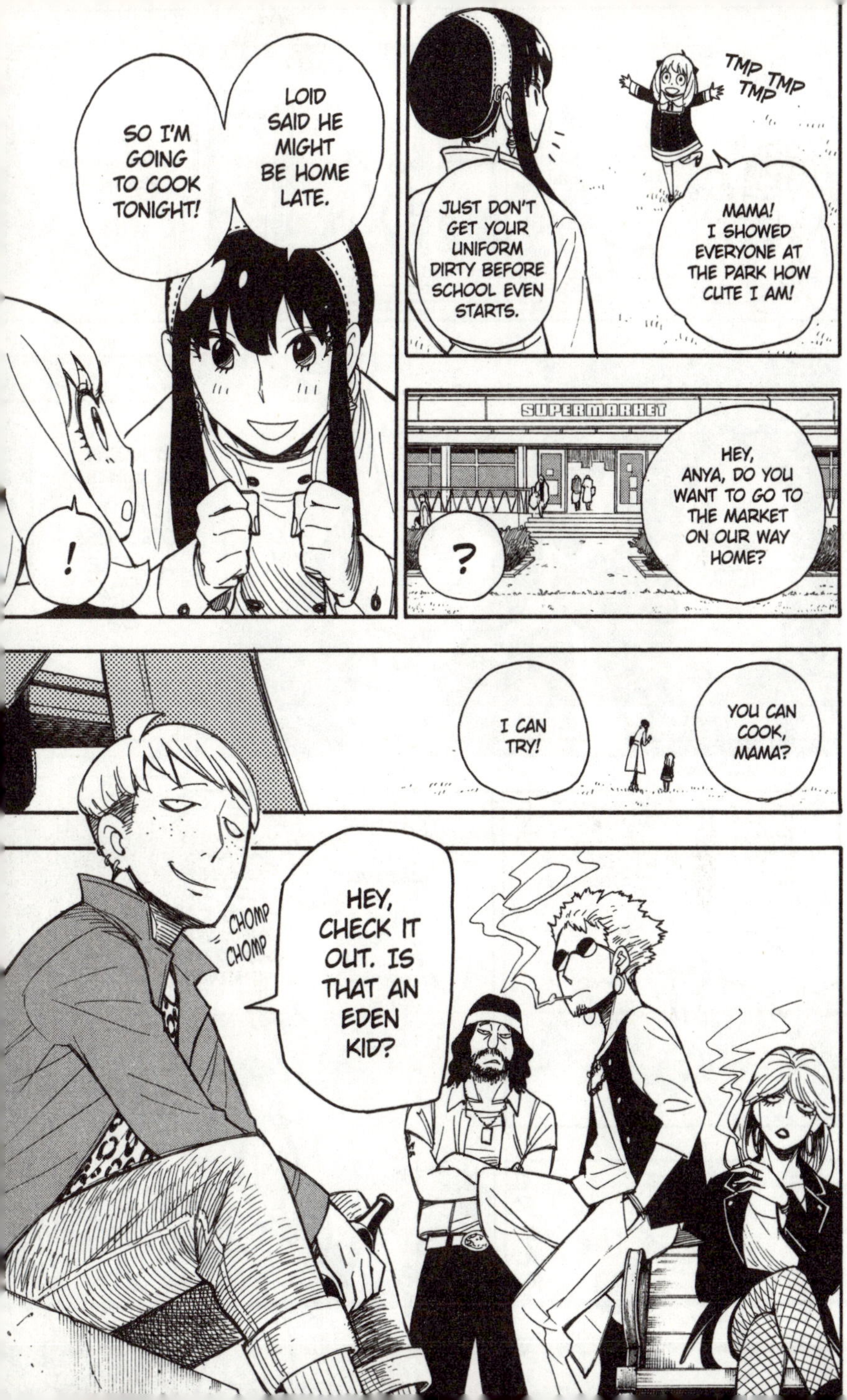
TMP TMP TMP
MAMA! I SHOWED EVERYONE AT THE PARK HOW CUTE I AM!
JUST DON'T GET YOUR UNIFORM DIRTY BEFORE SCHOOL EVEN STARTS.
SUPERMARKET
HEY, ANYA, DO YOU WANT TO GO TO THE MARKET ON OUR WAY HOME?
?
LOID SAID HE MIGHT BE HOME LATE.
SO I'M GOING TO COOK TONIGHT!
!
YOU CAN COOK, MAMA?
I CAN TRY!
HEY, CHECK IT OUT. IS THAT AN EDEN KID?
CHOMP CHOMP

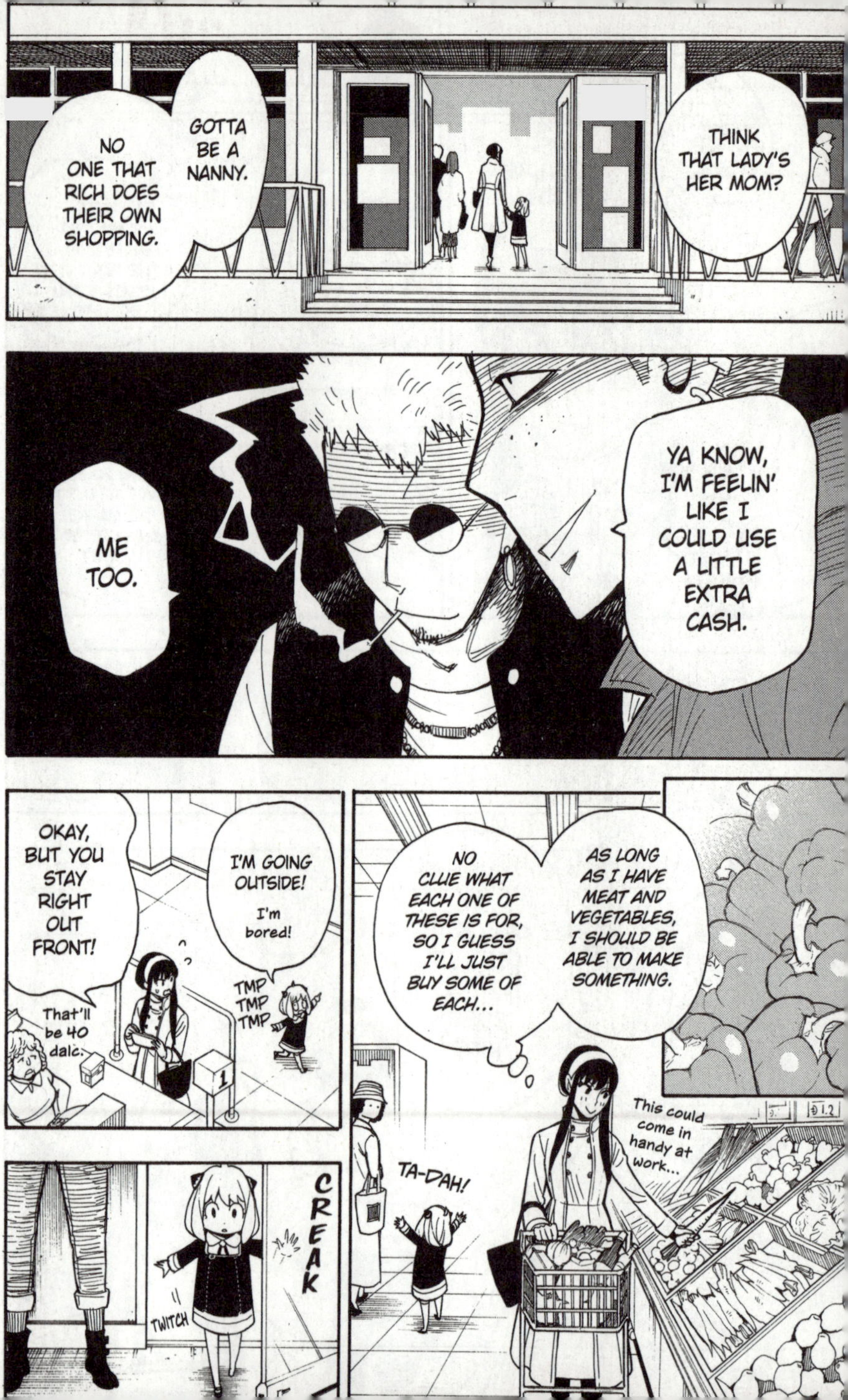
THINK THAT LADY'S HER MOM?
GOTTA BE A NANNY.
NO ONE THAT RICH DOES THEIR OWN SHOPPING.
YA KNOW, I'M FEELIN' LIKE I COULD USE A LITTLE EXTRA CASH.
ME TOO.
AS LONG AS I HAVE MEAT AND VEGETABLES, I SHOULD BE ABLE TO MAKE SOMETHING.
NO CLUE WHAT EACH ONE OF THESE IS FOR, SO I GUESS I'LL JUST BUY SOME OF EACH...
This could come in handy at work...
TA-DAH!
I'M GOING OUTSIDE!
I'm bored!
OKAY, BUT YOU STAY RIGHT OUT FRONT!
TMP TMP TMP
That'll be 40 dalc.
CREAK
TWITCH

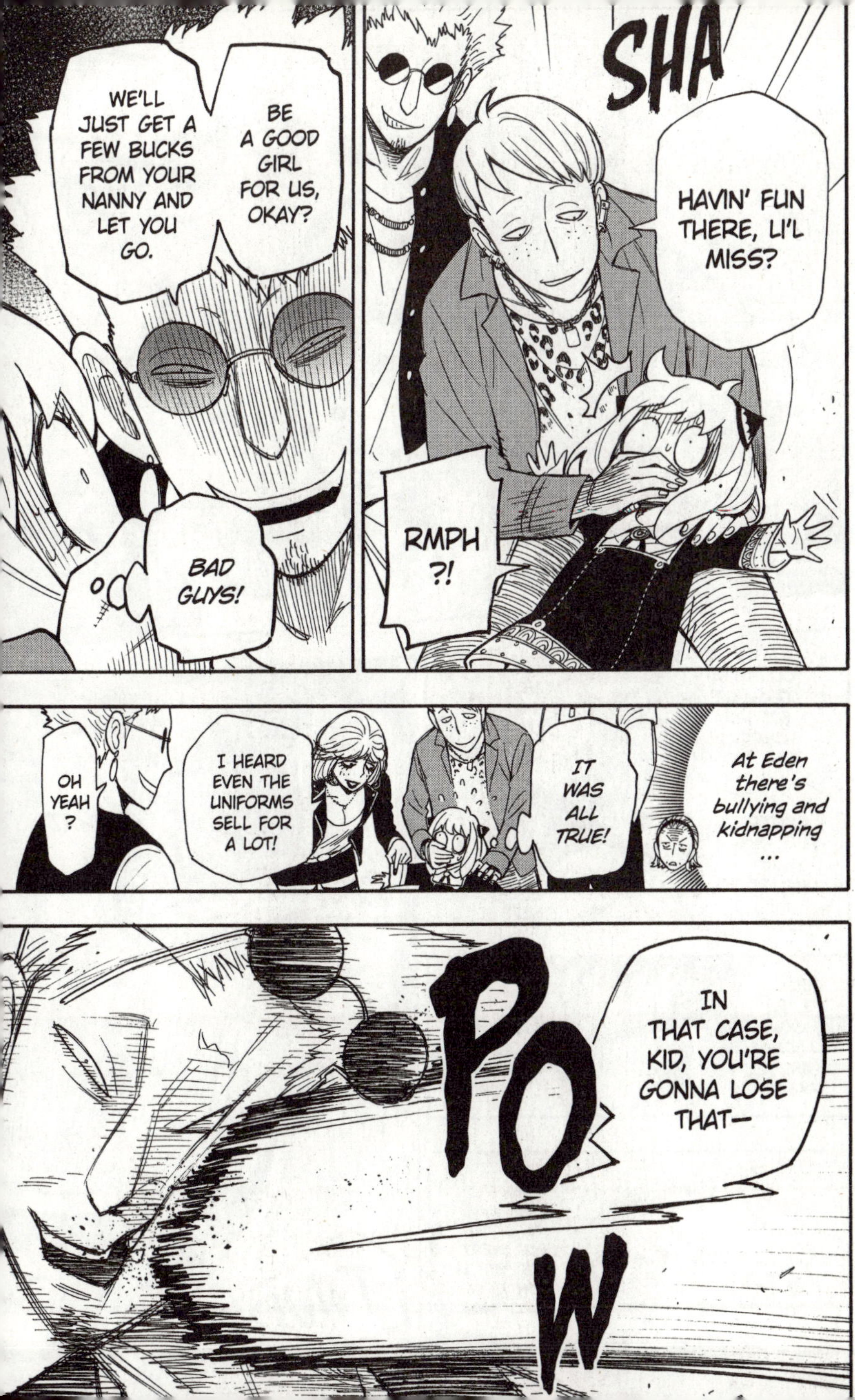
SHA
HAVIN' FUN THERE, LI'L MISS?
RMPH ?!
BE A GOOD GIRL FOR US, OKAY?
WE'LL JUST GET A FEW BUCKS FROM YOUR NANNY AND LET YOU GO.
BAD GUYS!
At Eden there's bullying and kidnapping ...
IT WAS ALL TRUE!
I HEARD EVEN THE UNIFORMS SELL FOR A LOT!
OH YEAH ?
IN THAT CASE, KID, YOU'RE GONNA LOSE THAT—
POW

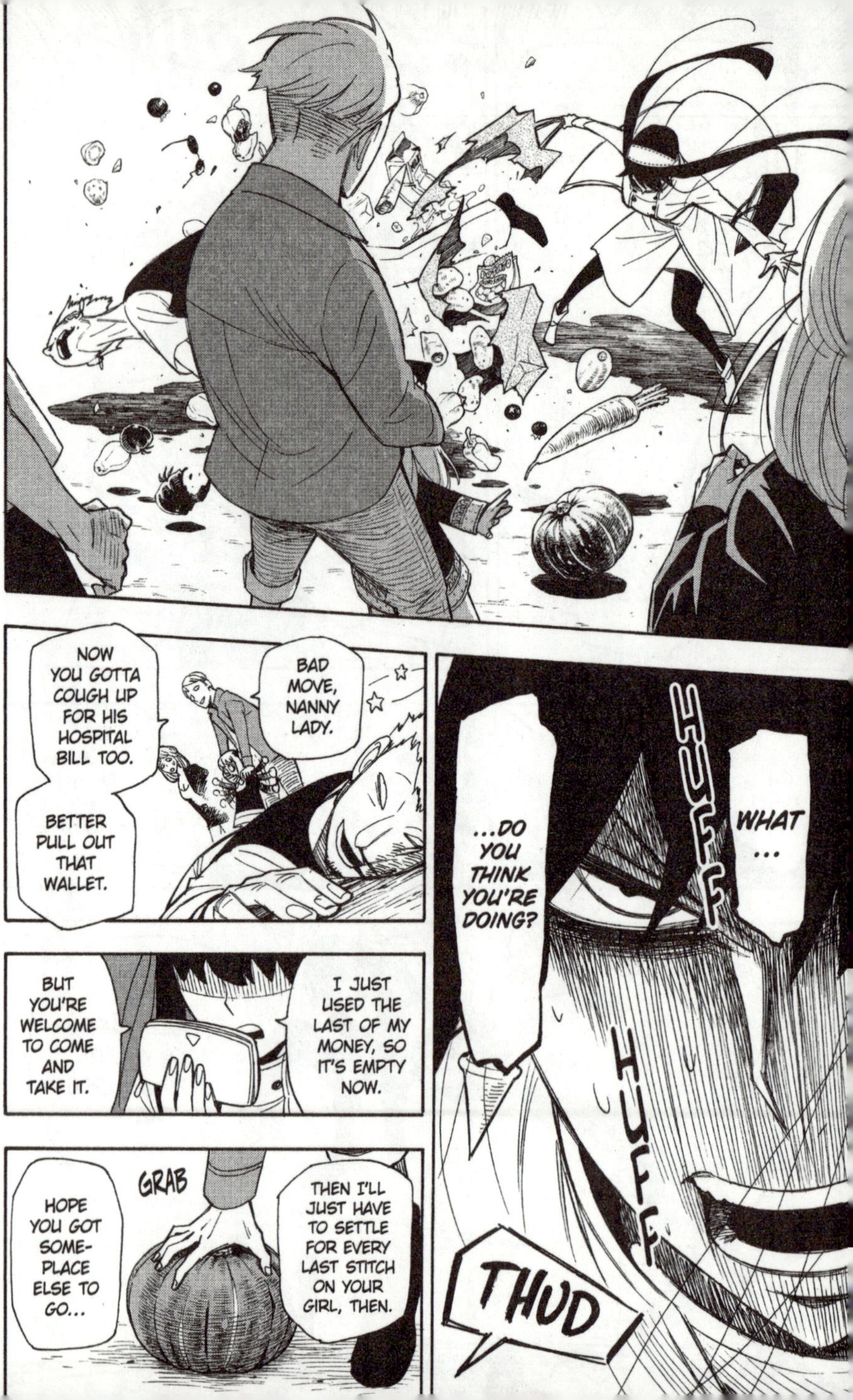

HUFF
WHAT ...
...DO YOU THINK YOU'RE DOING?
HUFF
THUD
BAD MOVE, NANNY LADY.
NOW YOU GOTTA COUGH UP FOR HIS HOSPITAL BILL TOO.
BETTER PULL OUT THAT WALLET.
I JUST USED THE LAST OF MY MONEY, SO IT'S EMPTY NOW.
BUT YOU'RE WELCOME TO COME AND TAKE IT.
THEN I'LL JUST HAVE TO SETTLE FOR EVERY LAST STITCH ON YOUR GIRL, THEN.
GRAB
HOPE YOU GOT SOME-PLACE ELSE TO GO...

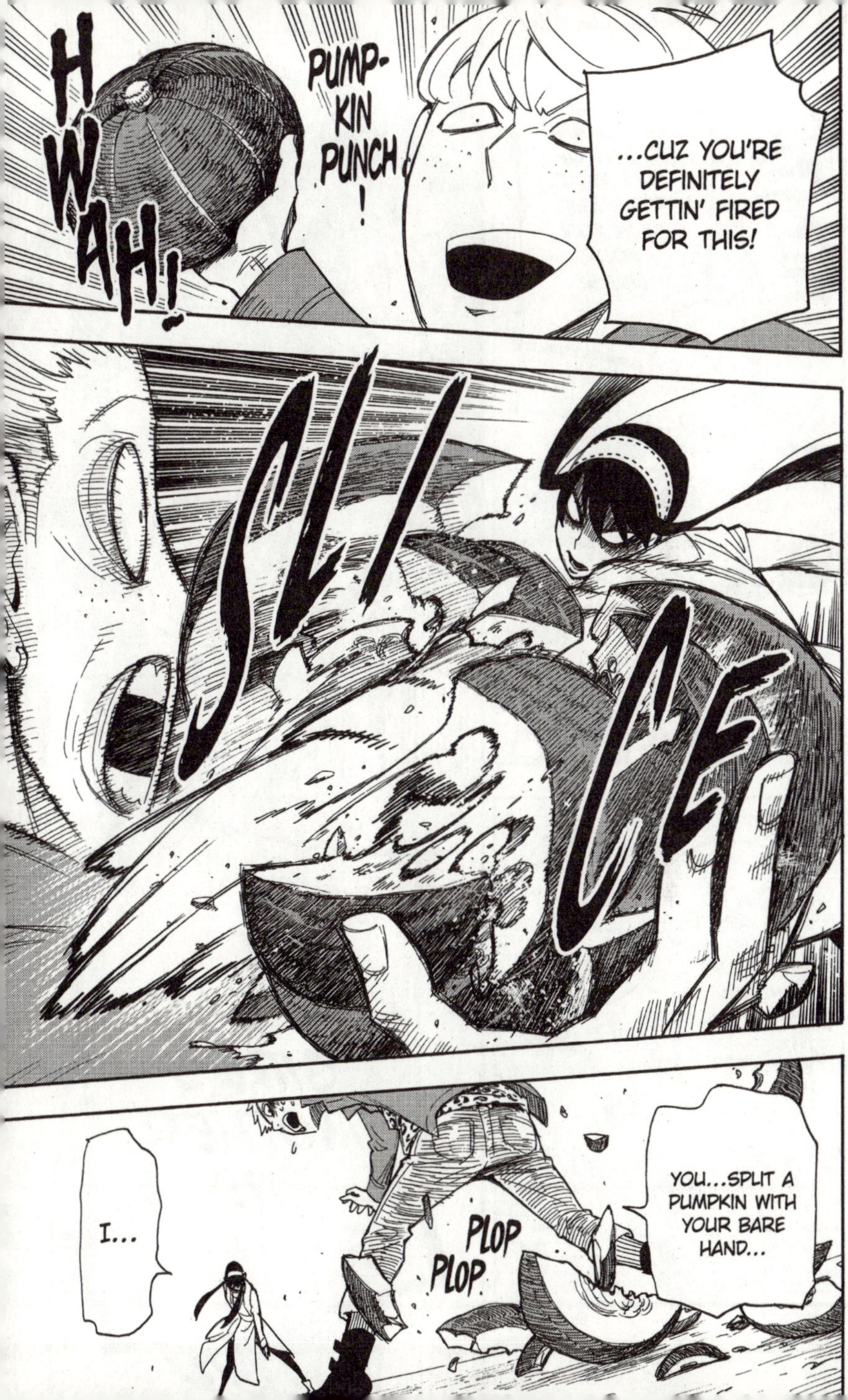
...CUZ YOU'RE DEFINITELY GETTIN' FIRED FOR THIS!
PUMP-KIN PUNCH!
HWAH!
SLICE
YOU...SPLIT A PUMPKIN WITH YOUR BARE HAND...
PLOP PLOP
I...

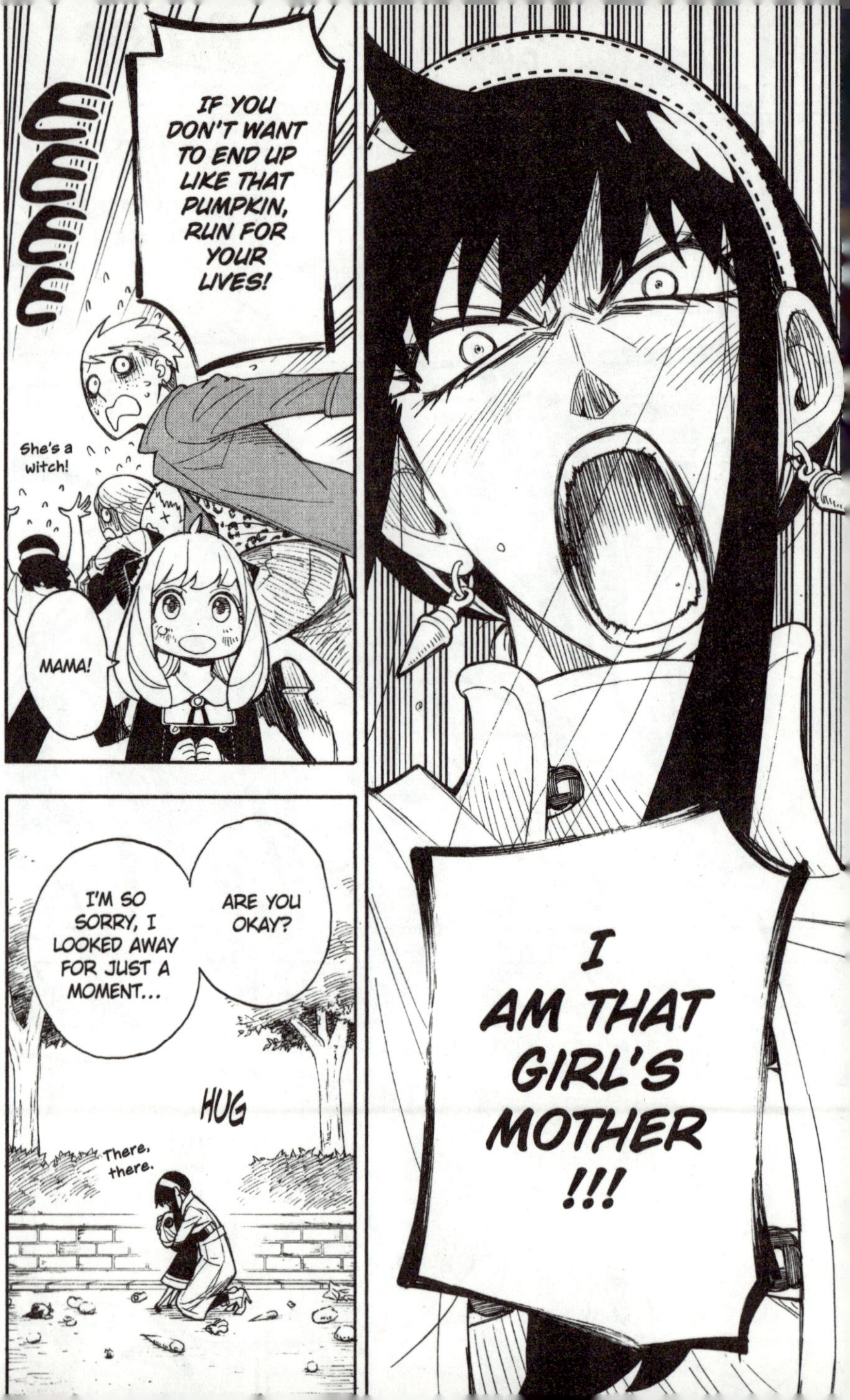
I AM THAT GIRL'S MOTHER !!!
IF YOU DON'T WANT TO END UP LIKE THAT PUMPKIN, RUN FOR YOUR LIVES!
She's a witch!
MAMA!
ARE YOU OKAY?
I'M SO SORRY, I LOOKED AWAY FOR JUST A MOMENT...
HUG
There, there.

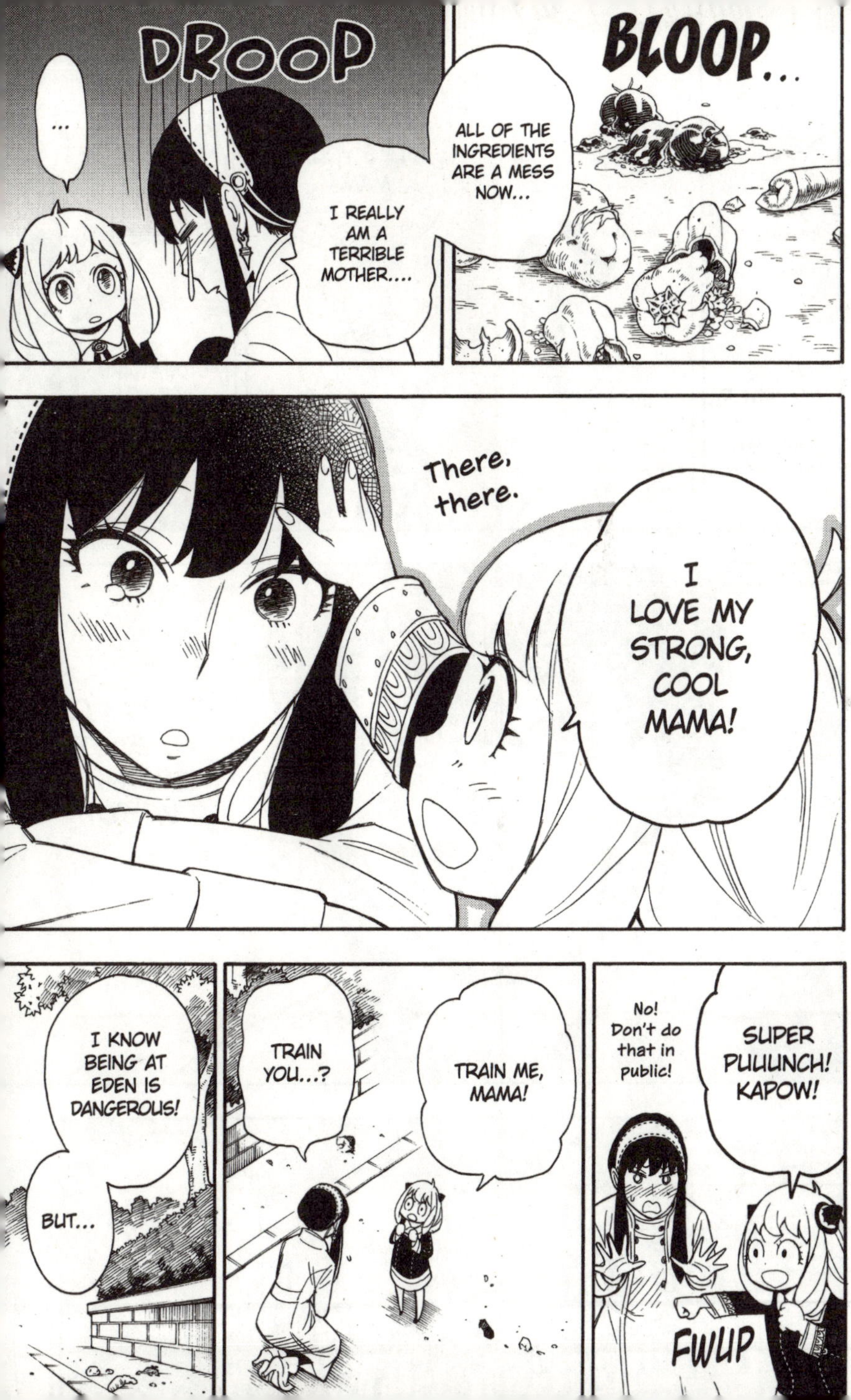
BLOOP...
DROOP
ALL OF THE INGREDIENTS ARE A MESS NOW...
I REALLY AM A TERRIBLE MOTHER....
...
I LOVE MY STRONG, COOL MAMA!
There, there.
SUPER PUUUNCH! KAPOW!
No! Don't do that in public!
FWUP
TRAIN ME, MAMA!
TRAIN YOU...?
I KNOW BEING AT EDEN IS DANGEROUS!
BUT...

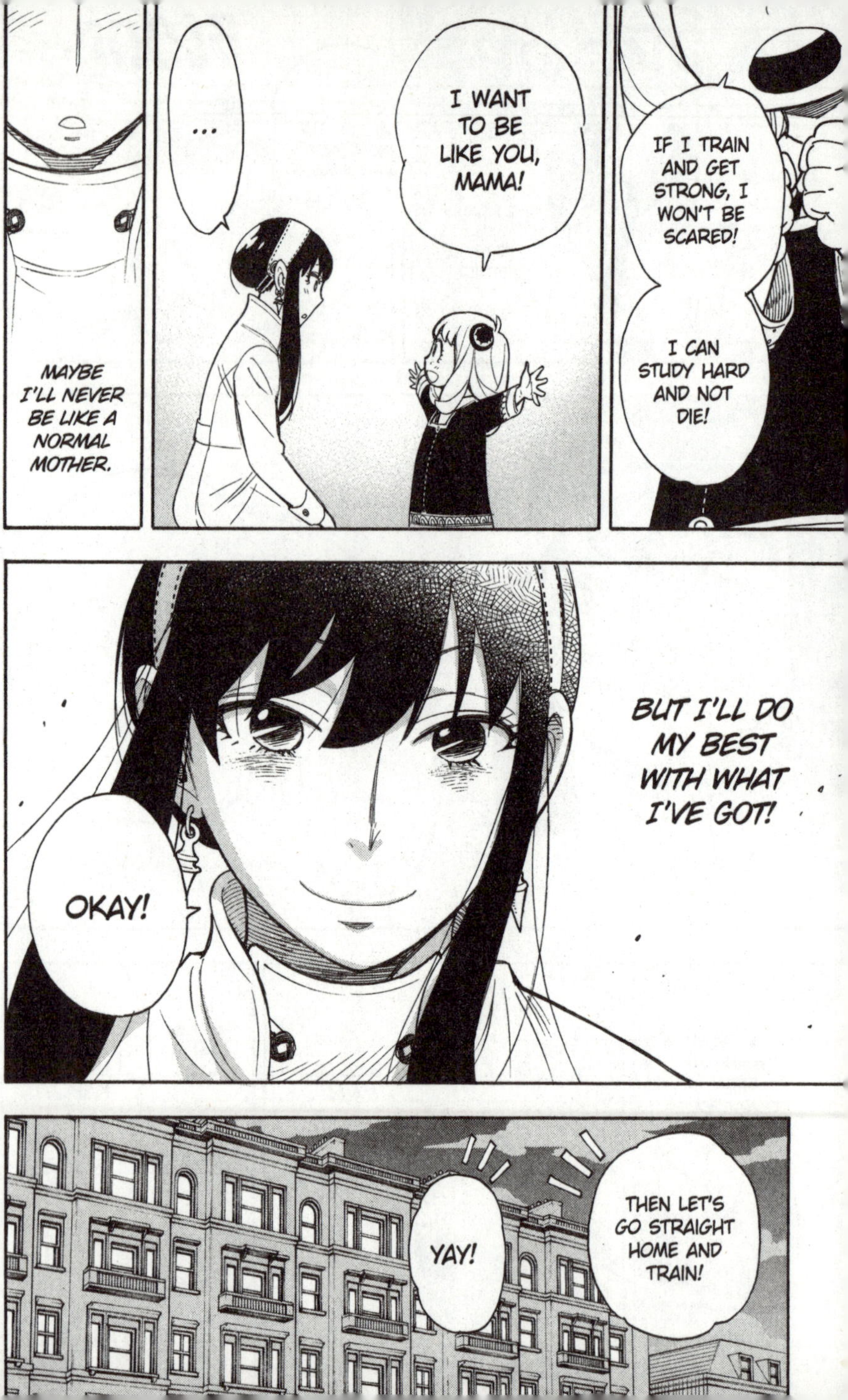
IF I TRAIN AND GET STRONG, I WON'T BE SCARED!
I CAN STUDY HARD AND NOT DIE!
I WANT TO BE LIKE YOU, MAMA!
...
MAYBE I'LL NEVER BE LIKE A NORMAL MOTHER.
BUT I'LL DO MY BEST WITH WHAT I'VE GOT!
OKAY!
THEN LET'S GO STRAIGHT HOME AND TRAIN!
YAY!

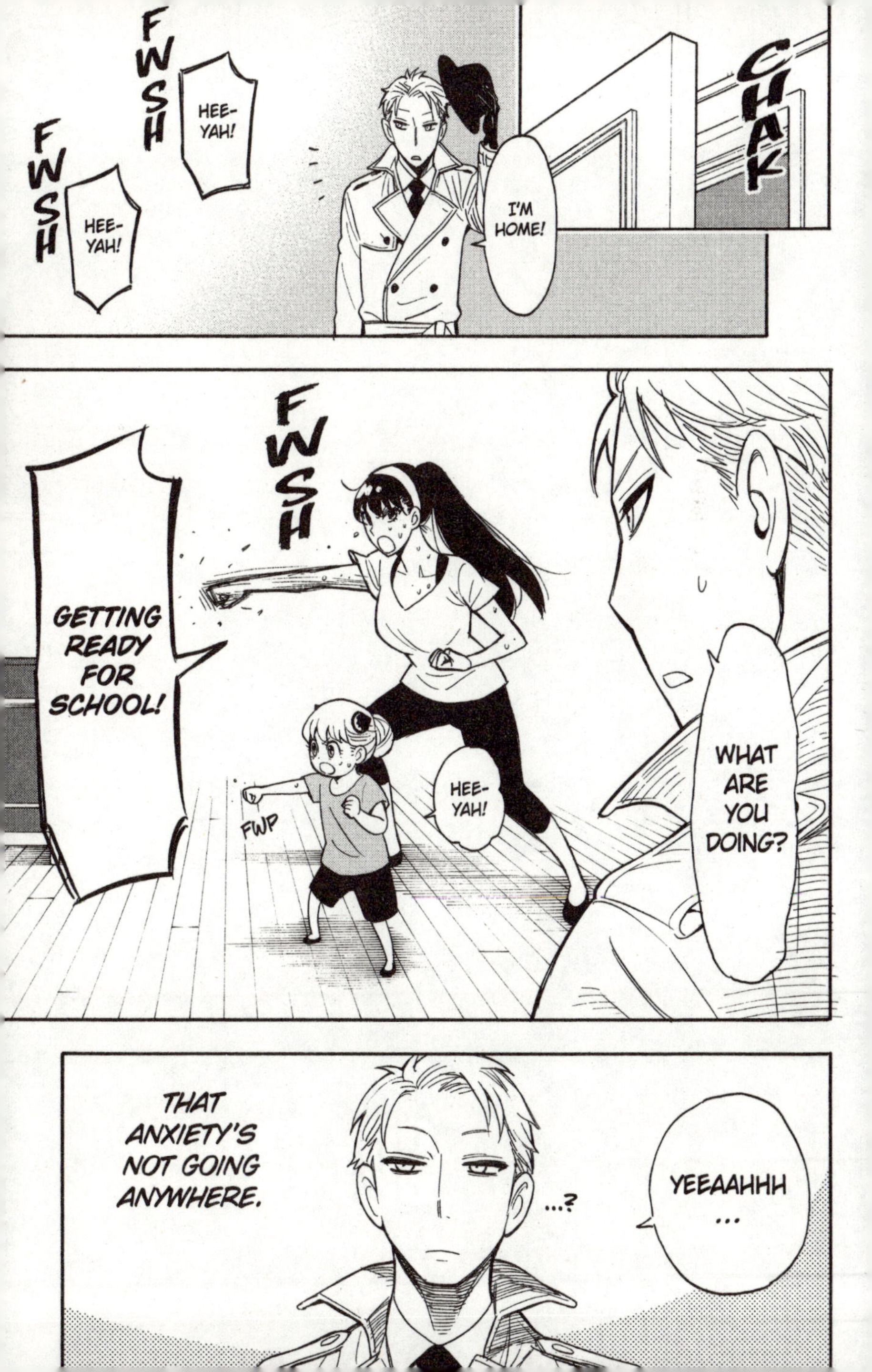
CHAK
I'M HOME!
FWSH
HEE-YAH!
FWSH
HEE-YAH!
WHAT ARE YOU DOING?
FWSH
HEE-YAH!
FWP
GETTING READY FOR SCHOOL!
YEEAAHHH ...
...?
THAT ANXIETY'S NOT GOING ANYWHERE.

SPY×FAMILY

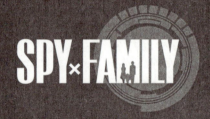

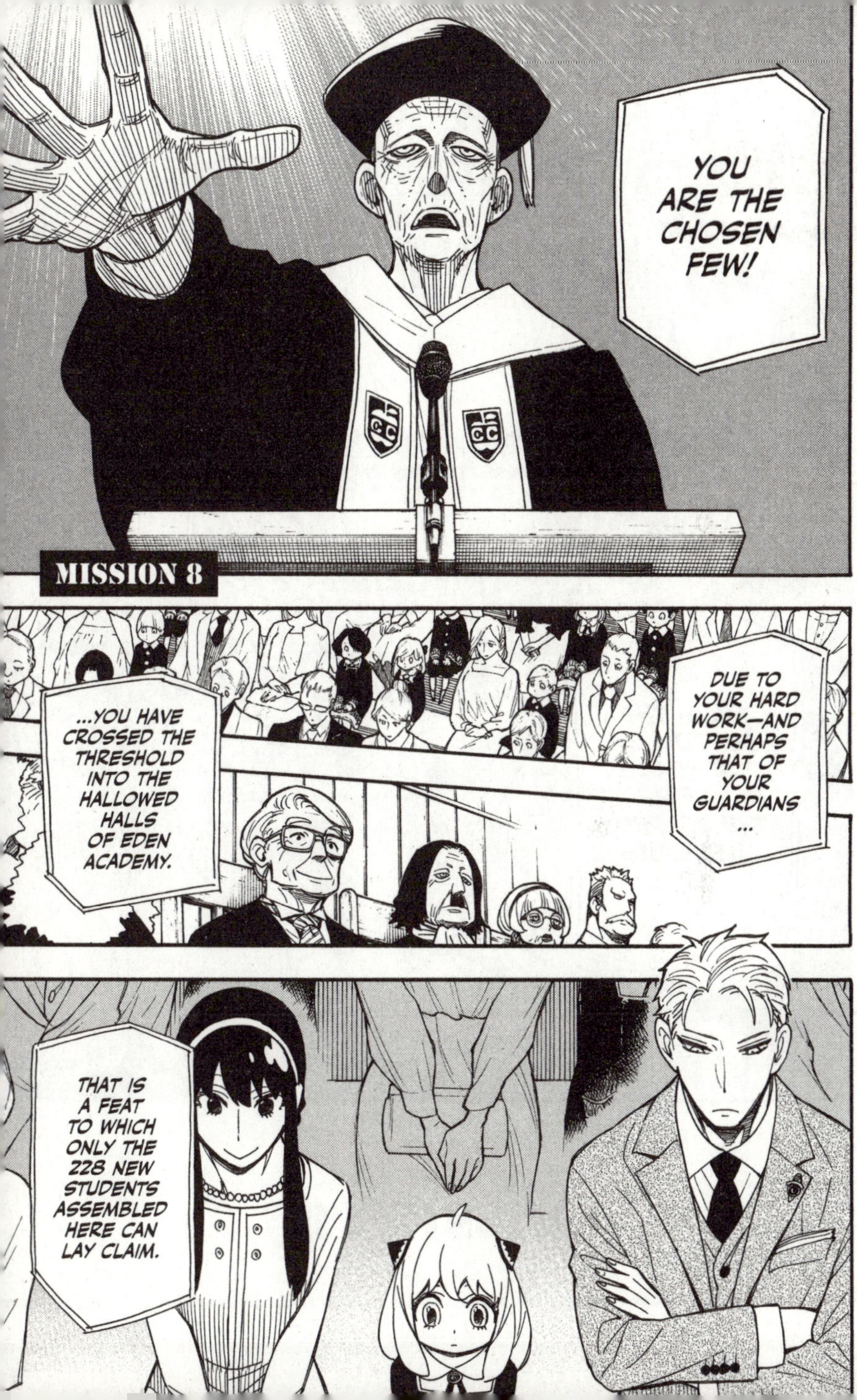
YOU ARE THE CHOSEN FEW!
MISSION 8
DUE TO YOUR HARD WORK—AND PERHAPS THAT OF YOUR GUARDIANS ...
...YOU HAVE CROSSED THE THRESHOLD INTO THE HALLOWED HALLS OF EDEN ACADEMY.
THAT IS A FEAT TO WHICH ONLY THE 228 NEW STUDENTS ASSEMBLED HERE CAN LAY CLAIM.

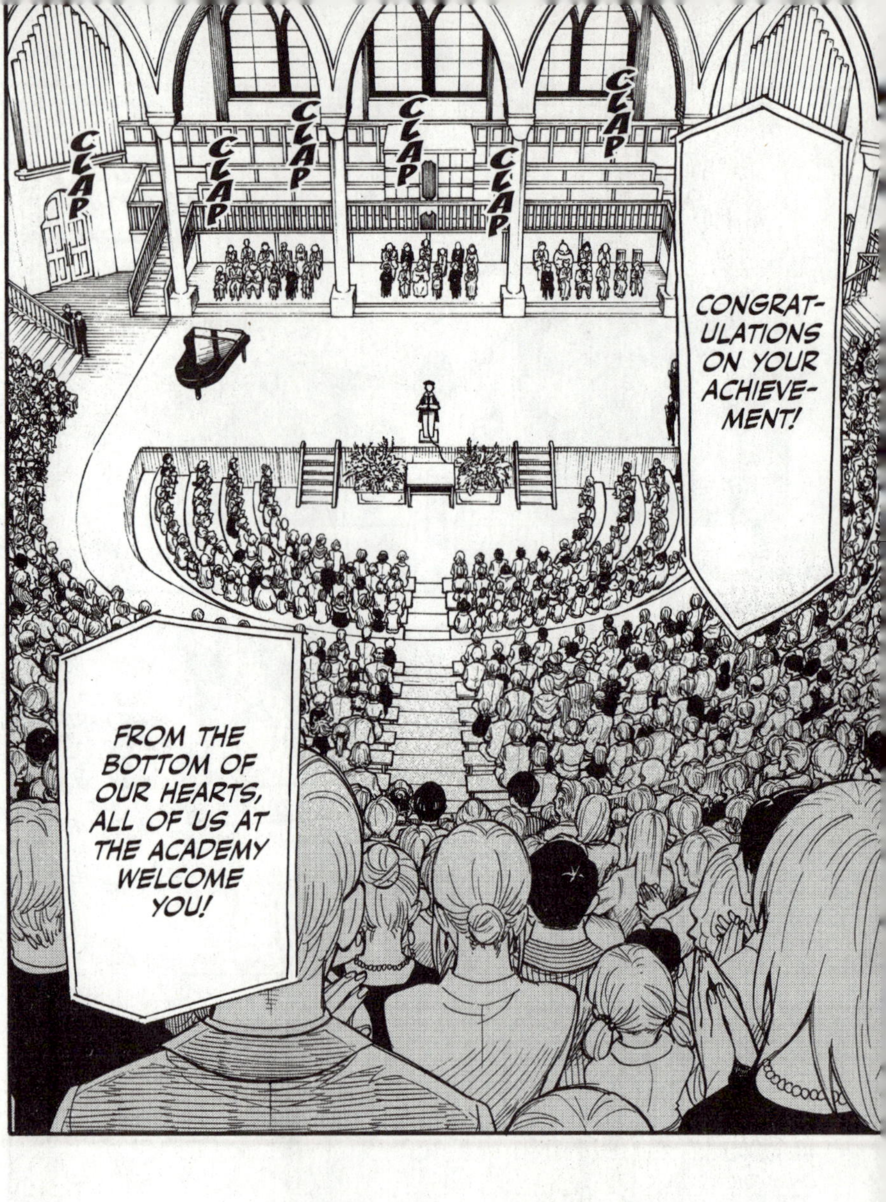
CLAP CLAP CLAP CLAP CLAP CLAP
CONGRATULATIONS ON YOUR ACHIEVEMENT!
FROM THE BOTTOM OF OUR HEARTS, ALL OF US AT THE ACADEMY WELCOME YOU!

MISSION 8

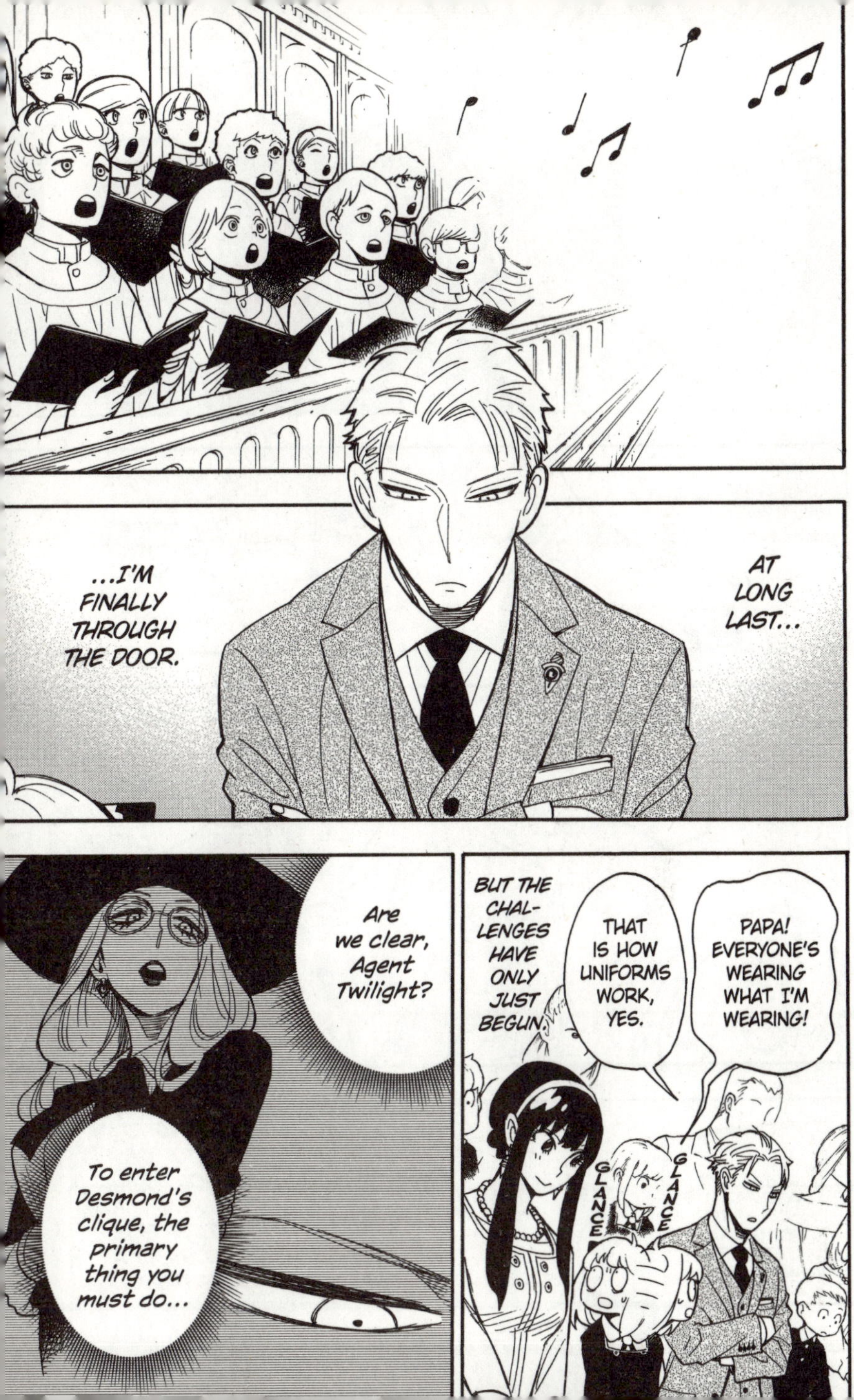
AT LONG LAST...
...I'M FINALLY THROUGH THE DOOR.
PAPA! EVERYONE'S WEARING WHAT I'M WEARING!
THAT IS HOW UNIFORMS WORK, YES.
BUT THE CHAL-LENGES HAVE ONLY JUST BEGUN.
GLANCE
GLANCE
Are we clear, Agent Twilight?
To enter Desmond's clique, the primary thing you must do...

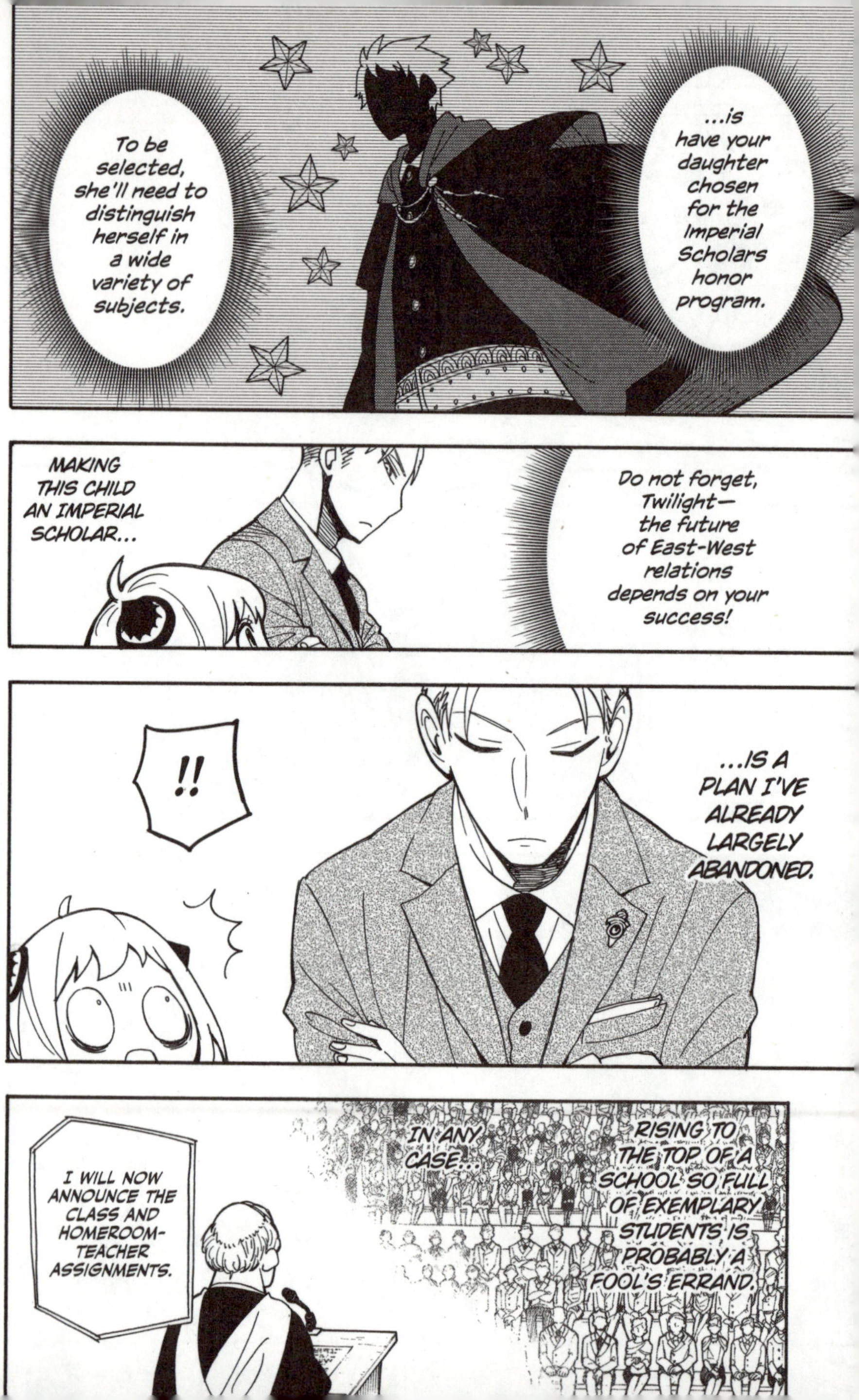
...is have your daughter chosen for the Imperial Scholars honor program.
To be selected, she'll need to distinguish herself in a wide variety of subjects.
Do not forget, Twilight— the future of East-West relations depends on your success!
MAKING THIS CHILD AN IMPERIAL SCHOLAR...
...IS A PLAN I'VE ALREADY LARGELY ABANDONED.
!!
RISING TO THE TOP OF A SCHOOL SO FULL OF EXEMPLARY STUDENTS IS PROBABLY A FOOL'S ERRAND.
IN ANY CASE...
I WILL NOW ANNOUNCE THE CLASS AND HOMEROOM-TEACHER ASSIGNMENTS.

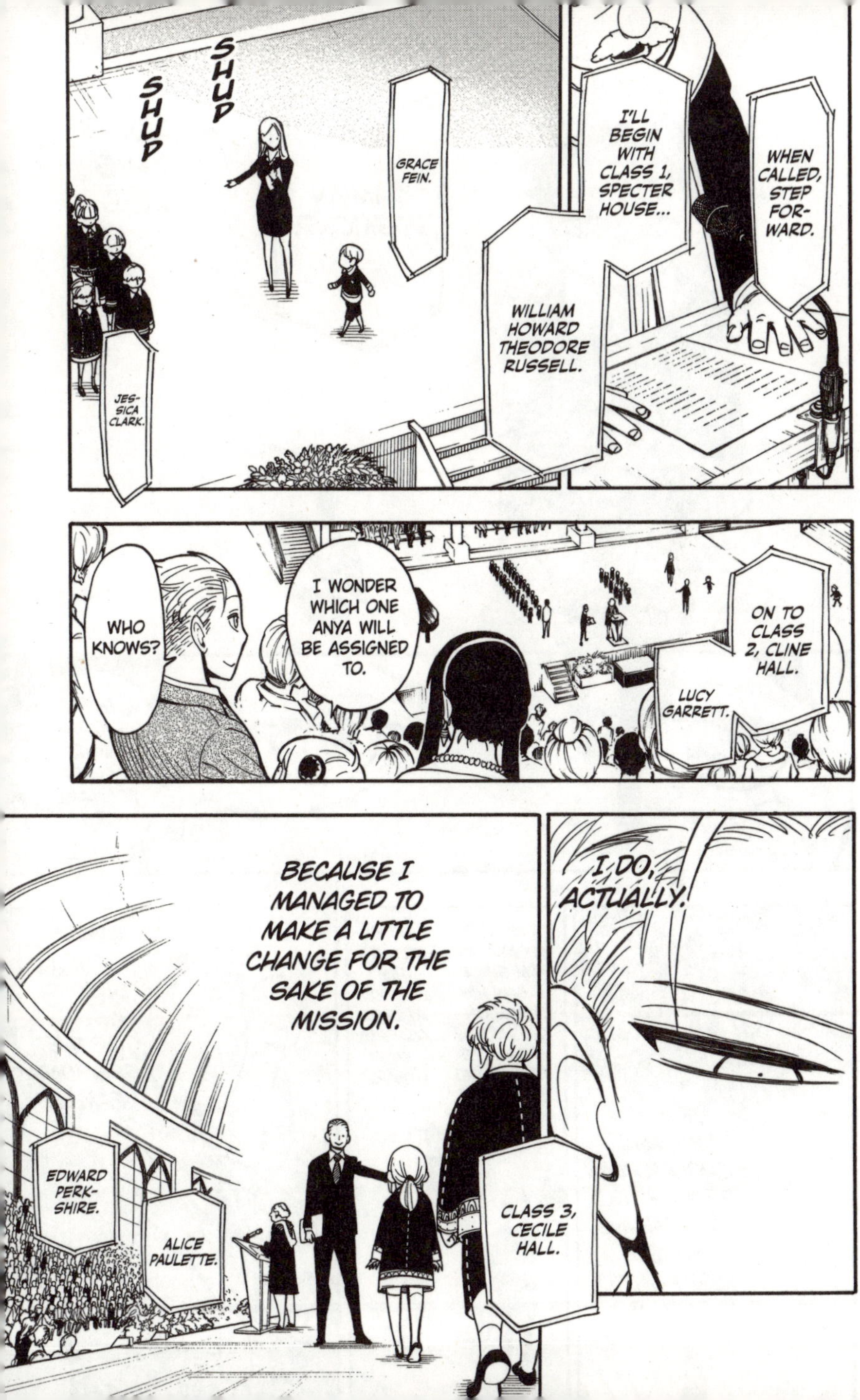
WHEN CALLED, STEP FORWARD.
I'LL BEGIN WITH CLASS 1, SPECTER HOUSE...
WILLIAM HOWARD THEODORE RUSSELL.
SHUP
SHUP
GRACE FEIN.
JESSICA CLARK.
ON TO CLASS 2, CLINE HALL.
LUCY GARRETT.
I WONDER WHICH ONE ANYA WILL BE ASSIGNED TO.
WHO KNOWS?
I DO, ACTUALLY.
BECAUSE I MANAGED TO MAKE A LITTLE CHANGE FOR THE SAKE OF THE MISSION.
CLASS 3, CECILE HALL.
ALICE PAULETTE.
EDWARD PERKSHIRE.

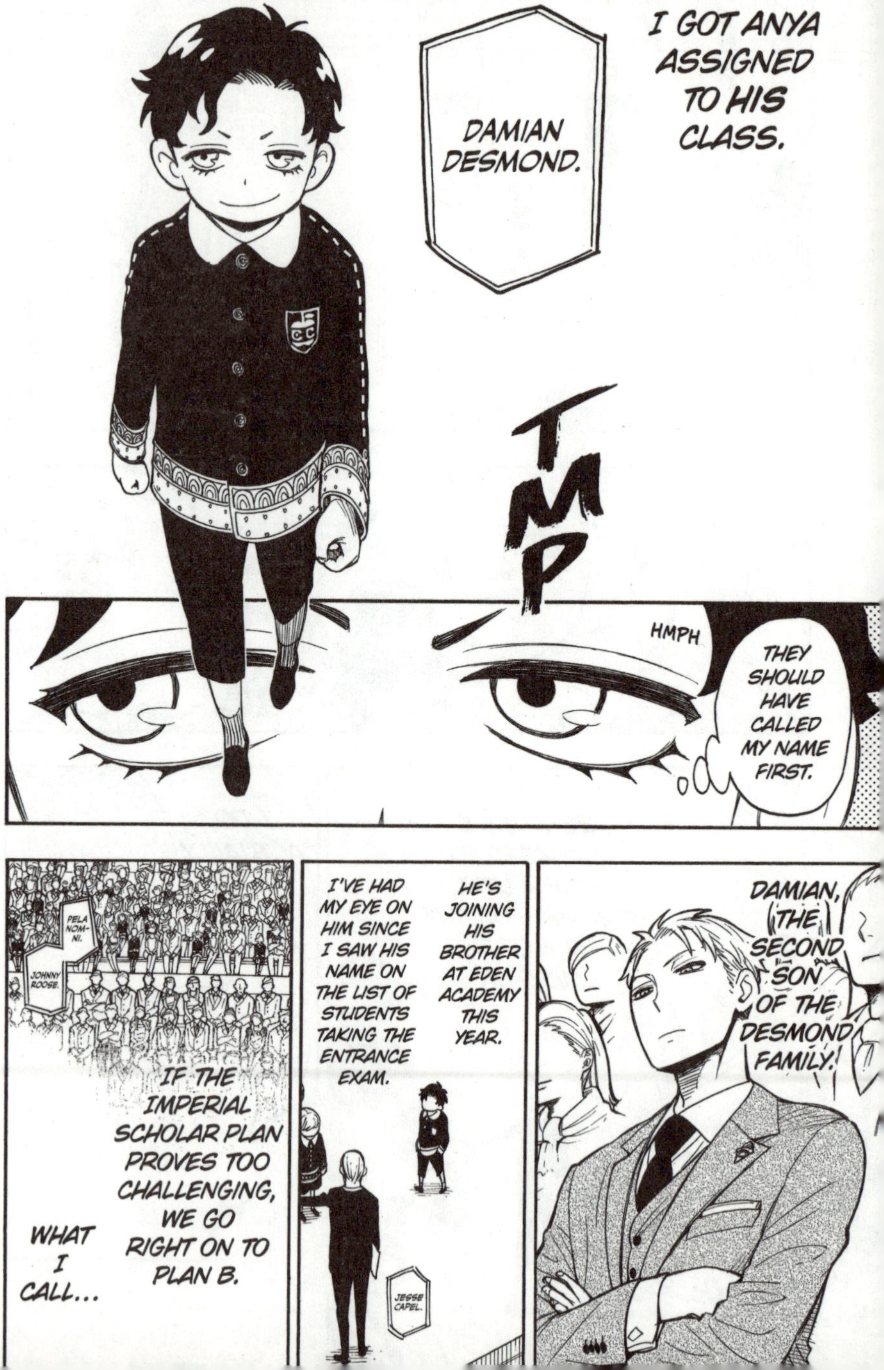
I GOT ANYA ASSIGNED TO HIS CLASS.
DAMIAN DESMOND.
TMP
HMPH
THEY SHOULD HAVE CALLED MY NAME FIRST.
DAMIAN, THE SECOND SON OF THE DESMOND FAMILY!
HE'S JOINING HIS BROTHER AT EDEN ACADEMY THIS YEAR.
I'VE HAD MY EYE ON HIM SINCE I SAW HIS NAME ON THE LIST OF STUDENTS TAKING THE ENTRANCE EXAM.
JESSE CAPEL.
PELA NOMNI.
JOHNNY ROOSE.
IF THE IMPERIAL SCHOLAR PLAN PROVES TOO CHALLENGING, WE GO RIGHT ON TO PLAN B.
WHAT I CALL...

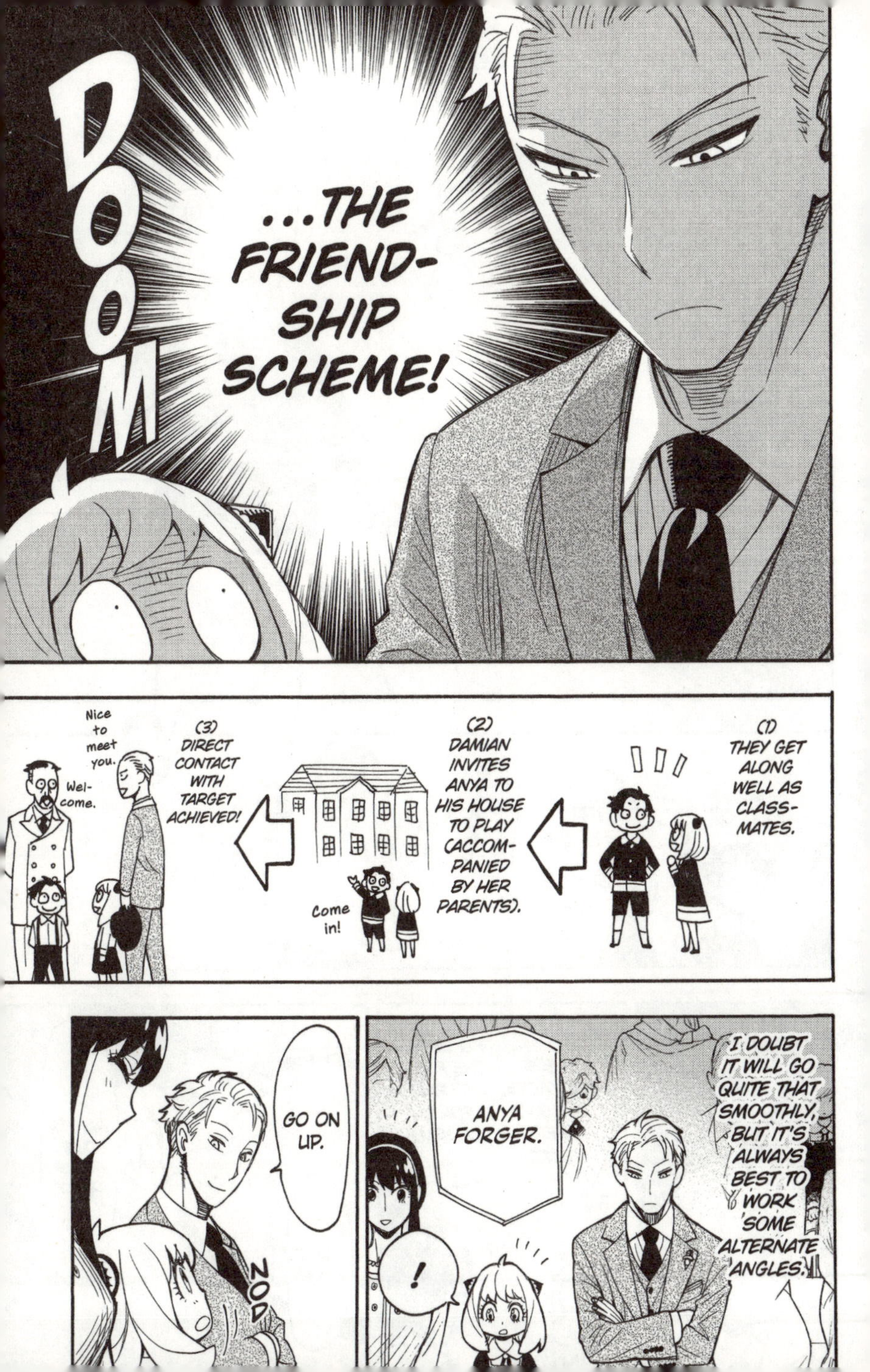
DOOM
...THE FRIEND-SHIP SCHEME!
(1) THEY GET ALONG WELL AS CLASS-MATES.
(2) DAMIAN INVITES ANYA TO HIS HOUSE TO PLAY (ACCOM-PANIED BY HER PARENTS).
Come in!
(3) DIRECT CONTACT WITH TARGET ACHIEVED!
Nice to meet you.
Wel-come.
I DOUBT IT WILL GO QUITE THAT SMOOTHLY, BUT IT'S ALWAYS BEST TO WORK SOME ALTERNATE ANGLES.
ANYA FORGER.
!
GO ON UP.
NOD

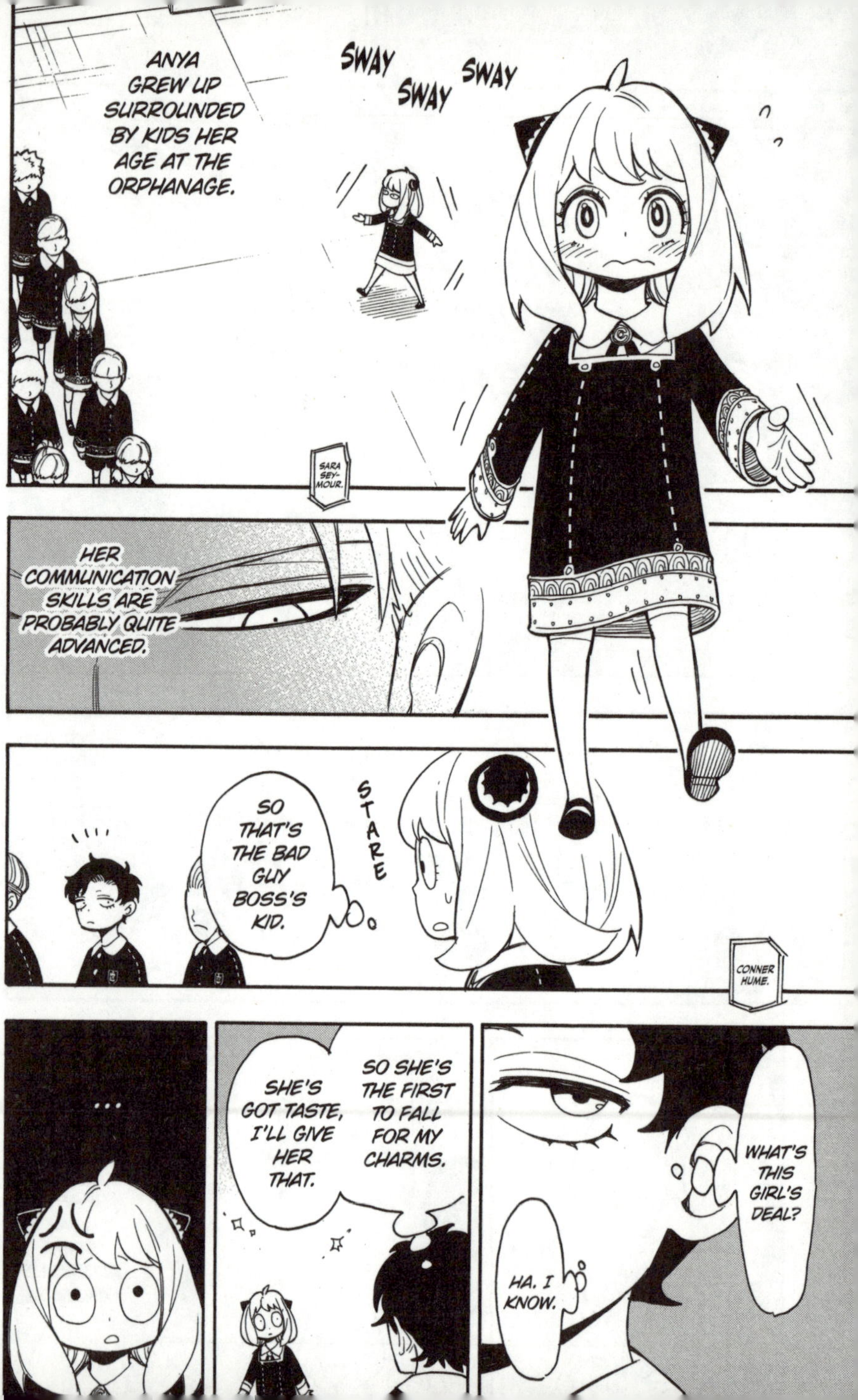
SWAY SWAY SWAY
ANYA GREW UP SURROUNDED BY KIDS HER AGE AT THE ORPHANAGE.
SARA SEYMOUR.
HER COMMUNICATION SKILLS ARE PROBABLY QUITE ADVANCED.
STARE
SO THAT'S THE BAD GUY BOSS'S KID.
CONNER HUME.
WHAT'S THIS GIRL'S DEAL?
HA. I KNOW.
SO SHE'S THE FIRST TO FALL FOR MY CHARMS.
SHE'S GOT TASTE, I'LL GIVE HER THAT.
...

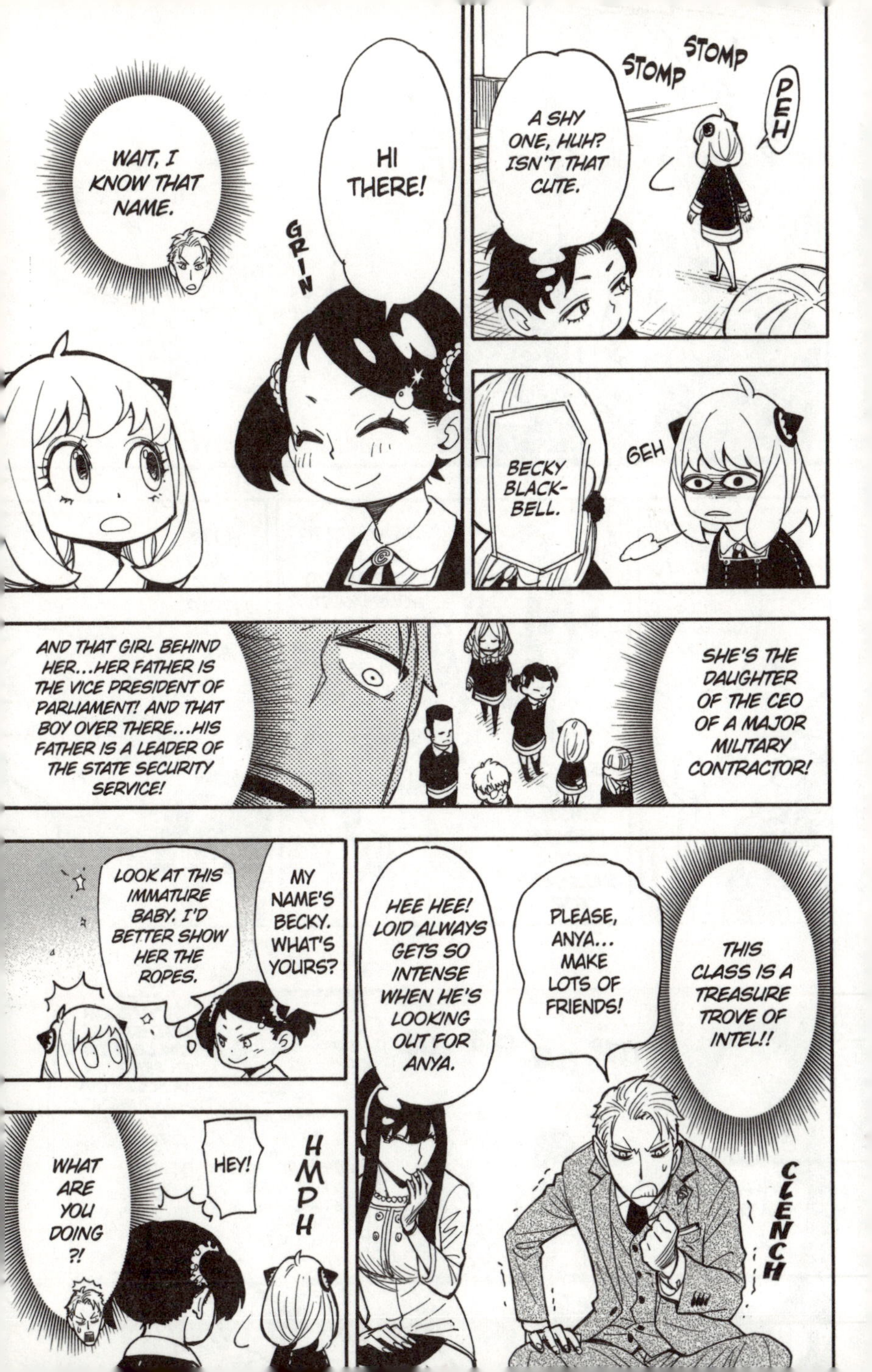
PEH
STOMP STOMP
A SHY ONE, HUH? ISN'T THAT CUTE.
GEH
BECKY BLACK-BELL.
HI THERE!
GRIN
WAIT, I KNOW THAT NAME.
SHE'S THE DAUGHTER OF THE CEO OF A MAJOR MILITARY CONTRACTOR!
AND THAT GIRL BEHIND HER...HER FATHER IS THE VICE PRESIDENT OF PARLIAMENT! AND THAT BOY OVER THERE...HIS FATHER IS A LEADER OF THE STATE SECURITY SERVICE!
THIS CLASS IS A TREASURE TROVE OF INTEL!!
CLENCH
PLEASE, ANYA... MAKE LOTS OF FRIENDS!
HEE HEE! LOID ALWAYS GETS SO INTENSE WHEN HE'S LOOKING OUT FOR ANYA.
MY NAME'S BECKY. WHAT'S YOURS?
LOOK AT THIS IMMATURE BABY. I'D BETTER SHOW HER THE ROPES.
HMPH
HEY!
WHAT ARE YOU DOING ?!

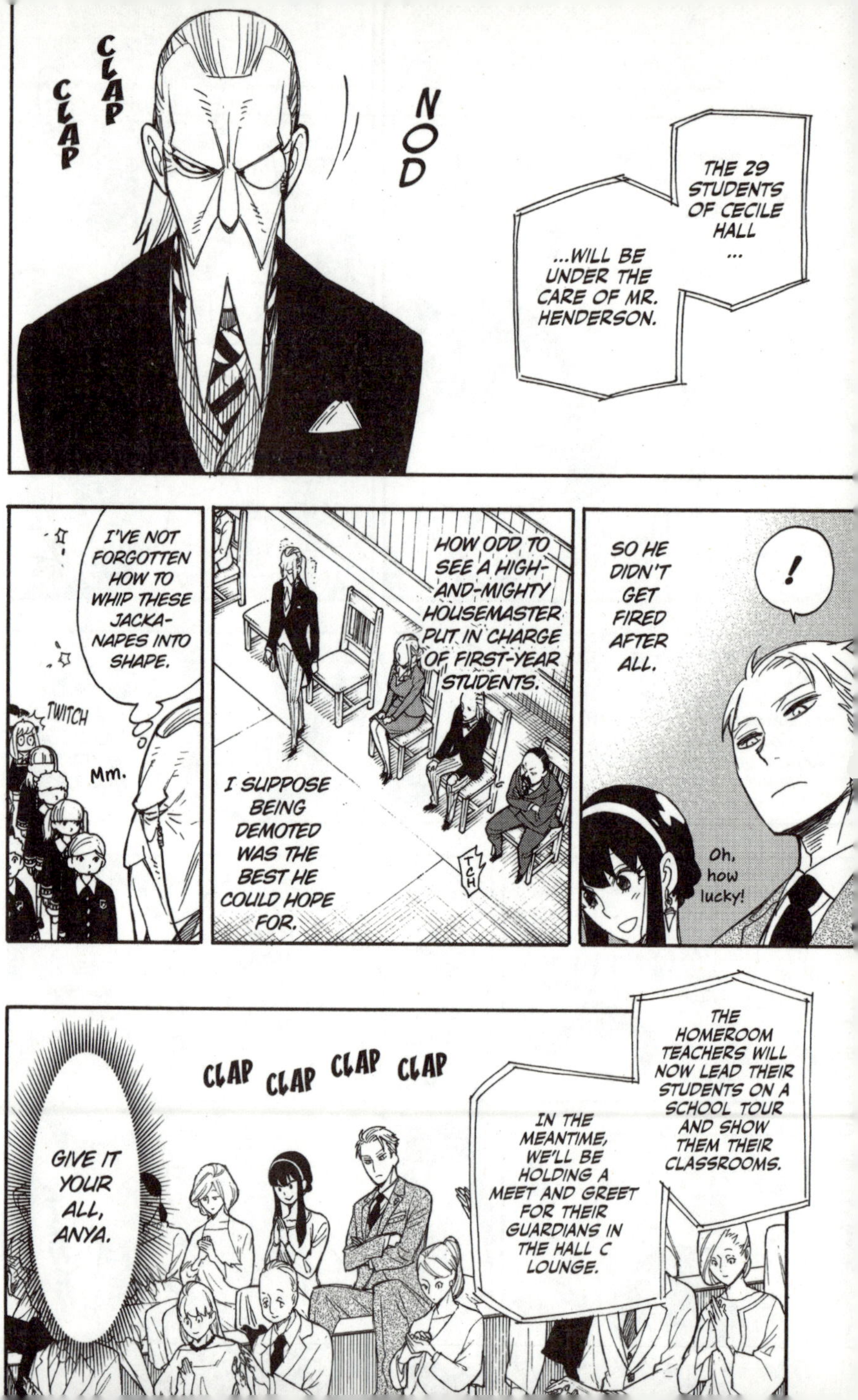
THE 29 STUDENTS OF CECILE HALL ...
...WILL BE UNDER THE CARE OF MR. HENDERSON.
NOD
CLAP CLAP
CLAP
!
SO HE DIDN'T GET FIRED AFTER ALL.
Oh, how lucky!
HOW ODD TO SEE A HIGH-AND-MIGHTY HOUSEMASTER PUT IN CHARGE OF FIRST-YEAR STUDENTS.
I SUPPOSE BEING DEMOTED WAS THE BEST HE COULD HOPE FOR.
TCH
I'VE NOT FORGOTTEN HOW TO WHIP THESE JACKANAPES INTO SHAPE.
Mm.
TWITCH
THE HOMEROOM TEACHERS WILL NOW LEAD THEIR STUDENTS ON A SCHOOL TOUR AND SHOW THEM THEIR CLASSROOMS.
IN THE MEANTIME, WE'LL BE HOLDING A MEET AND GREET FOR THEIR GUARDIANS IN THE HALL C LOUNGE.
CLAP CLAP CLAP CLAP
GIVE IT YOUR ALL, ANYA.

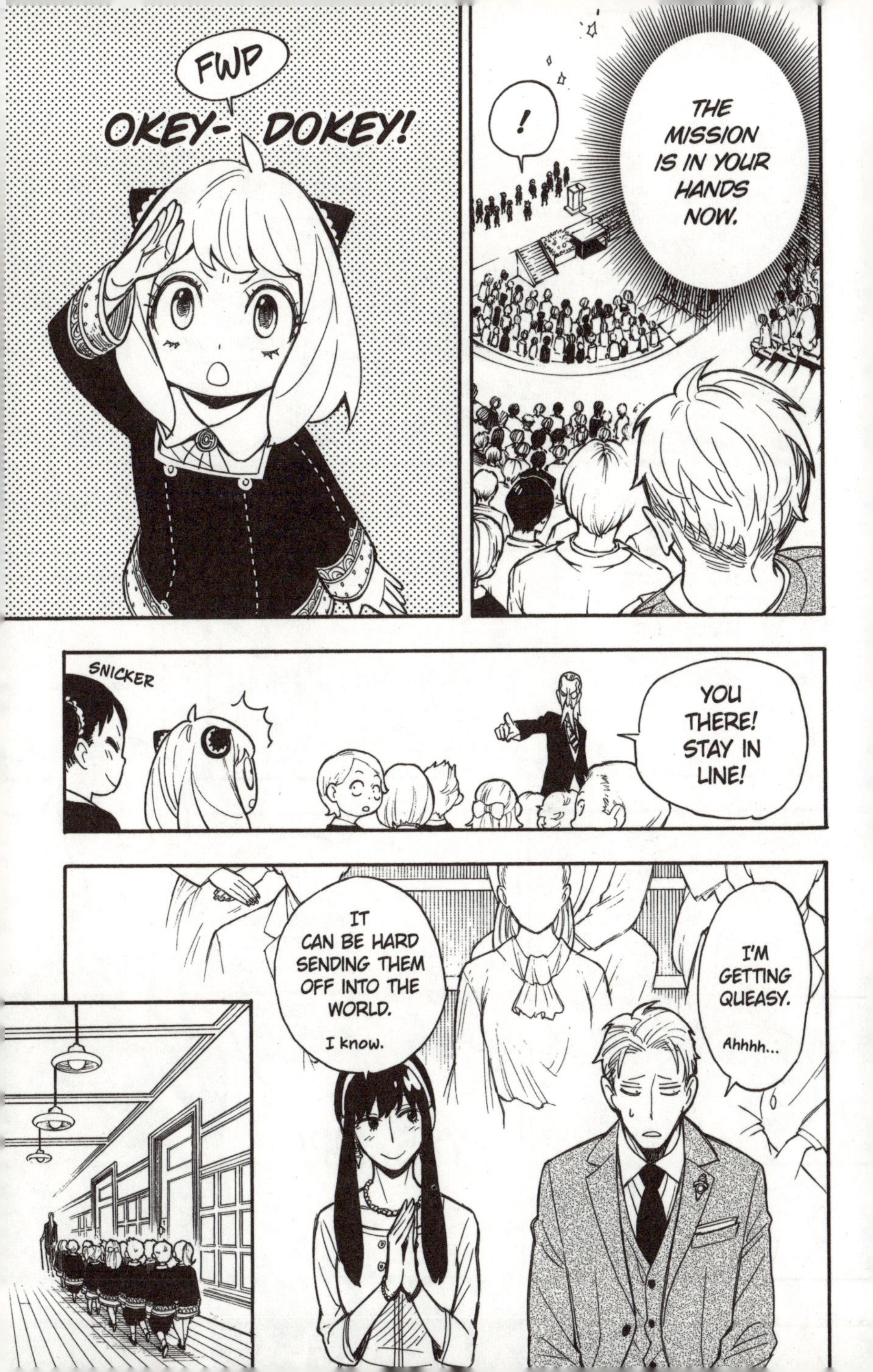
!
THE MISSION IS IN YOUR HANDS NOW.
FWP
OKEY- DOKEY!
YOU THERE! STAY IN LINE!
SNICKER
I'M GETTING QUEASY.
Ahhhh...
IT CAN BE HARD SENDING THEM OFF INTO THE WORLD.
I know.

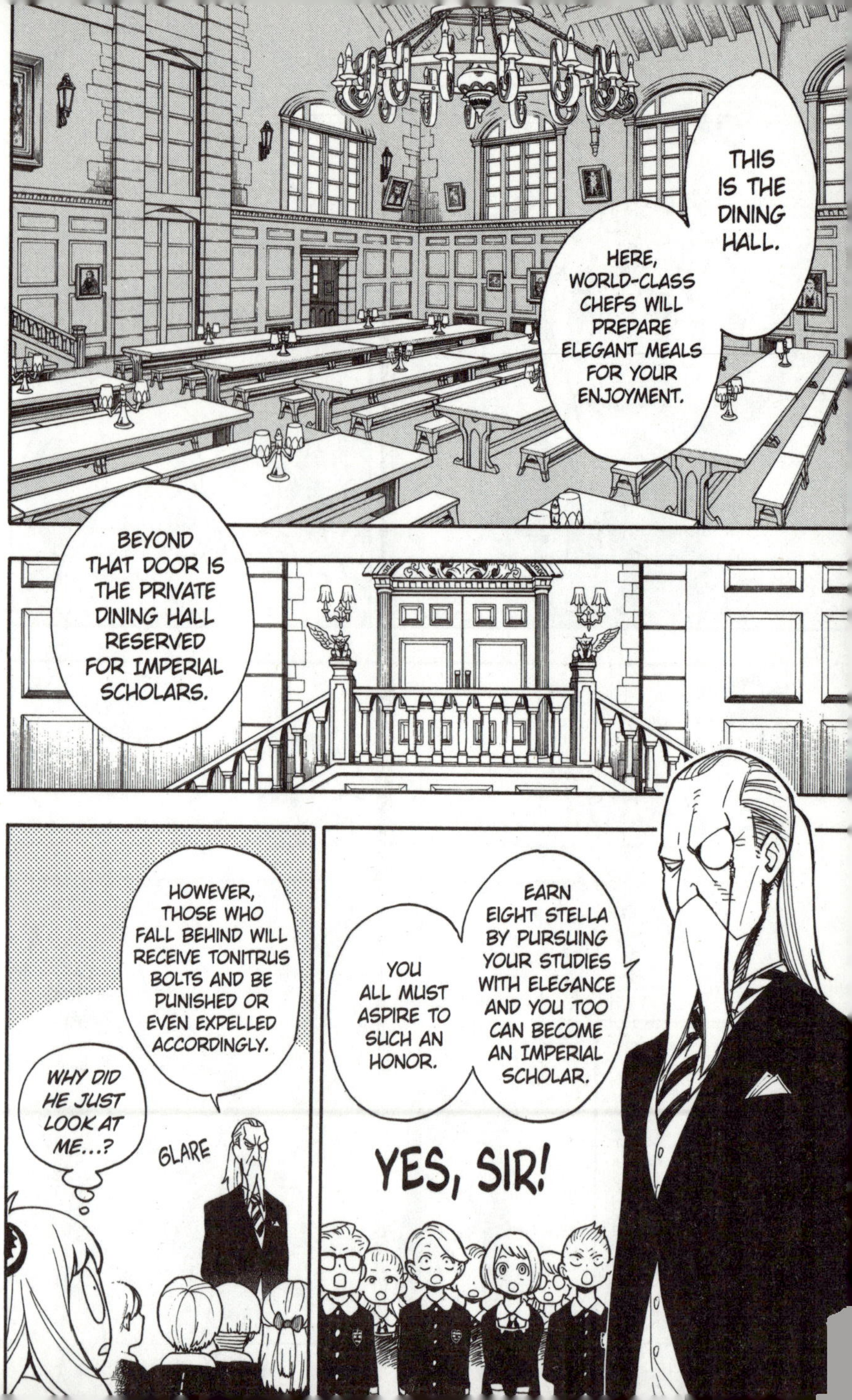
THIS IS THE DINING HALL.
HERE, WORLD-CLASS CHEFS WILL PREPARE ELEGANT MEALS FOR YOUR ENJOYMENT.
BEYOND THAT DOOR IS THE PRIVATE DINING HALL RESERVED FOR IMPERIAL SCHOLARS.
EARN EIGHT STELLA BY PURSUING YOUR STUDIES WITH ELEGANCE AND YOU TOO CAN BECOME AN IMPERIAL SCHOLAR.
YOU ALL MUST ASPIRE TO SUCH AN HONOR.
YES, SIR!
HOWEVER, THOSE WHO FALL BEHIND WILL RECEIVE TONITRUS BOLTS AND BE PUNISHED OR EVEN EXPELLED ACCORDINGLY.
GLARE
WHY DID HE JUST LOOK AT ME...?

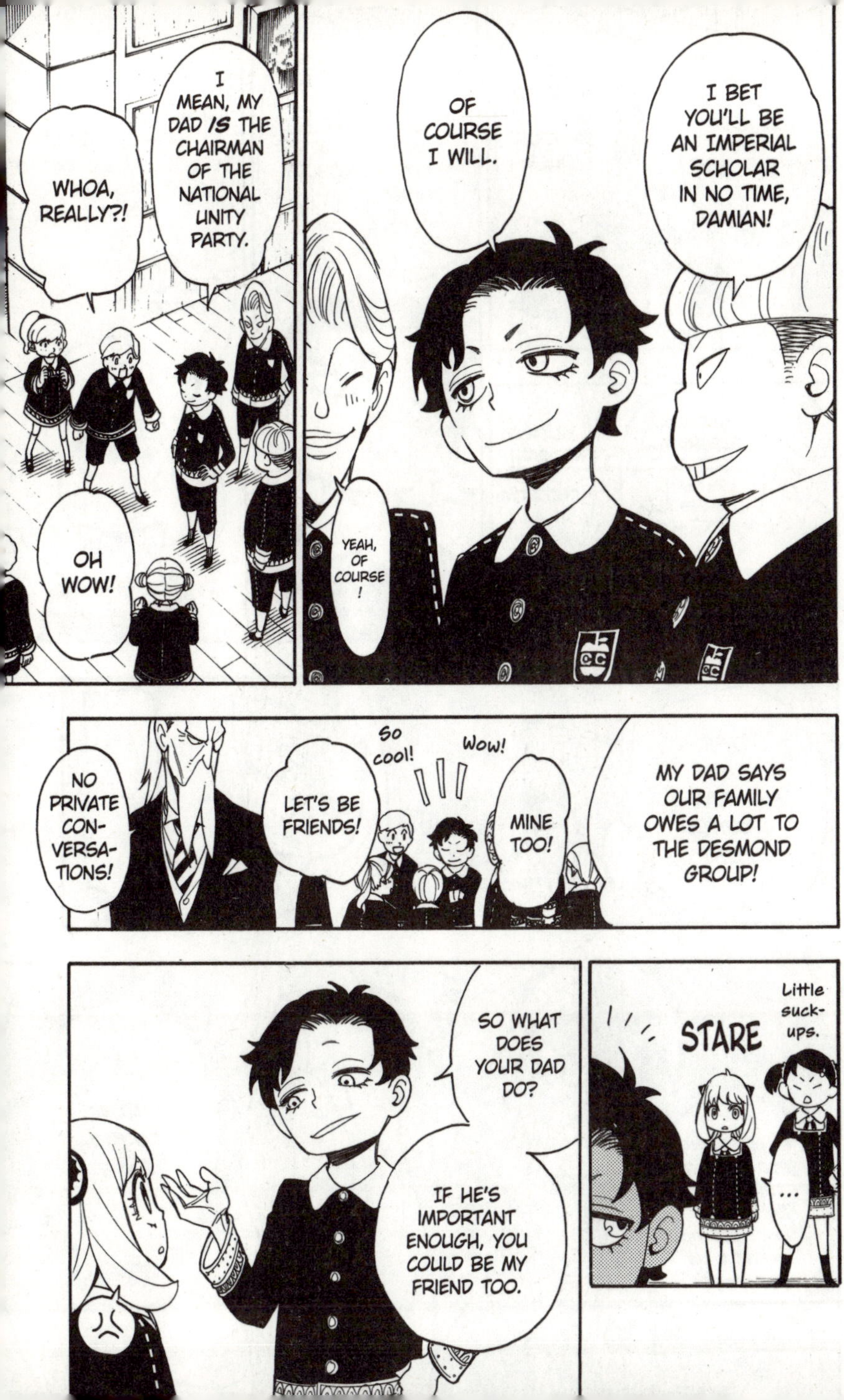
I BET YOU'LL BE AN IMPERIAL SCHOLAR IN NO TIME, DAMIAN!
OF COURSE I WILL.
YEAH, OF COURSE!
I MEAN, MY DAD IS THE CHAIRMAN OF THE NATIONAL UNITY PARTY.
WHOA, REALLY?!
OH WOW!
MY DAD SAYS OUR FAMILY OWES A LOT TO THE DESMOND GROUP!
Wow!
MINE TOO!
So cool!
LET'S BE FRIENDS!
NO PRIVATE CON-VERSA-TIONS!
Little suck-ups.
STARE
...
SO WHAT DOES YOUR DAD DO?
IF HE'S IMPORTANT ENOUGH, YOU COULD BE MY FRIEND TOO.

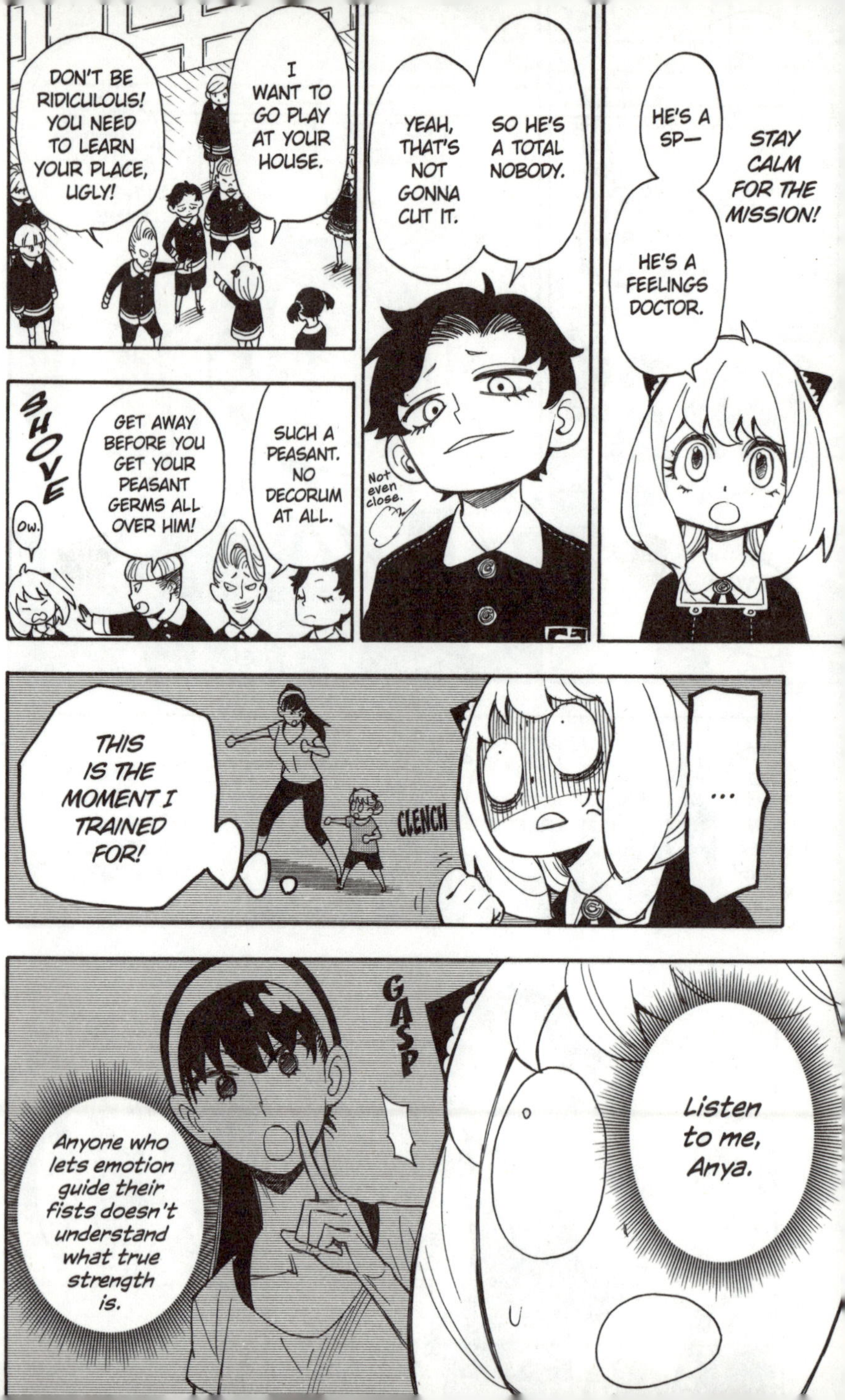
HE'S A SP—
STAY CALM FOR THE MISSION!
HE'S A FEELINGS DOCTOR.
SO HE'S A TOTAL NOBODY.
YEAH, THAT'S NOT GONNA CUT IT.
Not even close.
I WANT TO GO PLAY AT YOUR HOUSE.
DON'T BE RIDICULOUS! YOU NEED TO LEARN YOUR PLACE, UGLY!
SUCH A PEASANT. NO DECORUM AT ALL.
GET AWAY BEFORE YOU GET YOUR PEASANT GERMS ALL OVER HIM!
SHOVE
Ow.
...
CLENCH
THIS IS THE MOMENT I TRAINED FOR!
Listen to me, Anya.
GASP
Anyone who lets emotion guide their fists doesn't understand what true strength is.

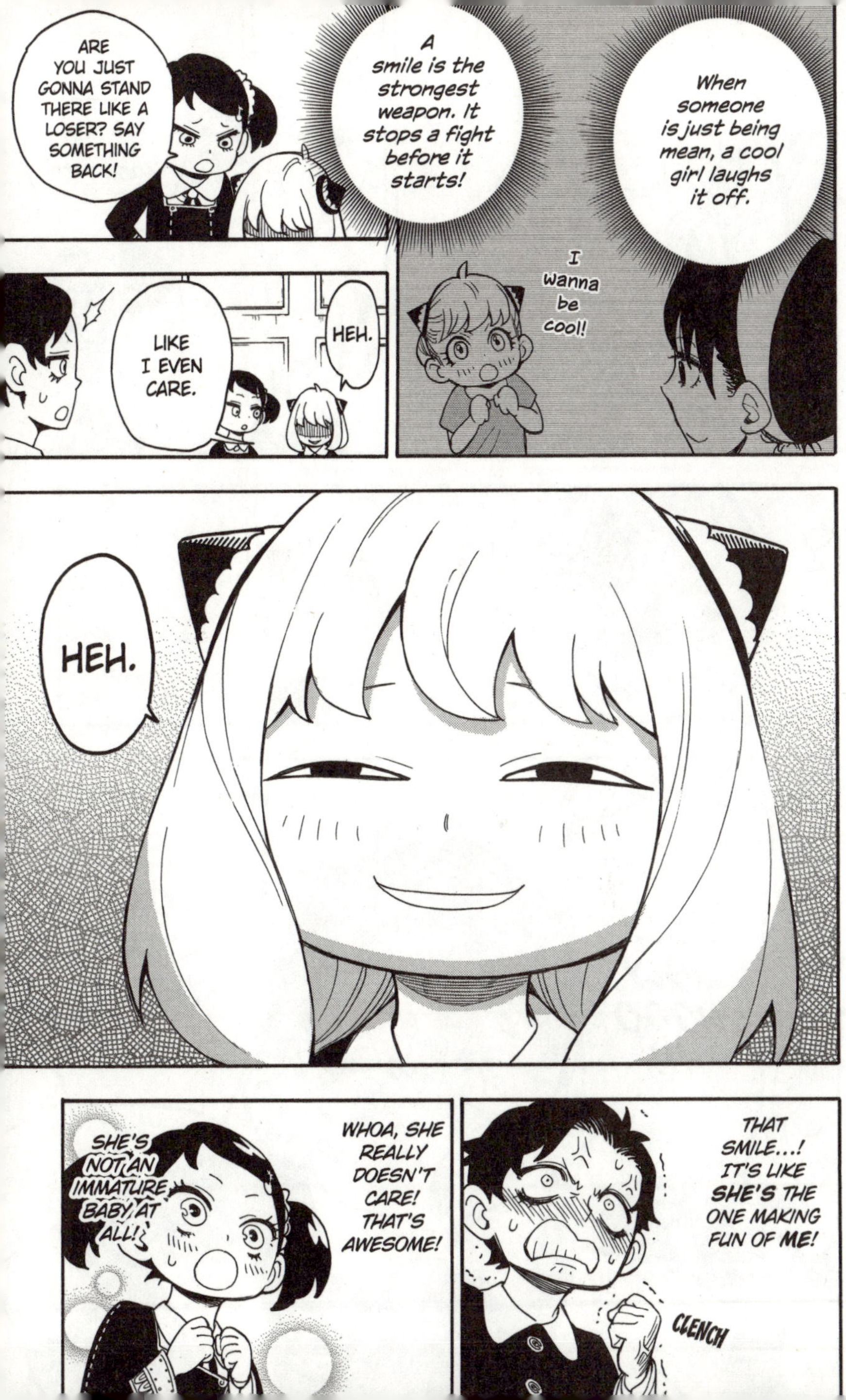
When someone is just being mean, a cool girl laughs it off.
A smile is the strongest weapon. It stops a fight before it starts!
I wanna be cool!
ARE YOU JUST GONNA STAND THERE LIKE A LOSER? SAY SOMETHING BACK!
HEH.
LIKE I EVEN CARE.
HEH.
THAT SMILE...! IT'S LIKE SHE'S THE ONE MAKING FUN OF ME!
CLENCH
WHOA, SHE REALLY DOESN'T CARE! THAT'S AWESOME!
SHE'S NOT AN IMMATURE BABY AT ALL!

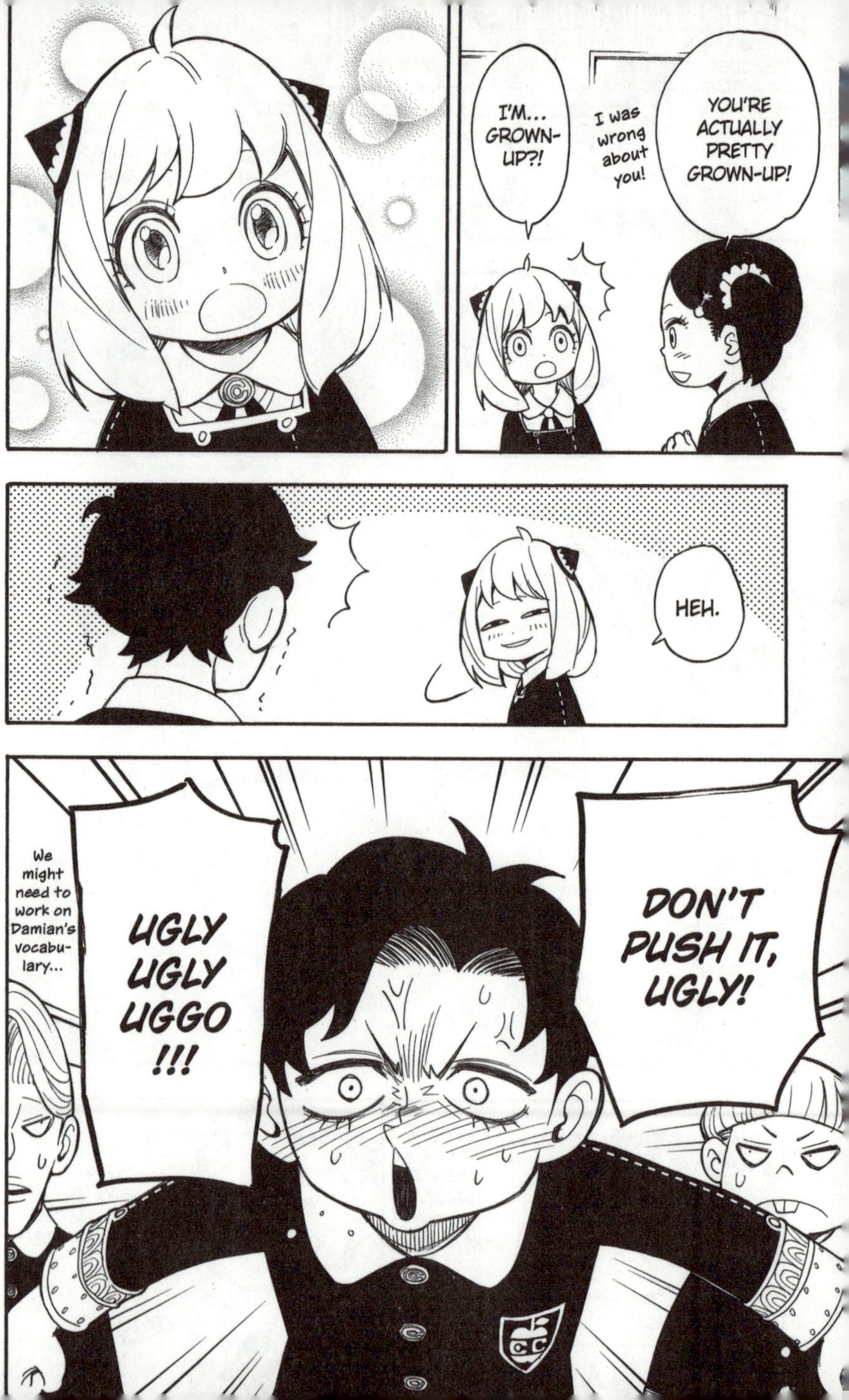
YOU'RE ACTUALLY PRETTY GROWN-UP!
I was wrong about you!
I'M... GROWN-UP?!
HEH.
DON'T PUSH IT, UGLY!
UGLY UGLY UGGO!!!
We might need to work on Damian's vocabulary...

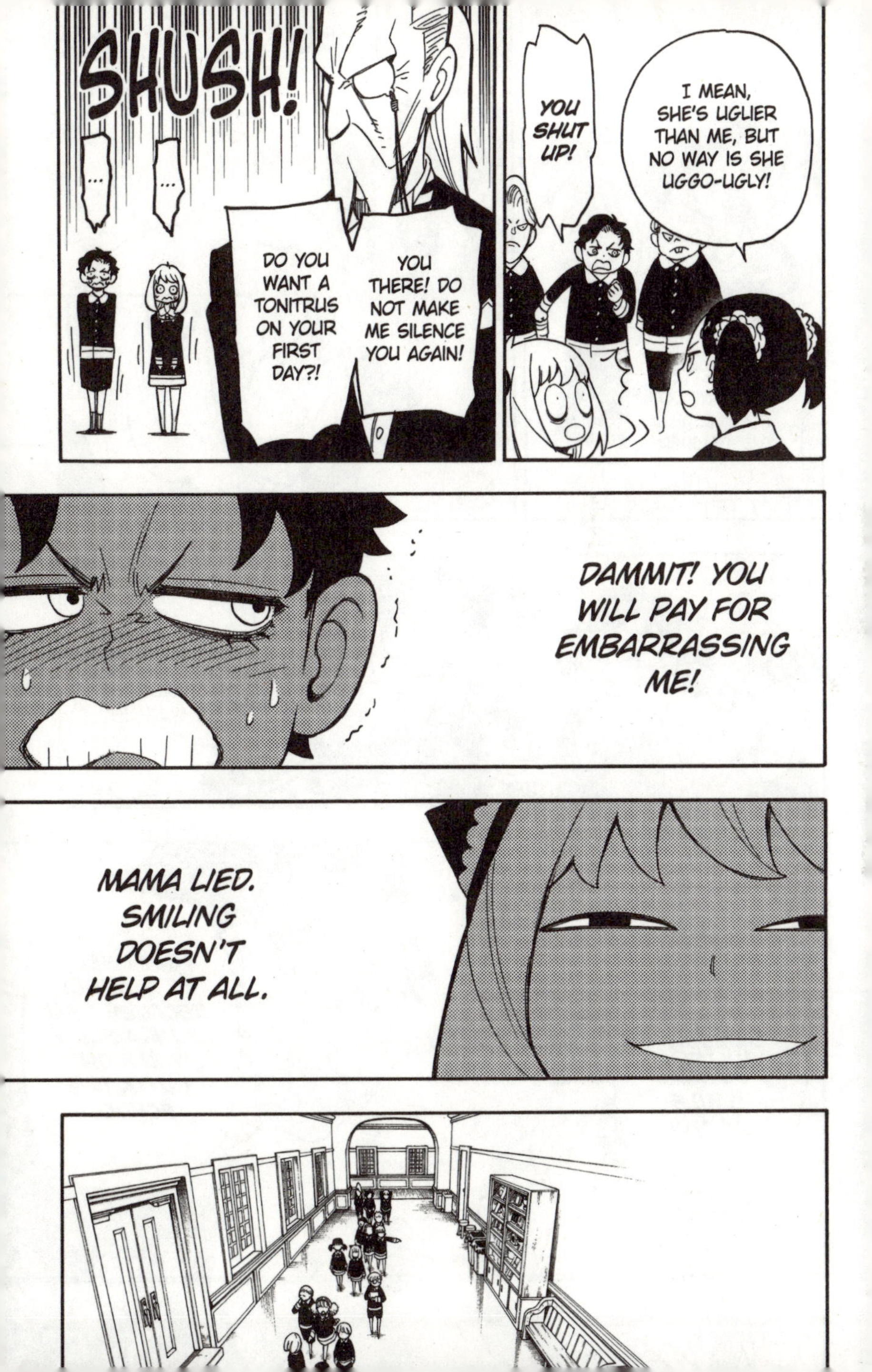
I MEAN, SHE'S UGLIER THAN ME, BUT NO WAY IS SHE UGGO-UGLY!
YOU SHUT UP!
SHUSH!
...
...
YOU THERE! DO NOT MAKE ME SILENCE YOU AGAIN!
DO YOU WANT A TONITRUS ON YOUR FIRST DAY?!
DAMMIT! YOU WILL PAY FOR EMBARRASSING ME!
MAMA LIED. SMILING DOESN'T HELP AT ALL.

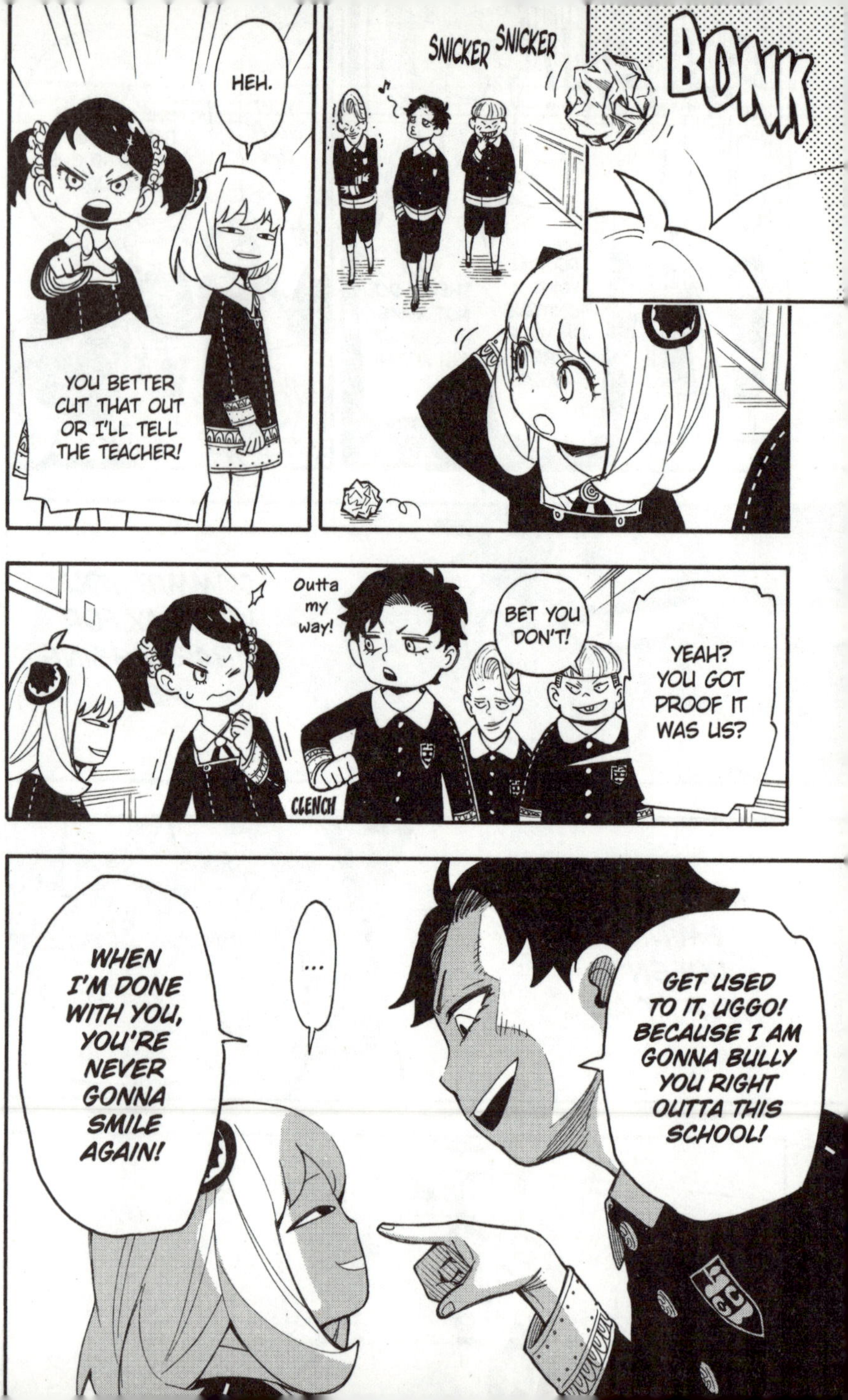
BONK
SNICKER SNICKER
HEH.
YOU BETTER CUT THAT OUT OR I'LL TELL THE TEACHER!
YEAH? YOU GOT PROOF IT WAS US?
BET YOU DON'T!
Outta my way!
CLENCH
GET USED TO IT, UGGO! BECAUSE I AM GONNA BULLY YOU RIGHT OUTTA THIS SCHOOL!
...
WHEN I'M DONE WITH YOU, YOU'RE NEVER GONNA SMILE AGAIN!

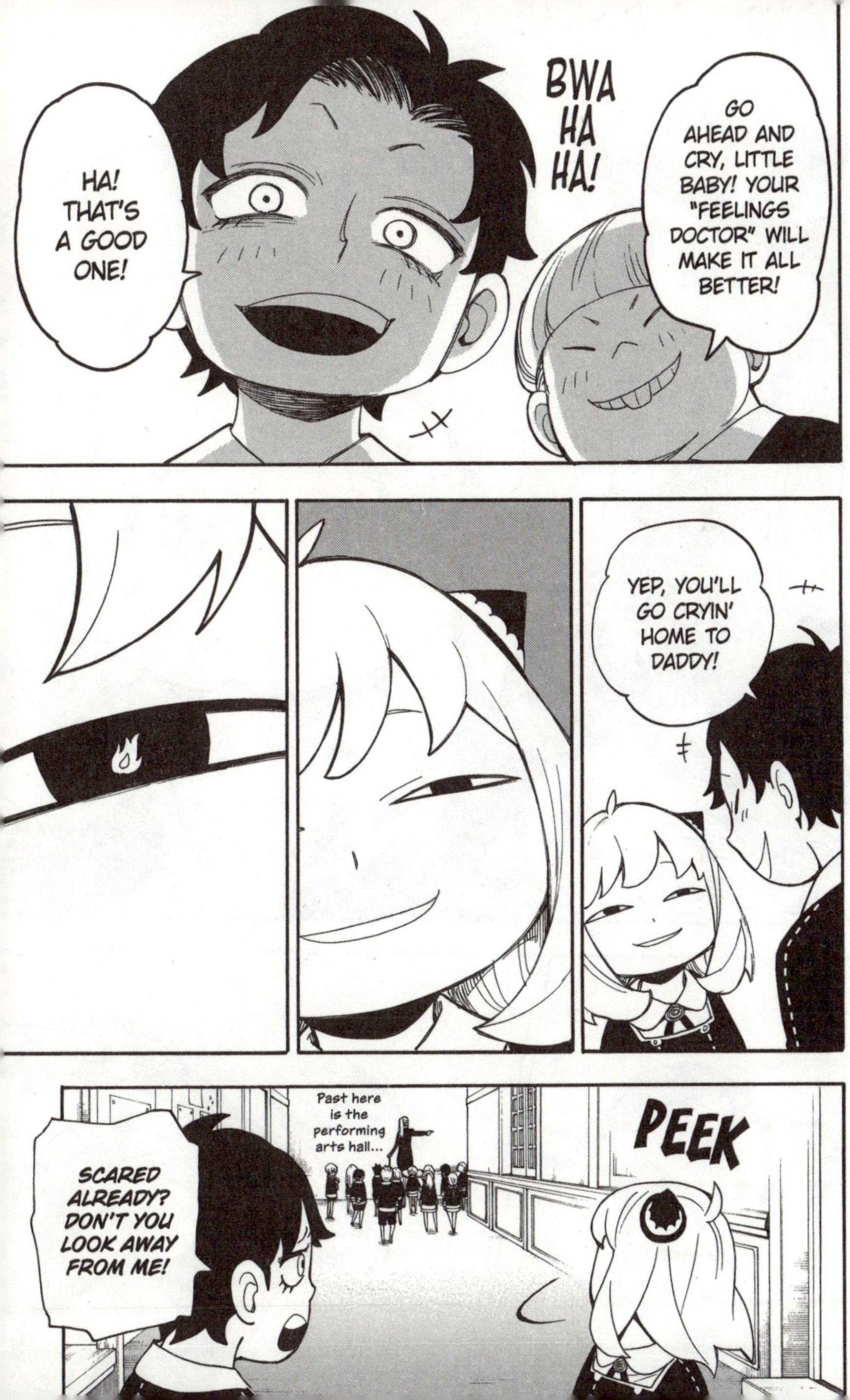
GO AHEAD AND CRY, LITTLE BABY! YOUR "FEELINGS DOCTOR" WILL MAKE IT ALL BETTER!
BWA HA HA!
HA! THAT'S A GOOD ONE!
YEP, YOU'LL GO CRYIN' HOME TO DADDY!
PEEK
Past here is the performing arts hall...
SCARED ALREADY? DON'T YOU LOOK AWAY FROM ME!

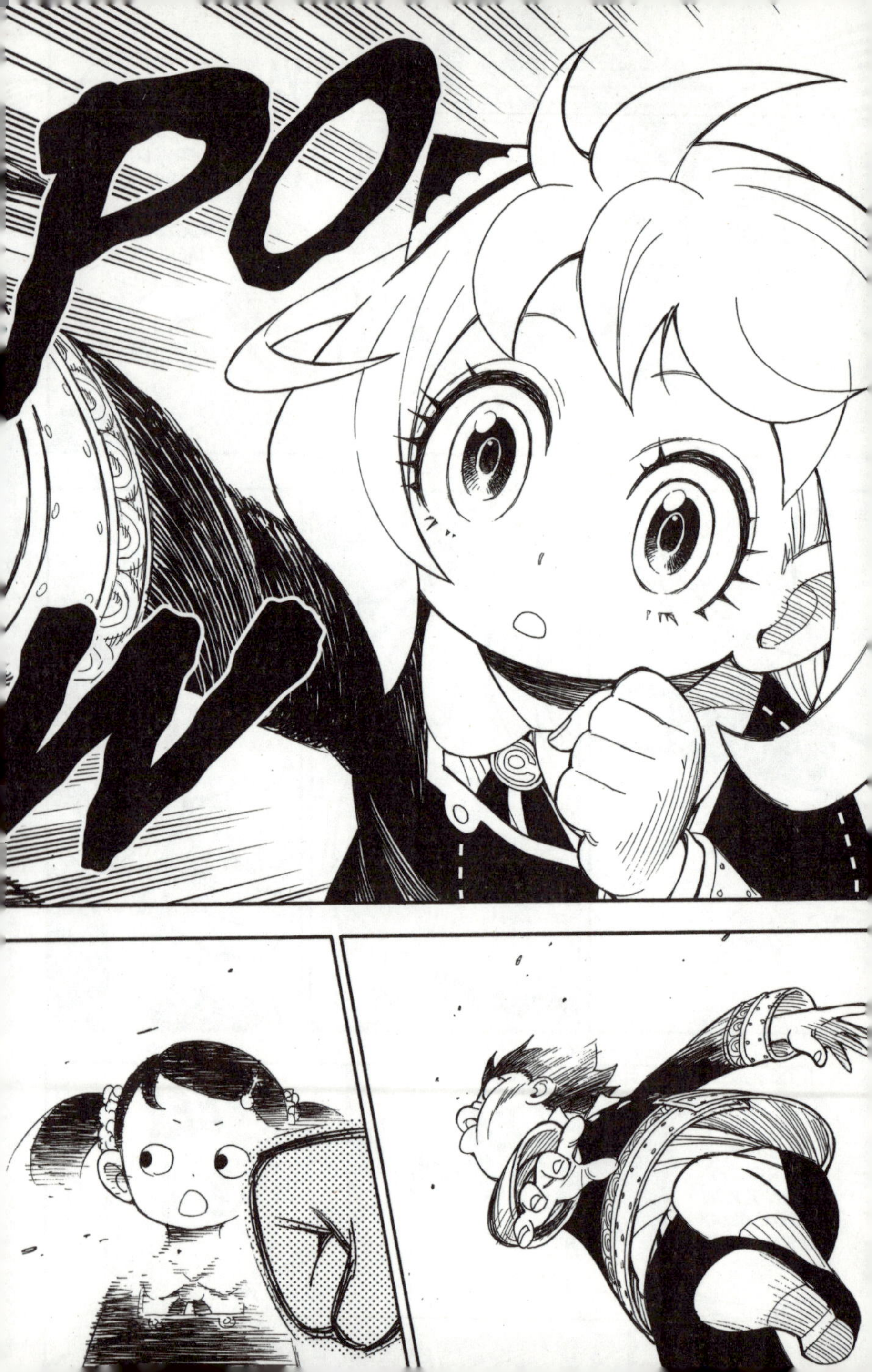
POW

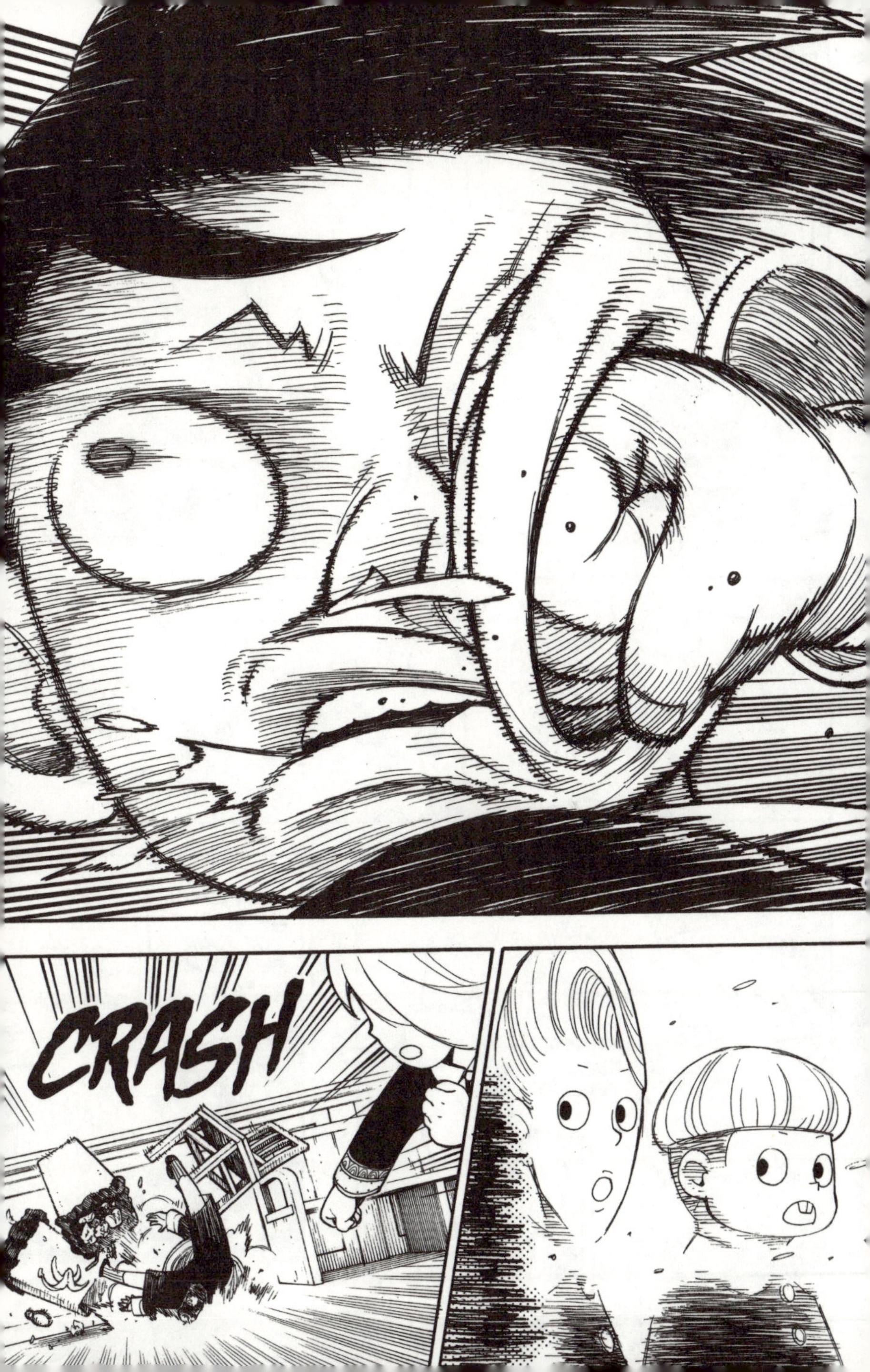
CRASH

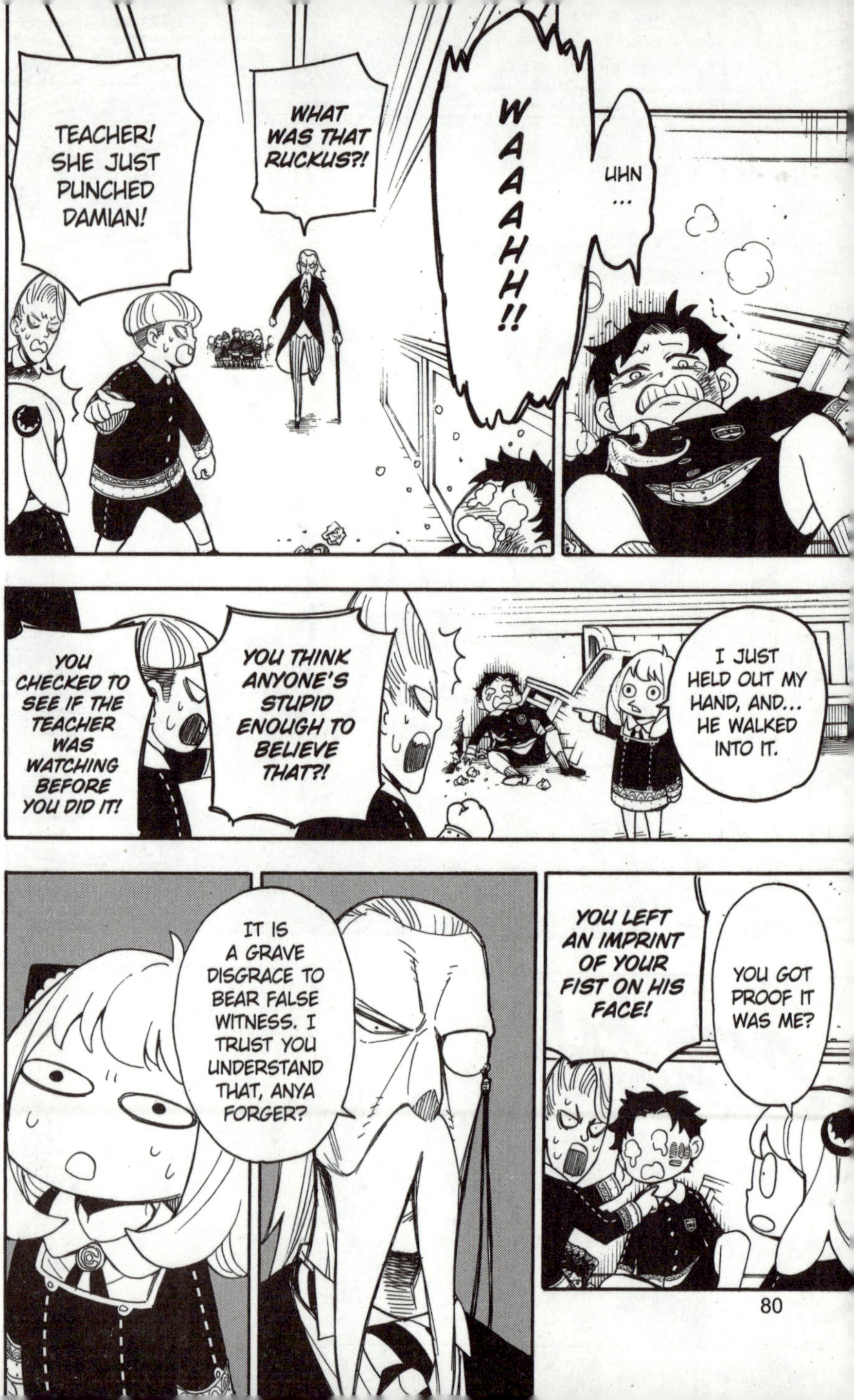
UHN ...
WAAAAHH!!
WHAT WAS THAT RUCKUS?!
TEACHER! SHE JUST PUNCHED DAMIAN!
I JUST HELD OUT MY HAND, AND... HE WALKED INTO IT.
YOU THINK ANYONE'S STUPID ENOUGH TO BELIEVE THAT?!
YOU CHECKED TO SEE IF THE TEACHER WAS WATCHING BEFORE YOU DID IT!
YOU GOT PROOF IT WAS ME?
YOU LEFT AN IMPRINT OF YOUR FIST ON HIS FACE!
IT IS A GRAVE DISGRACE TO BEAR FALSE WITNESS. I TRUST YOU UNDERSTAND THAT, ANYA FORGER?

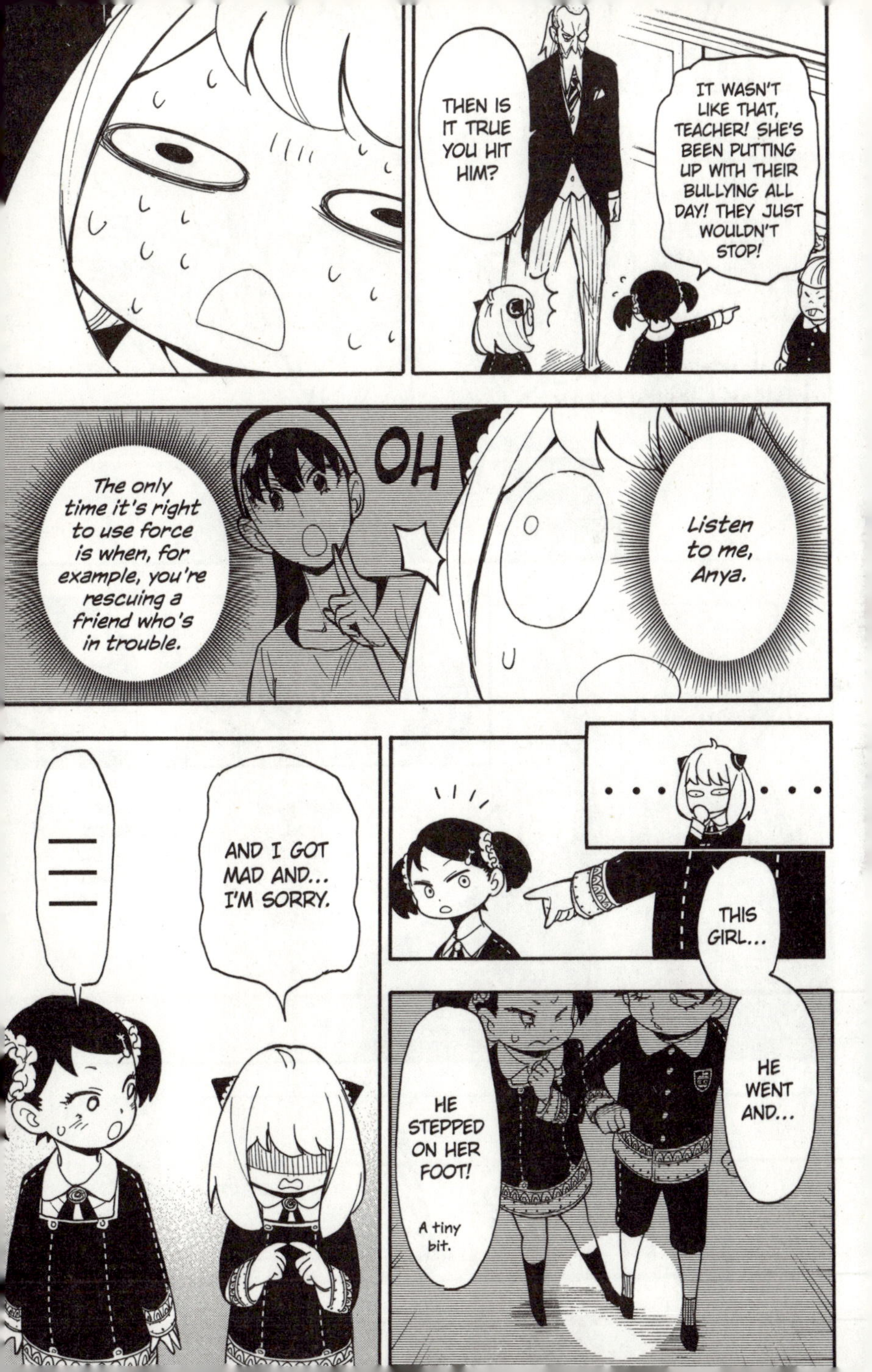
IT WASN'T LIKE THAT, TEACHER! SHE'S BEEN PUTTING UP WITH THEIR BULLYING ALL DAY! THEY JUST WOULDN'T STOP!
THEN IS IT TRUE YOU HIT HIM?
Listen to me, Anya.
OH
The only time it's right to use force is when, for example, you're rescuing a friend who's in trouble.
• • • • • •
THIS GIRL...
HE WENT AND...
HE STEPPED ON HER FOOT!
A tiny bit.
AND I GOT MAD AND... I'M SORRY.
———

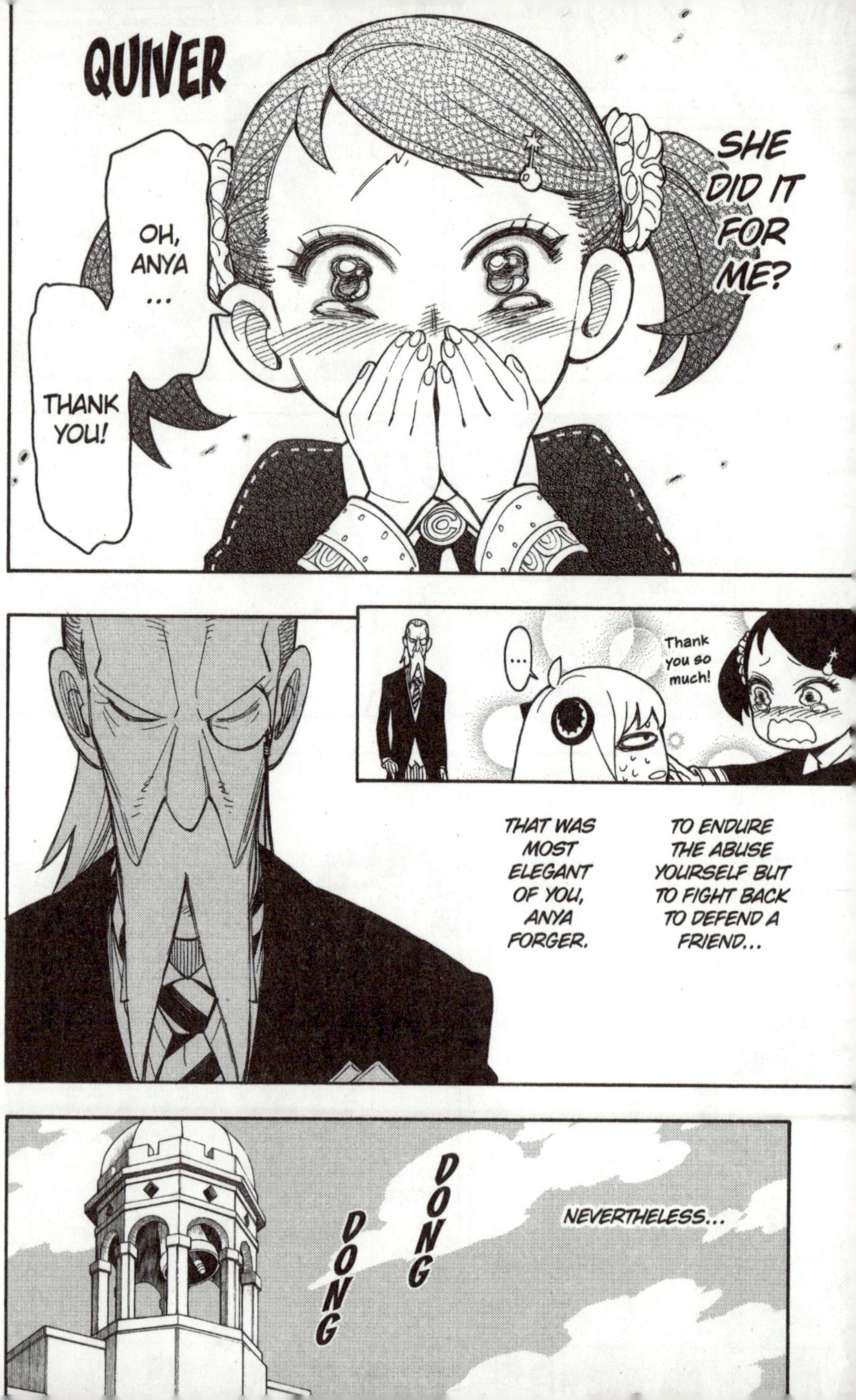
SHE DID IT FOR ME?
QUIVER
OH, ANYA...
THANK YOU!
Thank you so much!
...
TO ENDURE THE ABUSE YOURSELF BUT TO FIGHT BACK TO DEFEND A FRIEND...
THAT WAS MOST ELEGANT OF YOU, ANYA FORGER.
NEVERTHELESS...
DONG
DONG

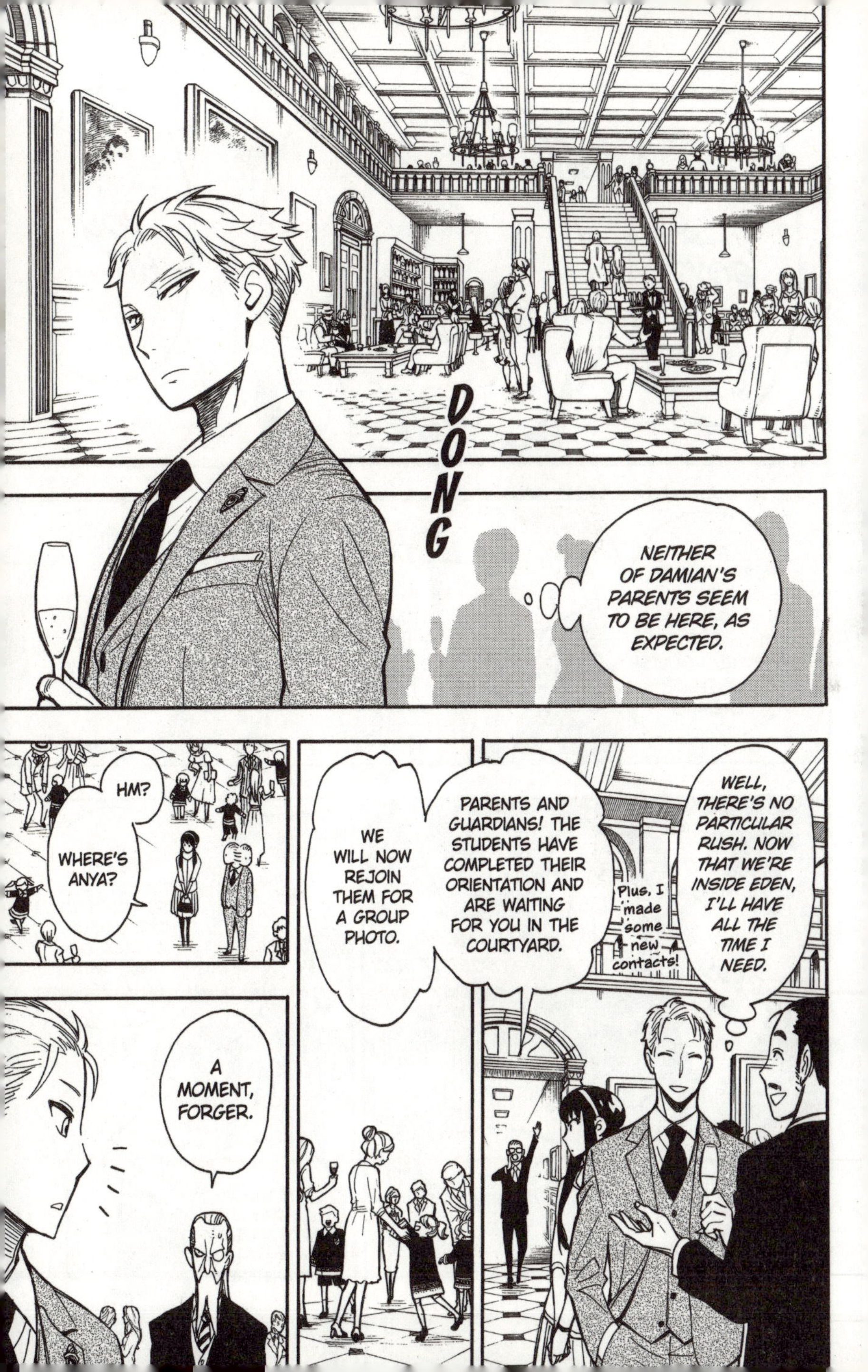
DONG
NEITHER OF DAMIAN'S PARENTS SEEM TO BE HERE, AS EXPECTED.
WELL, THERE'S NO PARTICULAR RUSH. NOW THAT WE'RE INSIDE EDEN, I'LL HAVE ALL THE TIME I NEED.
Plus, I made some new contacts!
PARENTS AND GUARDIANS! THE STUDENTS HAVE COMPLETED THEIR ORIENTATION AND ARE WAITING FOR YOU IN THE COURTYARD.
WE WILL NOW REJOIN THEM FOR A GROUP PHOTO.
HM?
WHERE'S ANYA?
A MOMENT, FORGER.

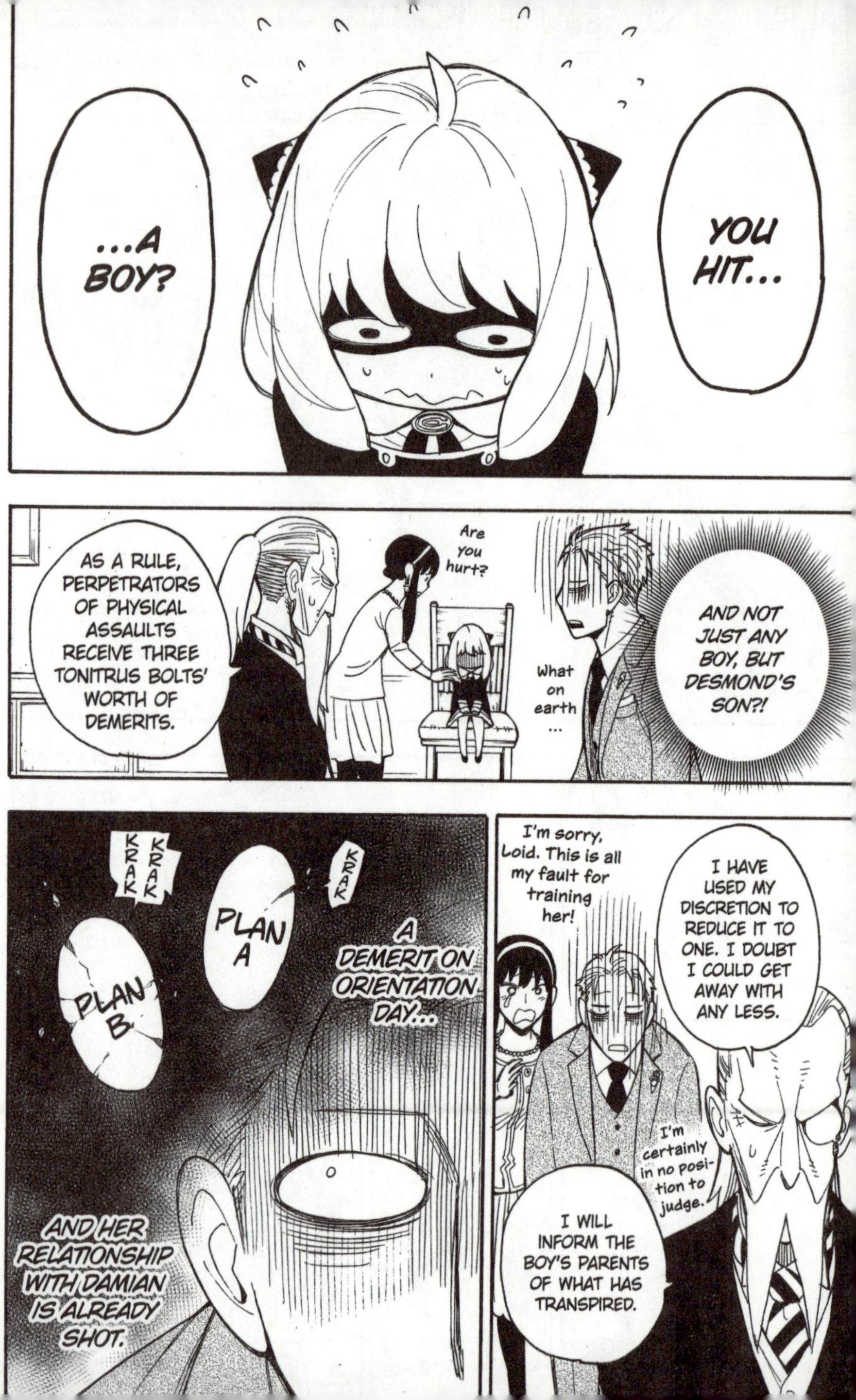

YOU HIT...
...A BOY?
AND NOT JUST ANY BOY, BUT DESMOND'S SON?!
What on earth ...
Are you hurt?
AS A RULE, PERPETRATORS OF PHYSICAL ASSAULTS RECEIVE THREE TONITRUS BOLTS' WORTH OF DEMERITS.
I HAVE USED MY DISCRETION TO REDUCE IT TO ONE. I DOUBT I COULD GET AWAY WITH ANY LESS.
I'm sorry, Loid. This is all my fault for training her!
I'm certainly in no position to judge.
I WILL INFORM THE BOY'S PARENTS OF WHAT HAS TRANSPIRED.
KRAK
KRAK KRAK
PLAN A
PLAN B
A DEMERIT ON ORIENTATION DAY...
AND HER RELATIONSHIP WITH DAMIAN IS ALREADY SHOT.

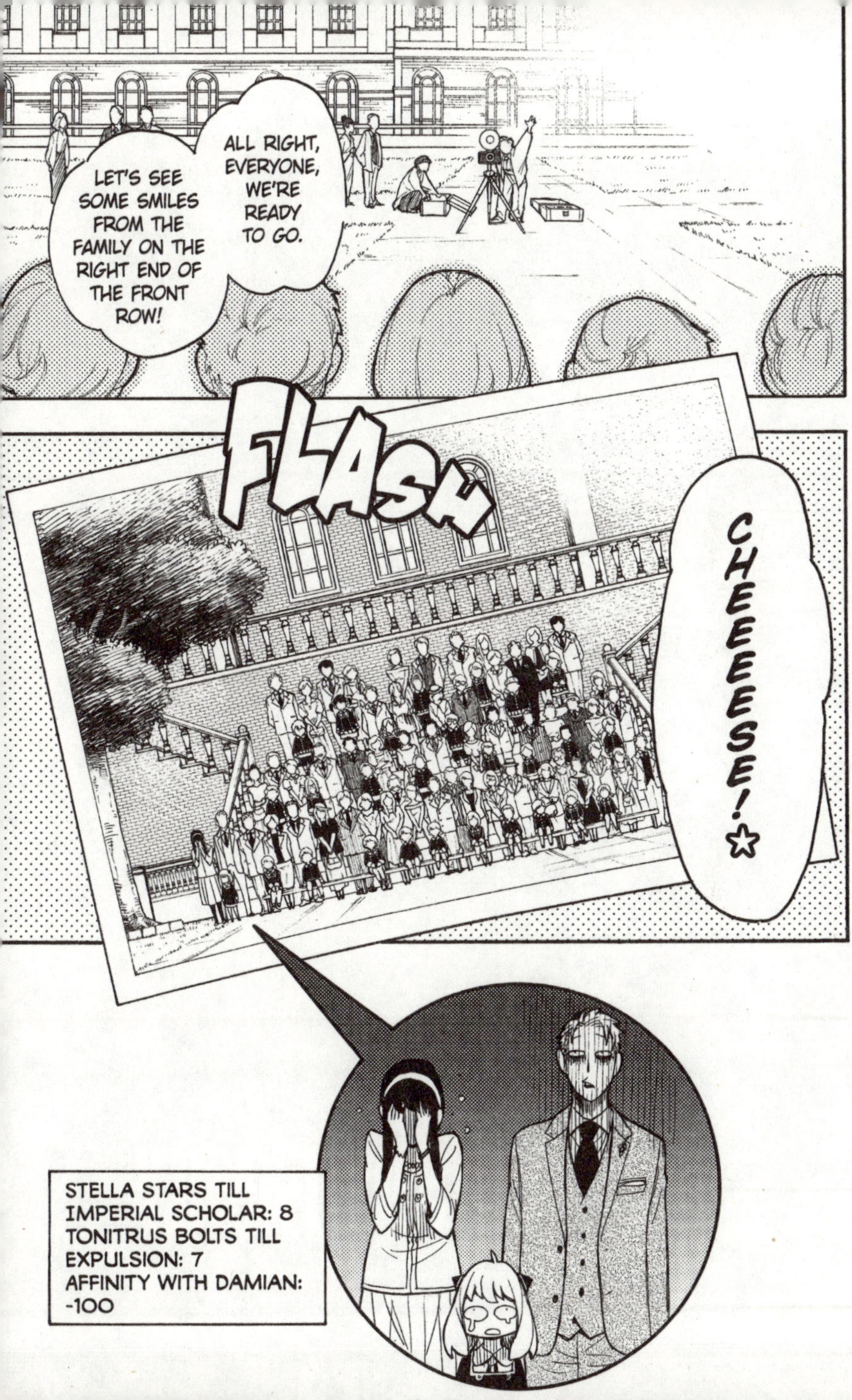
ALL RIGHT, EVERYONE, WE'RE READY TO GO.
LET'S SEE SOME SMILES FROM THE FAMILY ON THE RIGHT END OF THE FRONT ROW!
CHEEEESE!☆
FLASH
STELLA STARS TILL IMPERIAL SCHOLAR: 8
TONITRUS BOLTS TILL EXPULSION: 7
AFFINITY WITH DAMIAN: -100

SPY×FAMILY

MISSION 9

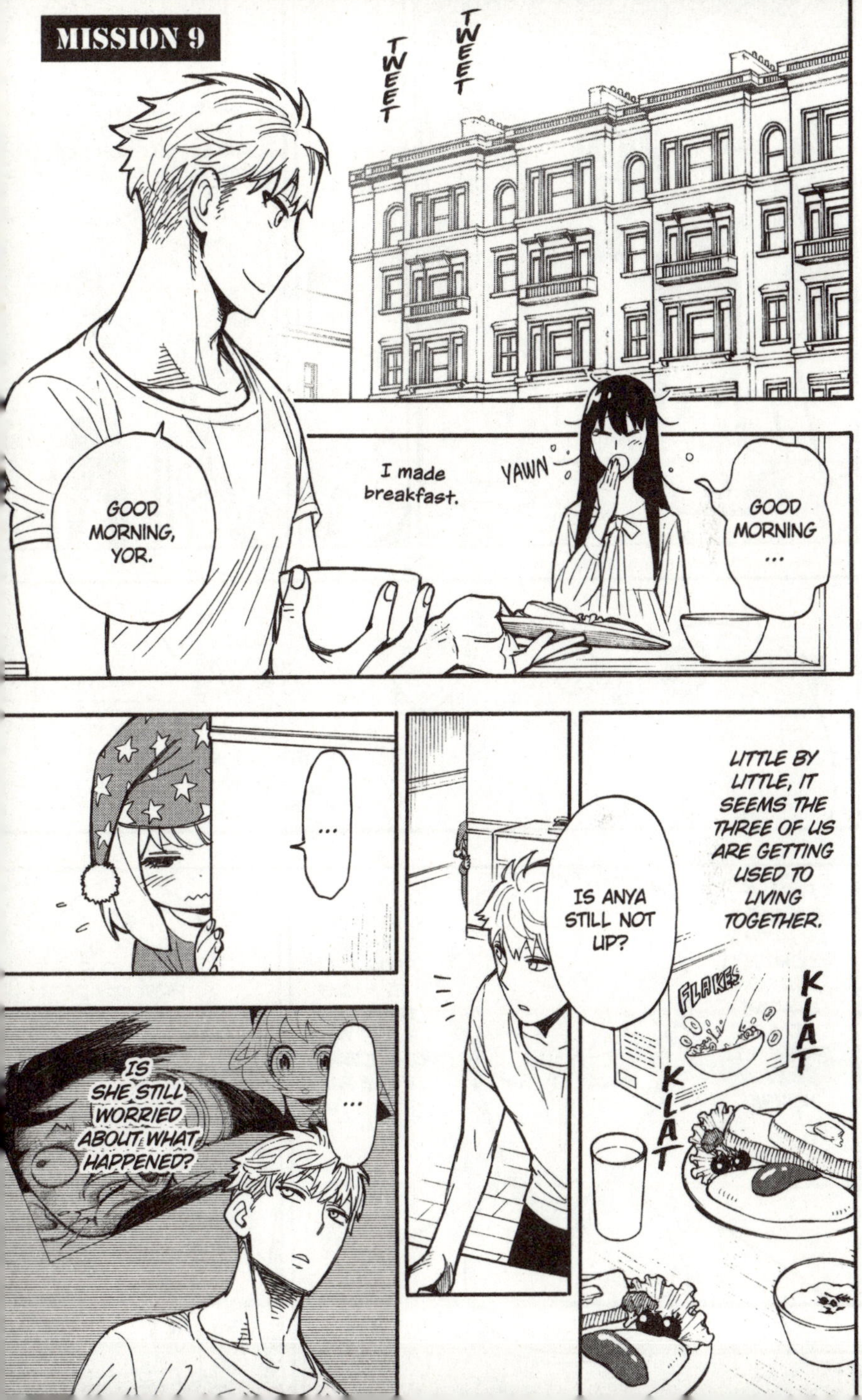
TWEET
TWEET
GOOD MORNING ...
YAWN
I made breakfast.
GOOD MORNING, YOR.
LITTLE BY LITTLE, IT SEEMS THE THREE OF US ARE GETTING USED TO LIVING TOGETHER.
KLAT
KLAT
FLAKES
IS ANYA STILL NOT UP?
...
...
IS SHE STILL WORRIED ABOUT WHAT HAPPENED?

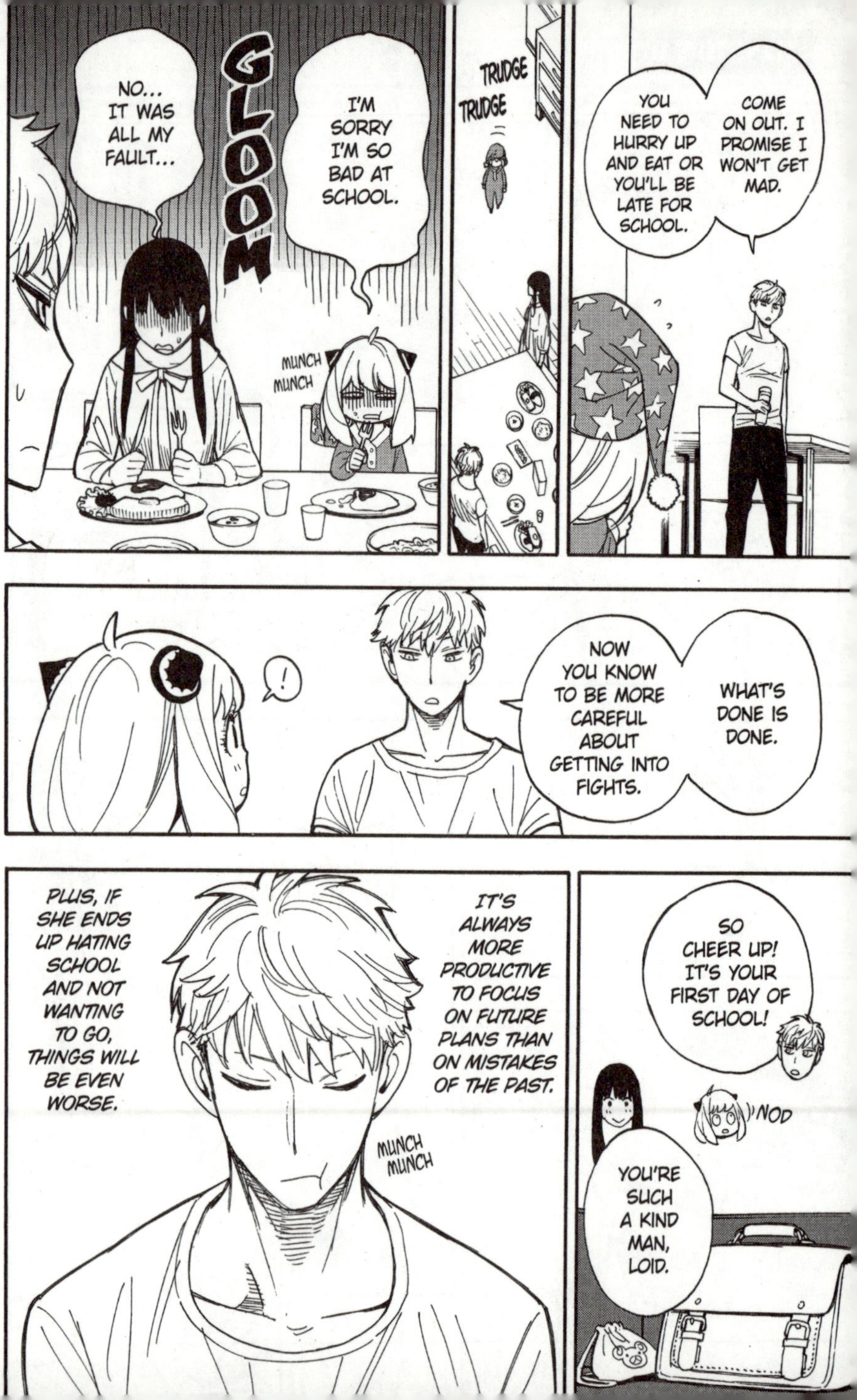
COME ON OUT. I PROMISE I WON'T GET MAD.
YOU NEED TO HURRY UP AND EAT OR YOU'LL BE LATE FOR SCHOOL.
TRUDGE
TRUDGE
I'M SORRY I'M SO BAD AT SCHOOL.
GLOOM
NO... IT WAS ALL MY FAULT...
MUNCH MUNCH
WHAT'S DONE IS DONE.
NOW YOU KNOW TO BE MORE CAREFUL ABOUT GETTING INTO FIGHTS.
!
SO CHEER UP! IT'S YOUR FIRST DAY OF SCHOOL!
NOD
YOU'RE SUCH A KIND MAN, LOID.
IT'S ALWAYS MORE PRODUCTIVE TO FOCUS ON FUTURE PLANS THAN ON MISTAKES OF THE PAST.
PLUS, IF SHE ENDS UP HATING SCHOOL AND NOT WANTING TO GO, THINGS WILL BE EVEN WORSE.
MUNCH MUNCH

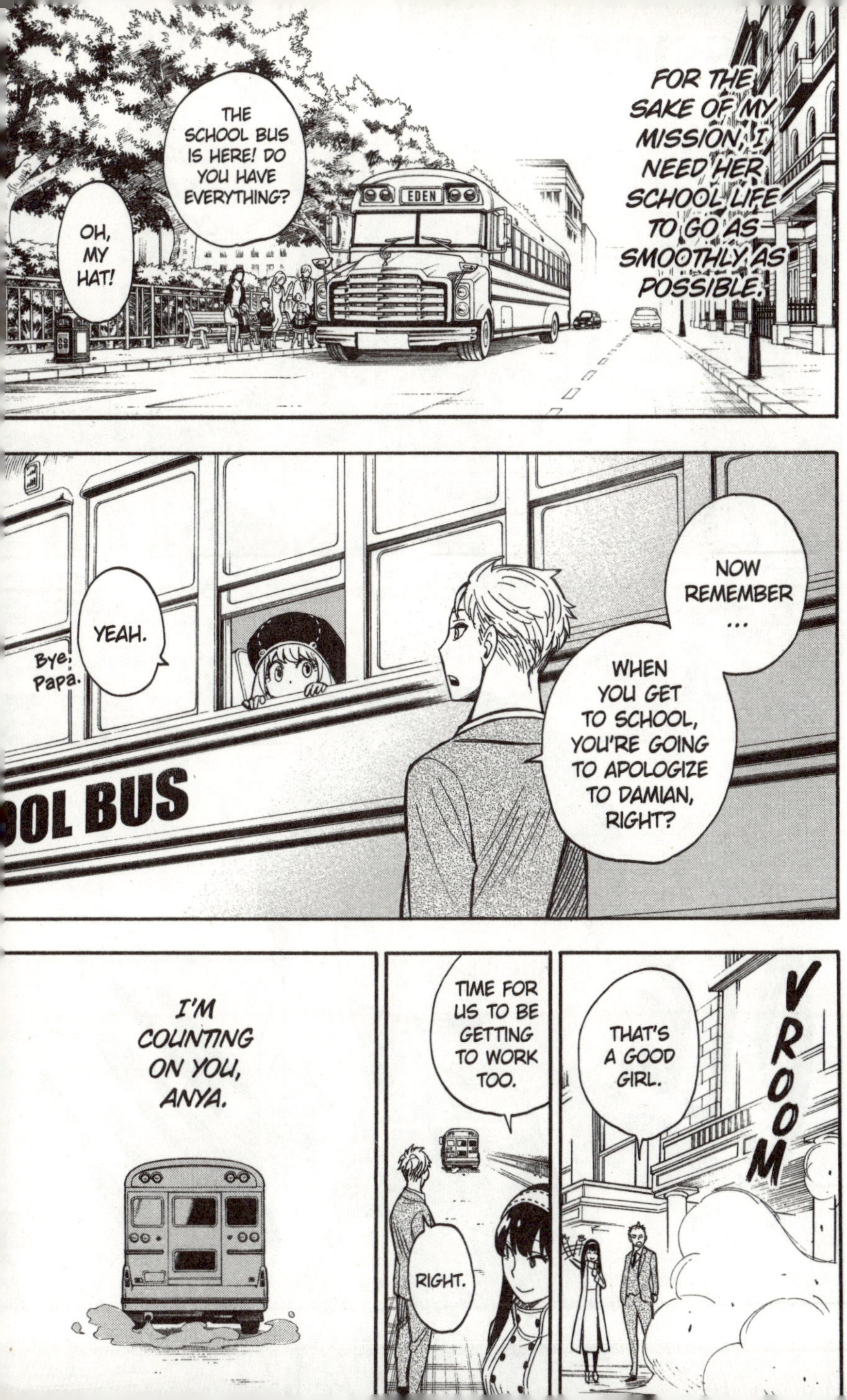
FOR THE SAKE OF MY MISSION, I NEED HER SCHOOL LIFE TO GO AS SMOOTHLY AS POSSIBLE.
EDEN
THE SCHOOL BUS IS HERE! DO YOU HAVE EVERYTHING?
OH, MY HAT!
NOW REMEMBER ...
WHEN YOU GET TO SCHOOL, YOU'RE GOING TO APOLOGIZE TO DAMIAN, RIGHT?
YEAH.
Bye, Papa.
OOL BUS
VROOM
THAT'S A GOOD GIRL.
TIME FOR US TO BE GETTING TO WORK TOO.
RIGHT.
I'M COUNTING ON YOU, ANYA.

MISSION 9

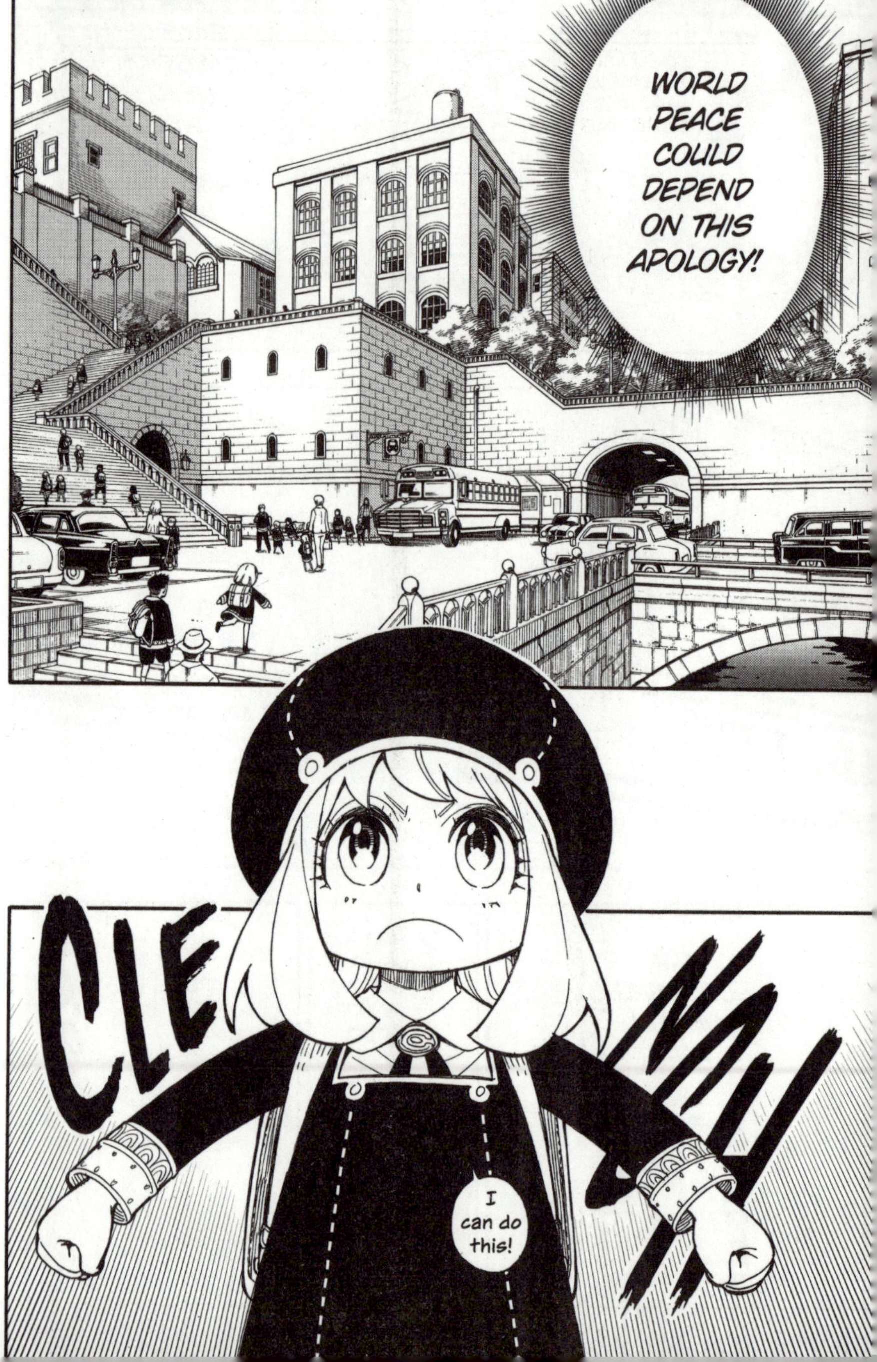
WORLD PEACE COULD DEPEND ON THIS APOLOGY!
CLENCH
I can do this!

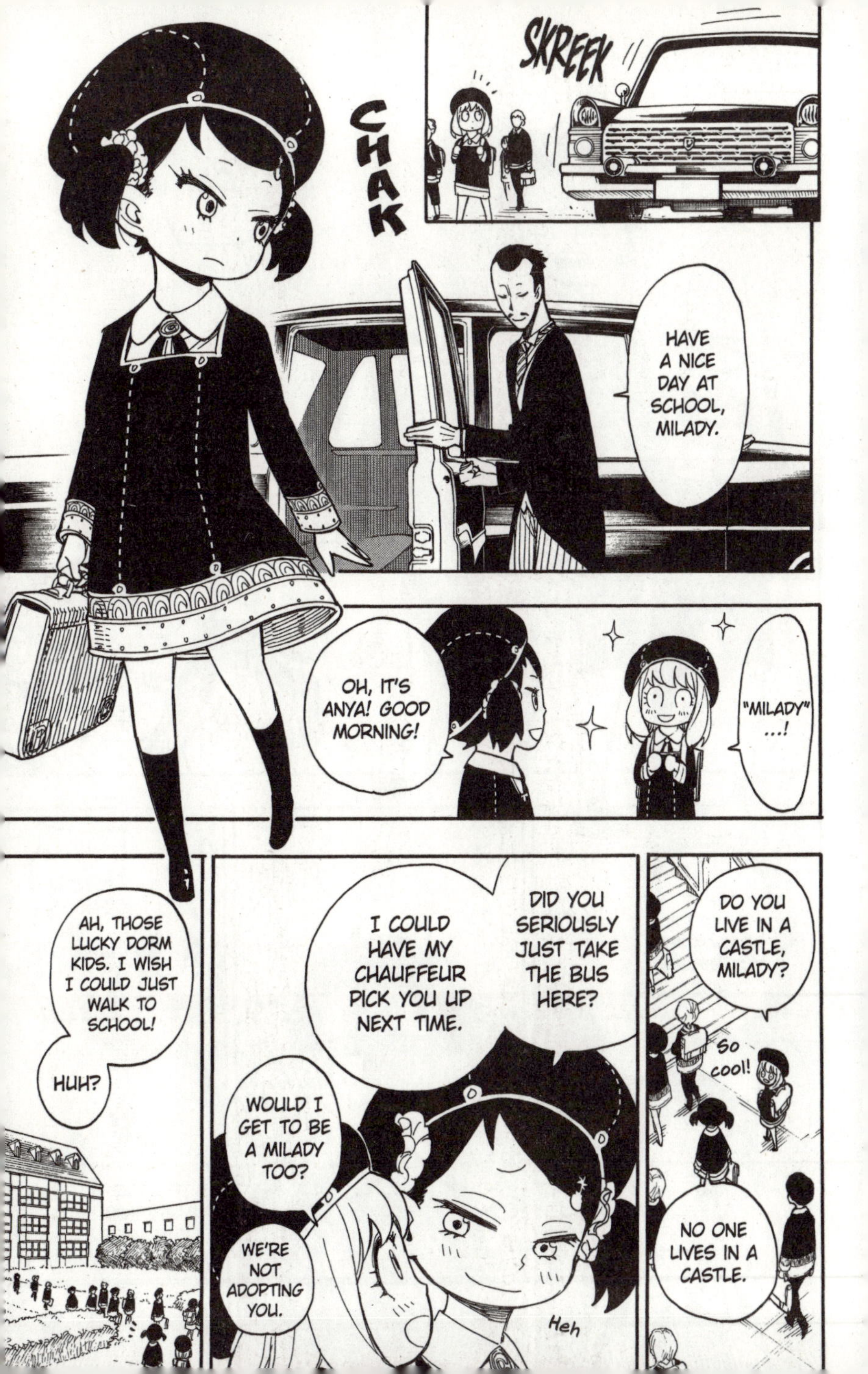
SKREEK
CHAK
HAVE A NICE DAY AT SCHOOL, MILADY.
"MILADY" ...!
OH, IT'S ANYA! GOOD MORNING!
DO YOU LIVE IN A CASTLE, MILADY?
So cool!
NO ONE LIVES IN A CASTLE.
DID YOU SERIOUSLY JUST TAKE THE BUS HERE?
I COULD HAVE MY CHAUFFEUR PICK YOU UP NEXT TIME.
WOULD I GET TO BE A MILADY TOO?
WE'RE NOT ADOPTING YOU.
Heh
AH, THOSE LUCKY DORM KIDS. I WISH I COULD JUST WALK TO SCHOOL!
HUH?

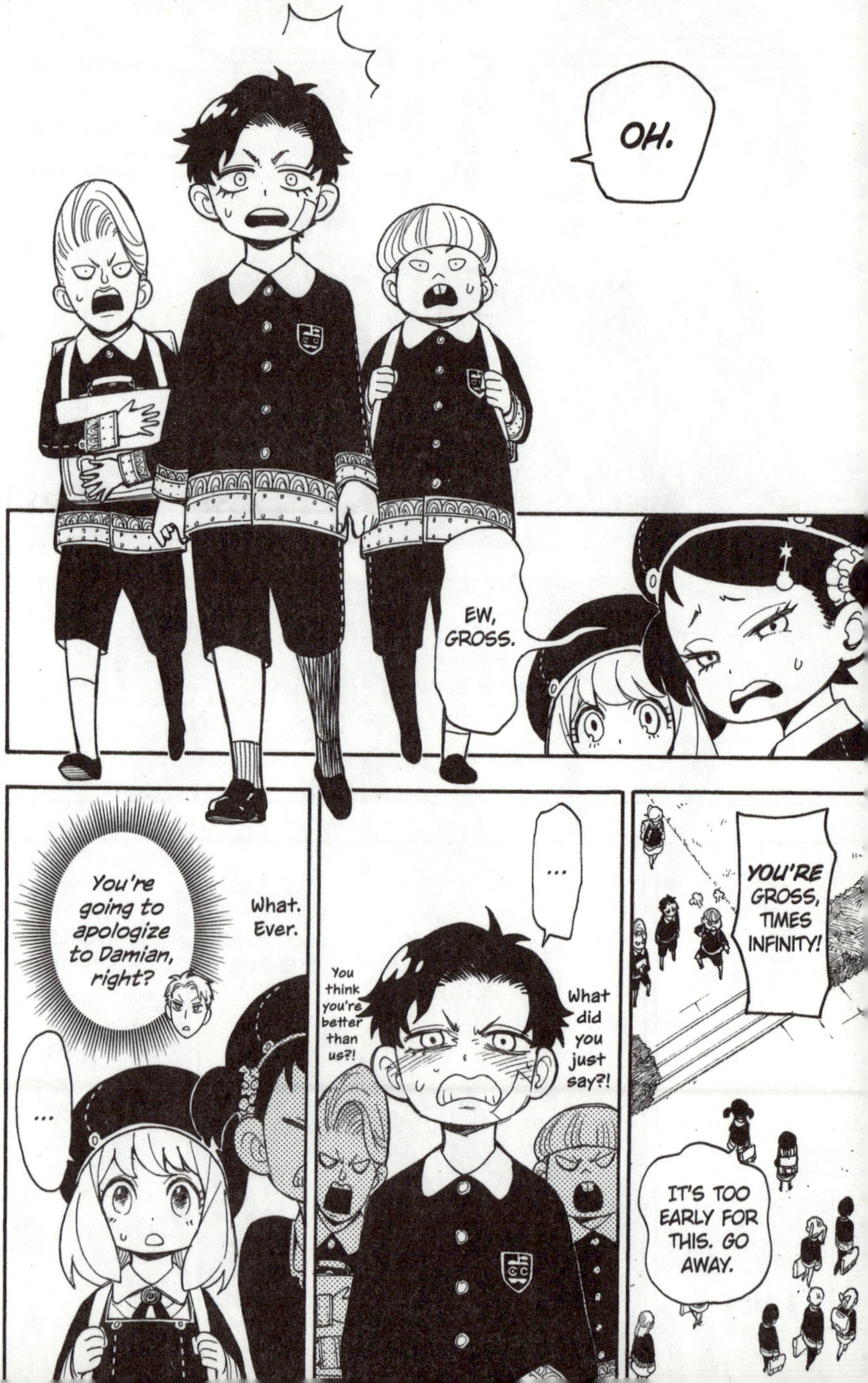
OH.
EW, GROSS.
YOU'RE GROSS, TIMES INFINITY!
IT'S TOO EARLY FOR THIS. GO AWAY.
...
What did you just say?!
You think you're better than us?!
You're going to apologize to Damian, right?
What. Ever.
...

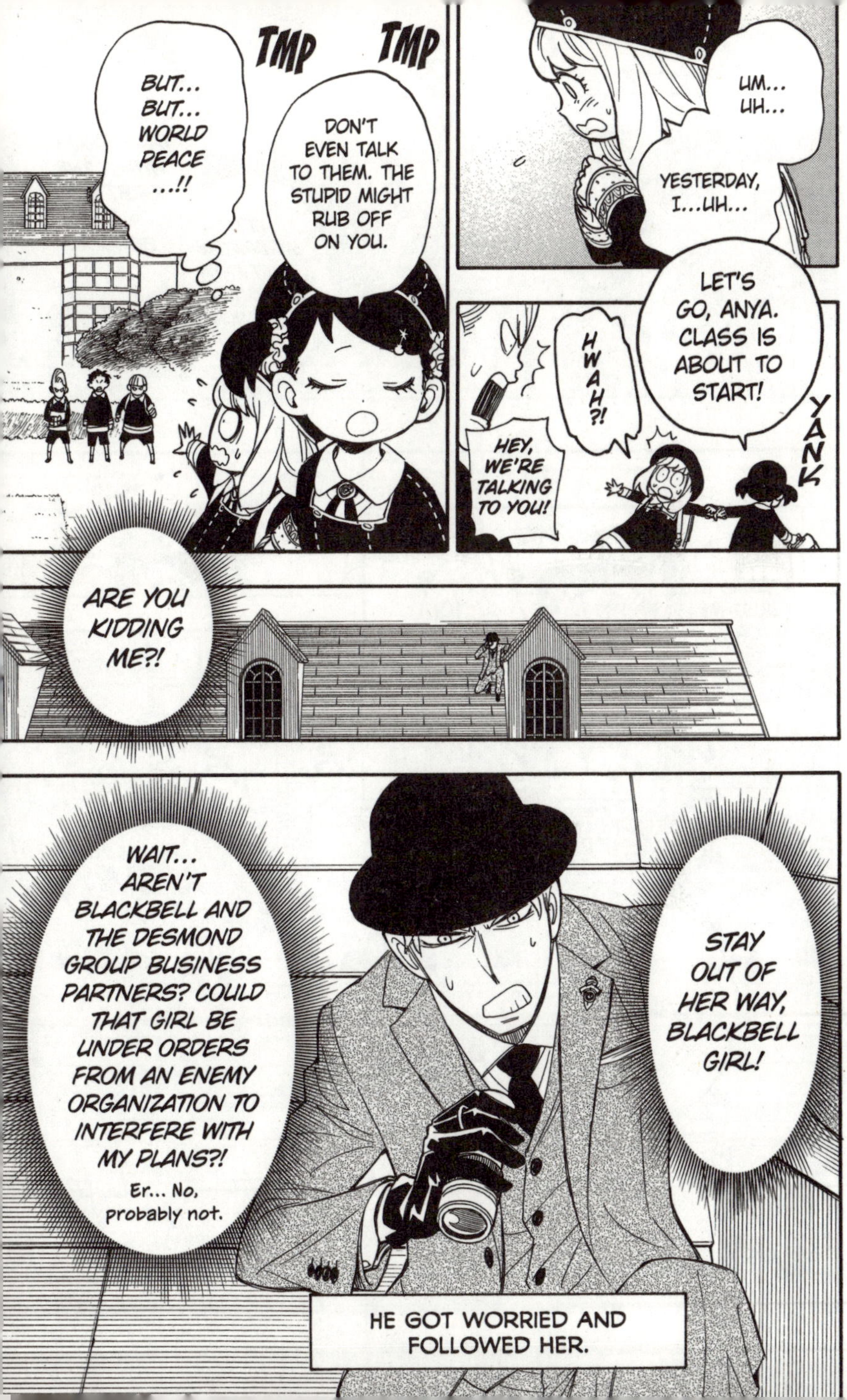
UM... UH...
YESTERDAY, I...UH...
LET'S GO, ANYA. CLASS IS ABOUT TO START!
YANK
HWAH?!
HEY, WE'RE TALKING TO YOU!
TMP TMP
DON'T EVEN TALK TO THEM. THE STUPID MIGHT RUB OFF ON YOU.
BUT... BUT... WORLD PEACE ...!!
ARE YOU KIDDING ME?!
STAY OUT OF HER WAY, BLACKBELL GIRL!
WAIT... AREN'T BLACKBELL AND THE DESMOND GROUP BUSINESS PARTNERS? COULD THAT GIRL BE UNDER ORDERS FROM AN ENEMY ORGANIZATION TO INTERFERE WITH MY PLANS?!
Er... No, probably not.
HE GOT WORRIED AND FOLLOWED HER.

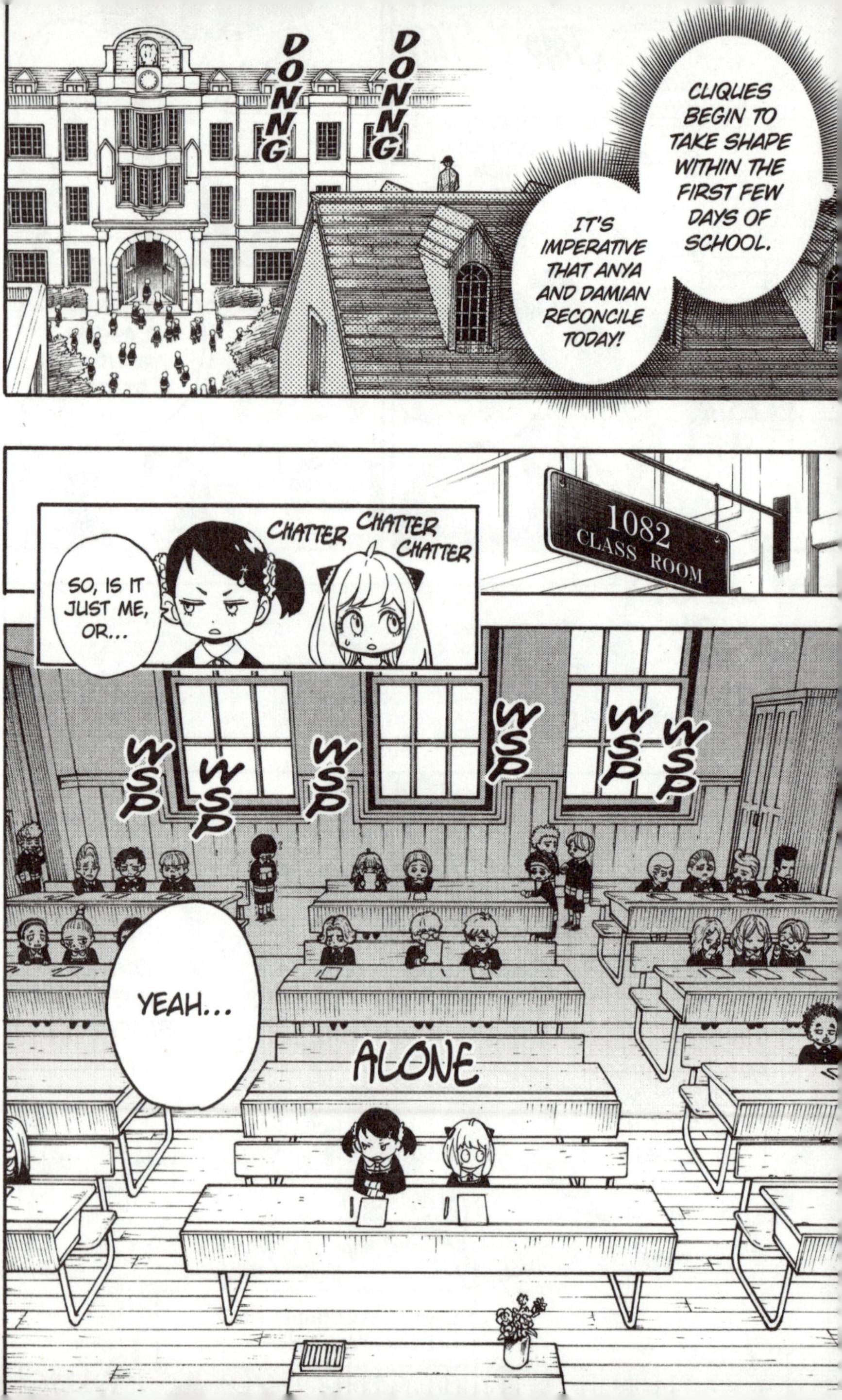
DONNG DONNG
CLIQUES BEGIN TO TAKE SHAPE WITHIN THE FIRST FEW DAYS OF SCHOOL.
IT'S IMPERATIVE THAT ANYA AND DAMIAN RECONCILE TODAY!
1082 CLASS ROOM
CHATTER CHATTER CHATTER
SO, IS IT JUST ME, OR...
WSP WSP WSP WSP WSP WSP
YEAH...
ALONE

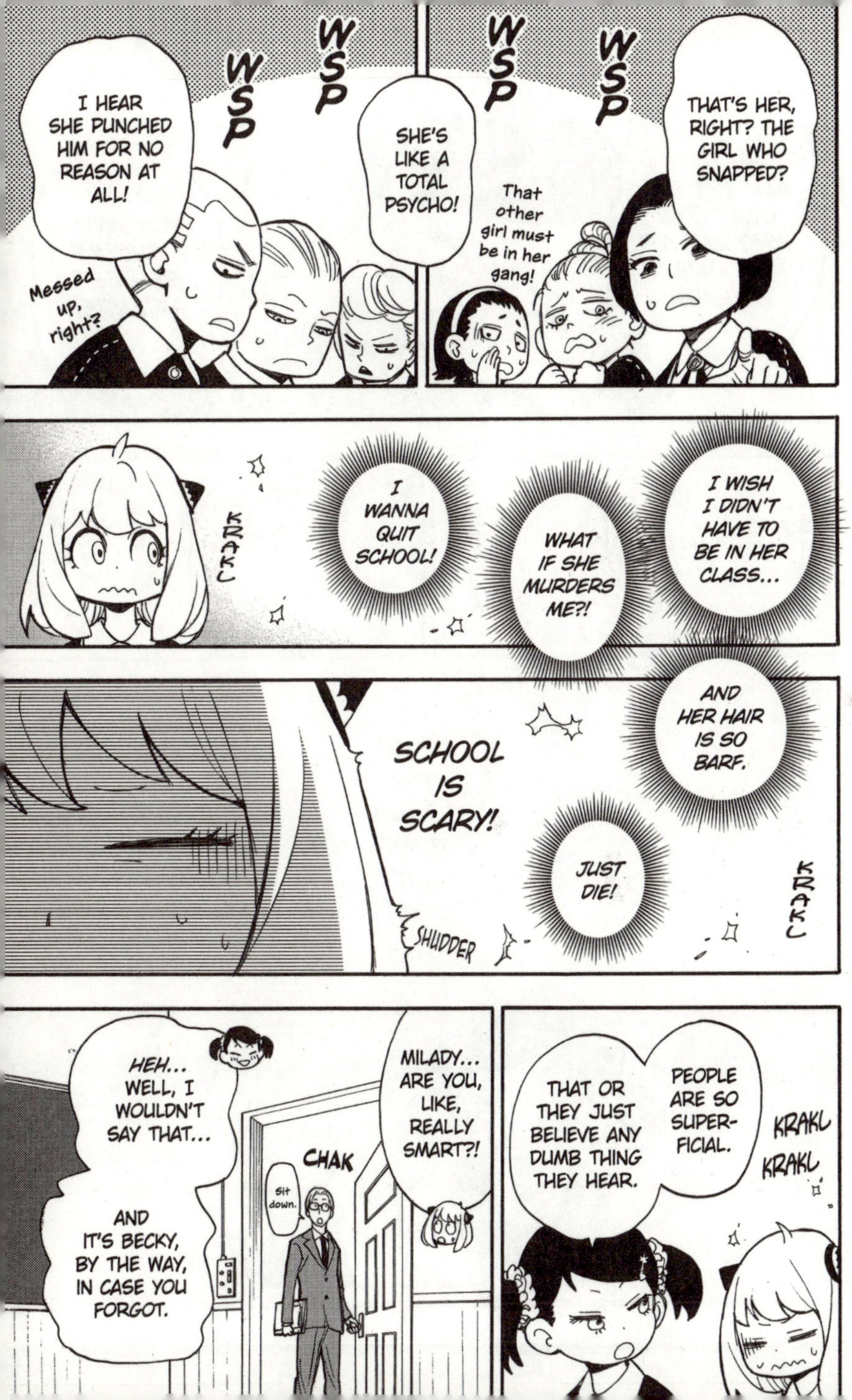
WSP
WSP
THAT'S HER, RIGHT? THE GIRL WHO SNAPPED?
That other girl must be in her gang!
WSP
SHE'S LIKE A TOTAL PSYCHO!
WSP
I HEAR SHE PUNCHED HIM FOR NO REASON AT ALL!
Messed up, right?
I WISH I DIDN'T HAVE TO BE IN HER CLASS...
WHAT IF SHE MURDERS ME?!
I WANNA QUIT SCHOOL!
KRAKL
AND HER HAIR IS SO BARF.
KRAKL
JUST DIE!
SCHOOL IS SCARY!
SHUDDER
PEOPLE ARE SO SUPER-FICIAL.
THAT OR THEY JUST BELIEVE ANY DUMB THING THEY HEAR.
KRAKL
KRAKL
MILADY... ARE YOU, LIKE, REALLY SMART?!
HEH... WELL, I WOULDN'T SAY THAT...
CHAK
Sit down.
AND IT'S BECKY, BY THE WAY, IN CASE YOU FORGOT.

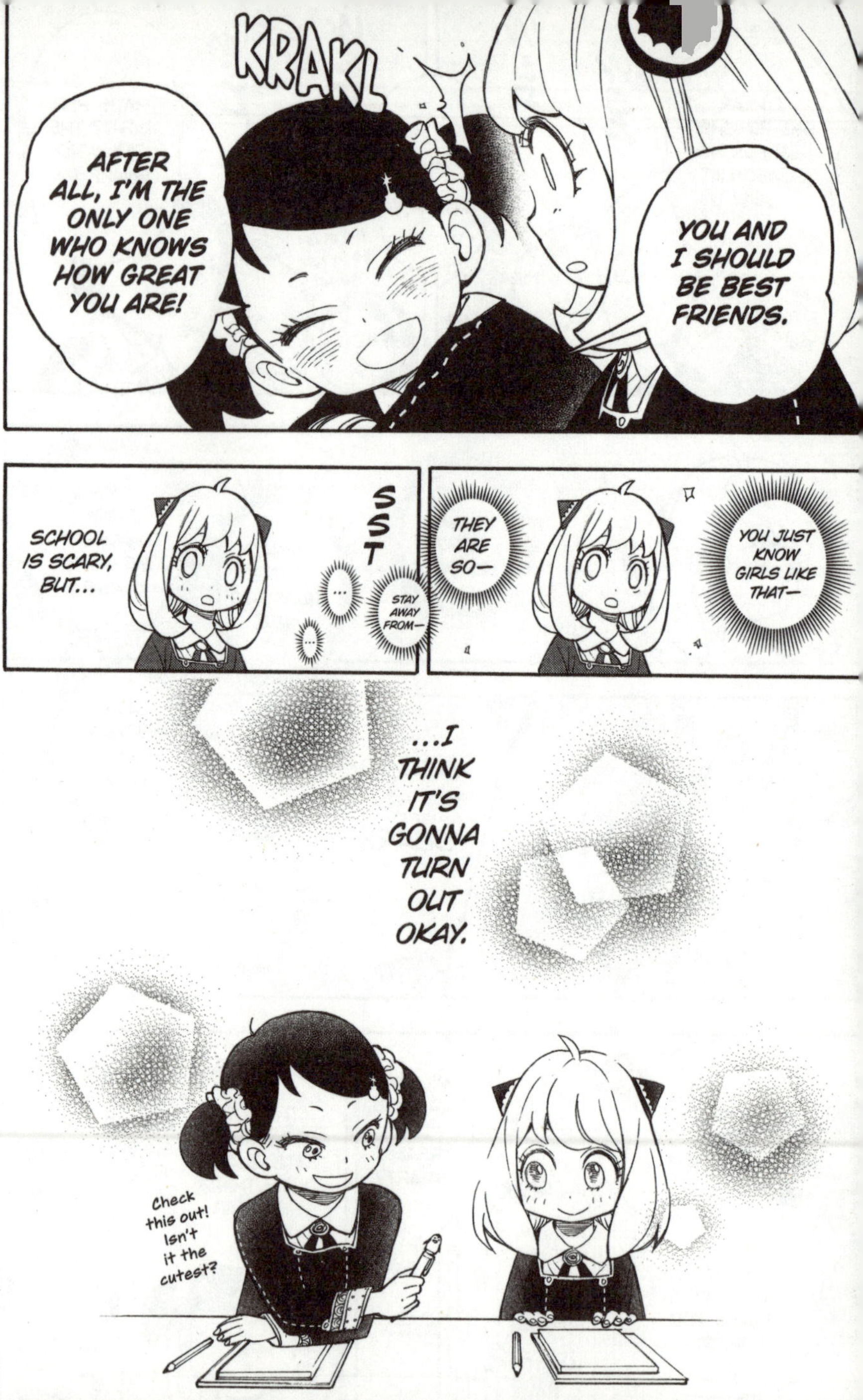
YOU AND I SHOULD BE BEST FRIENDS.
KRAKL
AFTER ALL, I'M THE ONLY ONE WHO KNOWS HOW GREAT YOU ARE!
YOU JUST KNOW GIRLS LIKE THAT—
THEY ARE SO—
STAY AWAY FROM—
SST
...
...
SCHOOL IS SCARY, BUT...
...I THINK IT'S GONNA TURN OUT OKAY.
Check this out! Isn't it the cutest?

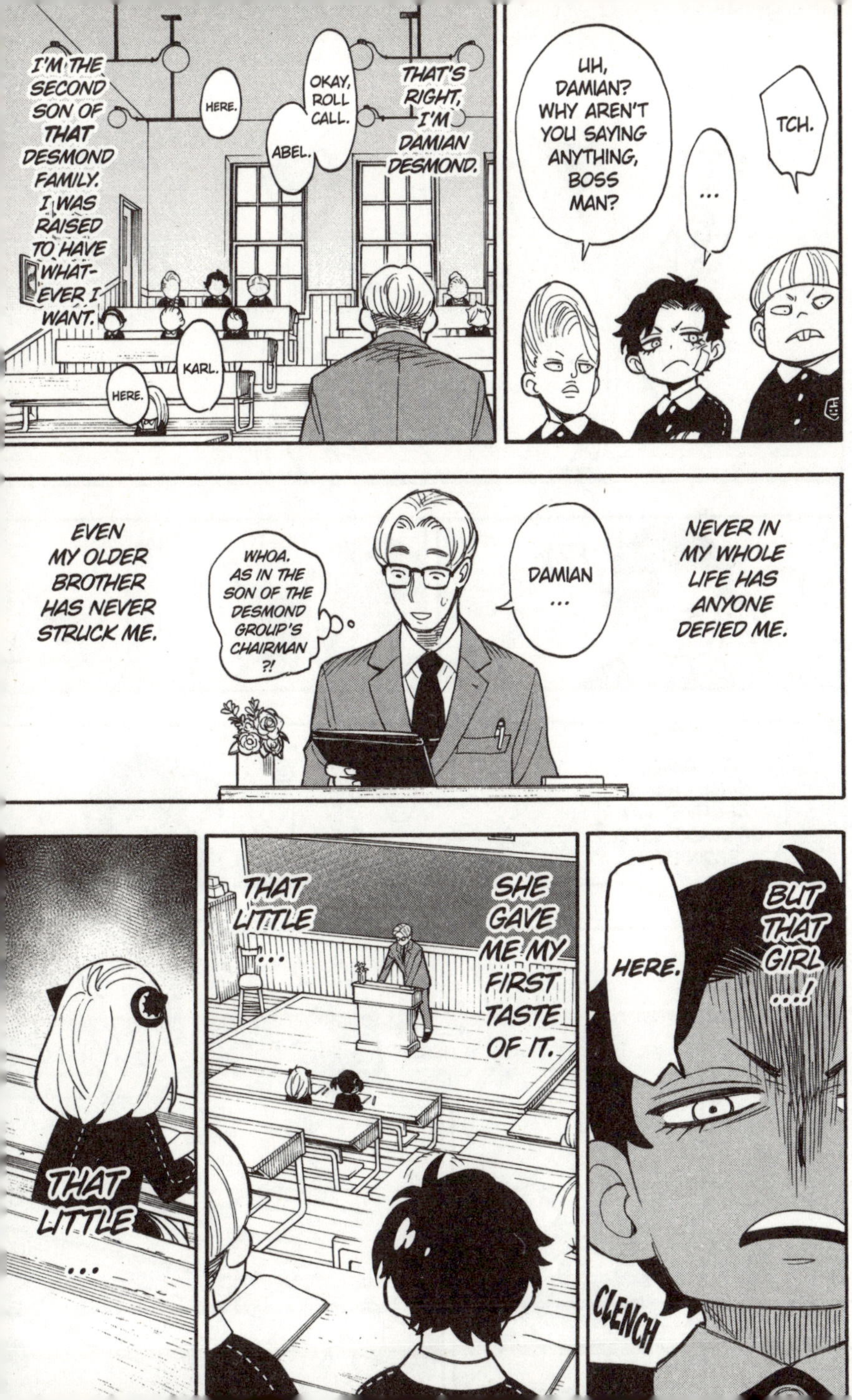
UH, DAMIAN? WHY AREN'T YOU SAYING ANYTHING, BOSS MAN?
...
TCH.
THAT'S RIGHT, I'M DAMIAN DESMOND.
OKAY, ROLL CALL.
ABEL.
HERE.
I'M THE SECOND SON OF THAT DESMOND FAMILY. I WAS RAISED TO HAVE WHATEVER I WANT.
KARL.
HERE.
NEVER IN MY WHOLE LIFE HAS ANYONE DEFIED ME.
DAMIAN ...
WHOA. AS IN THE SON OF THE DESMOND GROUP'S CHAIRMAN ?!
EVEN MY OLDER BROTHER HAS NEVER STRUCK ME.
BUT THAT GIRL ...!
HERE.
CLENCH
SHE GAVE ME MY FIRST TASTE OF IT.
THAT LITTLE ...
THAT LITTLE ...

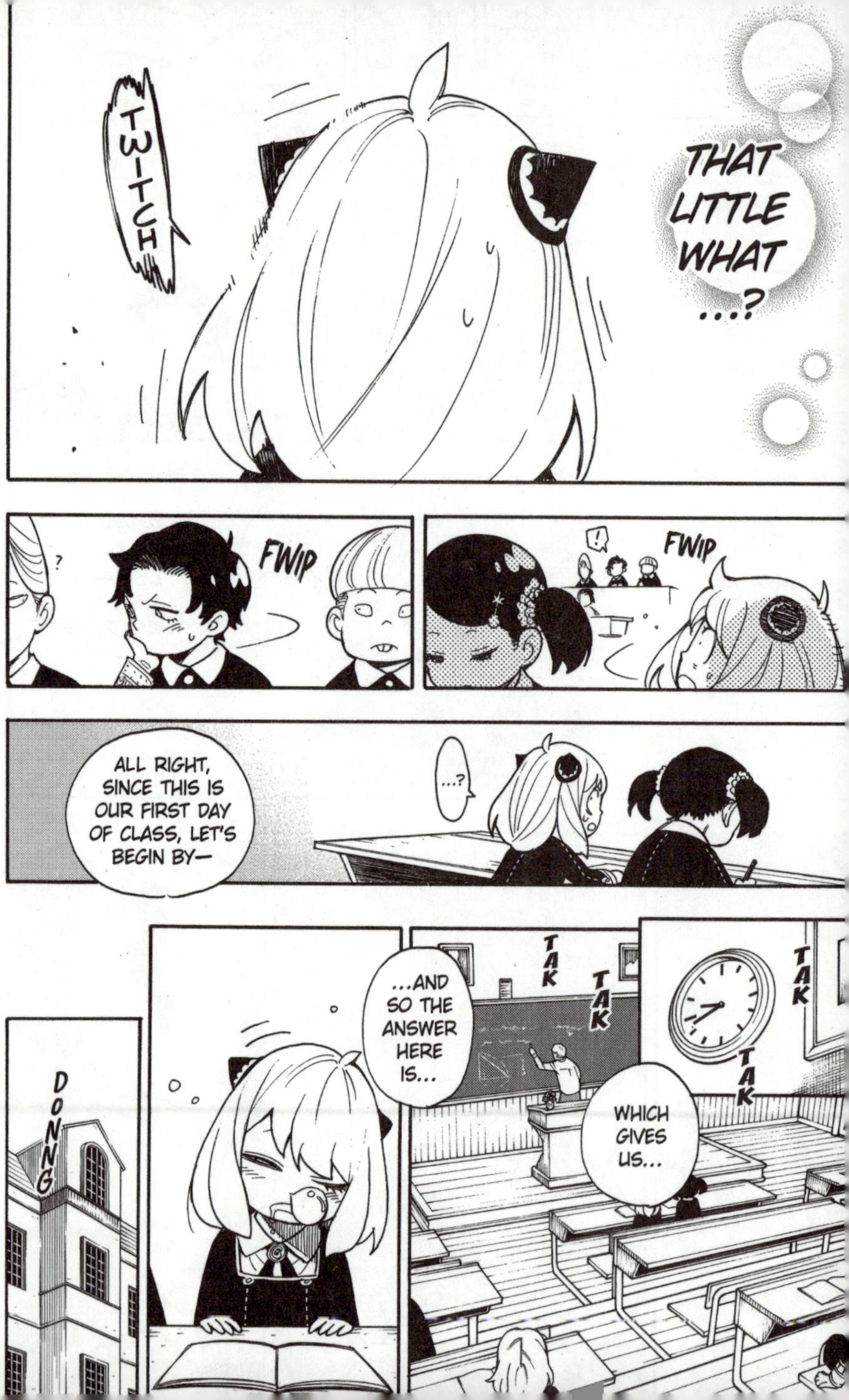
THAT LITTLE WHAT ...?
TWITCH
!
FWIP
FWIP
?
...?
ALL RIGHT, SINCE THIS IS OUR FIRST DAY OF CLASS, LET'S BEGIN BY—
TAK
TAK
TAK
TAK
...AND SO THE ANSWER HERE IS...
WHICH GIVES US...
DONNG

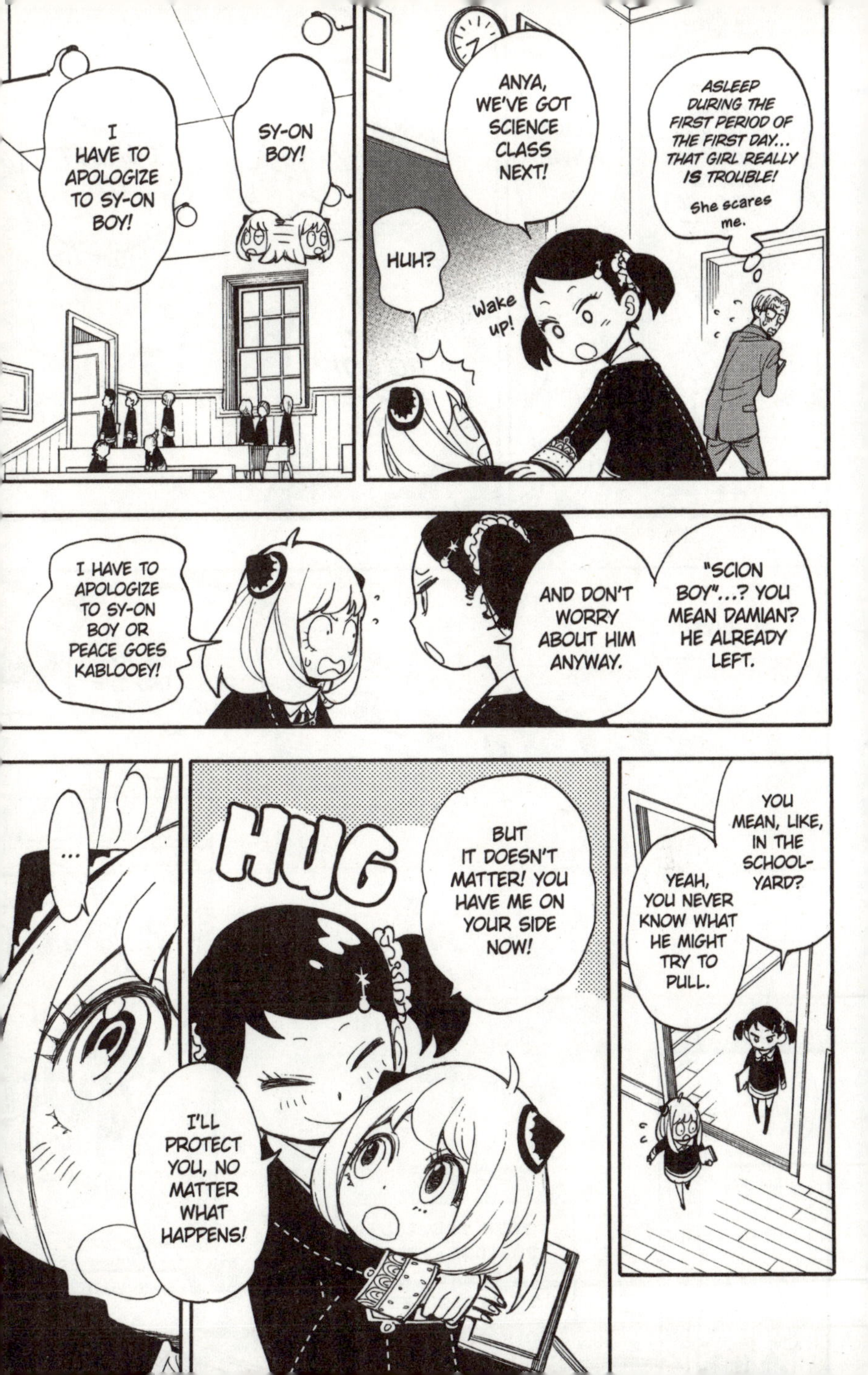
ASLEEP DURING THE FIRST PERIOD OF THE FIRST DAY... THAT GIRL REALLY IS TROUBLE!
She scares me.
ANYA, WE'VE GOT SCIENCE CLASS NEXT!
Wake up!
HUH?
SY-ON BOY!
I HAVE TO APOLOGIZE TO SY-ON BOY!
"SCION BOY"...? YOU MEAN DAMIAN? HE ALREADY LEFT.
AND DON'T WORRY ABOUT HIM ANYWAY.
I HAVE TO APOLOGIZE TO SY-ON BOY OR PEACE GOES KABLOOEY!
YOU MEAN, LIKE, IN THE SCHOOL-YARD?
YEAH, YOU NEVER KNOW WHAT HE MIGHT TRY TO PULL.
HUG
BUT IT DOESN'T MATTER! YOU HAVE ME ON YOUR SIDE NOW!
I'LL PROTECT YOU, NO MATTER WHAT HAPPENS!
...

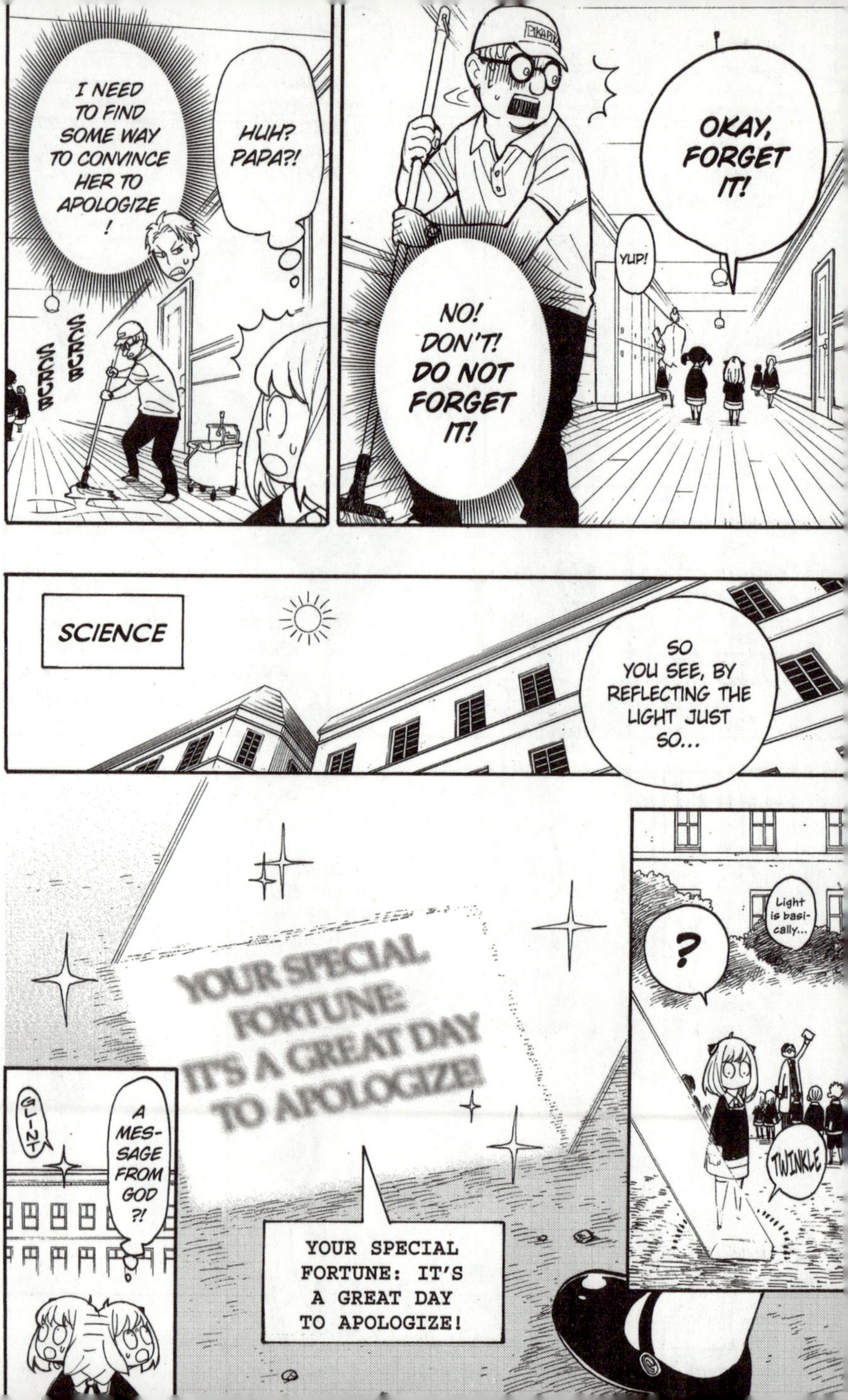
OKAY, FORGET IT!
YUP!
NO! DON'T! DO NOT FORGET IT!
HUH? PAPA?!
I NEED TO FIND SOME WAY TO CONVINCE HER TO APOLOGIZE!
SCRUB SCRUB
SCIENCE
SO YOU SEE, BY REFLECTING THE LIGHT JUST SO...
Light is basi-cally...
?
TWINKLE
YOUR SPECIAL FORTUNE: IT'S A GREAT DAY TO APOLOGIZE!
YOUR SPECIAL FORTUNE: IT'S A GREAT DAY TO APOLOGIZE!
GLINT
A MES-SAGE FROM GOD?!

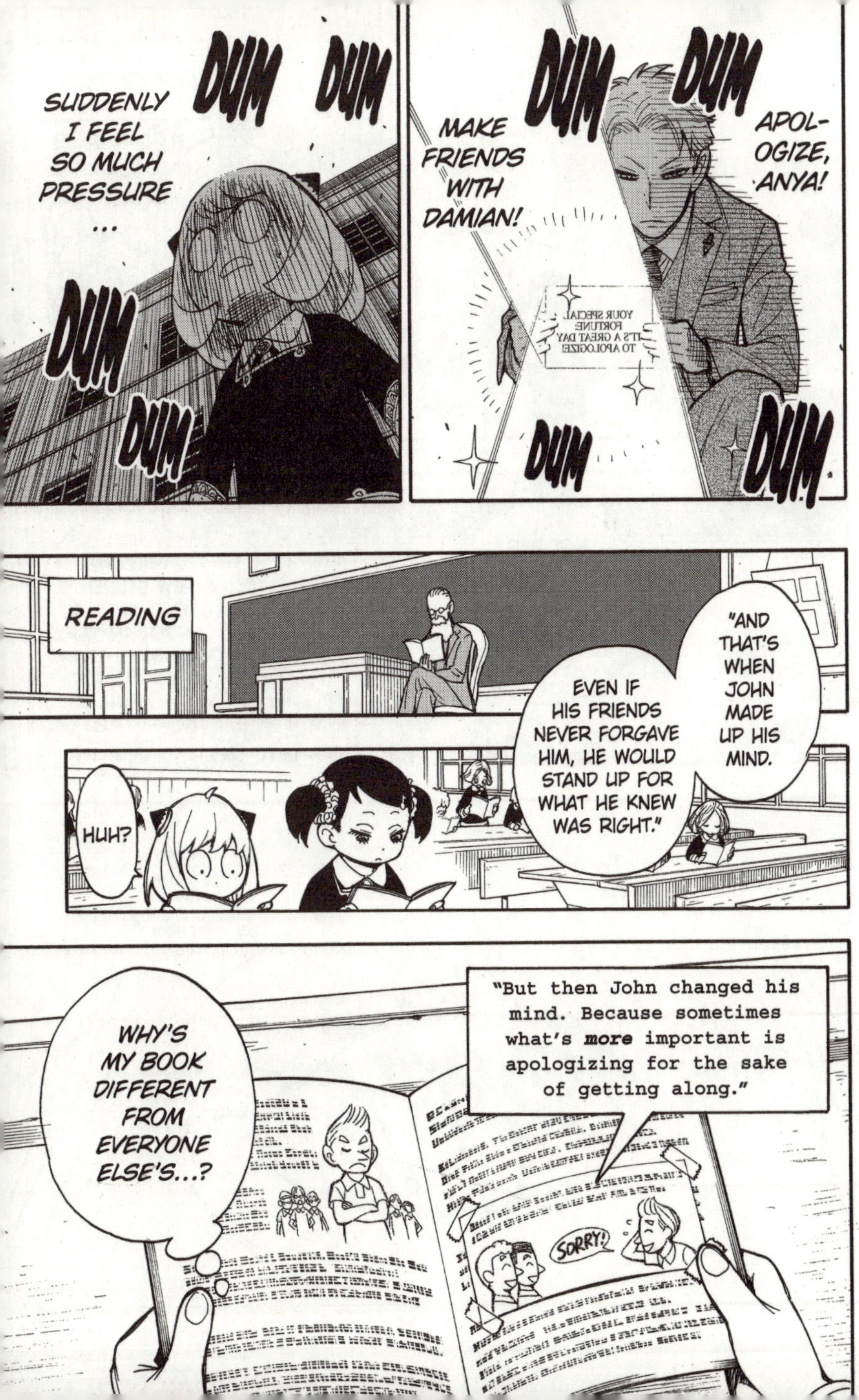
DUM DUM
APOLOGIZE, ANYA!
MAKE FRIENDS WITH DAMIAN!
YOUR SPECIAL FORTUNE: IT'S A GREAT DAY TO APOLOGIZE!
DUM DUM
DUM DUM
SUDDENLY I FEEL SO MUCH PRESSURE...
DUM DUM
READING
"AND THAT'S WHEN JOHN MADE UP HIS MIND.
EVEN IF HIS FRIENDS NEVER FORGAVE HIM, HE WOULD STAND UP FOR WHAT HE KNEW WAS RIGHT."
HUH?
"But then John changed his mind. Because sometimes what's *more* important is apologizing for the sake of getting along."
SORRY!
WHY'S MY BOOK DIFFERENT FROM EVERYONE ELSE'S...?

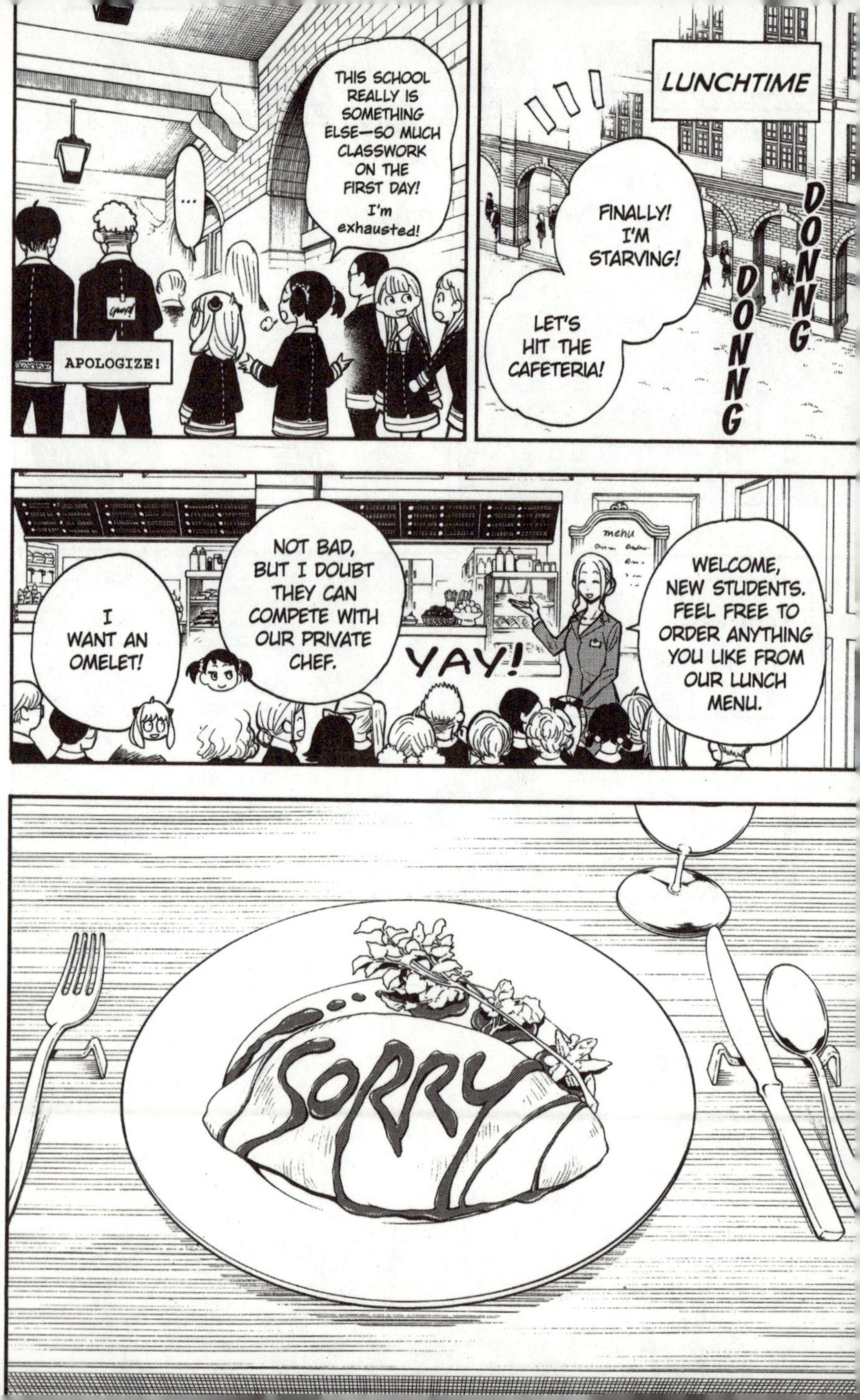
LUNCHTIME
DONNG
DONNG
FINALLY! I'M STARVING!
LET'S HIT THE CAFETERIA!
THIS SCHOOL REALLY IS SOMETHING ELSE—SO MUCH CLASSWORK ON THE FIRST DAY! I'm exhausted!
...
APOLOGIZE!
menu
WELCOME, NEW STUDENTS. FEEL FREE TO ORDER ANYTHING YOU LIKE FROM OUR LUNCH MENU.
YAY!
NOT BAD, BUT I DOUBT THEY CAN COMPETE WITH OUR PRIVATE CHEF.
I WANT AN OMELET!
SORRY

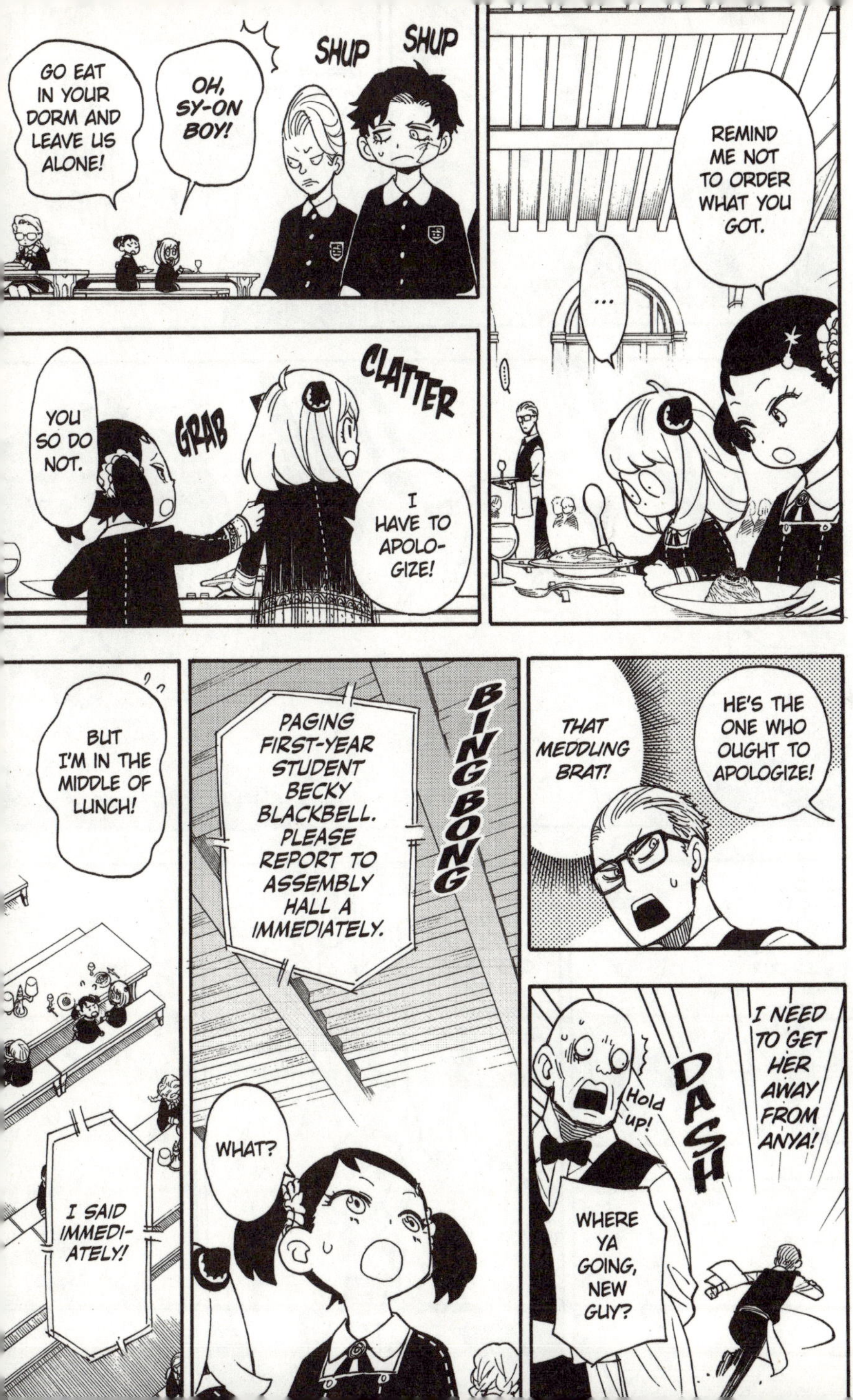
REMIND ME NOT TO ORDER WHAT YOU GOT.
...
...
SHUP
SHUP
OH, SY-ON BOY!
GO EAT IN YOUR DORM AND LEAVE US ALONE!
CLATTER
I HAVE TO APOLOGIZE!
GRAB
YOU SO DO NOT.
HE'S THE ONE WHO OUGHT TO APOLOGIZE!
THAT MEDDLING BRAT!
I NEED TO GET HER AWAY FROM ANYA!
DASH
Hold up!
WHERE YA GOING, NEW GUY?
BING BONG
PAGING FIRST-YEAR STUDENT BECKY BLACKBELL. PLEASE REPORT TO ASSEMBLY HALL A IMMEDIATELY.
WHAT?
BUT I'M IN THE MIDDLE OF LUNCH!
I SAID IMMEDI-ATELY!

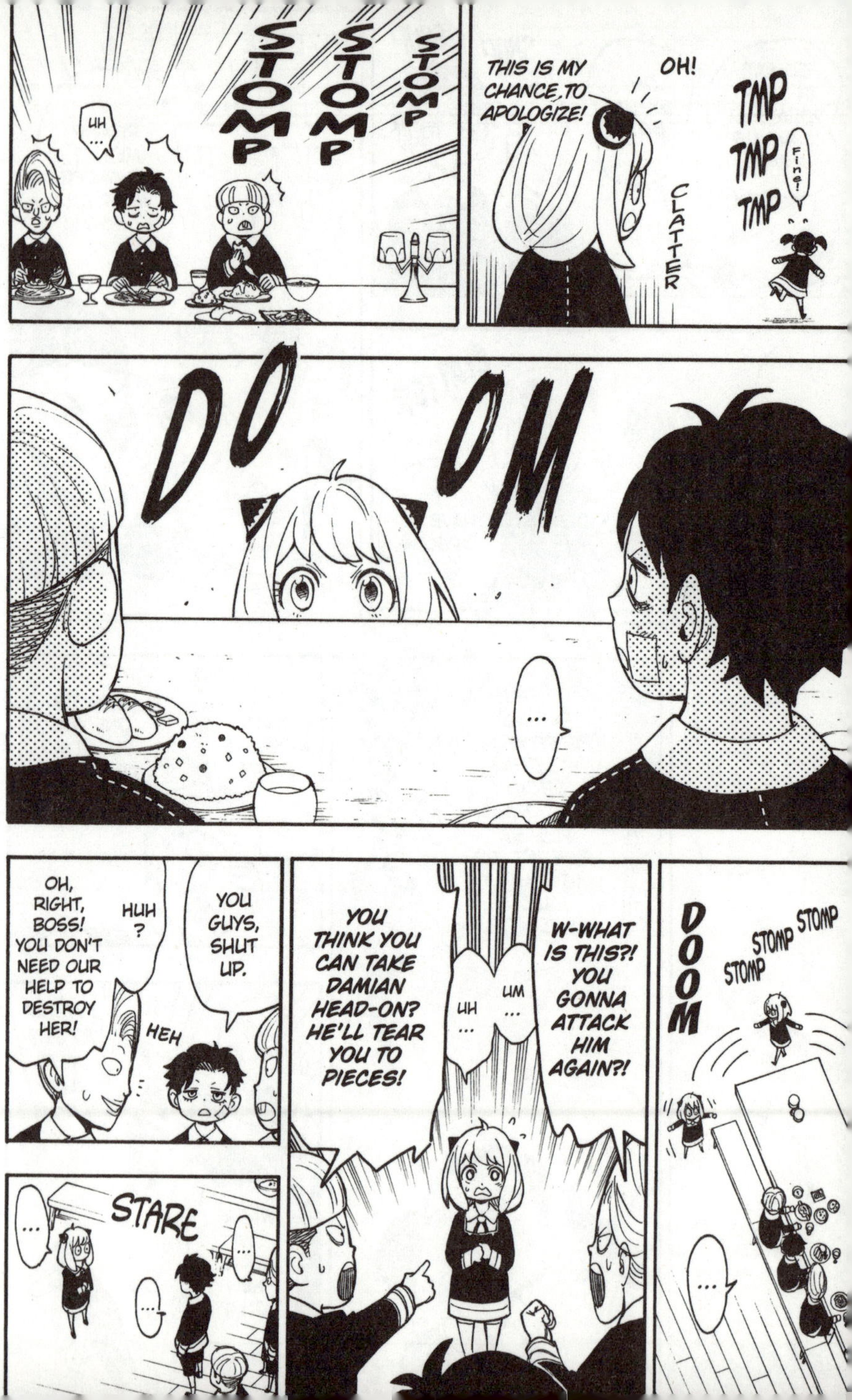
TMP
TMP
TMP
Fine!
OH!
THIS IS MY CHANCE TO APOLOGIZE!
CLATTER
STOMP
STOMP
STOMP
UH...
DO
OM
...
DOOM
STOMP
STOMP
STOMP
...
W-WHAT IS THIS?! YOU GONNA ATTACK HIM AGAIN?!
UM...
UH...
YOU THINK YOU CAN TAKE DAMIAN HEAD-ON? HE'LL TEAR YOU TO PIECES!
YOU GUYS, SHUT UP.
HUH?
OH, RIGHT, BOSS! YOU DON'T NEED OUR HELP TO DESTROY HER!
HEH
STARE
...
...
...

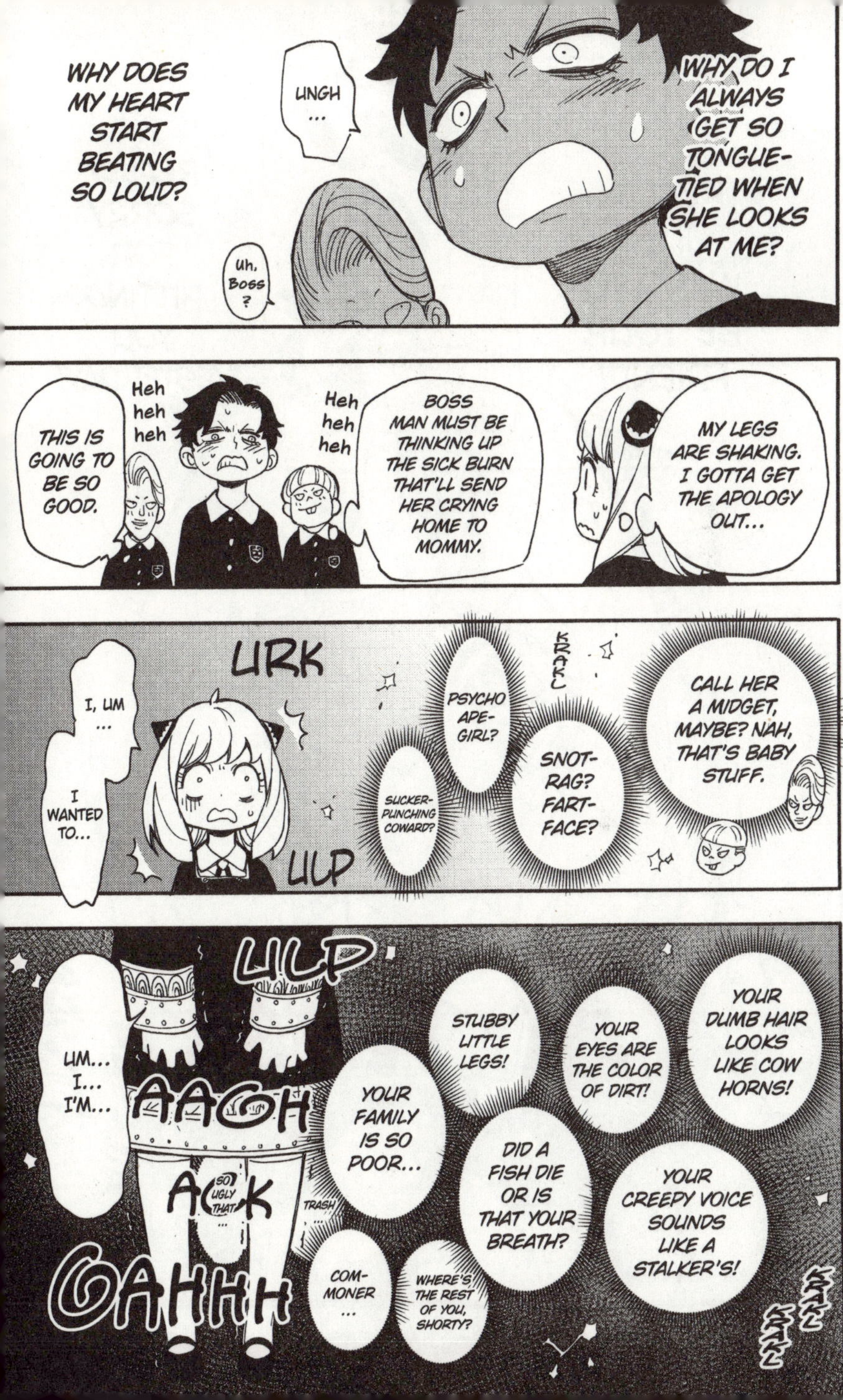
WHY DO I ALWAYS GET SO TONGUE-TIED WHEN SHE LOOKS AT ME?
UNGH ...
WHY DOES MY HEART START BEATING SO LOUD?
Uh, Boss?
MY LEGS ARE SHAKING. I GOTTA GET THE APOLOGY OUT...
BOSS MAN MUST BE THINKING UP THE SICK BURN THAT'LL SEND HER CRYING HOME TO MOMMY.
Heh heh heh
Heh heh heh
THIS IS GOING TO BE SO GOOD.
CALL HER A MIDGET, MAYBE? NAH, THAT'S BABY STUFF.
KRAKL
SNOT-RAG? FART-FACE?
PSYCHO APE-GIRL?
SUCKER-PUNCHING COWARD?
URK
ULP
I, UM ...
I WANTED TO...
KRAKL
KRAKL
YOUR DUMB HAIR LOOKS LIKE COW HORNS!
YOUR CREEPY VOICE SOUNDS LIKE A STALKER'S!
YOUR EYES ARE THE COLOR OF DIRT!
DID A FISH DIE OR IS THAT YOUR BREATH?
STUBBY LITTLE LEGS!
YOUR FAMILY IS SO POOR...
WHERE'S THE REST OF YOU, SHORTY?
COM-MONER ...
TRASH ...
SO UGLY THAT ...
ULP
AAGH
ACK
GAHHH
UM... I... I'M...

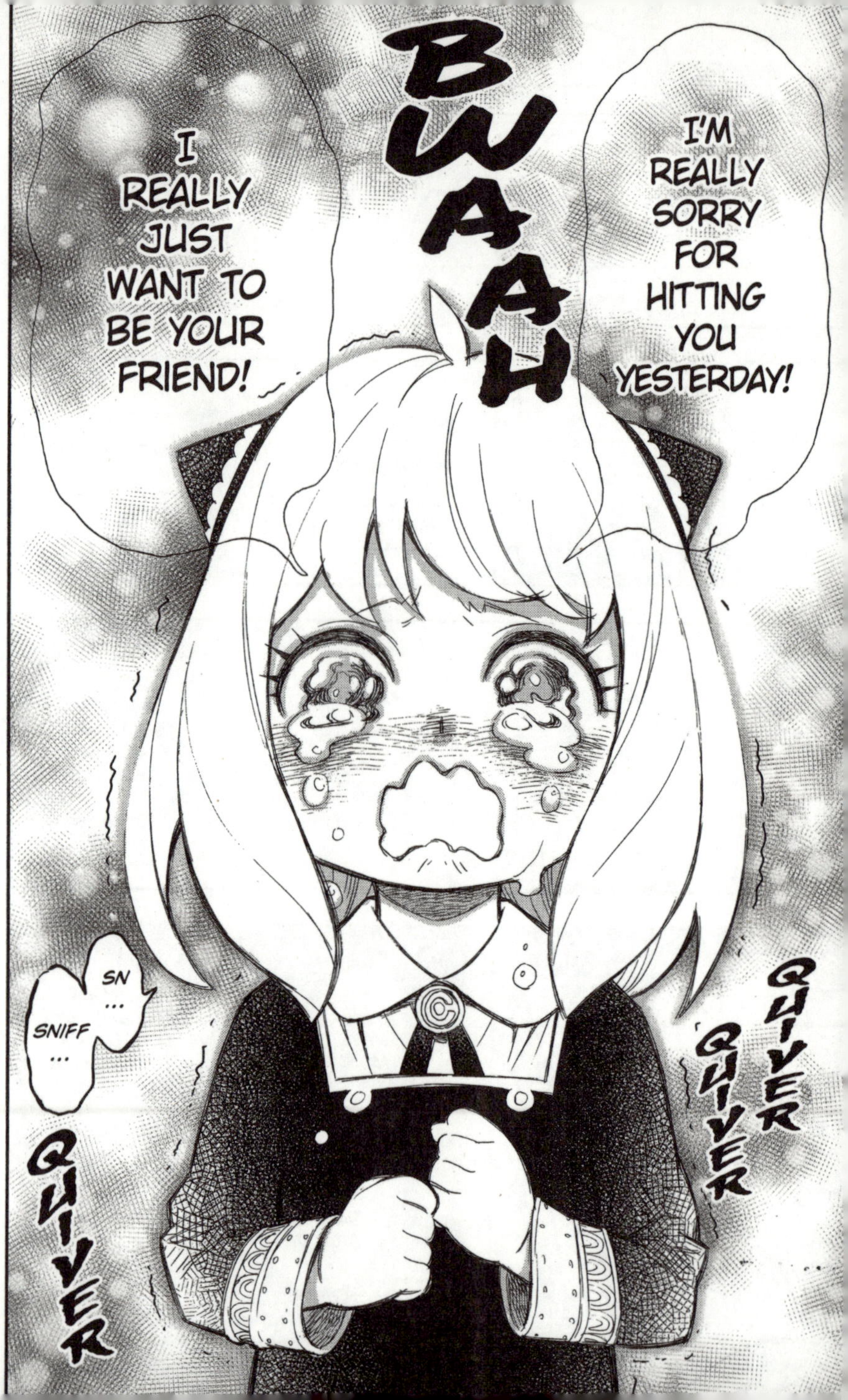
I'M REALLY SORRY FOR HITTING YOU YESTERDAY!
BWAAH
I REALLY JUST WANT TO BE YOUR FRIEND!
QUIVER QUIVER
QUIVER
SN... SNIFF...

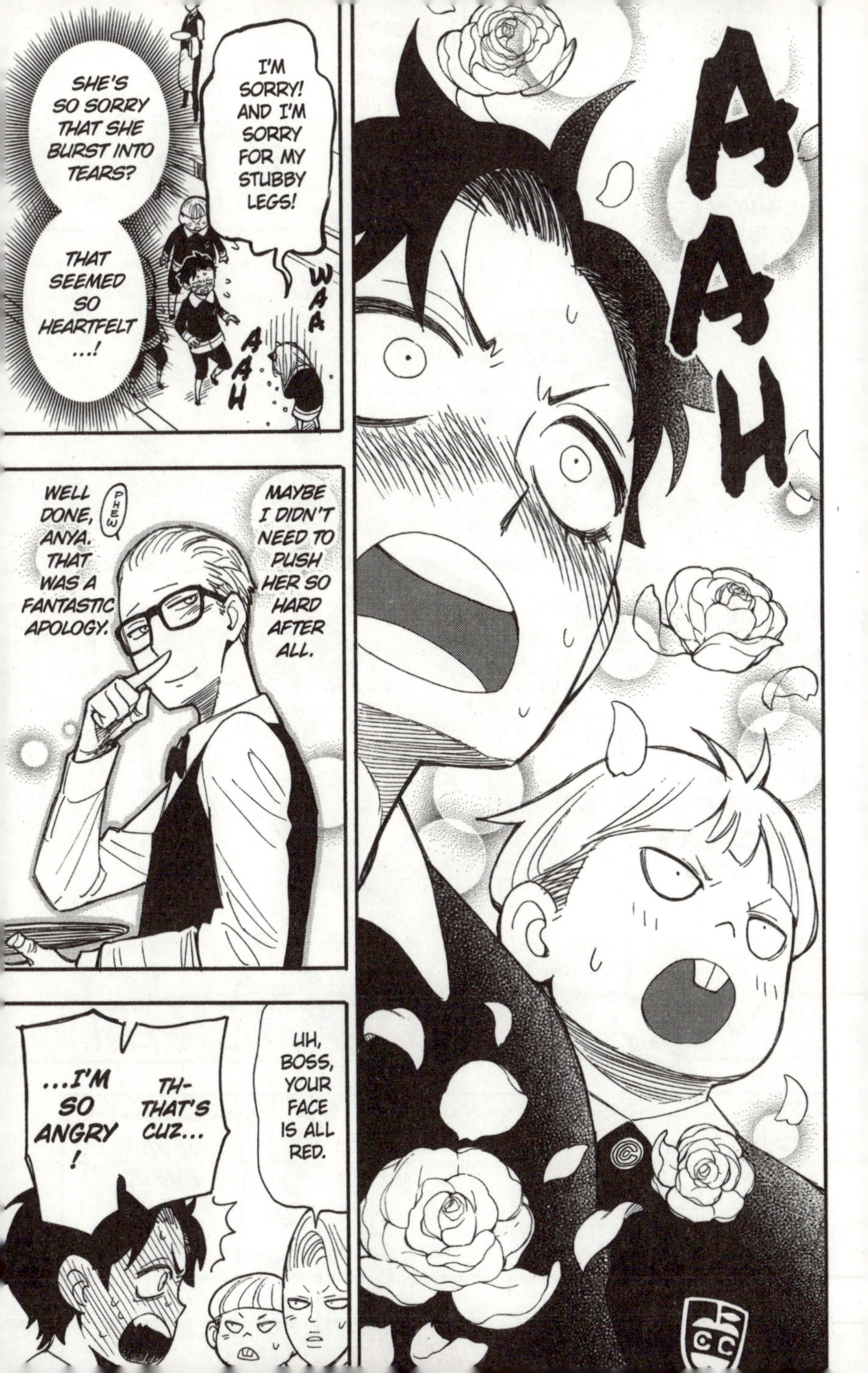
AAAH
I'M SORRY! AND I'M SORRY FOR MY STUBBY LEGS!
WAA
AAAH
SHE'S SO SORRY THAT SHE BURST INTO TEARS?
THAT SEEMED SO HEARTFELT ...!
MAYBE I DIDN'T NEED TO PUSH HER SO HARD AFTER ALL.
PHEW
WELL DONE, ANYA. THAT WAS A FANTASTIC APOLOGY.
UH, BOSS, YOUR FACE IS ALL RED.
TH- THAT'S CUZ...
...I'M SO ANGRY!

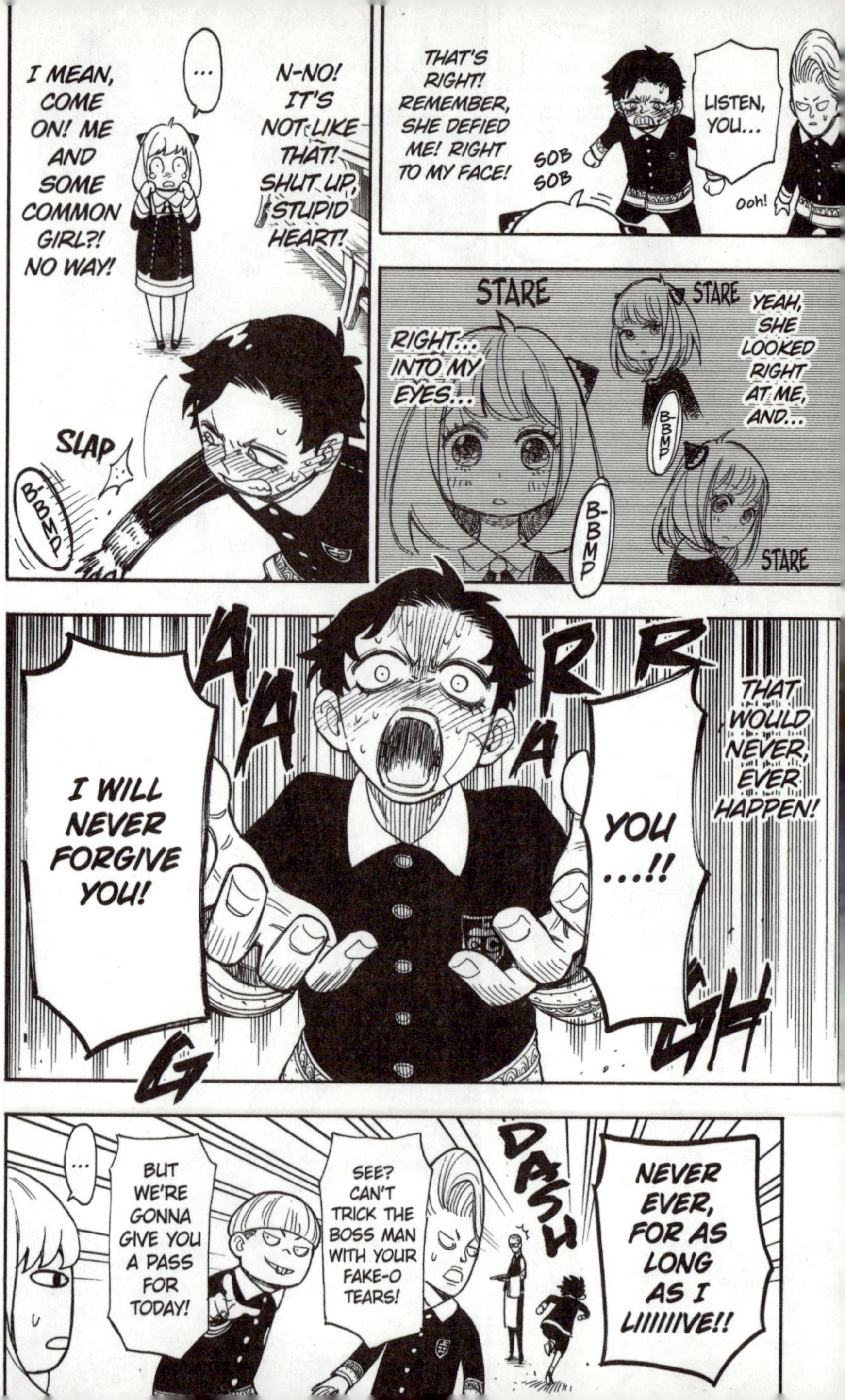
LISTEN, YOU...
Ooh!
THAT'S RIGHT! REMEMBER, SHE DEFIED ME! RIGHT TO MY FACE!
SOB SOB
STARE
YEAH, SHE LOOKED RIGHT AT ME, AND...
B-BBMP
RIGHT... INTO MY EYES...
STARE
B-BBMP
STARE
N-NO! IT'S NOT LIKE THAT! SHUT UP, STUPID HEART!
...
I MEAN, COME ON! ME AND SOME COMMON GIRL?! NO WAY!
SLAP
B-BBMP
THAT WOULD NEVER, EVER HAPPEN!
YOU ...!!
I WILL NEVER FORGIVE YOU!
GAARRAUH
NEVER EVER, FOR AS LONG AS I LIIIIIIVE!!
DASH
SEE? CAN'T TRICK THE BOSS MAN WITH YOUR FAKE-O TEARS!
BUT WE'RE GONNA GIVE YOU A PASS FOR TODAY!
...

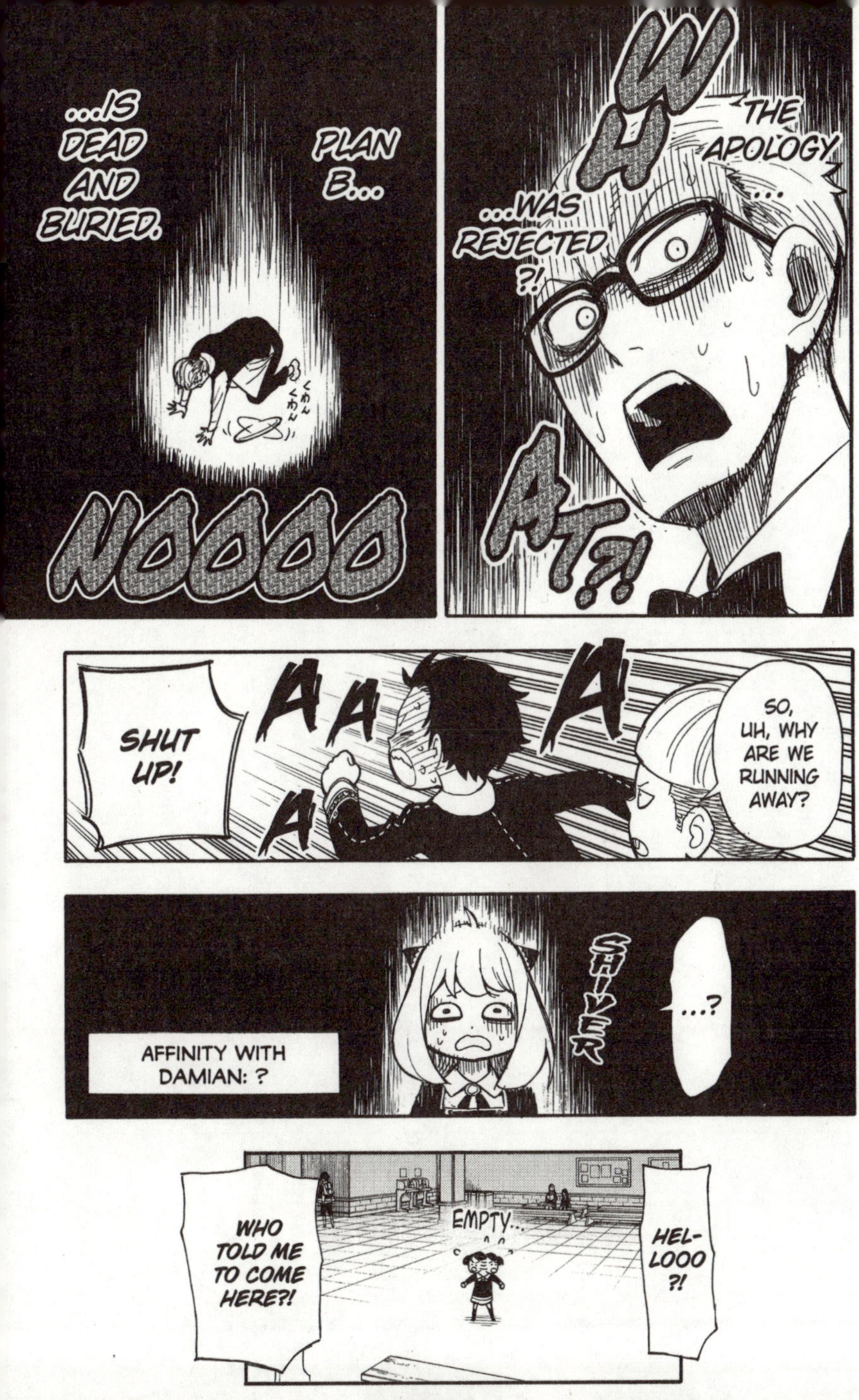
WH
THE APOLOGY...
...WAS REJECTED?!
AT?!
PLAN B...
...IS DEAD AND BURIED.
くわん くわん
NOOOO
SO, UH, WHY ARE WE RUNNING AWAY?
AAAA
SHUT UP!
...?
SHIVER
AFFINITY WITH DAMIAN: ?
HEL-LOOO?!
EMPTY...
WHO TOLD ME TO COME HERE?!

SPY×FAMILY

MISSION 10

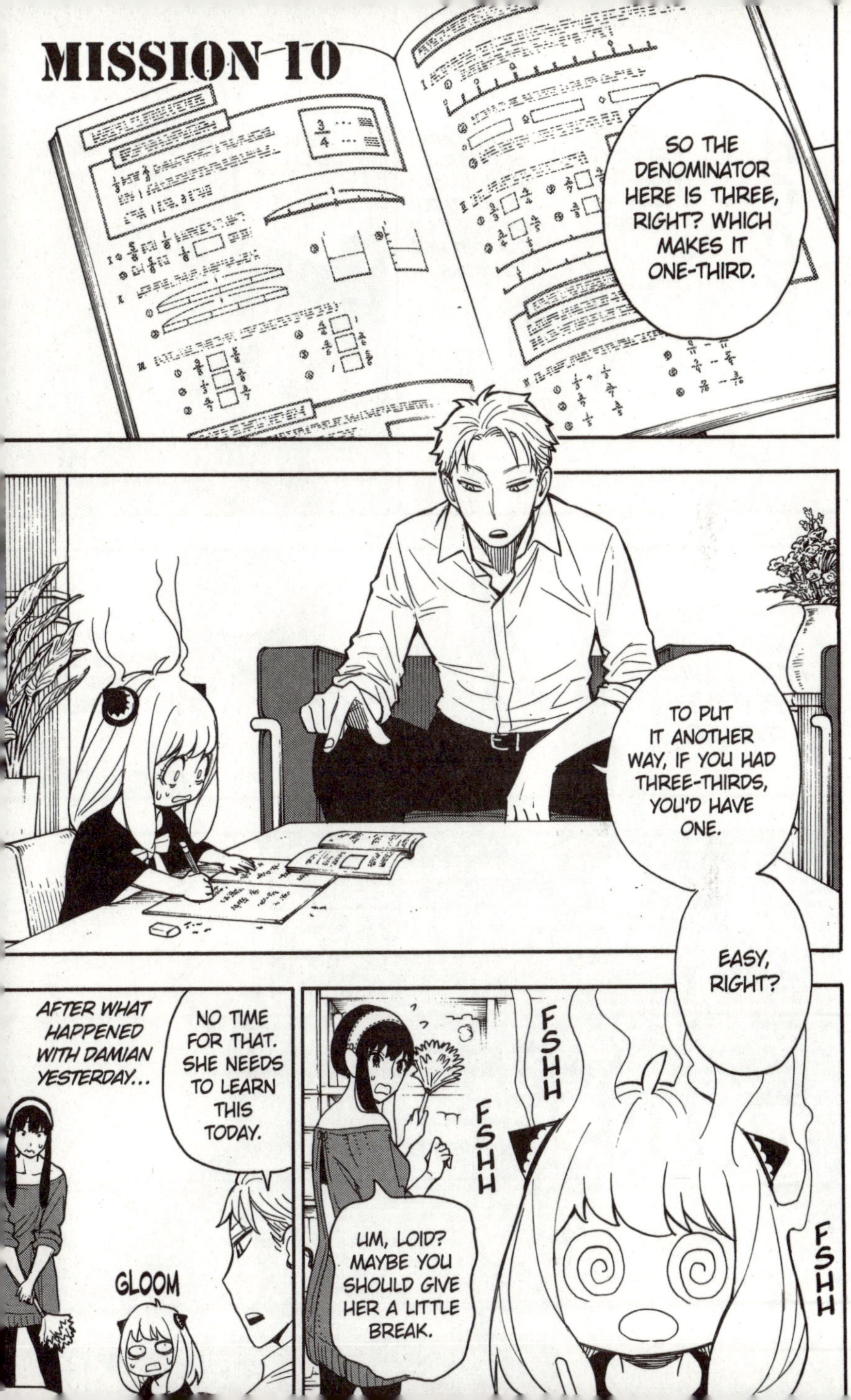
SO THE DENOMINATOR HERE IS THREE, RIGHT? WHICH MAKES IT ONE-THIRD.
TO PUT IT ANOTHER WAY, IF YOU HAD THREE-THIRDS, YOU'D HAVE ONE.
EASY, RIGHT?
FSHH
FSHH
FSHH
UM, LOID? MAYBE YOU SHOULD GIVE HER A LITTLE BREAK.
NO TIME FOR THAT. SHE NEEDS TO LEARN THIS TODAY.
AFTER WHAT HAPPENED WITH DAMIAN YESTERDAY...
GLOOM

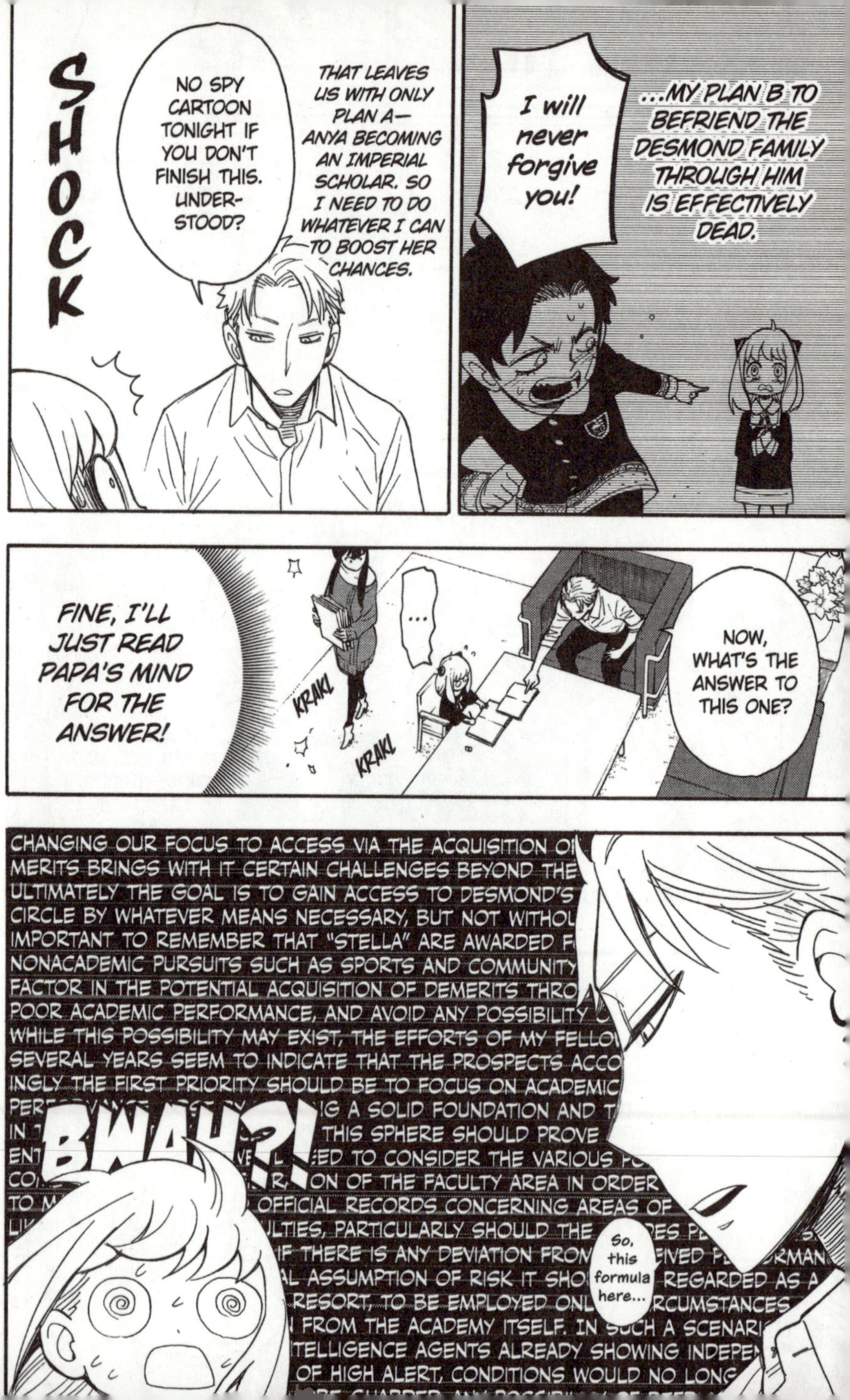
I will never forgive you!
...MY PLAN B TO BEFRIEND THE DESMOND FAMILY THROUGH HIM IS EFFECTIVELY DEAD.
THAT LEAVES US WITH ONLY PLAN A— ANYA BECOMING AN IMPERIAL SCHOLAR. SO I NEED TO DO WHATEVER I CAN TO BOOST HER CHANCES.
NO SPY CARTOON TONIGHT IF YOU DON'T FINISH THIS. UNDER-STOOD?
SHOCK
NOW, WHAT'S THE ANSWER TO THIS ONE?
...
KRAKL
KRAKL
FINE, I'LL JUST READ PAPA'S MIND FOR THE ANSWER!
So, this formula here...
BWAH?!
CHANGING OUR FOCUS TO ACCESS VIA THE ACQUISITION O
MERITS BRINGS WITH IT CERTAIN CHALLENGES BEYOND THE
ULTIMATELY THE GOAL IS TO GAIN ACCESS TO DESMOND'S
CIRCLE BY WHATEVER MEANS NECESSARY, BUT NOT WITHOU
IMPORTANT TO REMEMBER THAT "STELLA" ARE AWARDED F
NONACADEMIC PURSUITS SUCH AS SPORTS AND COMMUNITY
FACTOR IN THE POTENTIAL ACQUISITION OF DEMERITS THRO
POOR ACADEMIC PERFORMANCE, AND AVOID ANY POSSIBILITY
WHILE THIS POSSIBILITY MAY EXIST, THE EFFORTS OF MY FELLO
SEVERAL YEARS SEEM TO INDICATE THAT THE PROSPECTS ACCO
INGLY THE FIRST PRIORITY SHOULD BE TO FOCUS ON ACADEMIC
IG A SOLID FOUNDATION AND T
THIS SPHERE SHOULD PROVE
ED TO CONSIDER THE VARIOUS P
ON OF THE FACULTY AREA IN ORDER
OFFICIAL RECORDS CONCERNING AREAS OF
ULTIES, PARTICULARLY SHOULD THE
IF THERE IS ANY DEVIATION FROM
AL ASSUMPTION OF RISK IT SHO
REGARDED AS A
RESORT, TO BE EMPLOYED ONL
RCUMSTANCES
FROM THE ACADEMY ITSELF. IN SUCH A SCENARI
TELLIGENCE AGENTS ALREADY SHOWING INDEPE
OF HIGH ALERT, CONDITIONS WOULD NO LONG

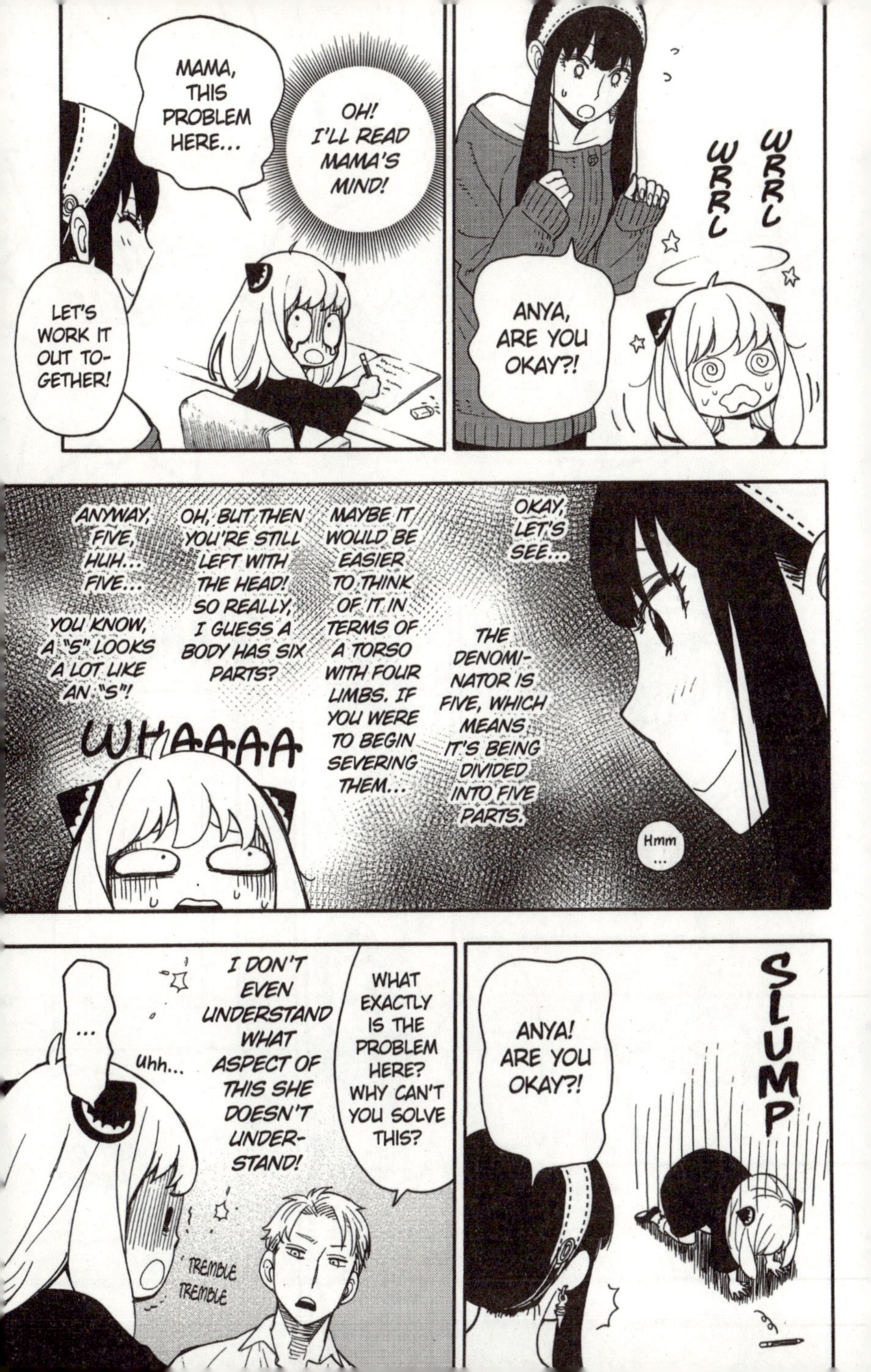
WRRL WRRL
ANYA, ARE YOU OKAY?!
MAMA, THIS PROBLEM HERE...
OH! I'LL READ MAMA'S MIND!
LET'S WORK IT OUT TO-GETHER!
OKAY, LET'S SEE...
Hmm...
THE DENOMI-NATOR IS FIVE, WHICH MEANS IT'S BEING DIVIDED INTO FIVE PARTS.
MAYBE IT WOULD BE EASIER TO THINK OF IT IN TERMS OF A TORSO WITH FOUR LIMBS. IF YOU WERE TO BEGIN SEVERING THEM...
OH, BUT THEN YOU'RE STILL LEFT WITH THE HEAD! SO REALLY, I GUESS A BODY HAS SIX PARTS?
ANYWAY, FIVE, HUH... FIVE...
YOU KNOW, A "5" LOOKS A LOT LIKE AN "S"!
WHAAAA
SLUMP
ANYA! ARE YOU OKAY?!
WHAT EXACTLY IS THE PROBLEM HERE? WHY CAN'T YOU SOLVE THIS?
I DON'T EVEN UNDERSTAND WHAT ASPECT OF THIS SHE DOESN'T UNDER-STAND!
...
Uhh...
TREMBLE TREMBLE

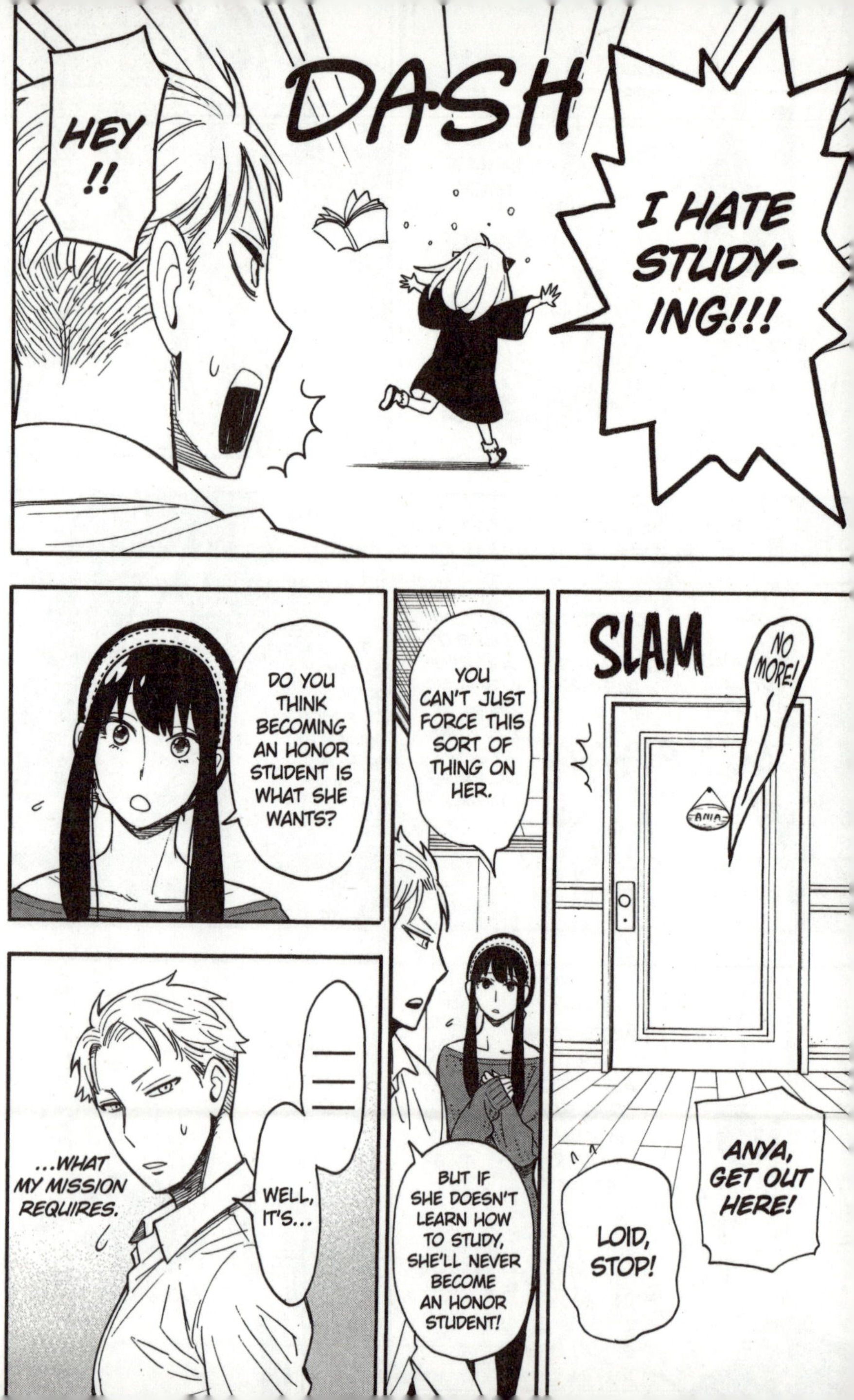
I HATE STUDYING!!!
DASH
HEY !!
SLAM
NO MORE!
ANIA
ANYA, GET OUT HERE!
LOID, STOP!
YOU CAN'T JUST FORCE THIS SORT OF THING ON HER.
BUT IF SHE DOESN'T LEARN HOW TO STUDY, SHE'LL NEVER BECOME AN HONOR STUDENT!
DO YOU THINK BECOMING AN HONOR STUDENT IS WHAT SHE WANTS?
———
WELL, IT'S...
...WHAT MY MISSION REQUIRES.

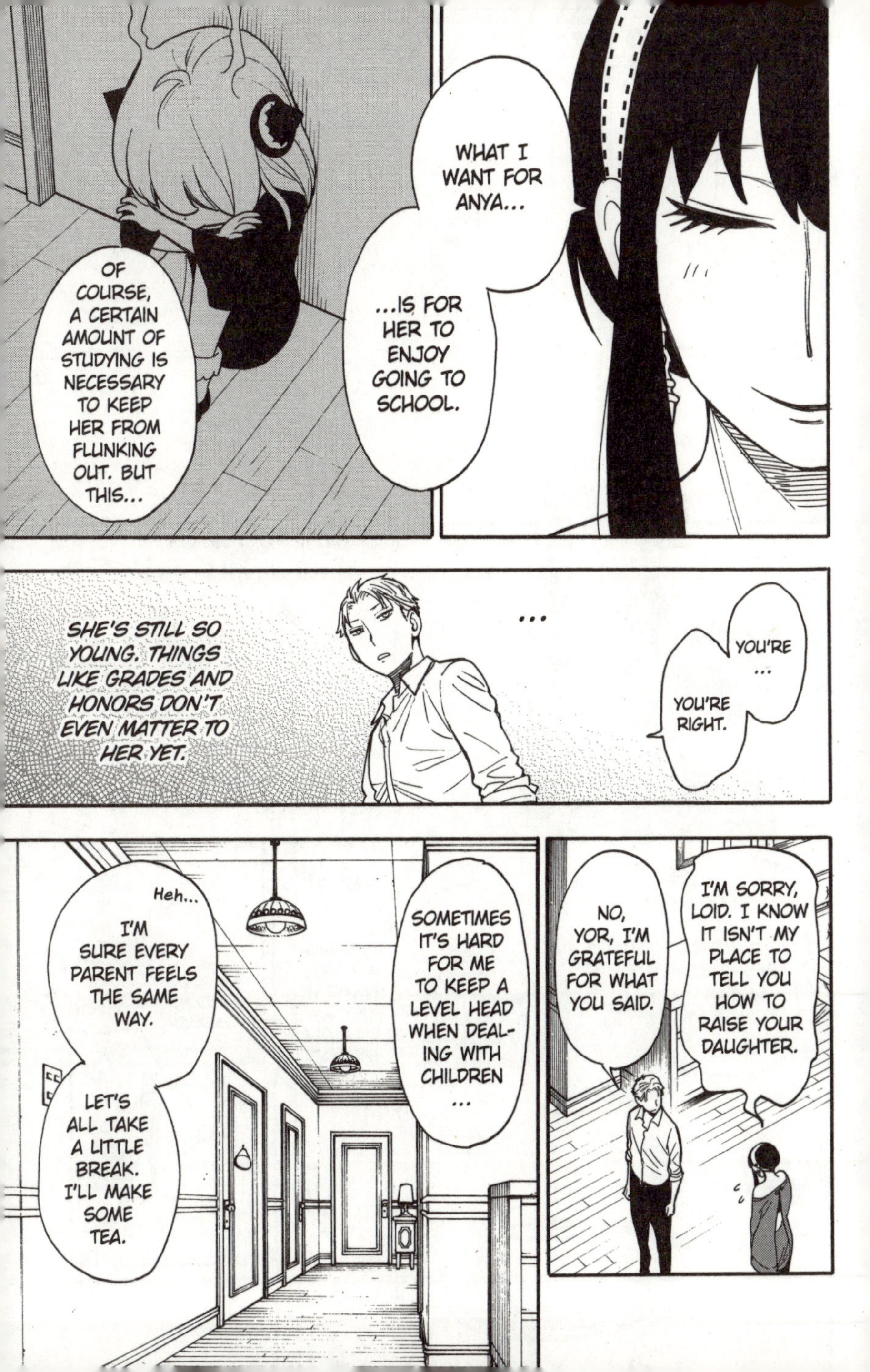
WHAT I WANT FOR ANYA...
...IS FOR HER TO ENJOY GOING TO SCHOOL.
OF COURSE, A CERTAIN AMOUNT OF STUDYING IS NECESSARY TO KEEP HER FROM FLUNKING OUT. BUT THIS...
YOU'RE ...
YOU'RE RIGHT.
...
SHE'S STILL SO YOUNG. THINGS LIKE GRADES AND HONORS DON'T EVEN MATTER TO HER YET.
I'M SORRY, LOID. I KNOW IT ISN'T MY PLACE TO TELL YOU HOW TO RAISE YOUR DAUGHTER.
NO, YOR, I'M GRATEFUL FOR WHAT YOU SAID.
SOMETIMES IT'S HARD FOR ME TO KEEP A LEVEL HEAD WHEN DEAL-ING WITH CHILDREN ...
Heh...
I'M SURE EVERY PARENT FEELS THE SAME WAY.
LET'S ALL TAKE A LITTLE BREAK. I'LL MAKE SOME TEA.

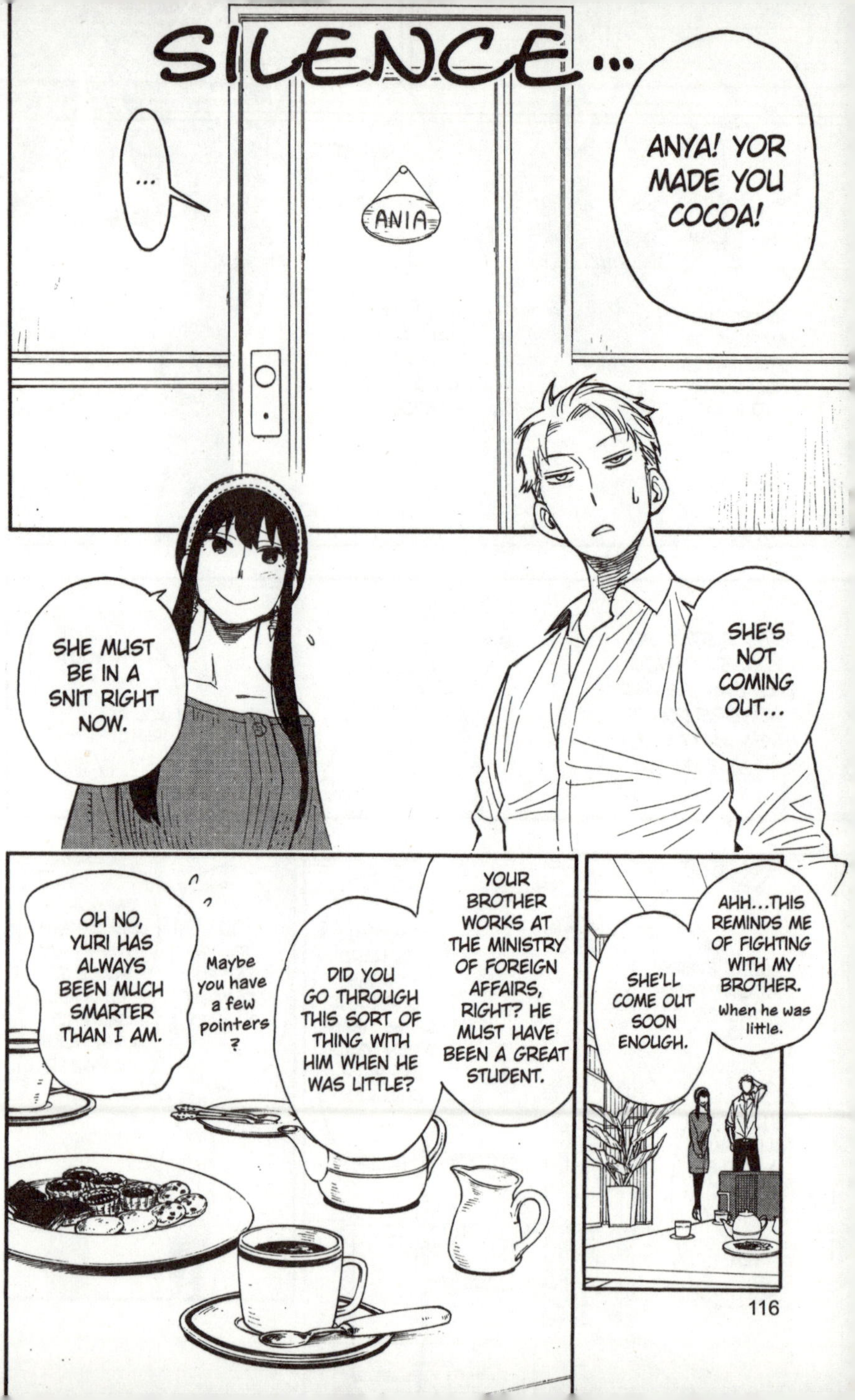
SILENCE...
ANYA! YOR MADE YOU COCOA!
...
SHE'S NOT COMING OUT...
SHE MUST BE IN A SNIT RIGHT NOW.
AHH...THIS REMINDS ME OF FIGHTING WITH MY BROTHER. When he was little.
SHE'LL COME OUT SOON ENOUGH.
YOUR BROTHER WORKS AT THE MINISTRY OF FOREIGN AFFAIRS, RIGHT? HE MUST HAVE BEEN A GREAT STUDENT.
DID YOU GO THROUGH THIS SORT OF THING WITH HIM WHEN HE WAS LITTLE?
Maybe you have a few pointers?
OH NO, YURI HAS ALWAYS BEEN MUCH SMARTER THAN I AM.

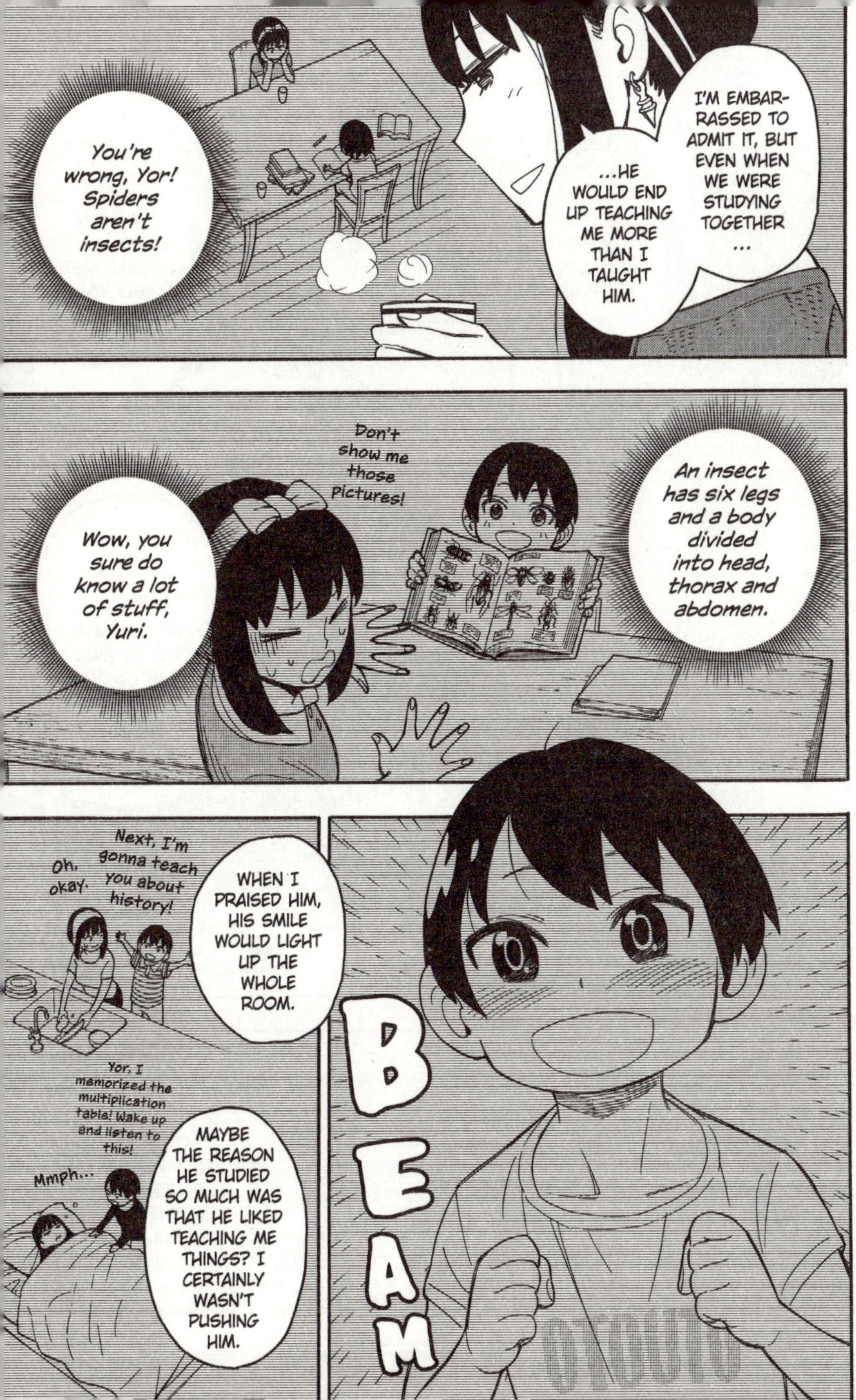
I'M EMBARRASSED TO ADMIT IT, BUT EVEN WHEN WE WERE STUDYING TOGETHER...
...HE WOULD END UP TEACHING ME MORE THAN I TAUGHT HIM.
You're wrong, Yor! Spiders aren't insects!
An insect has six legs and a body divided into head, thorax and abdomen.
Don't show me those pictures!
Wow, you sure do know a lot of stuff, Yuri.
BEAM
OTOUTO
WHEN I PRAISED HIM, HIS SMILE WOULD LIGHT UP THE WHOLE ROOM.
Next, I'm gonna teach you about history!
Oh, okay.
Yor, I memorized the multiplication table! Wake up and listen to this!
MAYBE THE REASON HE STUDIED SO MUCH WAS THAT HE LIKED TEACHING ME THINGS? I CERTAINLY WASN'T PUSHING HIM.
Mmph...

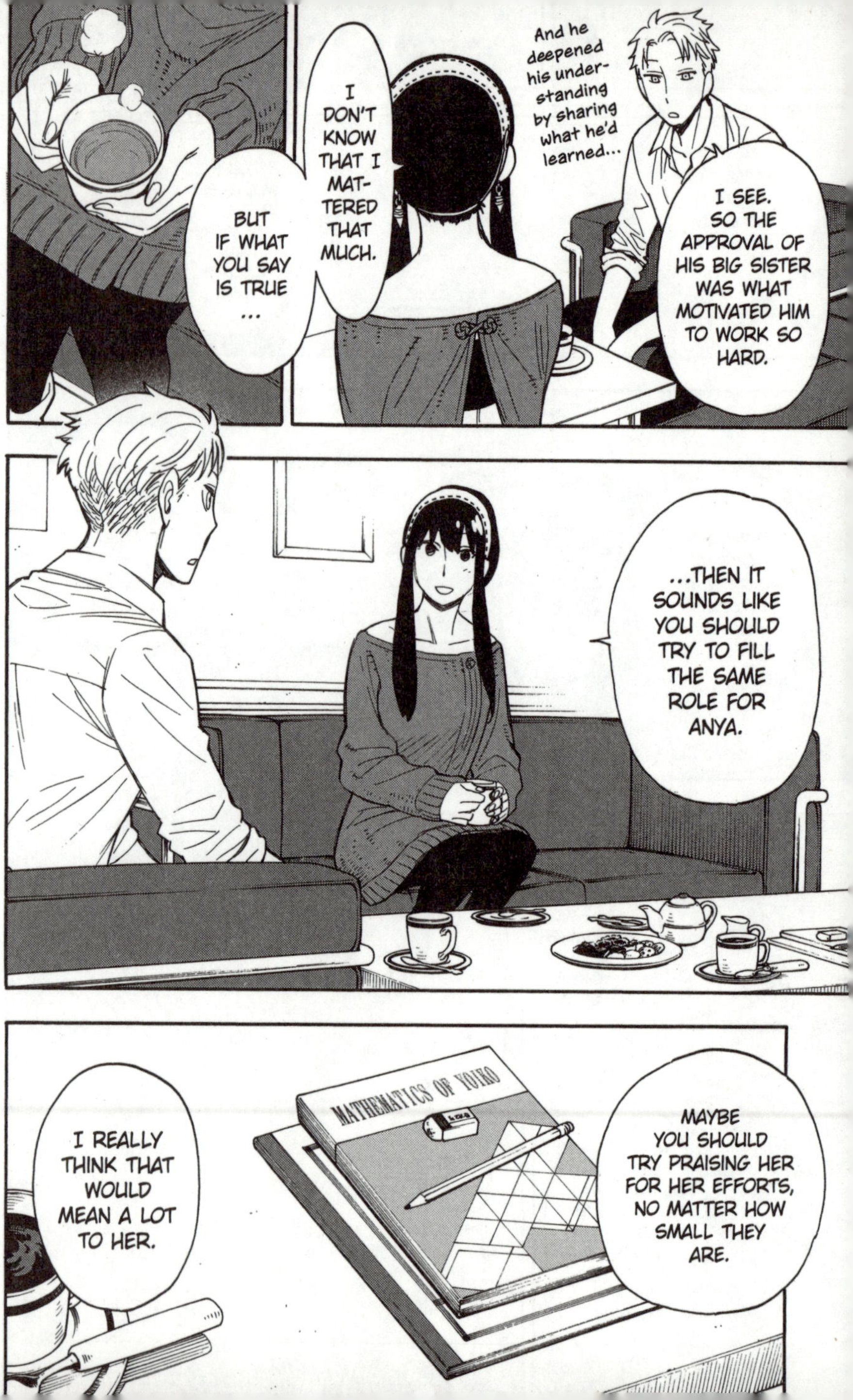
And he deepened his understanding by sharing what he'd learned...
I SEE. SO THE APPROVAL OF HIS BIG SISTER WAS WHAT MOTIVATED HIM TO WORK SO HARD.
I DON'T KNOW THAT I MATTERED THAT MUCH.
BUT IF WHAT YOU SAY IS TRUE ...
...THEN IT SOUNDS LIKE YOU SHOULD TRY TO FILL THE SAME ROLE FOR ANYA.
MATHEMATICS OF YOIKO
MAYBE YOU SHOULD TRY PRAISING HER FOR HER EFFORTS, NO MATTER HOW SMALL THEY ARE.
I REALLY THINK THAT WOULD MEAN A LOT TO HER.

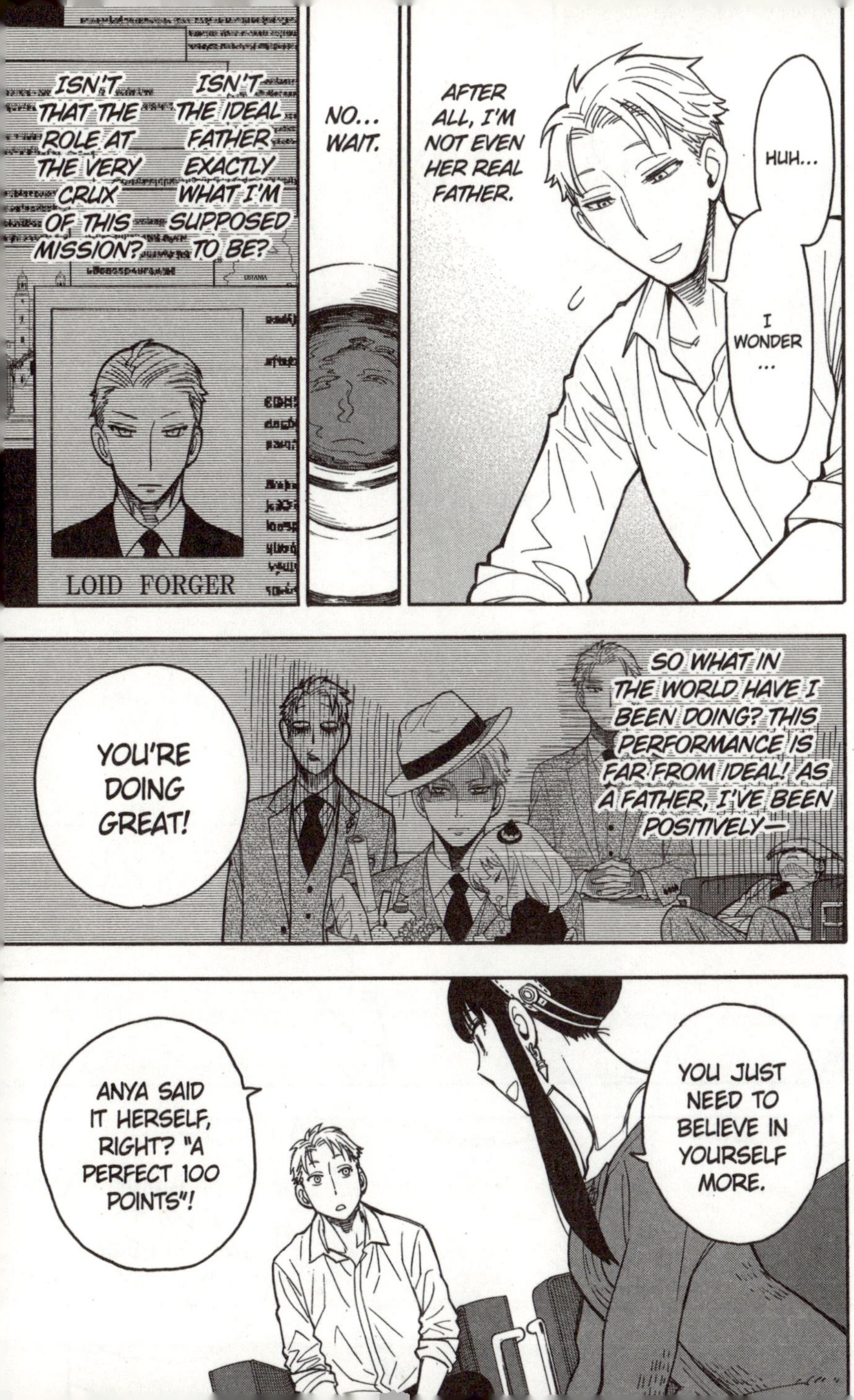
HUH... I WONDER...
AFTER ALL, I'M NOT EVEN HER REAL FATHER.
NO... WAIT.
ISN'T THE IDEAL FATHER EXACTLY WHAT I'M SUPPOSED TO BE?
ISN'T THAT THE ROLE AT THE VERY CRUX OF THIS MISSION?
LOID FORGER
SO WHAT IN THE WORLD HAVE I BEEN DOING? THIS PERFORMANCE IS FAR FROM IDEAL! AS A FATHER, I'VE BEEN POSITIVELY—
YOU'RE DOING GREAT!
YOU JUST NEED TO BELIEVE IN YOURSELF MORE.
ANYA SAID IT HERSELF, RIGHT? "A PERFECT 100 POINTS"!

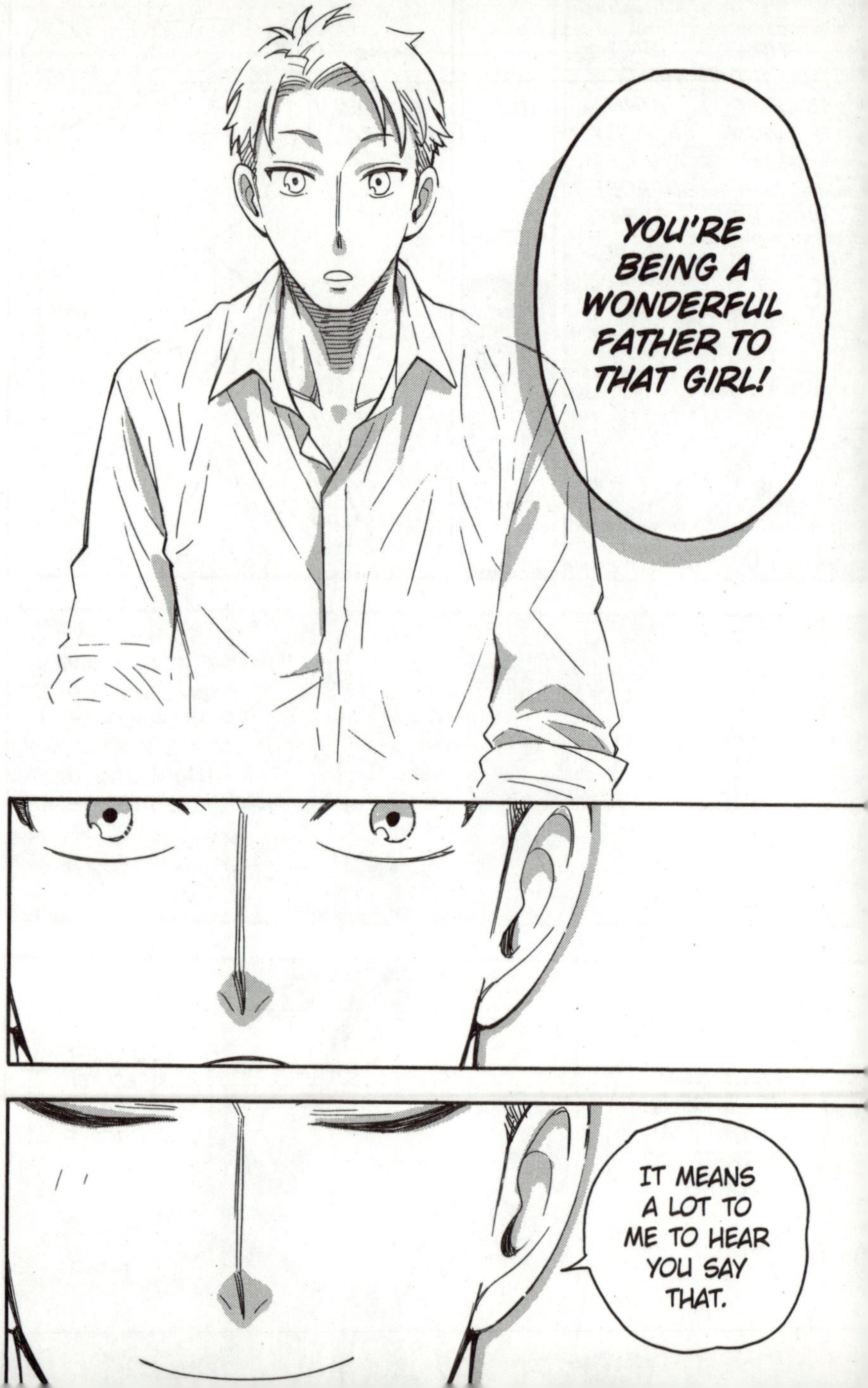
YOU'RE BEING A WONDERFUL FATHER TO THAT GIRL!
IT MEANS A LOT TO ME TO HEAR YOU SAY THAT.

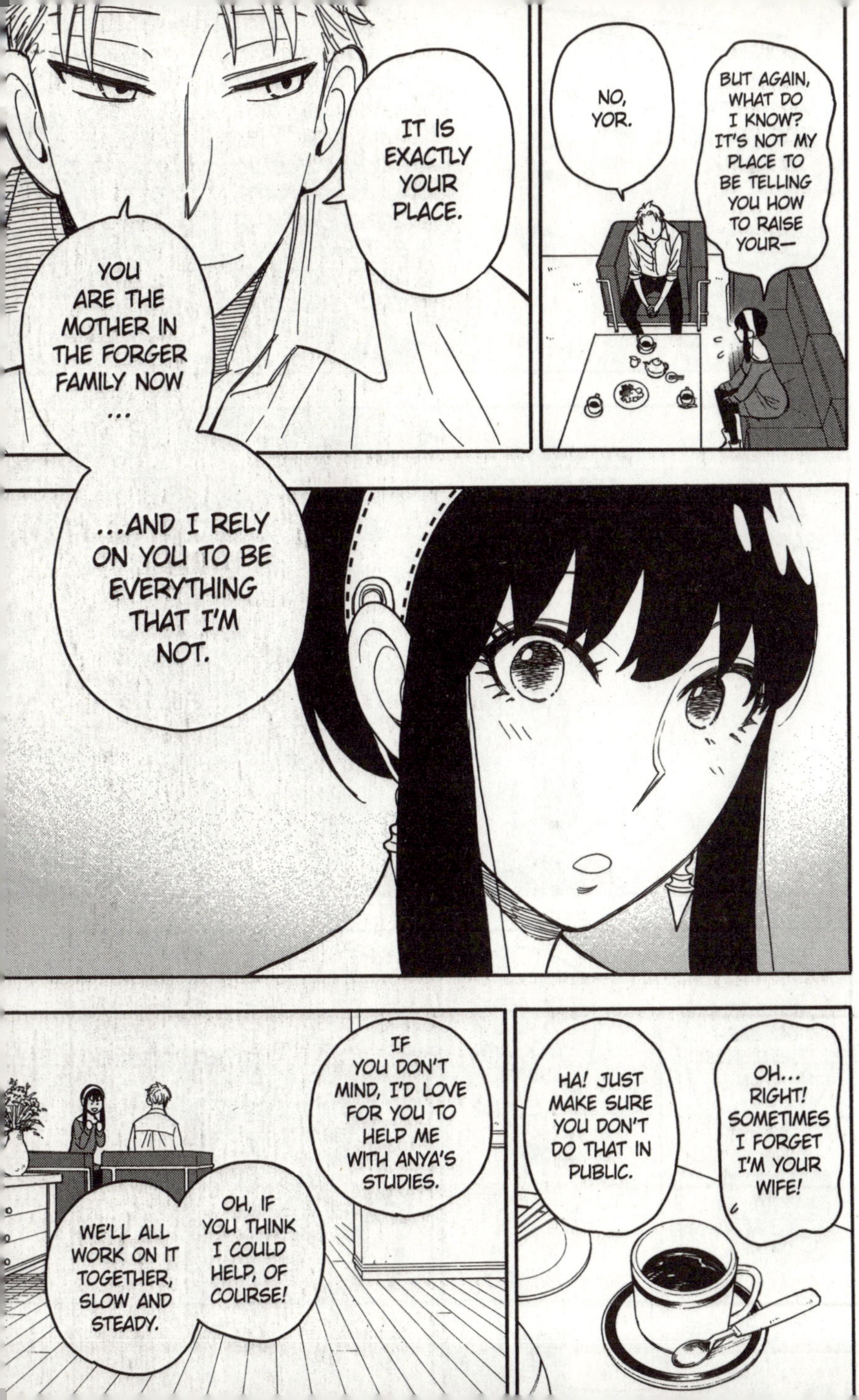
BUT AGAIN, WHAT DO I KNOW? IT'S NOT MY PLACE TO BE TELLING YOU HOW TO RAISE YOUR—
NO, YOR.
IT IS EXACTLY YOUR PLACE.
YOU ARE THE MOTHER IN THE FORGER FAMILY NOW ...
...AND I RELY ON YOU TO BE EVERYTHING THAT I'M NOT.
OH... RIGHT! SOMETIMES I FORGET I'M YOUR WIFE!
HA! JUST MAKE SURE YOU DON'T DO THAT IN PUBLIC.
IF YOU DON'T MIND, I'D LOVE FOR YOU TO HELP ME WITH ANYA'S STUDIES.
OH, IF YOU THINK I COULD HELP, OF COURSE!
WE'LL ALL WORK ON IT TOGETHER, SLOW AND STEADY.

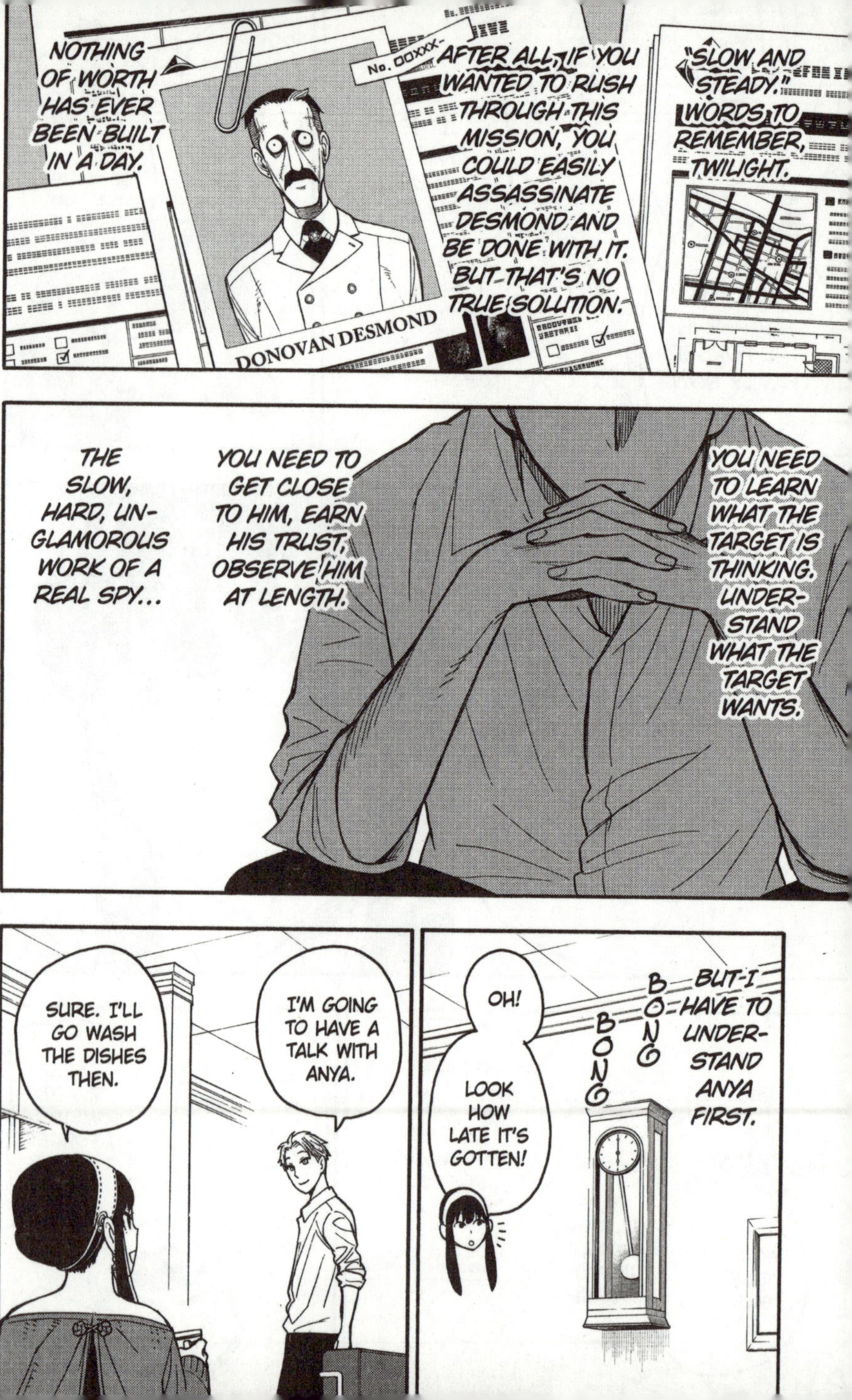
"SLOW AND STEADY." WORDS TO REMEMBER, TWILIGHT.
AFTER ALL, IF YOU WANTED TO RUSH THROUGH THIS MISSION, YOU COULD EASILY ASSASSINATE DESMOND AND BE DONE WITH IT. BUT THAT'S NO TRUE SOLUTION.
No. 00XXX-
DONOVAN DESMOND
NOTHING OF WORTH HAS EVER BEEN BUILT IN A DAY.
YOU NEED TO LEARN WHAT THE TARGET IS THINKING. UNDERSTAND WHAT THE TARGET WANTS.
YOU NEED TO GET CLOSE TO HIM, EARN HIS TRUST, OBSERVE HIM AT LENGTH.
THE SLOW, HARD, UNGLAMOROUS WORK OF A REAL SPY...
BUT I HAVE TO UNDERSTAND ANYA FIRST.
BONG
BONG
OH!
LOOK HOW LATE IT'S GOTTEN!
I'M GOING TO HAVE A TALK WITH ANYA.
SURE. I'LL GO WASH THE DISHES THEN.

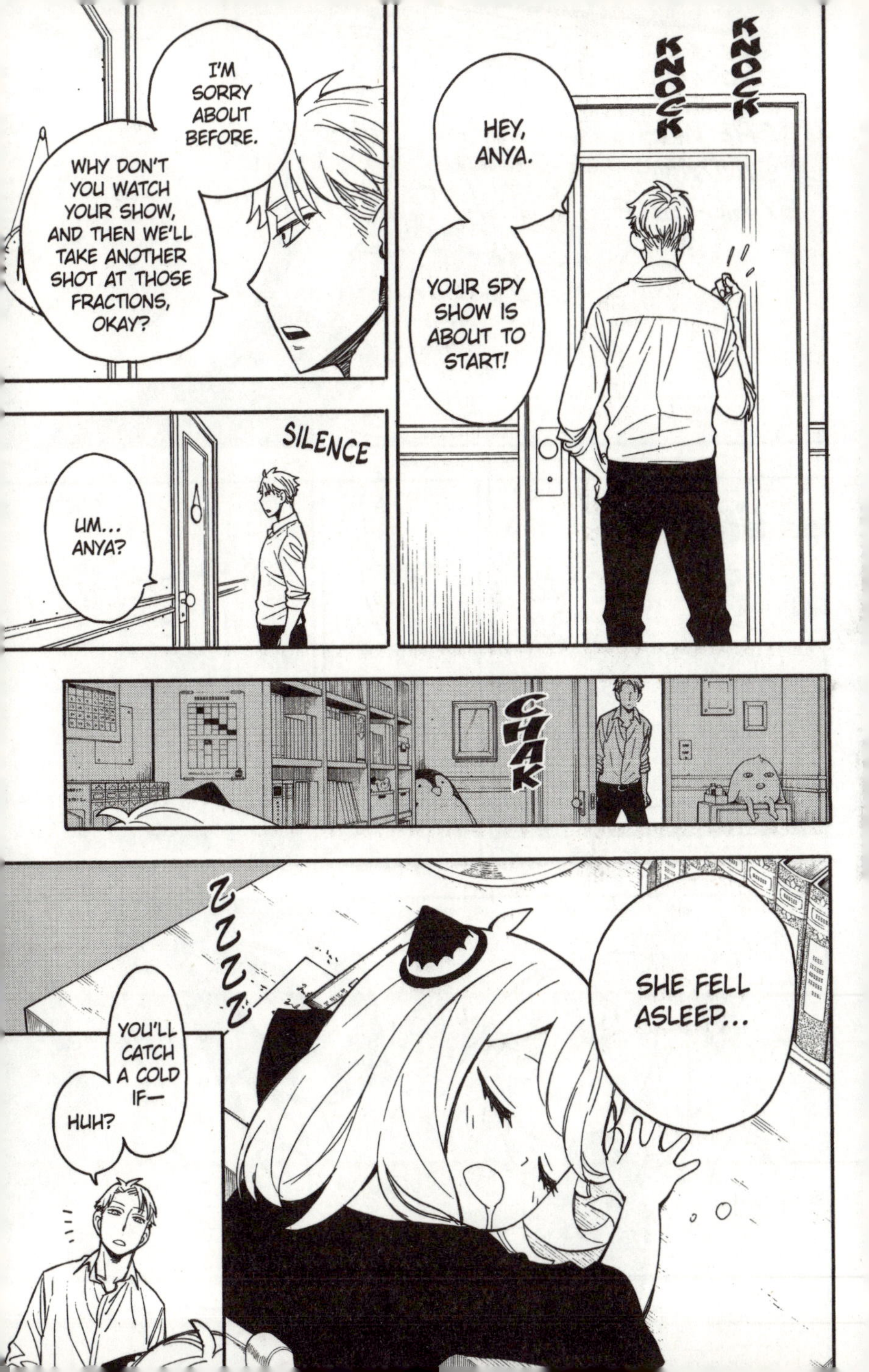
KNOCK KNOCK
HEY, ANYA.
YOUR SPY SHOW IS ABOUT TO START!
I'M SORRY ABOUT BEFORE.
WHY DON'T YOU WATCH YOUR SHOW, AND THEN WE'LL TAKE ANOTHER SHOT AT THOSE FRACTIONS, OKAY?
SILENCE
UM... ANYA?
CHAK
SHE FELL ASLEEP...
ZZZZ
YOU'LL CATCH A COLD IF—
HUH?

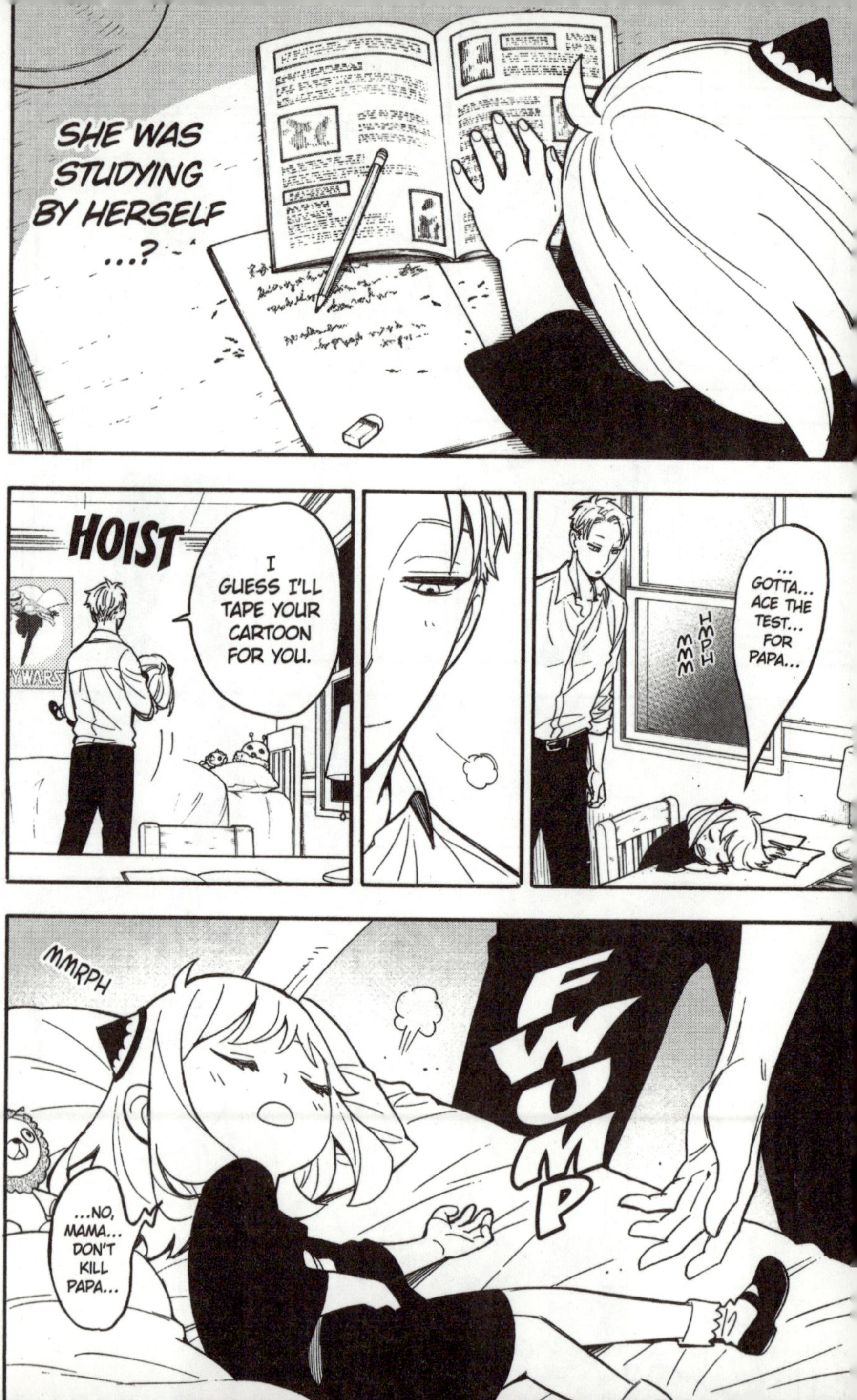
SHE WAS STUDYING BY HERSELF ...?
... GOTTA... ACE THE TEST... FOR PAPA...
HMPH
MMM
HOIST
I GUESS I'LL TAPE YOUR CARTOON FOR YOU.
FWUMP
MMRPH
...NO, MAMA... DON'T KILL PAPA...

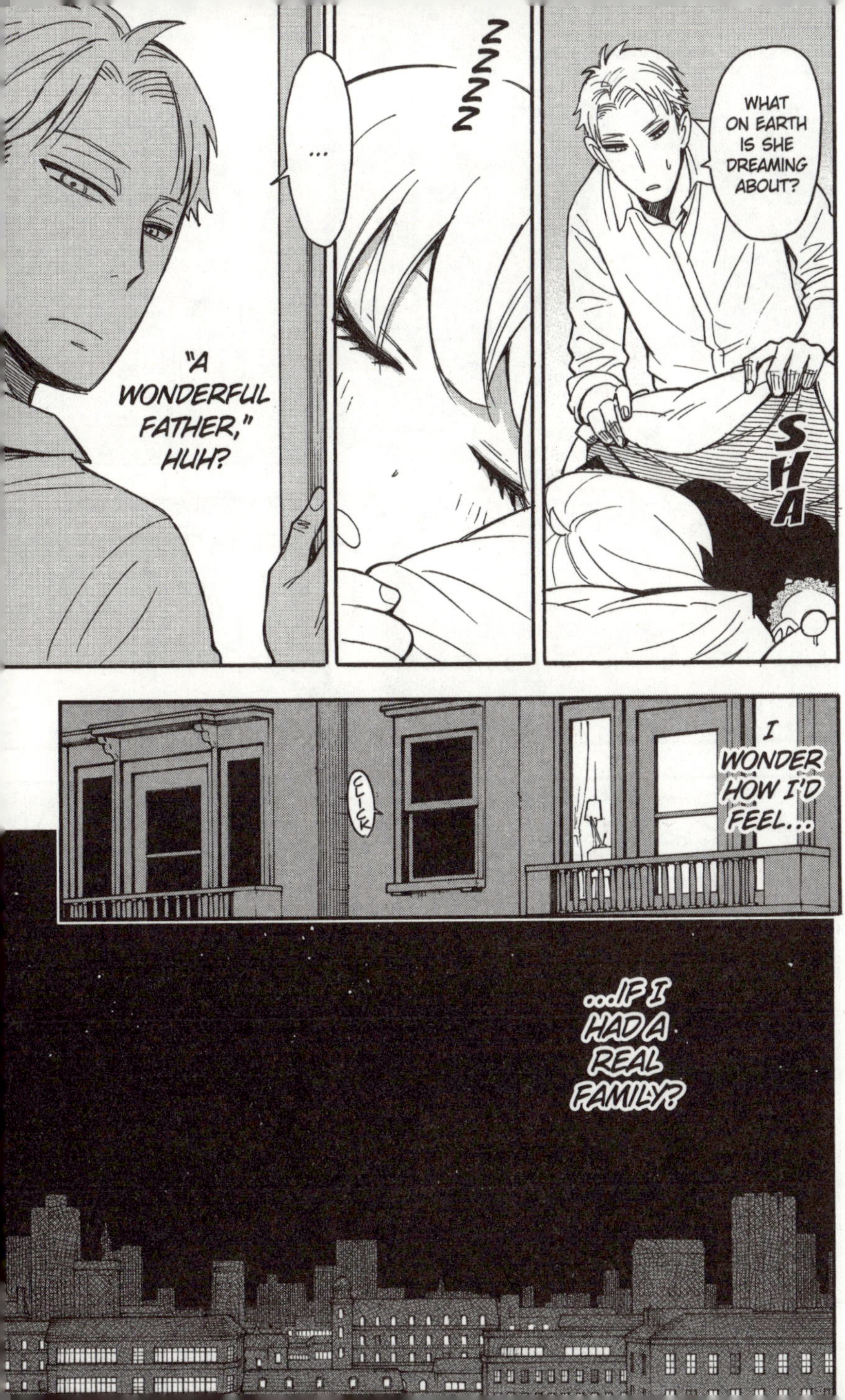
WHAT ON EARTH IS SHE DREAMING ABOUT?
SHA
ZZZZ
...
"A WONDERFUL FATHER," HUH?
I WONDER HOW I'D FEEL...
CLICK
...IF I HAD A REAL FAMILY?

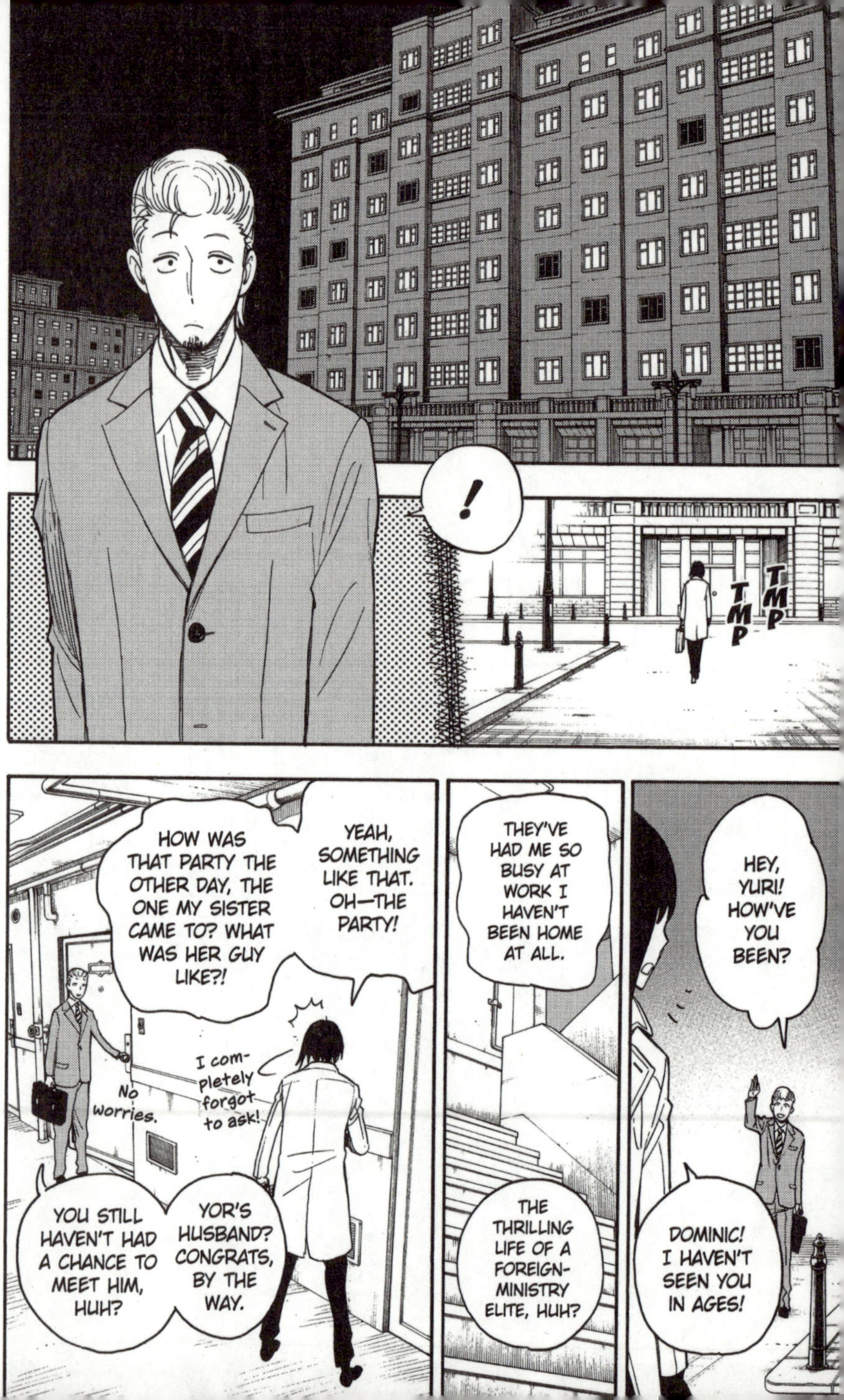
!
TMP TMP
HEY, YURI! HOW'VE YOU BEEN?
DOMINIC! I HAVEN'T SEEN YOU IN AGES!
THEY'VE HAD ME SO BUSY AT WORK I HAVEN'T BEEN HOME AT ALL.
THE THRILLING LIFE OF A FOREIGN-MINISTRY ELITE, HUH?
YEAH, SOMETHING LIKE THAT. OH—THE PARTY!
HOW WAS THAT PARTY THE OTHER DAY, THE ONE MY SISTER CAME TO? WHAT WAS HER GUY LIKE?!
I completely forgot to ask!
No worries.
YOR'S HUSBAND? CONGRATS, BY THE WAY.
YOU STILL HAVEN'T HAD A CHANCE TO MEET HIM, HUH?

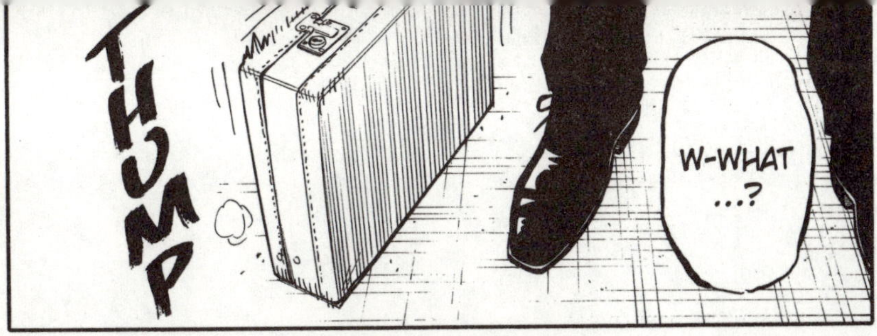
W-WHAT ...?
THUMP

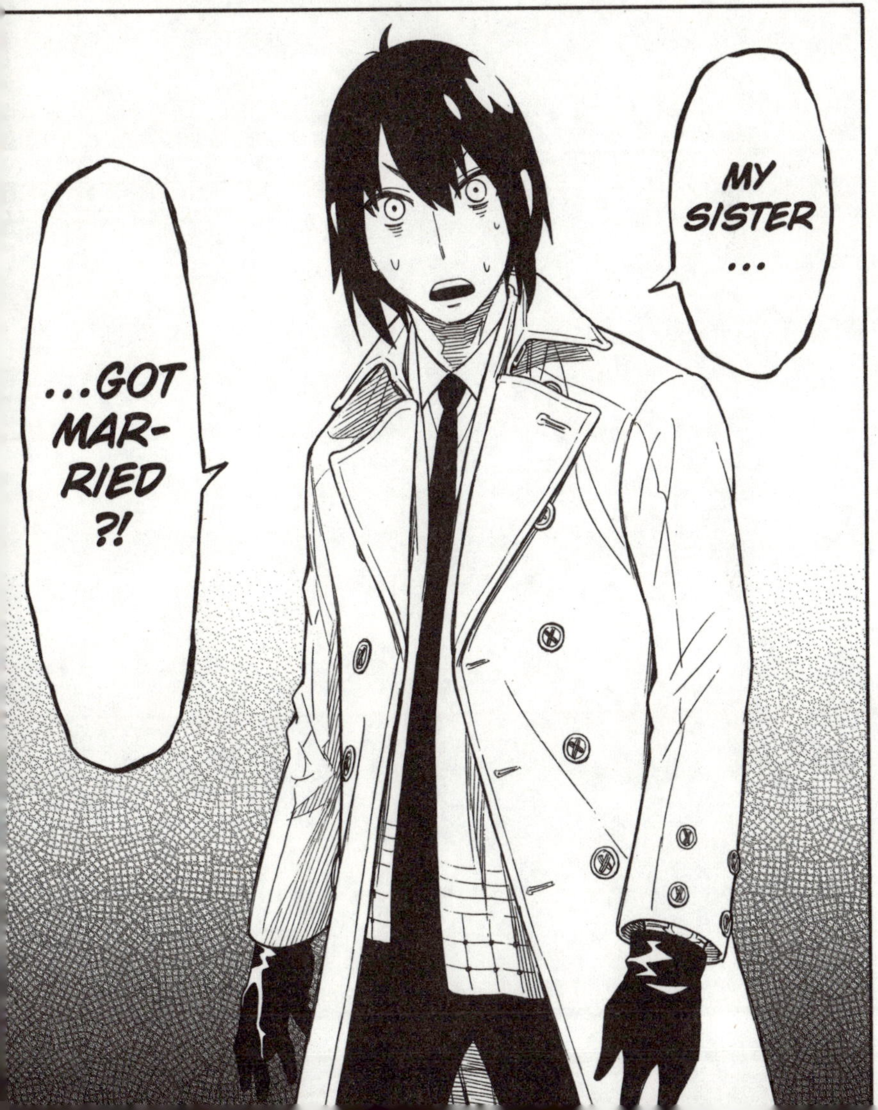
MY SISTER ...
...GOT MAR-RIED ?!

SPY×FAMILY

MISSION 11

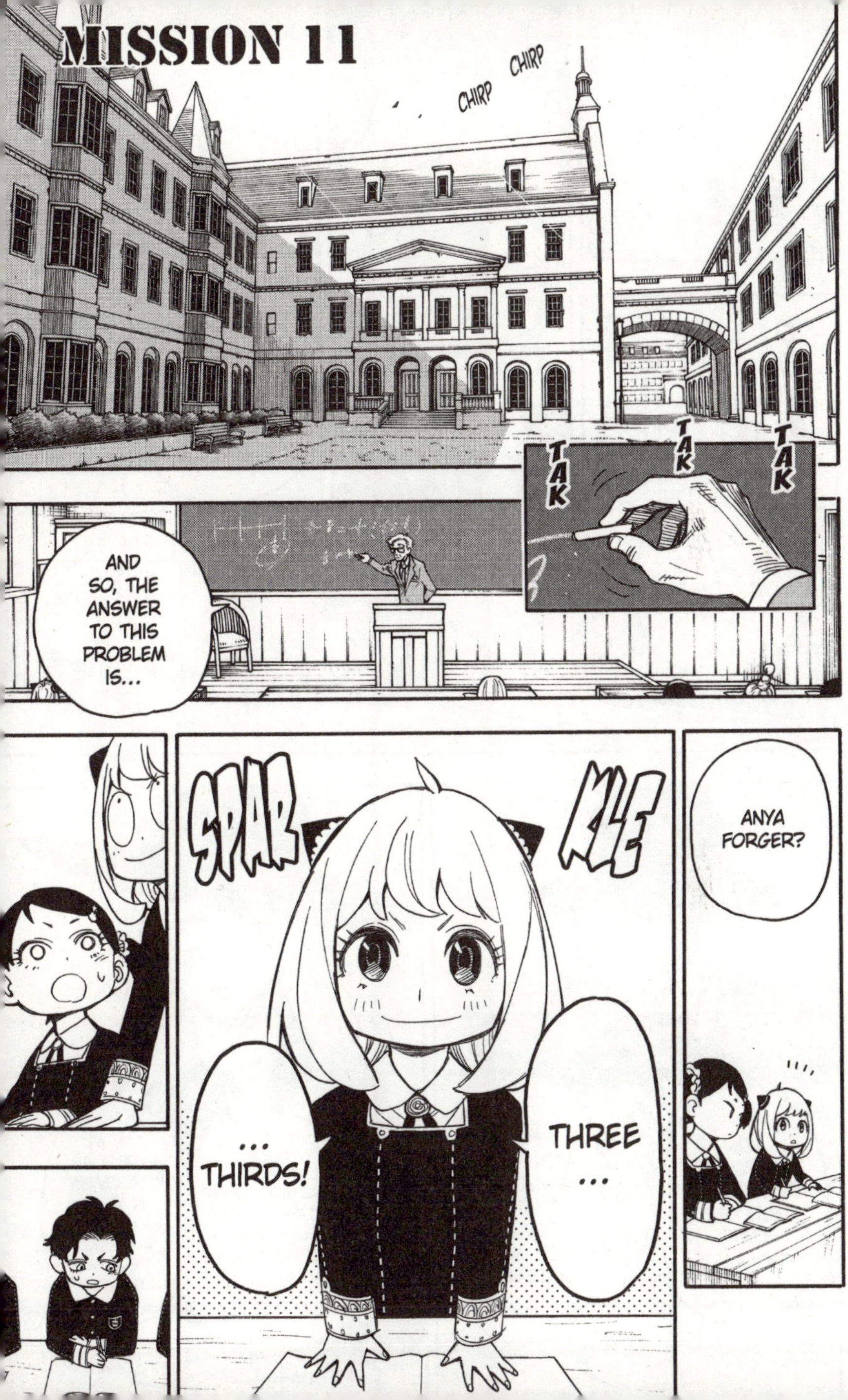
CHIRP CHIRP
TAK TAK TAK
AND SO, THE ANSWER TO THIS PROBLEM IS...
ANYA FORGER?
SPARKLE
THREE ...
... THIRDS!

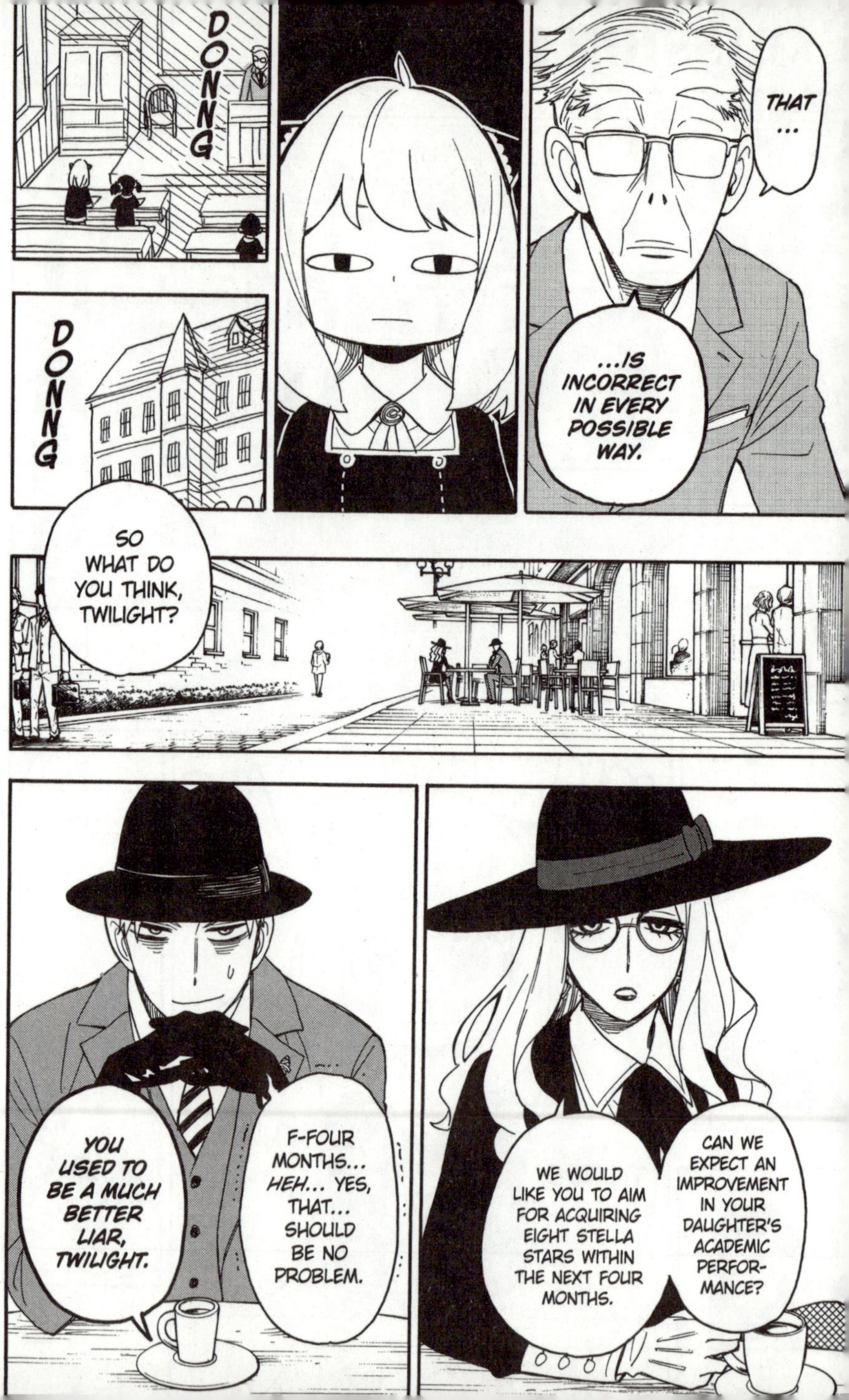
THAT...
...IS INCORRECT IN EVERY POSSIBLE WAY.
DONNG
DONNG
SO WHAT DO YOU THINK, TWILIGHT?
CAN WE EXPECT AN IMPROVEMENT IN YOUR DAUGHTER'S ACADEMIC PERFOR-MANCE?
WE WOULD LIKE YOU TO AIM FOR ACQUIRING EIGHT STELLA STARS WITHIN THE NEXT FOUR MONTHS.
F-FOUR MONTHS... HEH... YES, THAT... SHOULD BE NO PROBLEM.
YOU USED TO BE A MUCH BETTER LIAR, TWILIGHT.

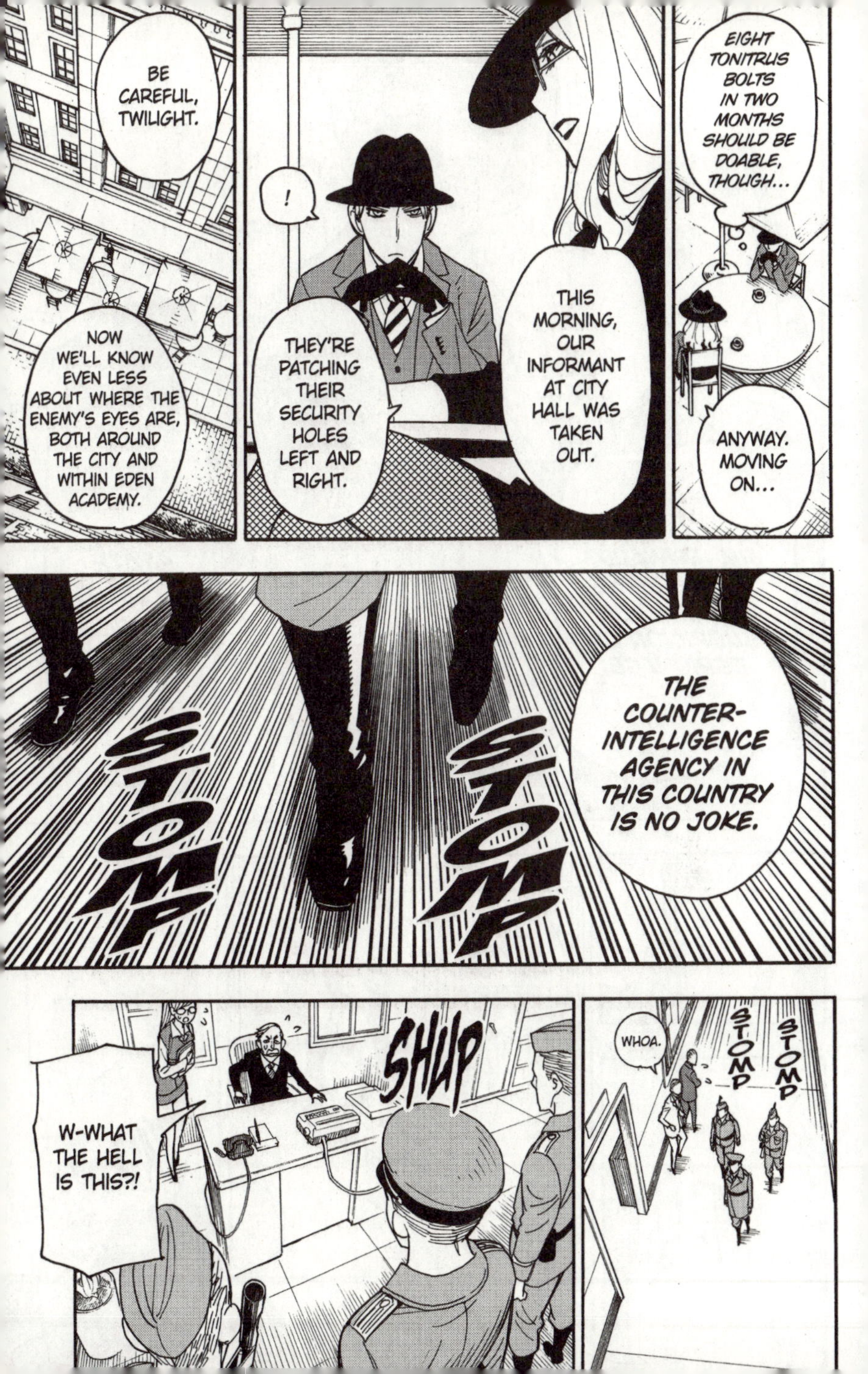
EIGHT TONITRUS BOLTS IN TWO MONTHS SHOULD BE DOABLE, THOUGH...
ANYWAY. MOVING ON...
THIS MORNING, OUR INFORMANT AT CITY HALL WAS TAKEN OUT.
!
THEY'RE PATCHING THEIR SECURITY HOLES LEFT AND RIGHT.
BE CAREFUL, TWILIGHT.
NOW WE'LL KNOW EVEN LESS ABOUT WHERE THE ENEMY'S EYES ARE, BOTH AROUND THE CITY AND WITHIN EDEN ACADEMY.
THE COUNTER-INTELLIGENCE AGENCY IN THIS COUNTRY IS NO JOKE.
STOMP
STOMP
WHOA.
STOMP
STOMP
SHUP
W-WHAT THE HELL IS THIS?!

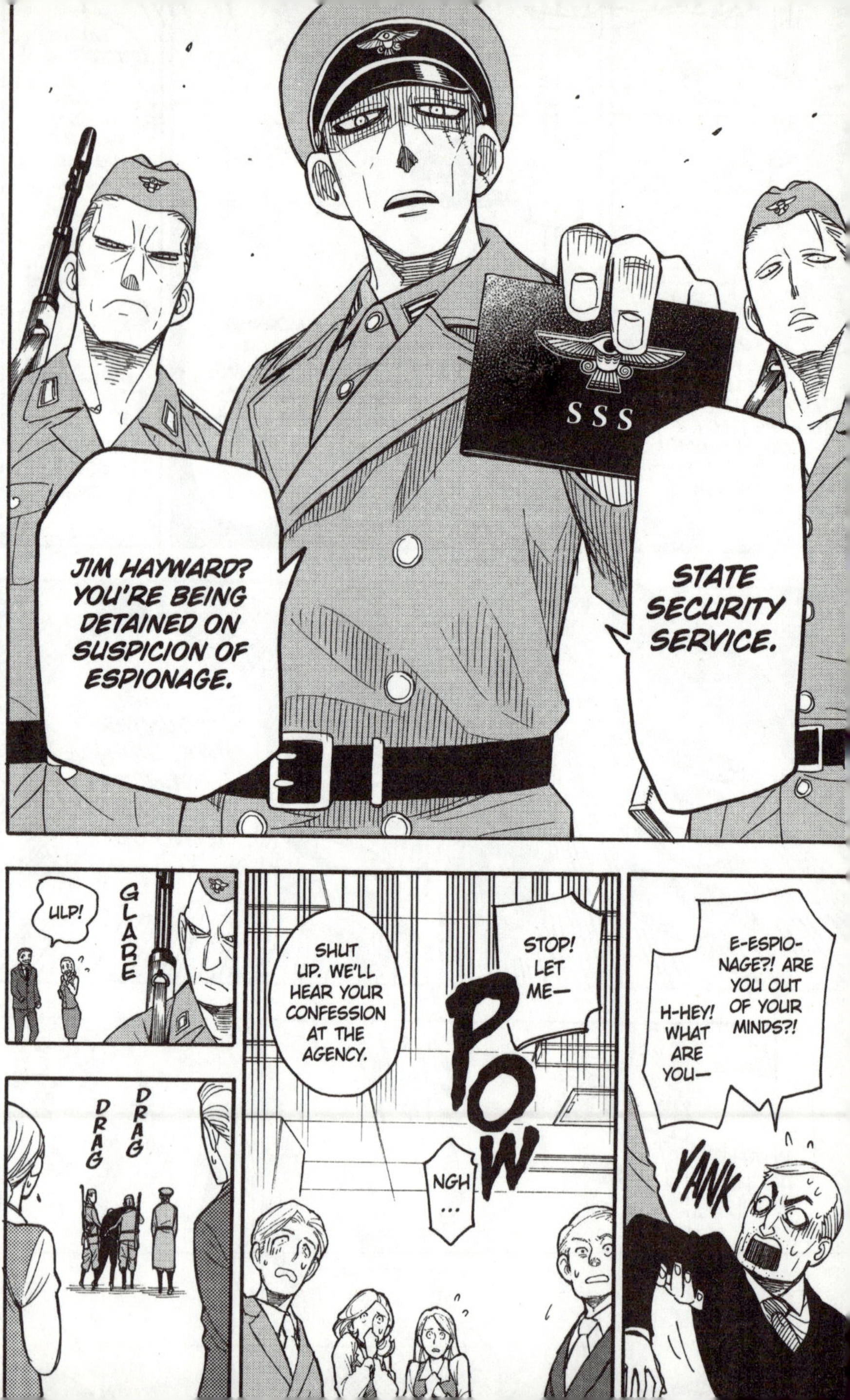
SSS
STATE SECURITY SERVICE.
JIM HAYWARD? YOU'RE BEING DETAINED ON SUSPICION OF ESPIONAGE.
E-ESPIONAGE?! ARE YOU OUT OF YOUR MINDS?!
H-HEY! WHAT ARE YOU—
YANK
STOP! LET ME—
POW
SHUT UP. WE'LL HEAR YOUR CONFESSION AT THE AGENCY.
NGH ...
GLARE
ULP!
DRAG DRAG

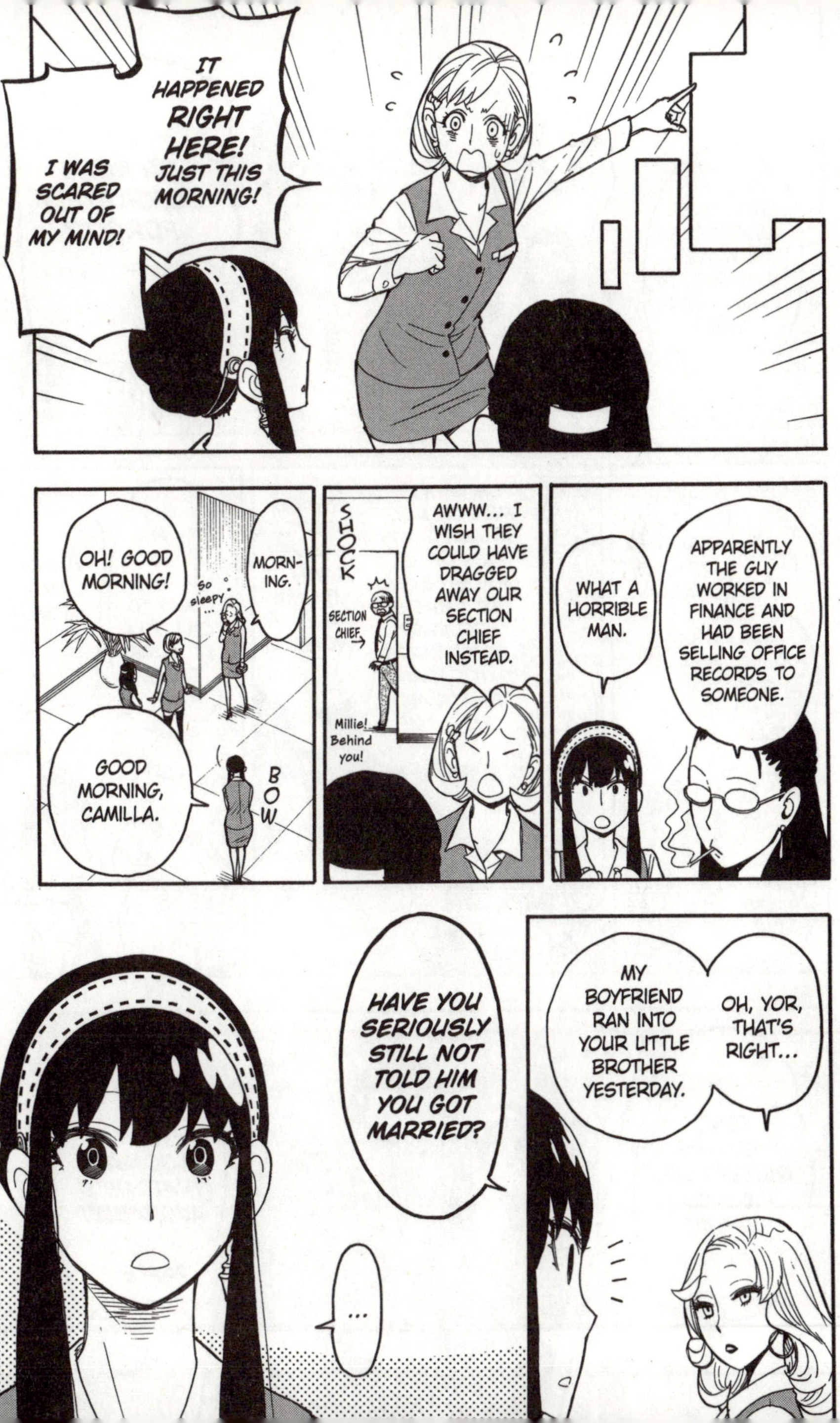
IT HAPPENED RIGHT HERE! JUST THIS MORNING!
I WAS SCARED OUT OF MY MIND!
APPARENTLY THE GUY WORKED IN FINANCE AND HAD BEEN SELLING OFFICE RECORDS TO SOMEONE.
WHAT A HORRIBLE MAN.
AWWW... I WISH THEY COULD HAVE DRAGGED AWAY OUR SECTION CHIEF INSTEAD.
SHOCK
SECTION CHIEF
Millie! Behind you!
MORNING.
So sleepy...
OH! GOOD MORNING!
BOW
GOOD MORNING, CAMILLA.
OH, YOR, THAT'S RIGHT...
MY BOYFRIEND RAN INTO YOUR LITTLE BROTHER YESTERDAY.
HAVE YOU SERIOUSLY STILL NOT TOLD HIM YOU GOT MARRIED?
...

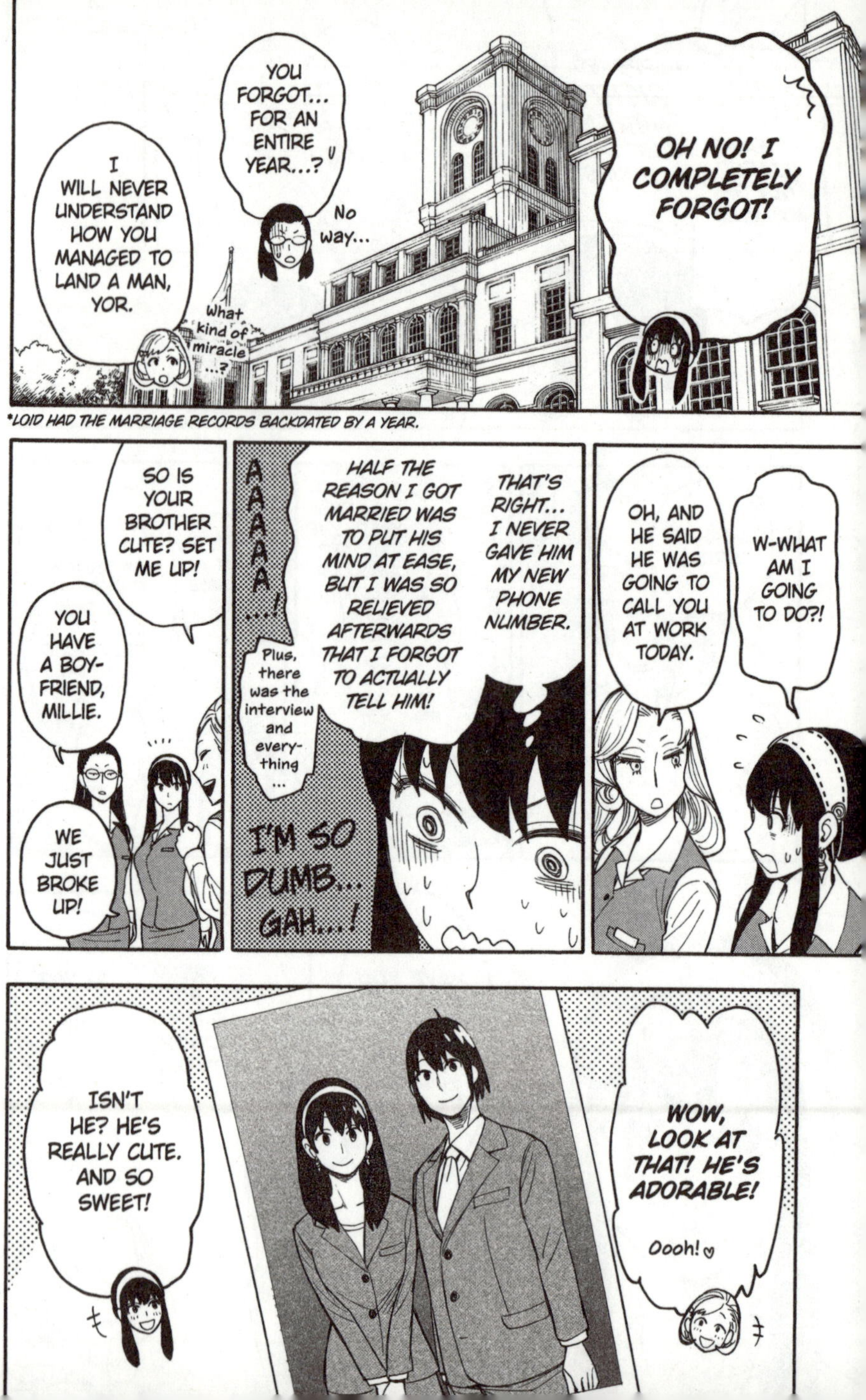
OH NO! I COMPLETELY FORGOT!
YOU FORGOT... FOR AN ENTIRE YEAR...?
No way...
I WILL NEVER UNDERSTAND HOW YOU MANAGED TO LAND A MAN, YOR.
What kind of miracle...?
*LOID HAD THE MARRIAGE RECORDS BACKDATED BY A YEAR.
W-WHAT AM I GOING TO DO?!
OH, AND HE SAID HE WAS GOING TO CALL YOU AT WORK TODAY.
THAT'S RIGHT... I NEVER GAVE HIM MY NEW PHONE NUMBER.
HALF THE REASON I GOT MARRIED WAS TO PUT HIS MIND AT EASE, BUT I WAS SO RELIEVED AFTERWARDS THAT I FORGOT TO ACTUALLY TELL HIM!
AAAAA...!
Plus, there was the interview and everything...
I'M SO DUMB... GAH...!
SO IS YOUR BROTHER CUTE? SET ME UP!
YOU HAVE A BOYFRIEND, MILLIE.
WE JUST BROKE UP!
WOW, LOOK AT THAT! HE'S ADORABLE!
Oooh!♡
ISN'T HE? HE'S REALLY CUTE. AND SO SWEET!

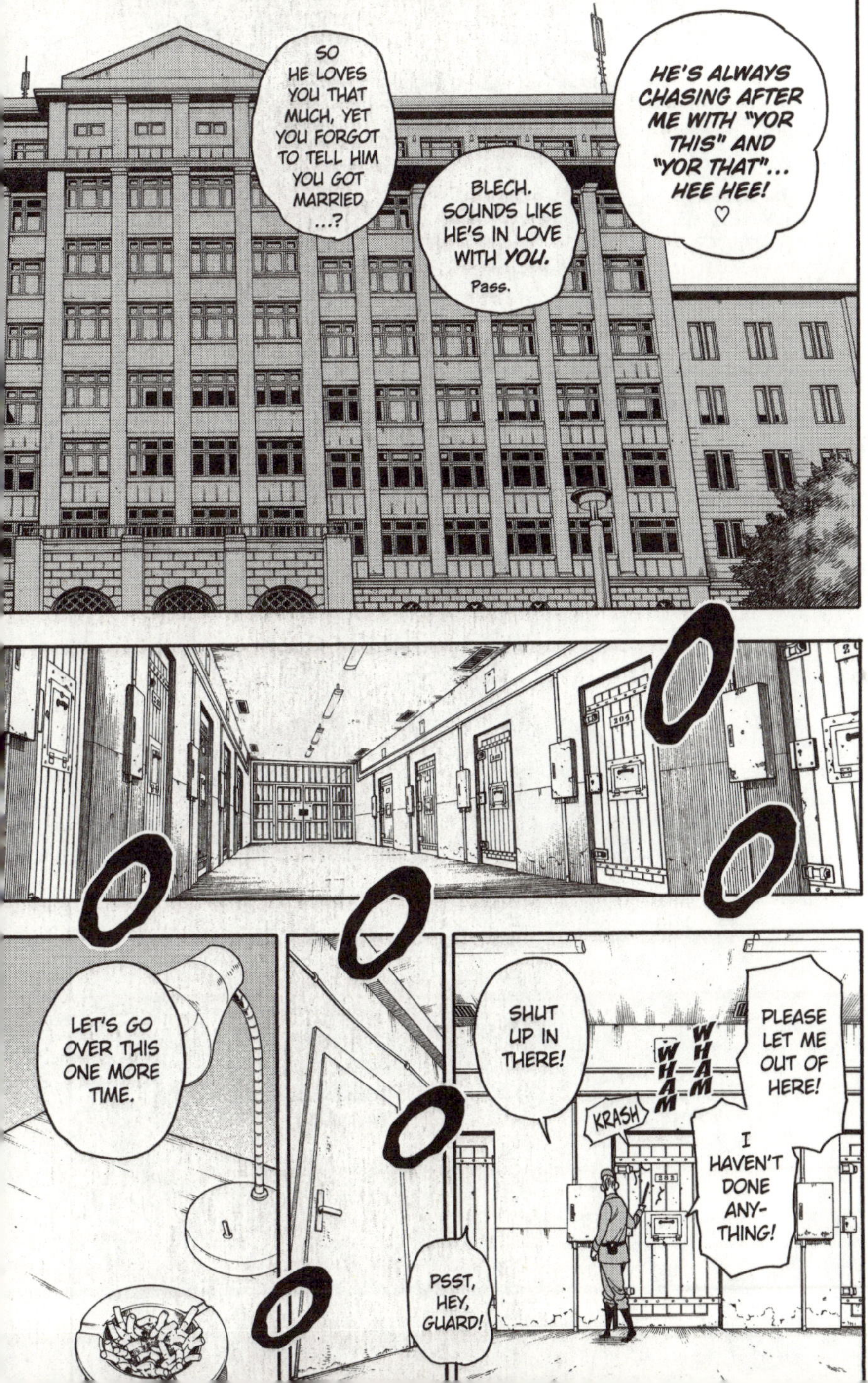
HE'S ALWAYS CHASING AFTER ME WITH "YOR THIS" AND "YOR THAT"... HEE HEE! ♡
BLECH. SOUNDS LIKE HE'S IN LOVE WITH YOU.
Pass.
SO HE LOVES YOU THAT MUCH, YET YOU FORGOT TO TELL HIM YOU GOT MARRIED ...?
PLEASE LET ME OUT OF HERE!
WHAM
WHAM
KRASH
I HAVEN'T DONE ANY-THING!
SHUT UP IN THERE!
PSST, HEY, GUARD!
LET'S GO OVER THIS ONE MORE TIME.

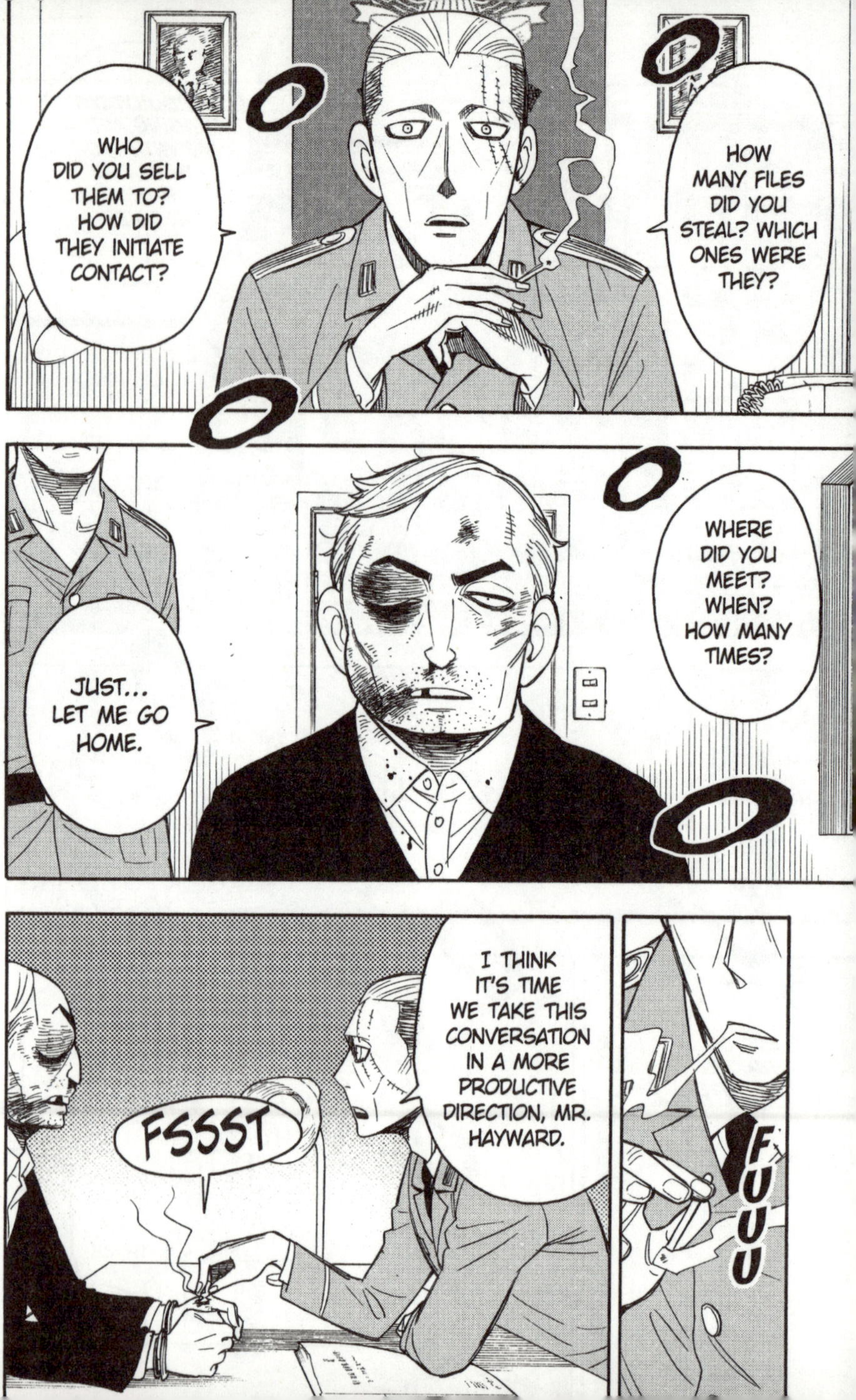
HOW MANY FILES DID YOU STEAL? WHICH ONES WERE THEY?
WHO DID YOU SELL THEM TO? HOW DID THEY INITIATE CONTACT?
WHERE DID YOU MEET? WHEN? HOW MANY TIMES?
JUST... LET ME GO HOME.
FUUU
I THINK IT'S TIME WE TAKE THIS CONVERSATION IN A MORE PRODUCTIVE DIRECTION, MR. HAYWARD.
FSSST

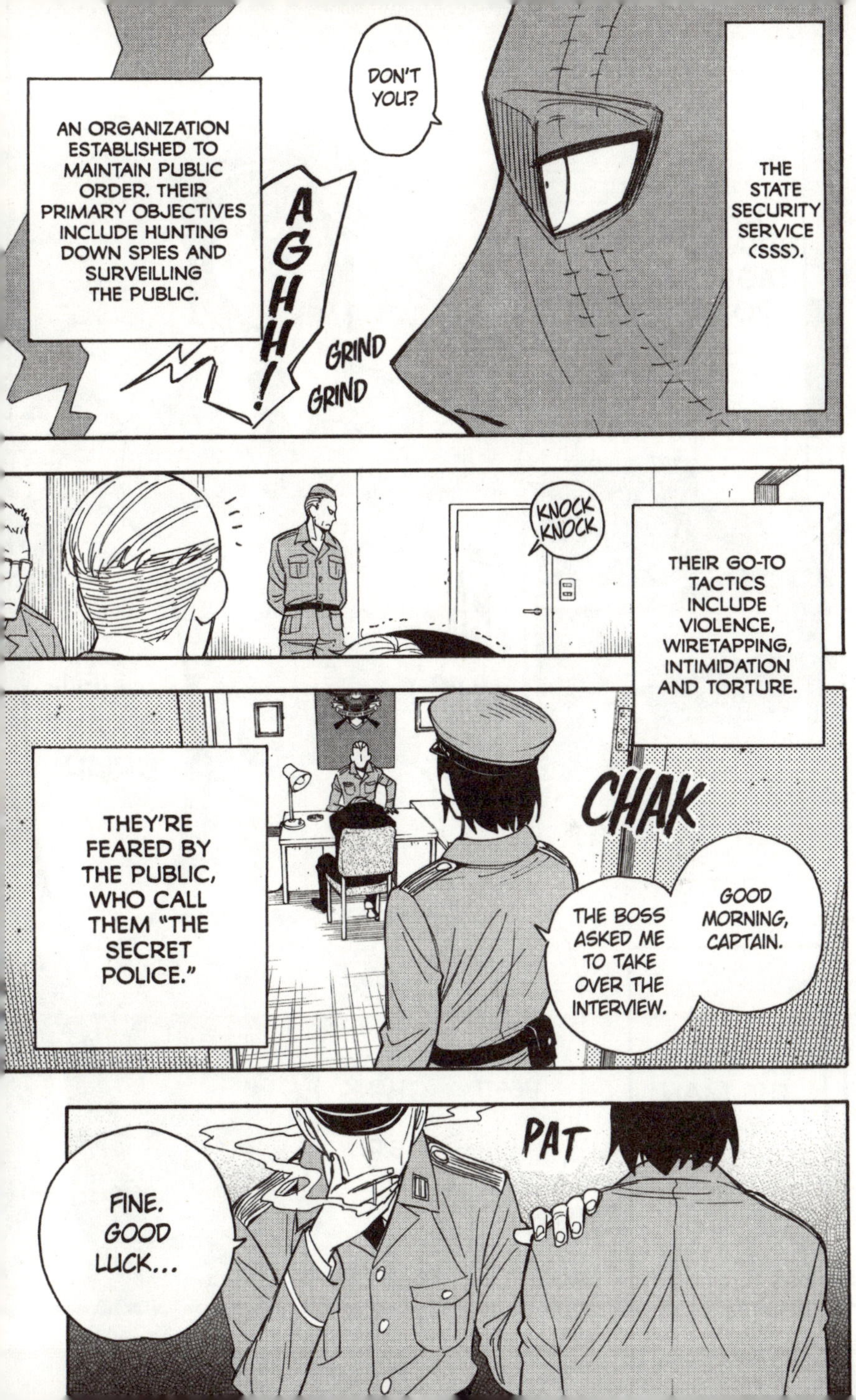
THE STATE SECURITY SERVICE (SSS).
DON'T YOU?
AGHHH!
AN ORGANIZATION ESTABLISHED TO MAINTAIN PUBLIC ORDER. THEIR PRIMARY OBJECTIVES INCLUDE HUNTING DOWN SPIES AND SURVEILLING THE PUBLIC.
GRIND
GRIND
THEIR GO-TO TACTICS INCLUDE VIOLENCE, WIRETAPPING, INTIMIDATION AND TORTURE.
KNOCK KNOCK
CHAK
GOOD MORNING, CAPTAIN.
THE BOSS ASKED ME TO TAKE OVER THE INTERVIEW.
THEY'RE FEARED BY THE PUBLIC, WHO CALL THEM "THE SECRET POLICE."
PAT
FINE. GOOD LUCK...

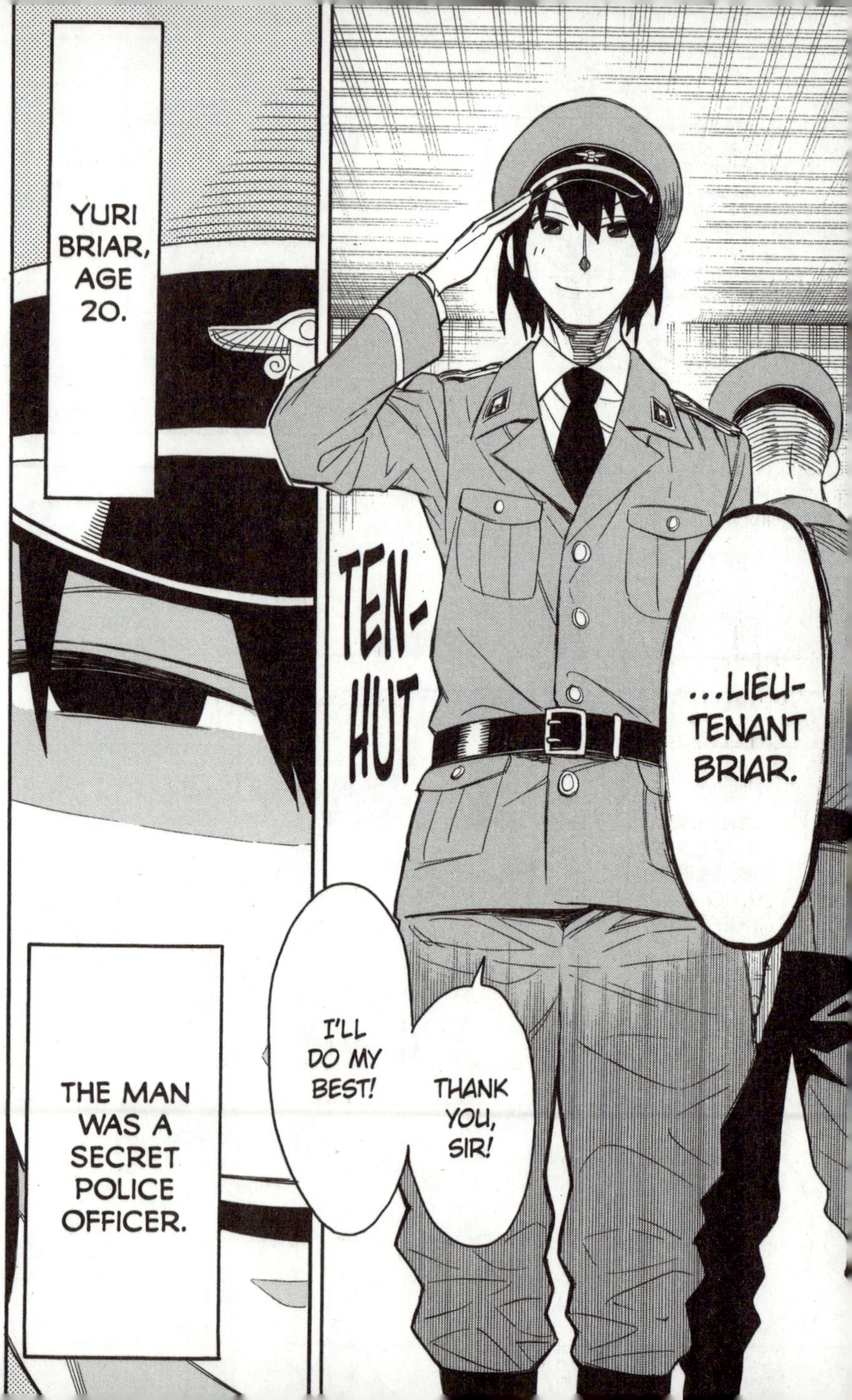
TEN-HUT
...LIEU-TENANT BRIAR.
THANK YOU, SIR!
I'LL DO MY BEST!
YURI BRIAR, AGE 20.
THE MAN WAS A SECRET POLICE OFFICER.

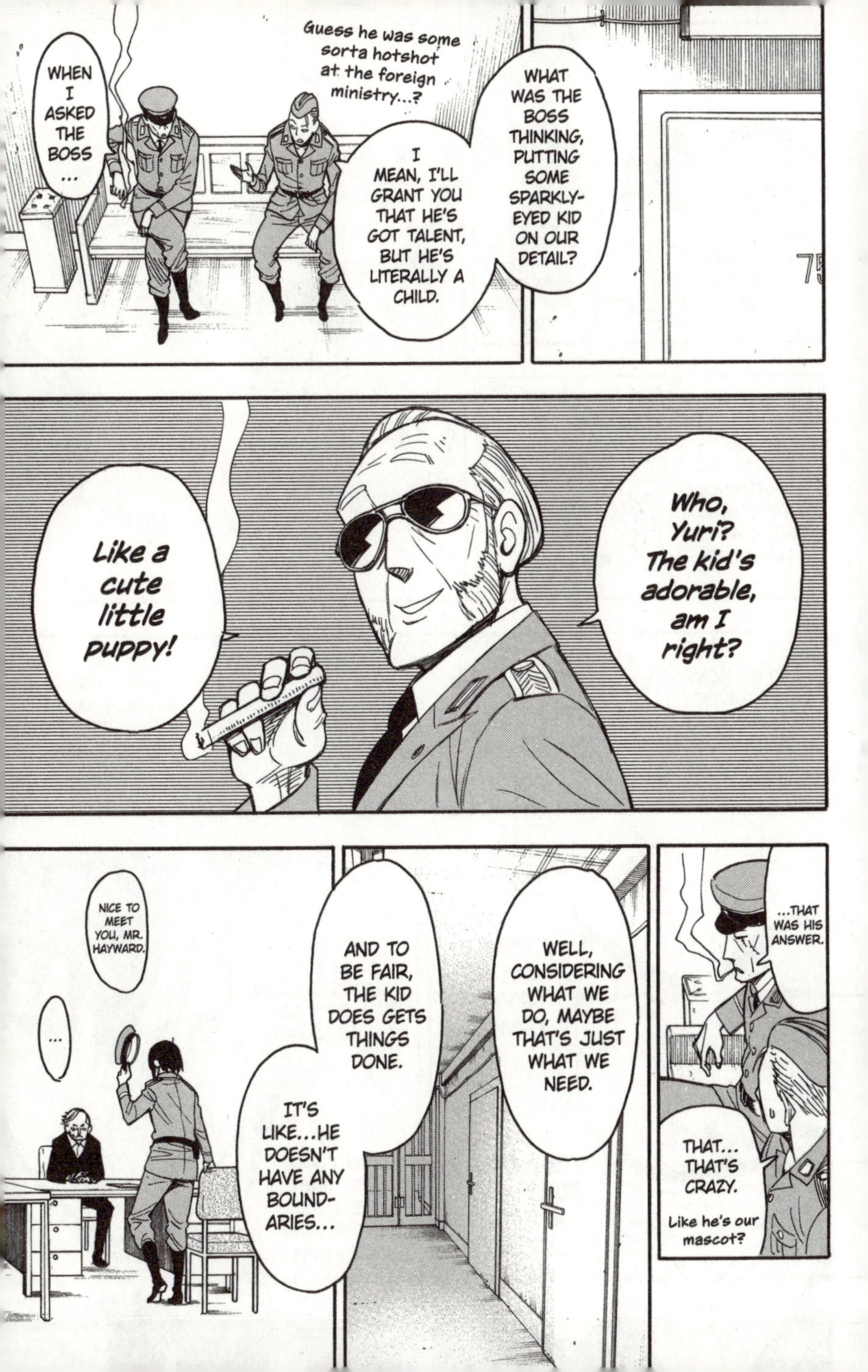
75
WHAT WAS THE BOSS THINKING, PUTTING SOME SPARKLY-EYED KID ON OUR DETAIL?
Guess he was some sorta hotshot at the foreign ministry...?
I MEAN, I'LL GRANT YOU THAT HE'S GOT TALENT, BUT HE'S LITERALLY A CHILD.
WHEN I ASKED THE BOSS...
Who, Yuri? The kid's adorable, am I right?
Like a cute little puppy!
...THAT WAS HIS ANSWER.
THAT... THAT'S CRAZY.
Like he's our mascot?
WELL, CONSIDERING WHAT WE DO, MAYBE THAT'S JUST WHAT WE NEED.
AND TO BE FAIR, THE KID DOES GETS THINGS DONE.
IT'S LIKE...HE DOESN'T HAVE ANY BOUND-ARIES...
NICE TO MEET YOU, MR. HAYWARD.
...

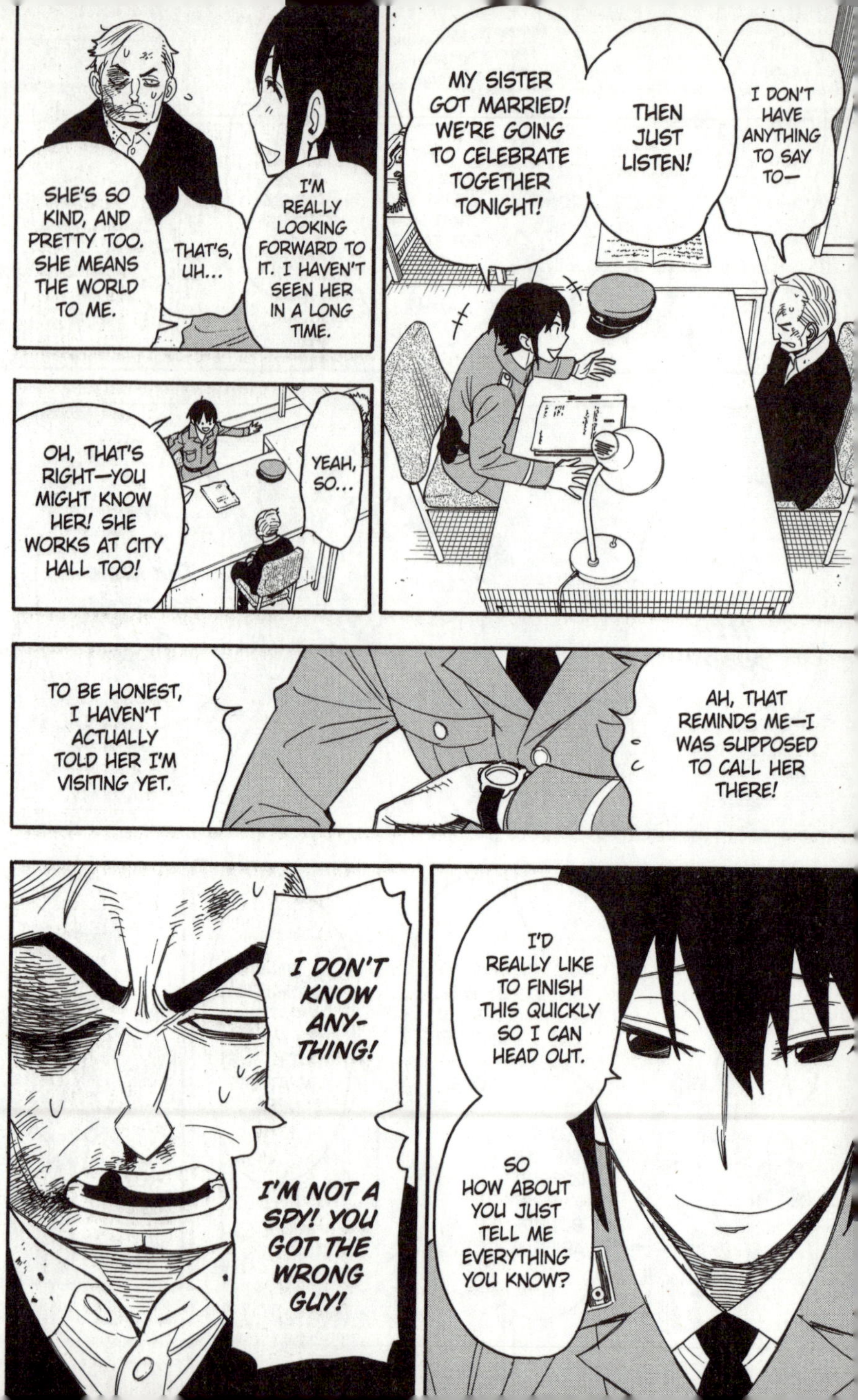
I DON'T HAVE ANYTHING TO SAY TO—
THEN JUST LISTEN!
MY SISTER GOT MARRIED! WE'RE GOING TO CELEBRATE TOGETHER TONIGHT!
I'M REALLY LOOKING FORWARD TO IT. I HAVEN'T SEEN HER IN A LONG TIME.
THAT'S, UH...
SHE'S SO KIND, AND PRETTY TOO. SHE MEANS THE WORLD TO ME.
YEAH, SO...
OH, THAT'S RIGHT—YOU MIGHT KNOW HER! SHE WORKS AT CITY HALL TOO!
AH, THAT REMINDS ME—I WAS SUPPOSED TO CALL HER THERE!
TO BE HONEST, I HAVEN'T ACTUALLY TOLD HER I'M VISITING YET.
I'D REALLY LIKE TO FINISH THIS QUICKLY SO I CAN HEAD OUT.
SO HOW ABOUT YOU JUST TELL ME EVERYTHING YOU KNOW?
I DON'T KNOW ANYTHING!
I'M NOT A SPY! YOU GOT THE WRONG GUY!

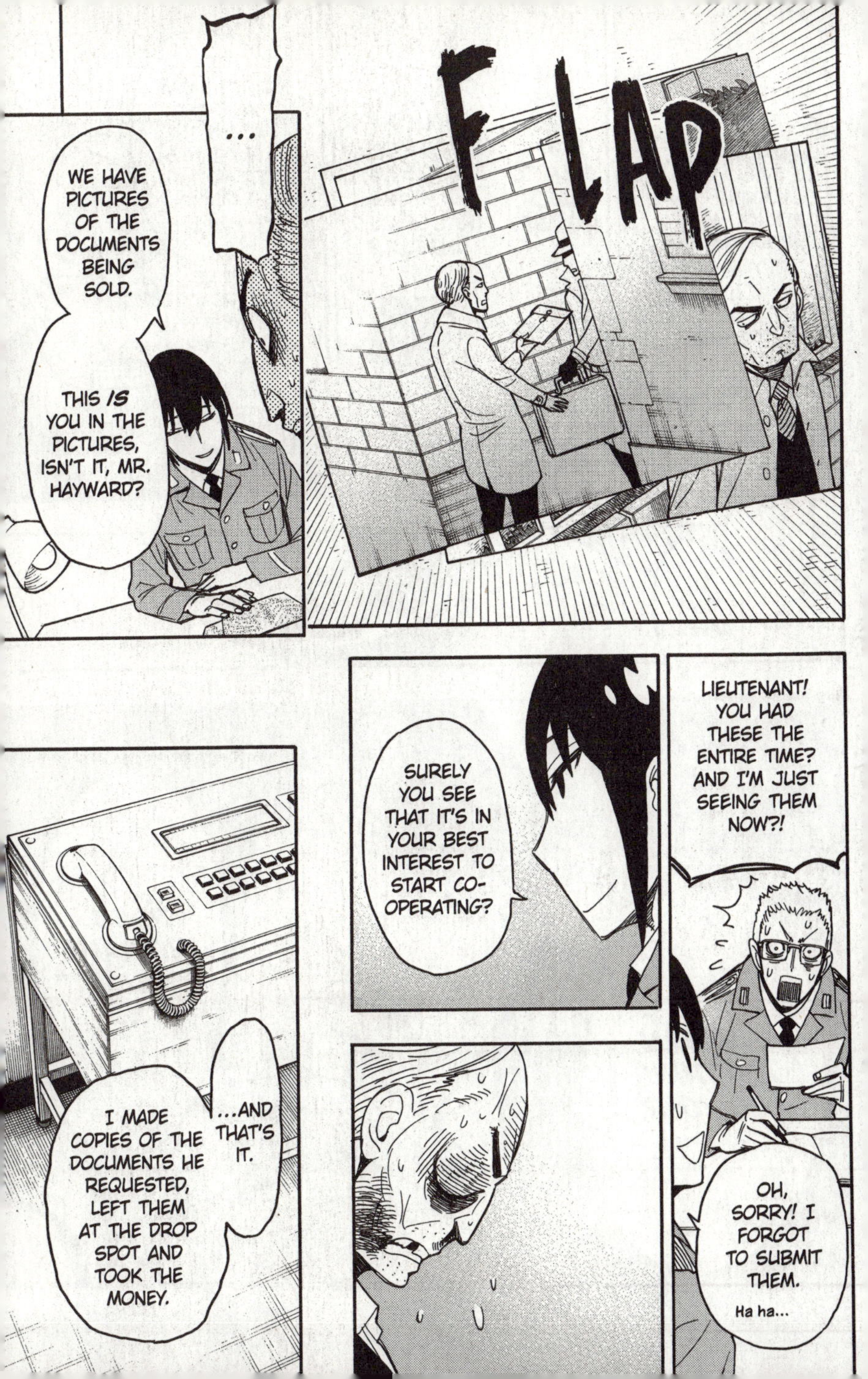
FLAP
...
WE HAVE PICTURES OF THE DOCUMENTS BEING SOLD.
THIS *IS* YOU IN THE PICTURES, ISN'T IT, MR. HAYWARD?
LIEUTENANT! YOU HAD THESE THE ENTIRE TIME? AND I'M JUST SEEING THEM NOW?!
OH, SORRY! I FORGOT TO SUBMIT THEM.
Ha ha...
SURELY YOU SEE THAT IT'S IN YOUR BEST INTEREST TO START CO-OPERATING?
I MADE COPIES OF THE DOCUMENTS HE REQUESTED, LEFT THEM AT THE DROP SPOT AND TOOK THE MONEY.
...AND THAT'S IT.

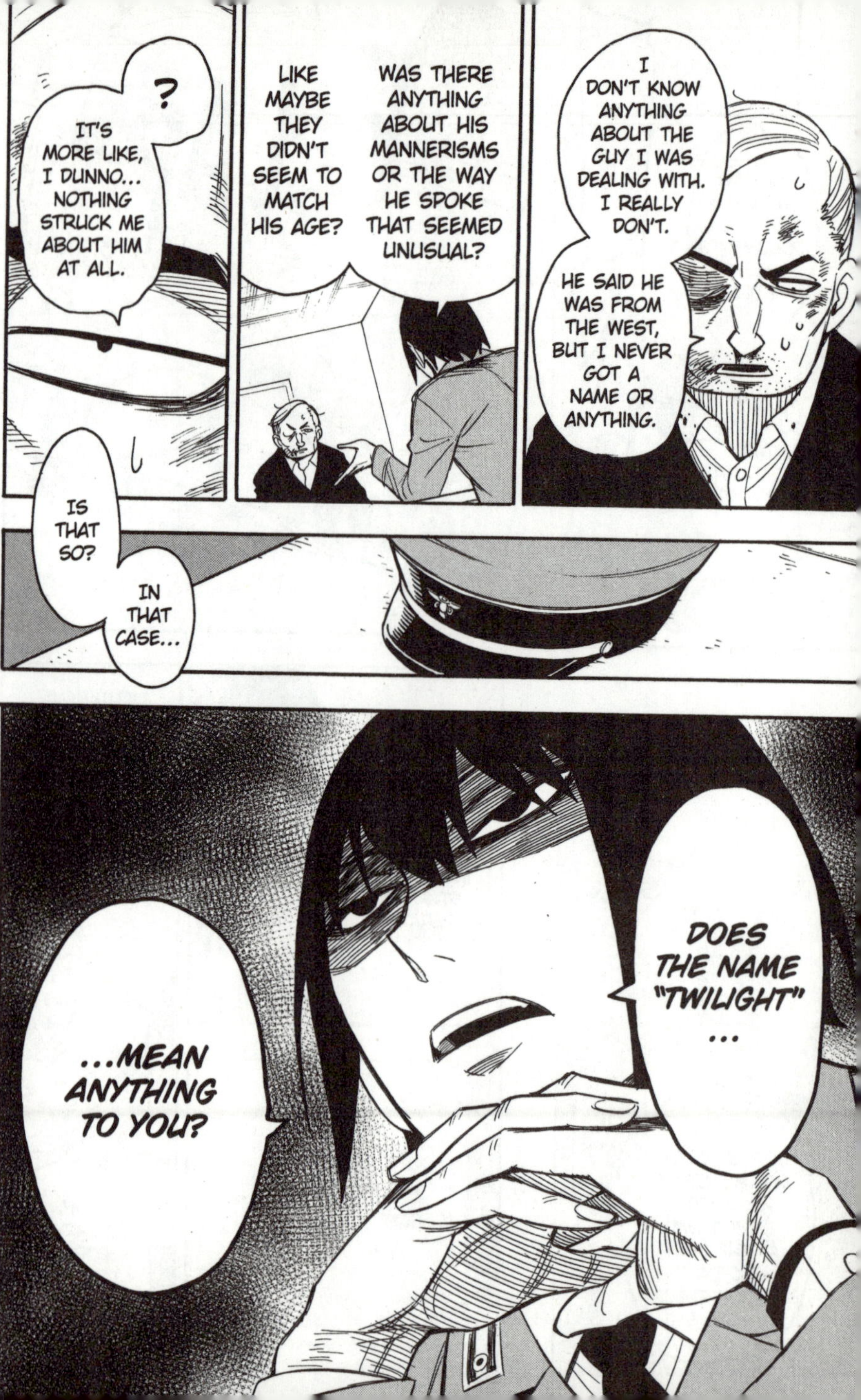
I DON'T KNOW ANYTHING ABOUT THE GUY I WAS DEALING WITH. I REALLY DON'T.
HE SAID HE WAS FROM THE WEST, BUT I NEVER GOT A NAME OR ANYTHING.
WAS THERE ANYTHING ABOUT HIS MANNERISMS OR THE WAY HE SPOKE THAT SEEMED UNUSUAL?
LIKE MAYBE THEY DIDN'T SEEM TO MATCH HIS AGE?
?
IT'S MORE LIKE, I DUNNO... NOTHING STRUCK ME ABOUT HIM AT ALL.
IS THAT SO?
IN THAT CASE...
DOES THE NAME "TWILIGHT" ...
...MEAN ANYTHING TO YOU?

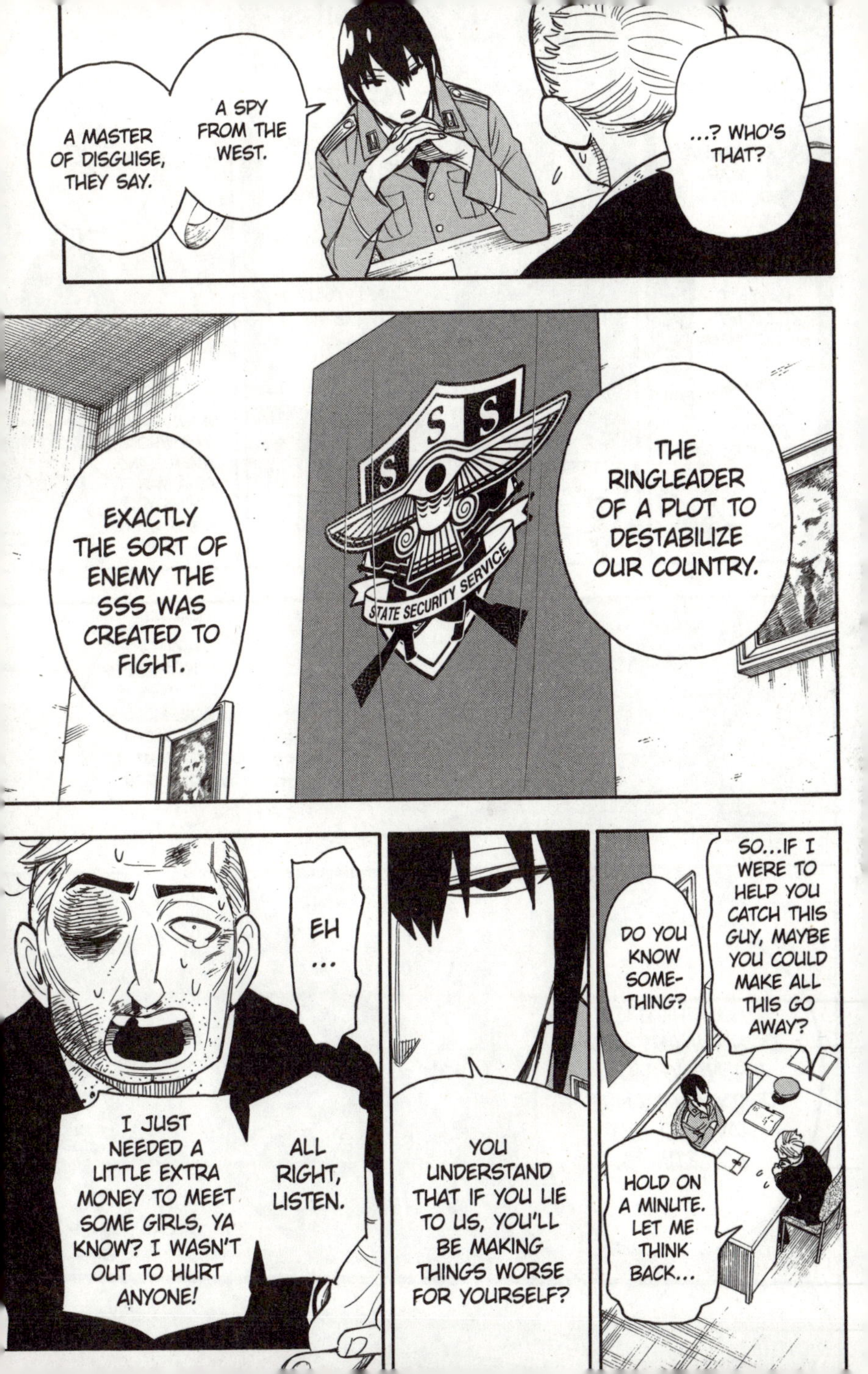
...? WHO'S THAT?
A SPY FROM THE WEST.
A MASTER OF DISGUISE, THEY SAY.
THE RINGLEADER OF A PLOT TO DESTABILIZE OUR COUNTRY.
S S S
STATE SECURITY SERVICE
EXACTLY THE SORT OF ENEMY THE SSS WAS CREATED TO FIGHT.
SO...IF I WERE TO HELP YOU CATCH THIS GUY, MAYBE YOU COULD MAKE ALL THIS GO AWAY?
DO YOU KNOW SOME-THING?
HOLD ON A MINUTE. LET ME THINK BACK...
YOU UNDERSTAND THAT IF YOU LIE TO US, YOU'LL BE MAKING THINGS WORSE FOR YOURSELF?
EH ...
ALL RIGHT, LISTEN.
I JUST NEEDED A LITTLE EXTRA MONEY TO MEET SOME GIRLS, YA KNOW? I WASN'T OUT TO HURT ANYONE!

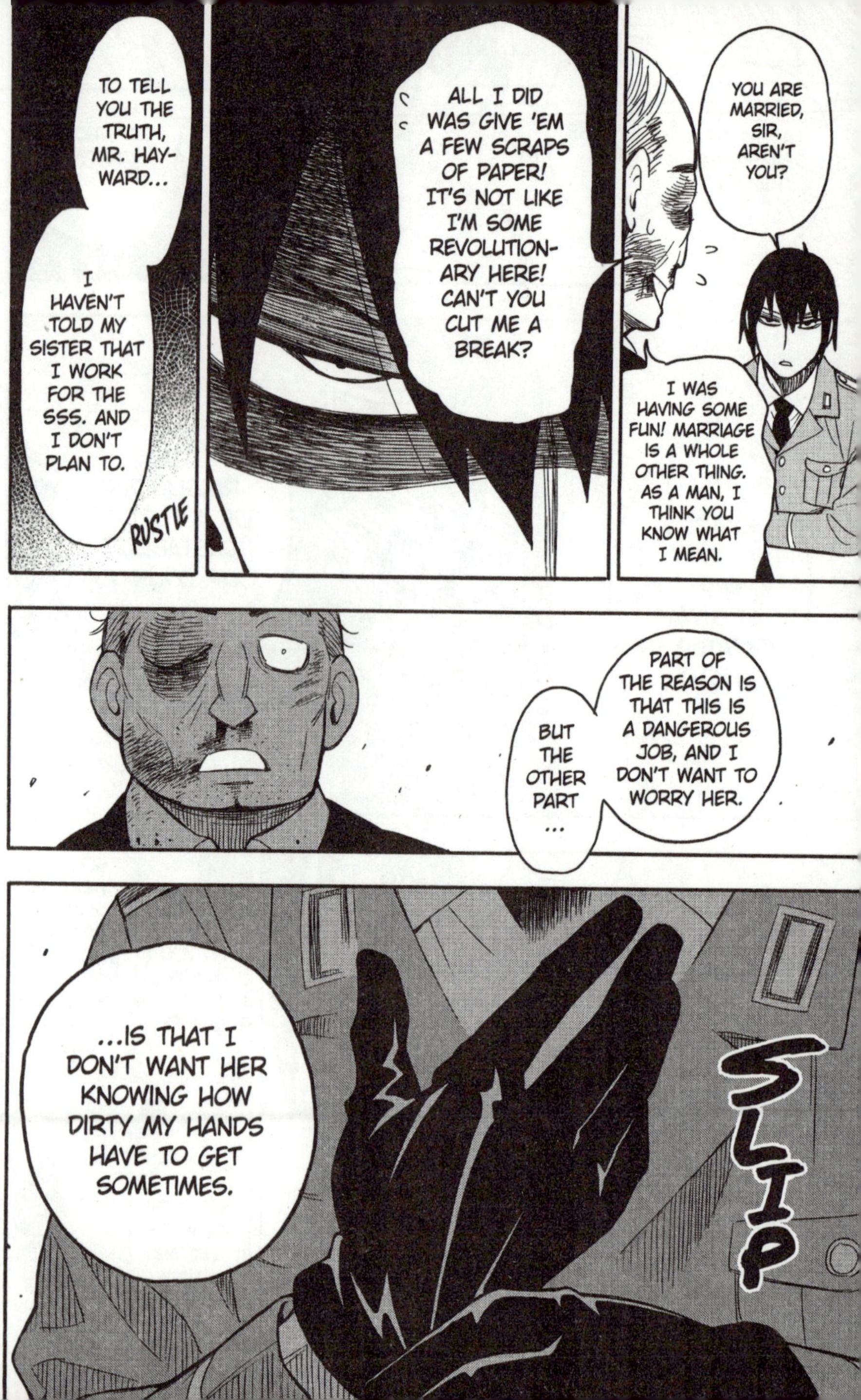
YOU ARE MARRIED, SIR, AREN'T YOU?
I WAS HAVING SOME FUN! MARRIAGE IS A WHOLE OTHER THING. AS A MAN, I THINK YOU KNOW WHAT I MEAN.
ALL I DID WAS GIVE 'EM A FEW SCRAPS OF PAPER! IT'S NOT LIKE I'M SOME REVOLUTIONARY HERE! CAN'T YOU CUT ME A BREAK?
TO TELL YOU THE TRUTH, MR. HAYWARD...
I HAVEN'T TOLD MY SISTER THAT I WORK FOR THE SSS. AND I DON'T PLAN TO.
RUSTLE
PART OF THE REASON IS THAT THIS IS A DANGEROUS JOB, AND I DON'T WANT TO WORRY HER.
BUT THE OTHER PART...
SLIP
...IS THAT I DON'T WANT HER KNOWING HOW DIRTY MY HANDS HAVE TO GET SOMETIMES.

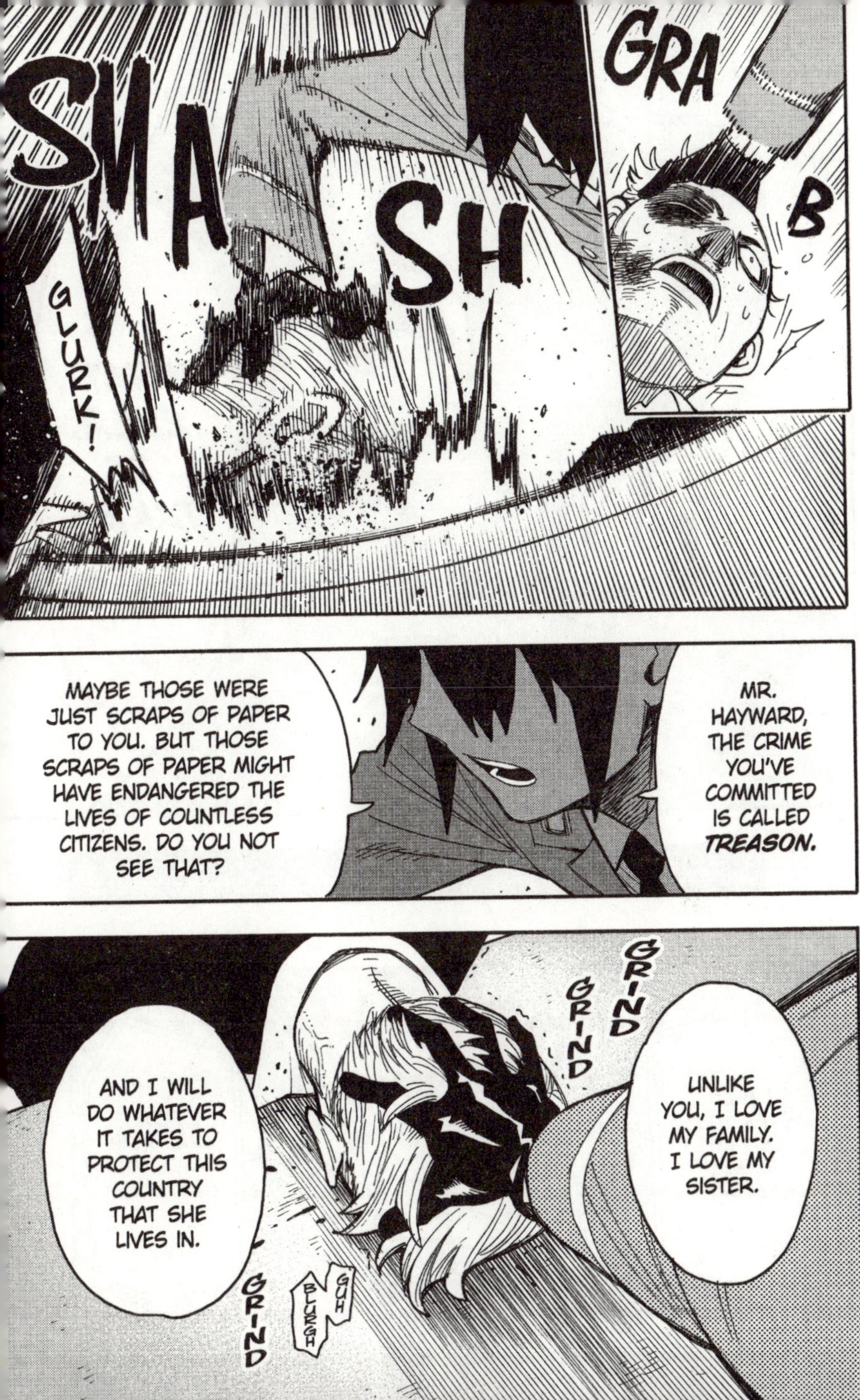
GRAB
SMASH
GLURK!
MR. HAYWARD, THE CRIME YOU'VE COMMITTED IS CALLED ***TREASON.***
MAYBE THOSE WERE JUST SCRAPS OF PAPER TO YOU. BUT THOSE SCRAPS OF PAPER MIGHT HAVE ENDANGERED THE LIVES OF COUNTLESS CITIZENS. DO YOU NOT SEE THAT?
GRIND
GRIND
UNLIKE YOU, I LOVE MY FAMILY. I LOVE MY SISTER.
AND I WILL DO WHATEVER IT TAKES TO PROTECT THIS COUNTRY THAT SHE LIVES IN.
GUH
BLUGH
GRIND

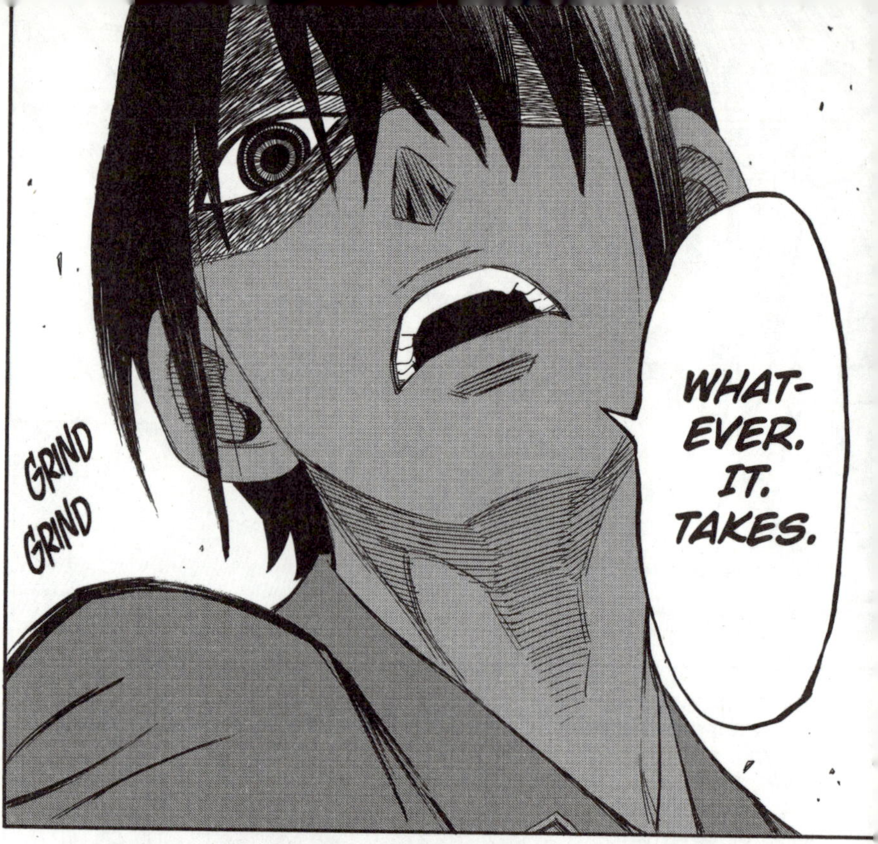
WHAT-EVER. IT. TAKES.
GRIND GRIND

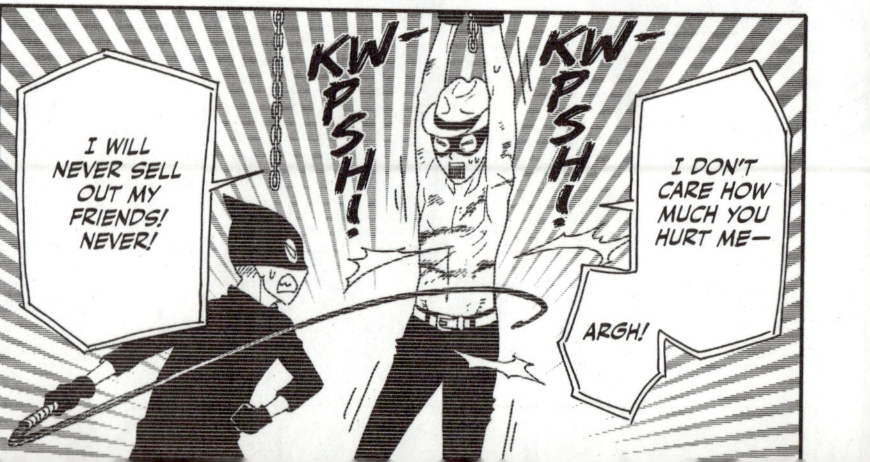
KW-PSH!
I DON'T CARE HOW MUCH YOU HURT ME—
ARGH!
KW-PSH!
I WILL NEVER SELL OUT MY FRIENDS! NEVER!

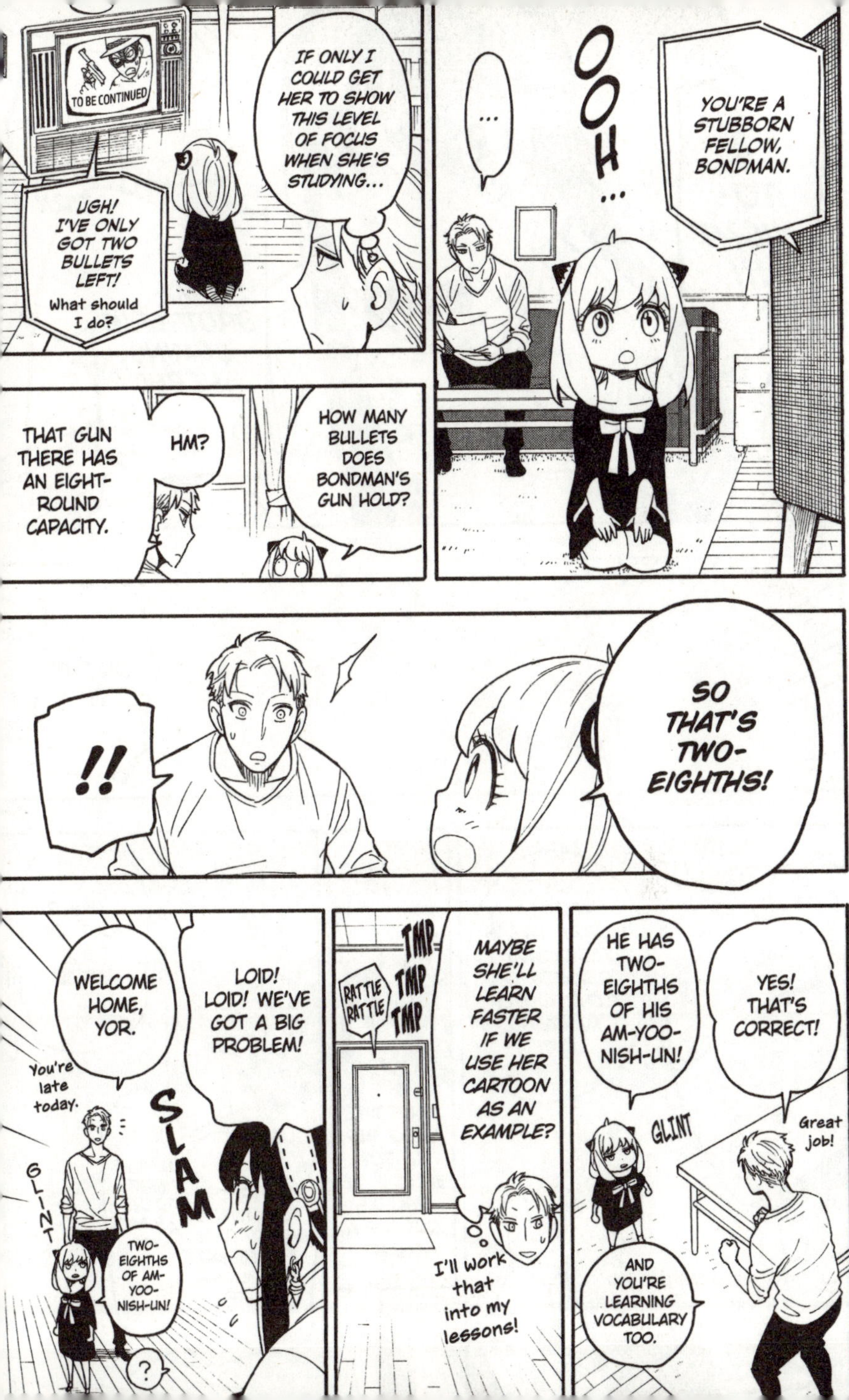
YOU'RE A STUBBORN FELLOW, BONDMAN.
OOH...
...
IF ONLY I COULD GET HER TO SHOW THIS LEVEL OF FOCUS WHEN SHE'S STUDYING...
TO BE CONTINUED
UGH! I'VE ONLY GOT TWO BULLETS LEFT!
What should I do?
HOW MANY BULLETS DOES BONDMAN'S GUN HOLD?
HM?
THAT GUN THERE HAS AN EIGHT-ROUND CAPACITY.
SO THAT'S TWO-EIGHTHS!
!!
YES! THAT'S CORRECT!
HE HAS TWO-EIGHTHS OF HIS AM-YOO-NISH-UN!
GLINT
Great job!
AND YOU'RE LEARNING VOCABULARY TOO.
TMP TMP TMP
MAYBE SHE'LL LEARN FASTER IF WE USE HER CARTOON AS AN EXAMPLE?
RATTLE RATTLE
I'll work that into my lessons!
LOID! LOID! WE'VE GOT A BIG PROBLEM!
WELCOME HOME, YOR.
SLAM
You're late today.
GLINT
TWO-EIGHTHS OF AM-YOO-NISH-UN!
?

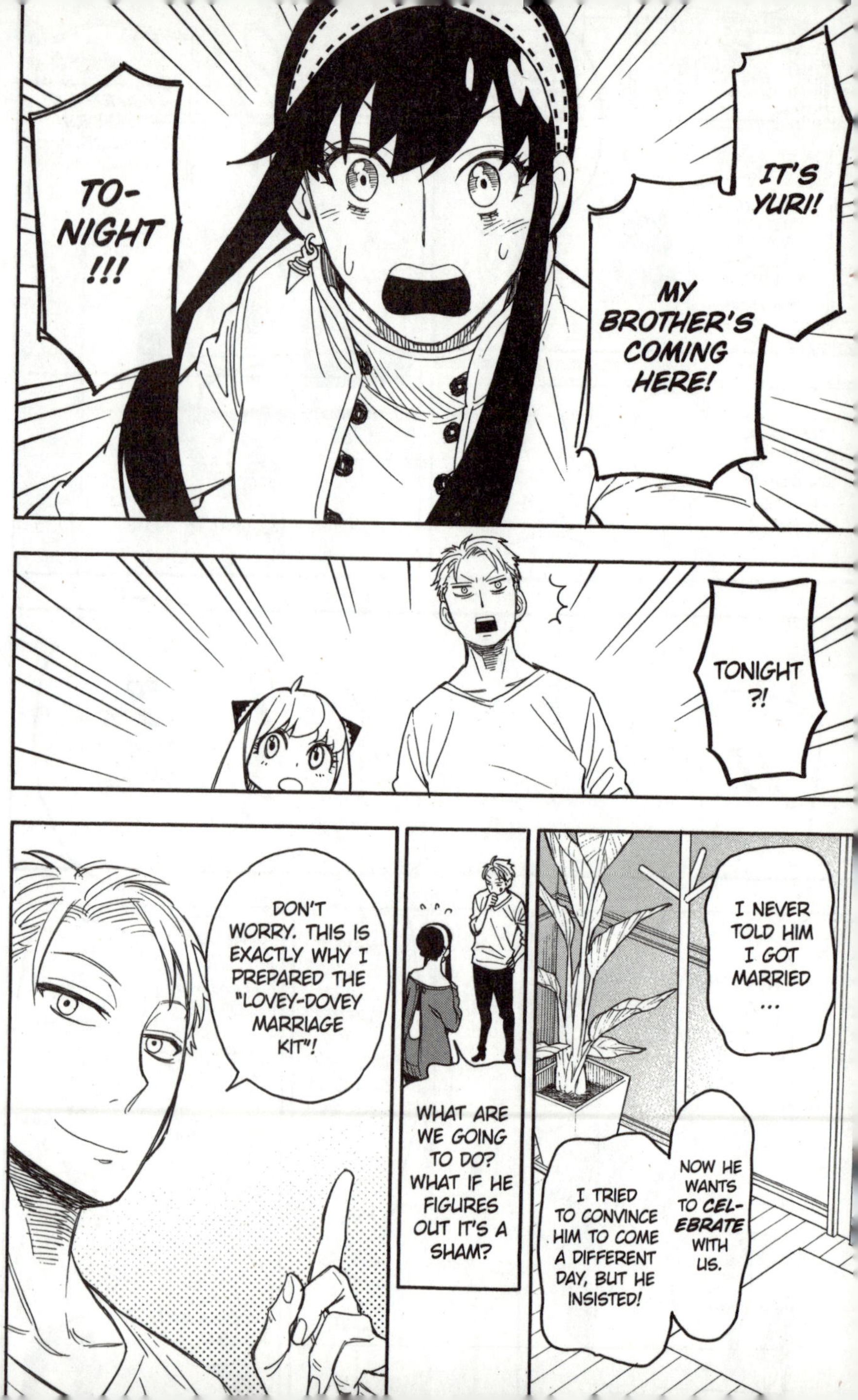
IT'S YURI!
MY BROTHER'S COMING HERE!
TO-NIGHT!!!
TONIGHT?!
I NEVER TOLD HIM I GOT MARRIED...
NOW HE WANTS TO CELEBRATE WITH US.
I TRIED TO CONVINCE HIM TO COME A DIFFERENT DAY, BUT HE INSISTED!
WHAT ARE WE GOING TO DO? WHAT IF HE FIGURES OUT IT'S A SHAM?
DON'T WORRY. THIS IS EXACTLY WHY I PREPARED THE "LOVEY-DOVEY MARRIAGE KIT"!

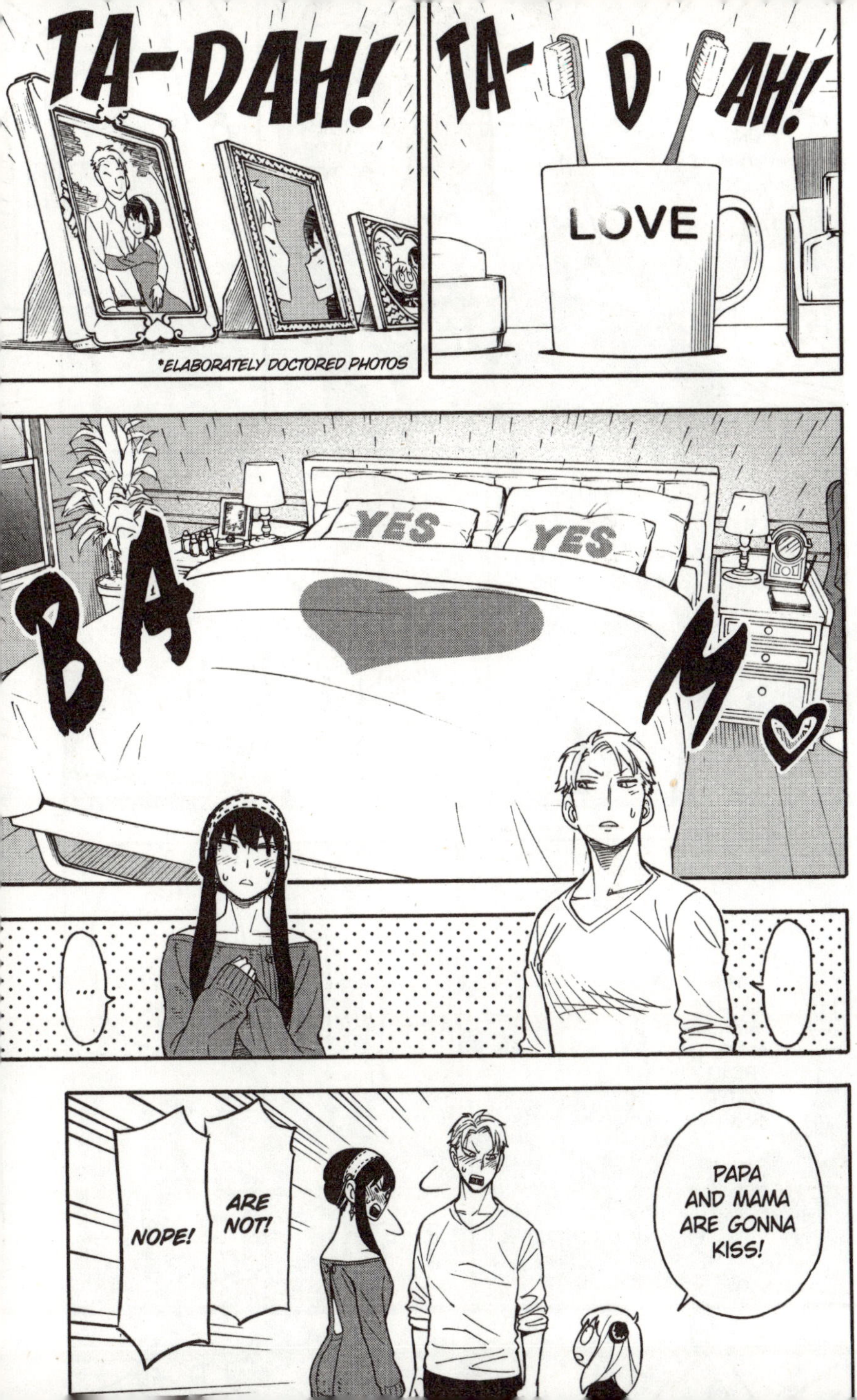
TA-DAH!
LOVE
TA-DAH!
*ELABORATELY DOCTORED PHOTOS
YES
YES
BAM
...
...
PAPA AND MAMA ARE GONNA KISS!
ARE NOT!
NOPE!

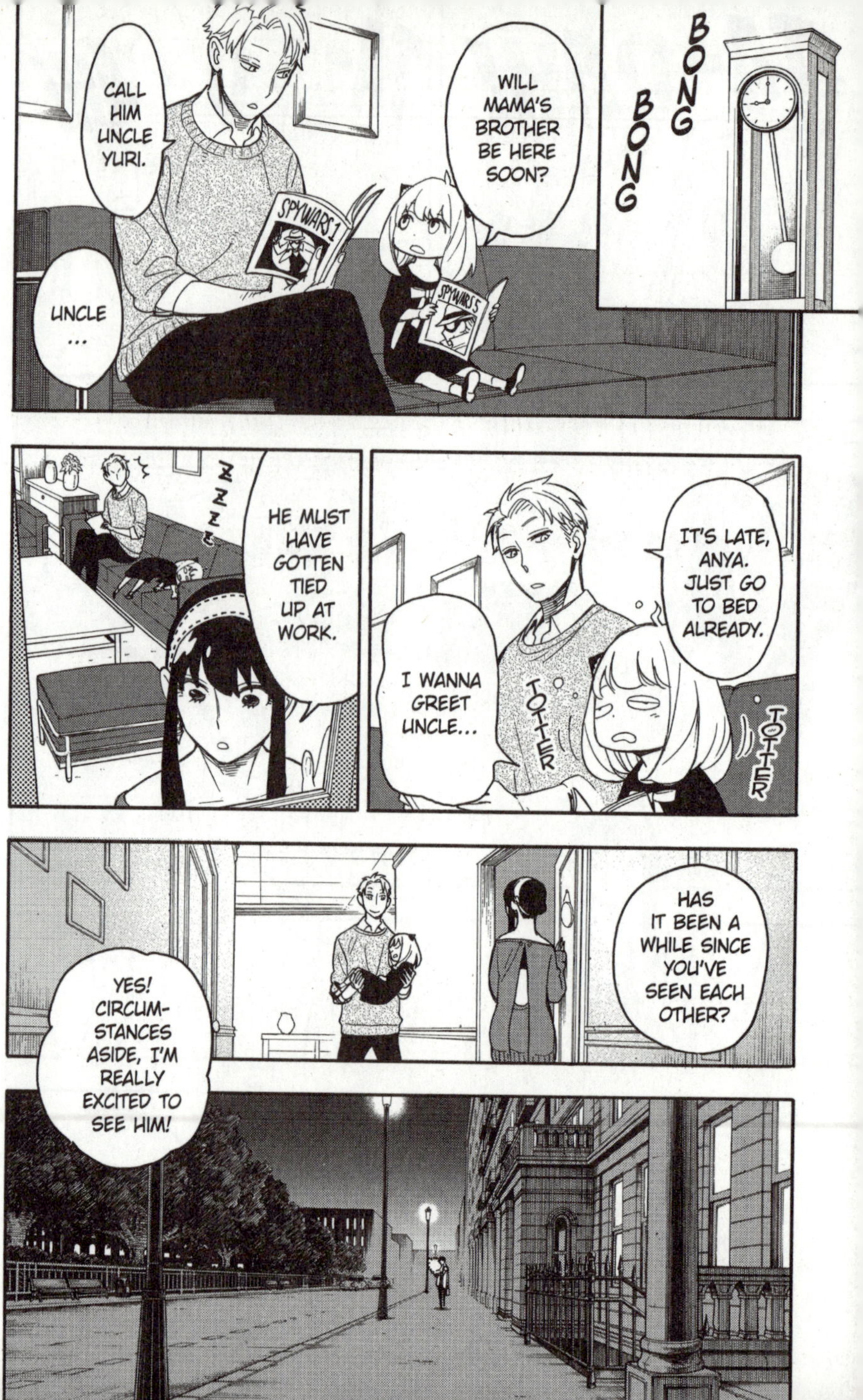
BONG BONG
WILL MAMA'S BROTHER BE HERE SOON?
CALL HIM UNCLE YURI.
UNCLE ...
IT'S LATE, ANYA. JUST GO TO BED ALREADY.
TOTTER
TOTTER
I WANNA GREET UNCLE...
ZZZ
HE MUST HAVE GOTTEN TIED UP AT WORK.
HAS IT BEEN A WHILE SINCE YOU'VE SEEN EACH OTHER?
YES! CIRCUM-STANCES ASIDE, I'M REALLY EXCITED TO SEE HIM!

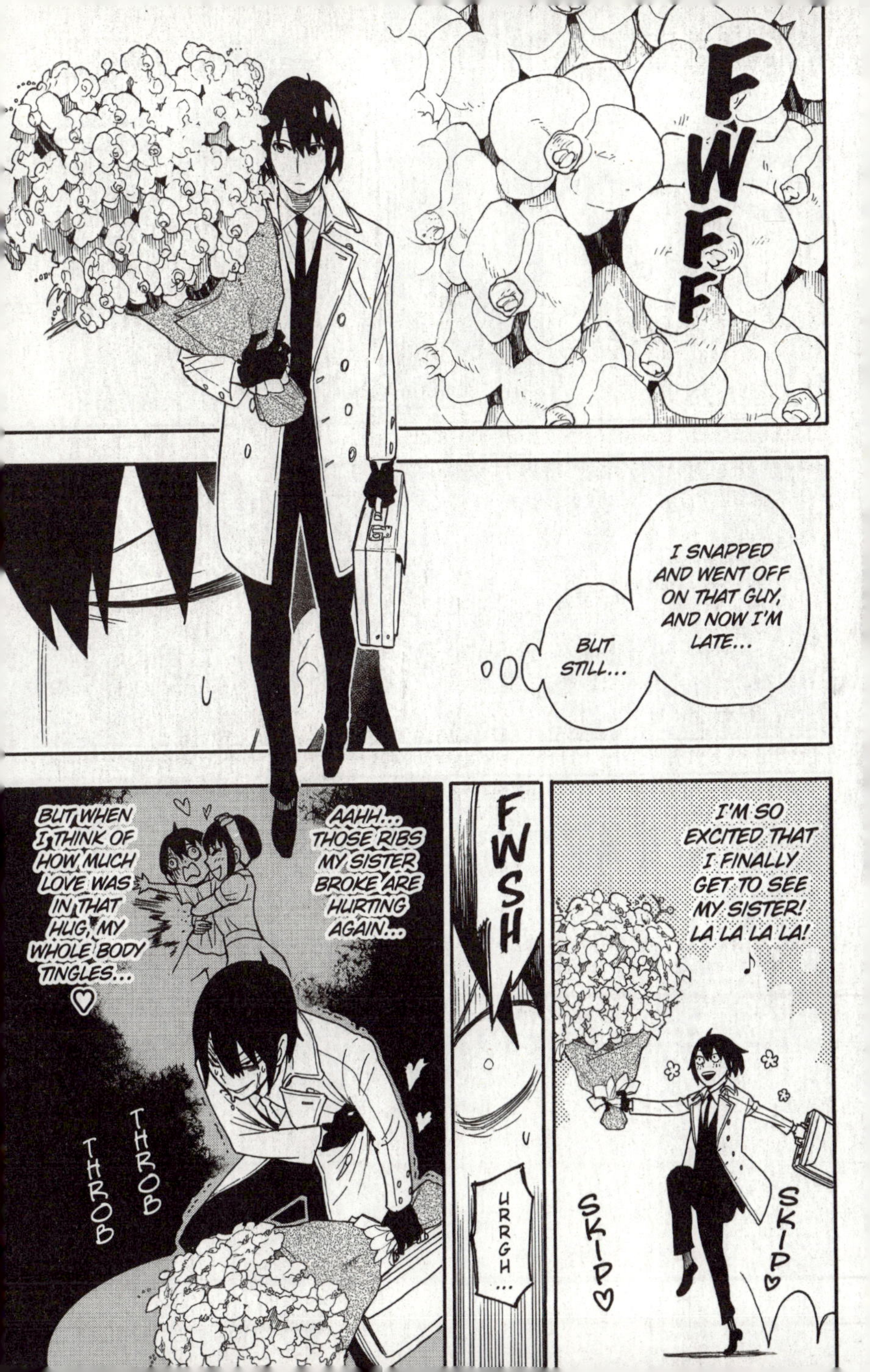
FWFF
I SNAPPED AND WENT OFF ON THAT GUY, AND NOW I'M LATE...
BUT STILL...
I'M SO EXCITED THAT I FINALLY GET TO SEE MY SISTER! LA LA LA LA! ♪
SKIP♡
SKIP♡
FWSH
URRGH...
AAHH... THOSE RIBS MY SISTER BROKE ARE HURTING AGAIN...
BUT WHEN I THINK OF HOW MUCH LOVE WAS IN THAT HUG, MY WHOLE BODY TINGLES... ♡
THROB
THROB

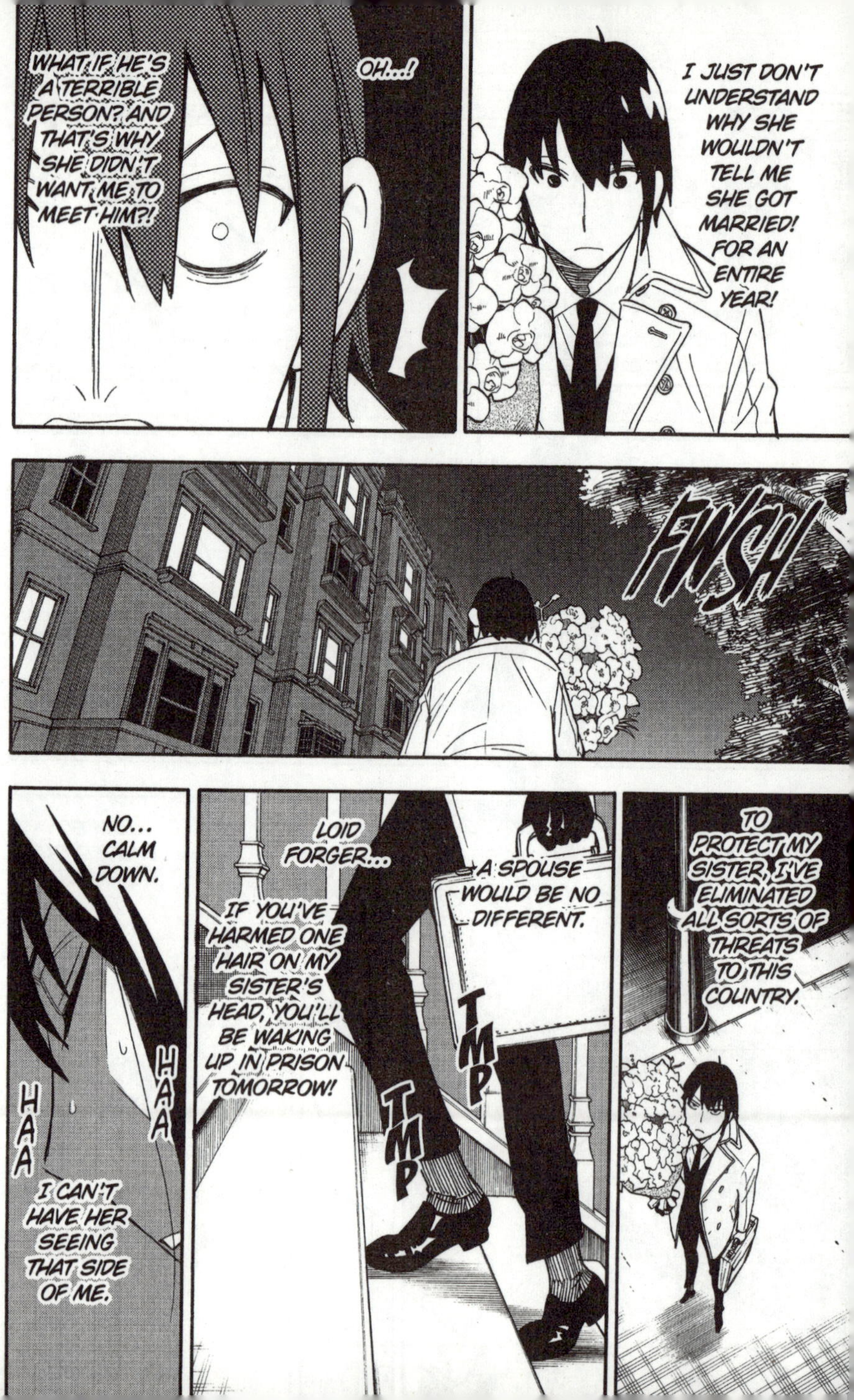
I JUST DON'T UNDERSTAND WHY SHE WOULDN'T TELL ME SHE GOT MARRIED! FOR AN ENTIRE YEAR!
OH...!
WHAT IF HE'S A TERRIBLE PERSON? AND THAT'S WHY SHE DIDN'T WANT ME TO MEET HIM?!
FWSH
TO PROTECT MY SISTER, I'VE ELIMINATED ALL SORTS OF THREATS TO THIS COUNTRY.
A SPOUSE WOULD BE NO DIFFERENT.
TMP
LOID FORGER...
IF YOU'VE HARMED ONE HAIR ON MY SISTER'S HEAD, YOU'LL BE WAKING UP IN PRISON TOMORROW!
TMP
NO... CALM DOWN.
HAA
HAA
I CAN'T HAVE HER SEEING THAT SIDE OF ME.

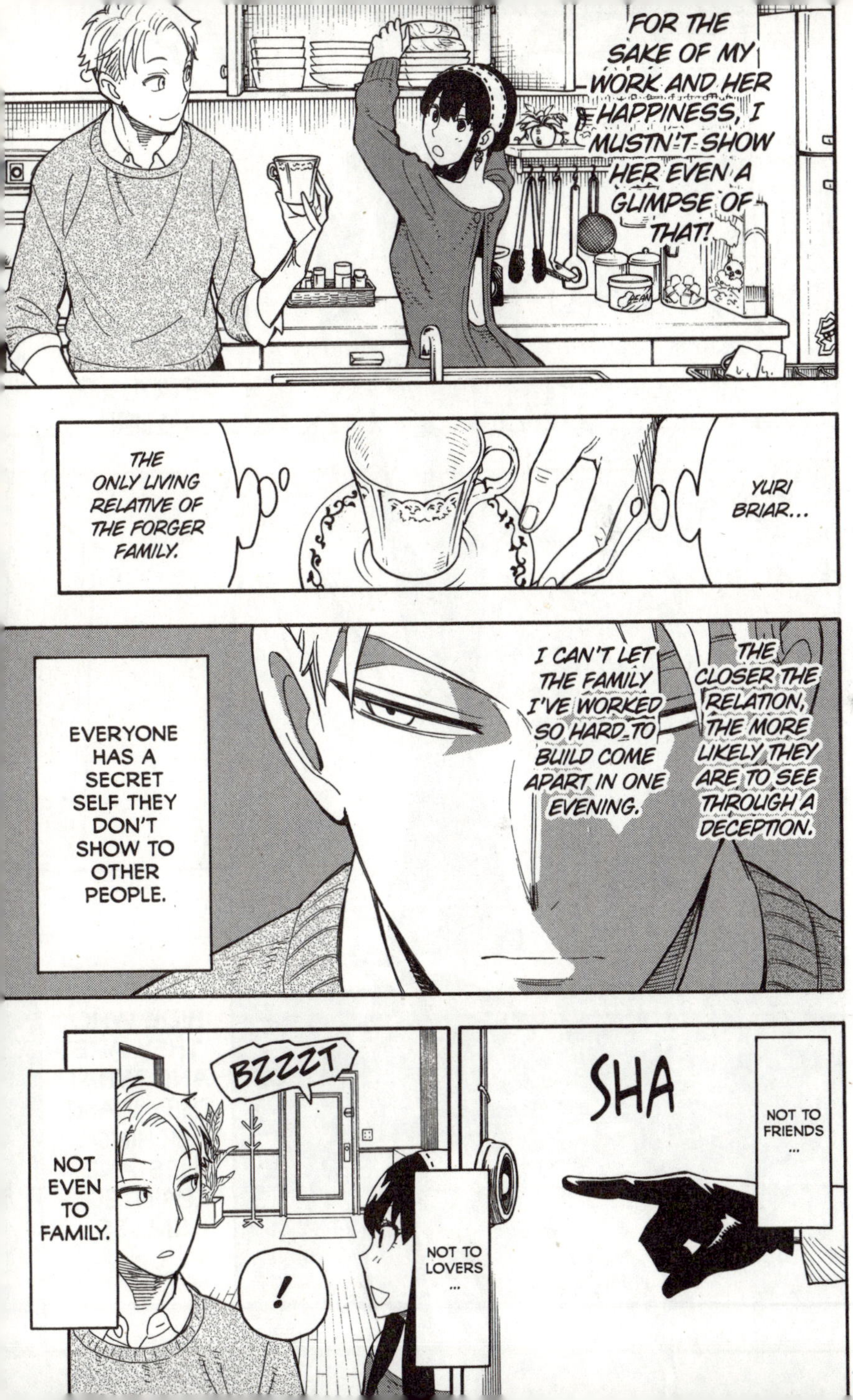
FOR THE SAKE OF MY WORK AND HER HAPPINESS, I MUSTN'T SHOW HER EVEN A GLIMPSE OF THAT!
YURI BRIAR...
THE ONLY LIVING RELATIVE OF THE FORGER FAMILY.
THE CLOSER THE RELATION, THE MORE LIKELY THEY ARE TO SEE THROUGH A DECEPTION.
I CAN'T LET THE FAMILY I'VE WORKED SO HARD TO BUILD COME APART IN ONE EVENING.
EVERYONE HAS A SECRET SELF THEY DON'T SHOW TO OTHER PEOPLE.
SHA
NOT TO FRIENDS...
BZZZT
NOT TO LOVERS...
!
NOT EVEN TO FAMILY.

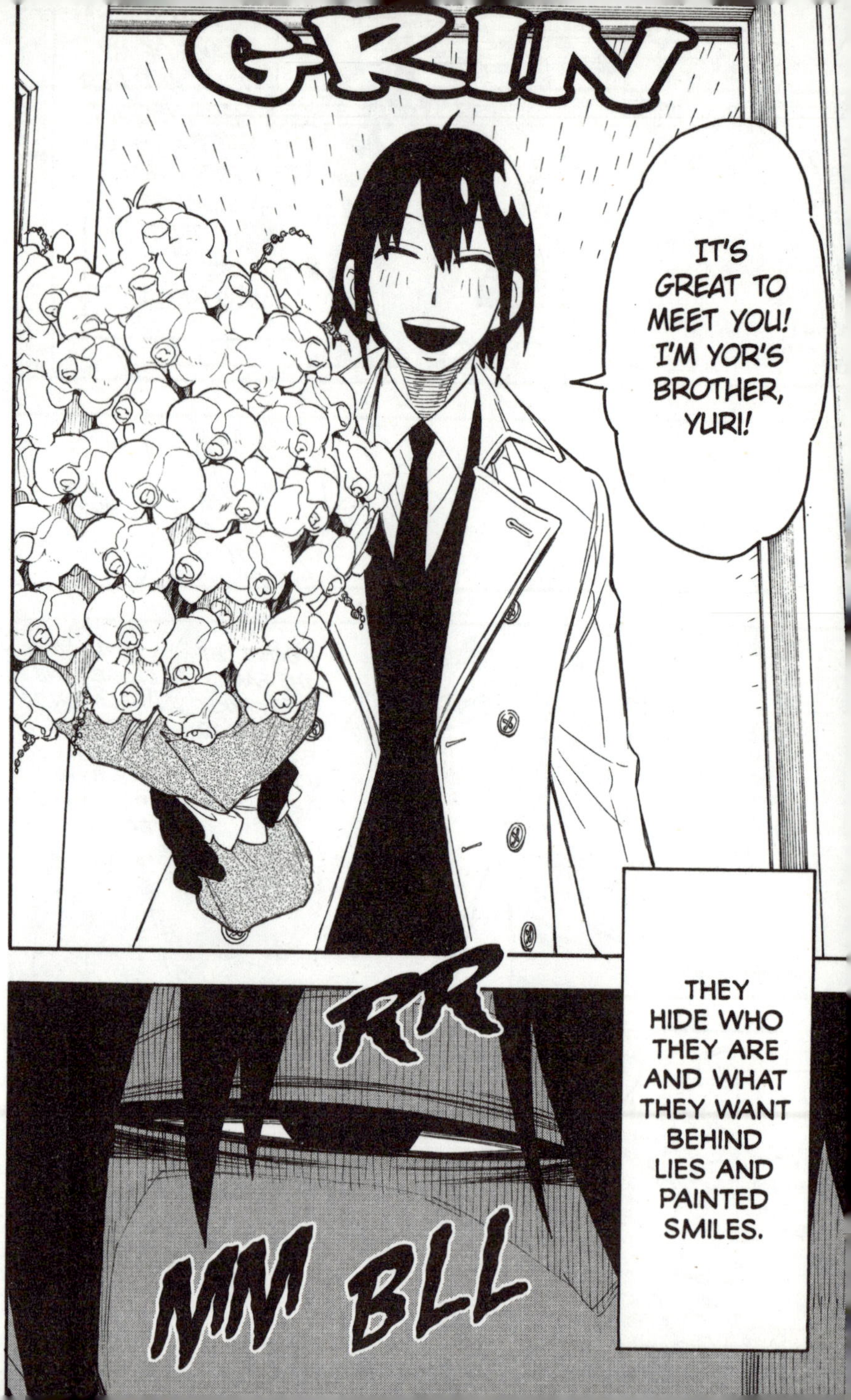
GRIN
IT'S GREAT TO MEET YOU! I'M YOR'S BROTHER, YURI!
THEY HIDE WHO THEY ARE AND WHAT THEY WANT BEHIND LIES AND PAINTED SMILES.
RR
MM BLL

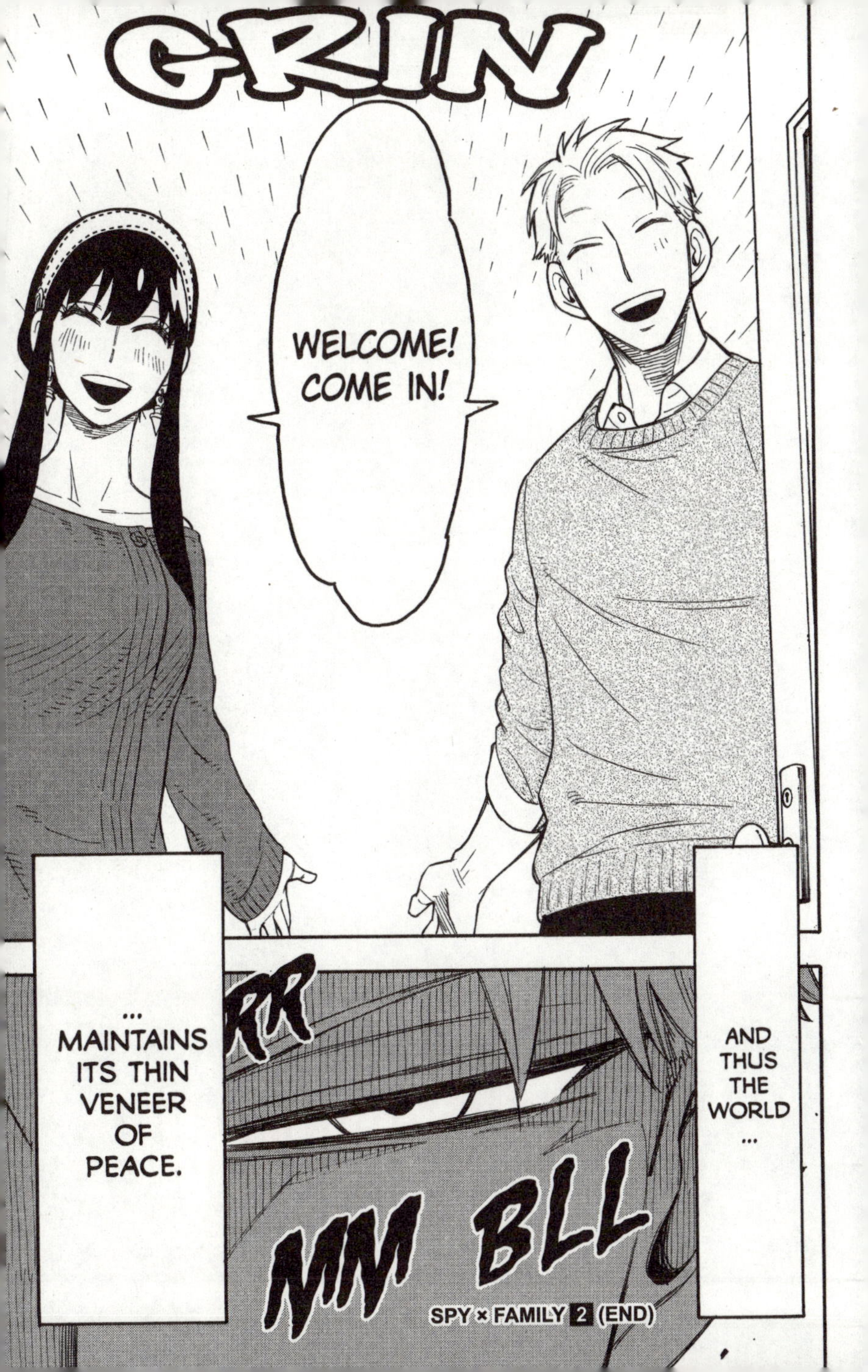
GRIN
WELCOME! COME IN!
AND THUS THE WORLD ...
RR
... MAINTAINS ITS THIN VENEER OF PEACE.
MM BLL
SPY × FAMILY 2 (END)

SPY×FAMILY

SPYxFAMILY CONFIDENTIAL FILES (BONUS)

TOP SECRET
EYES ONLY

FRANKY'S SECRET FILES

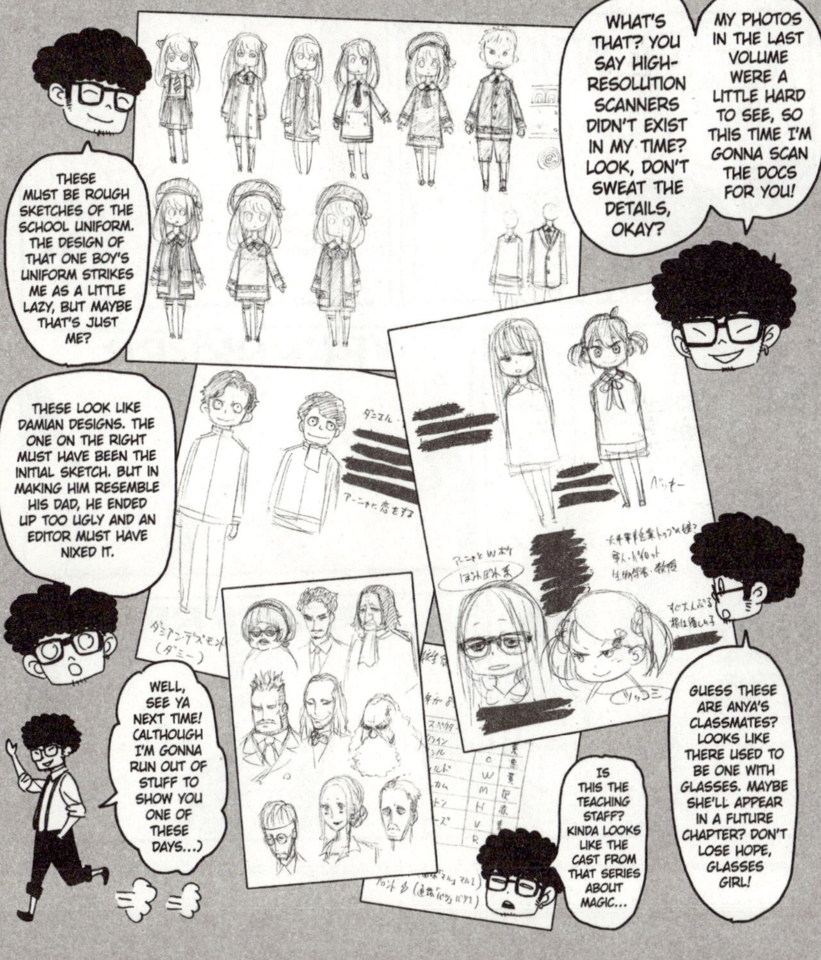
MY PHOTOS IN THE LAST VOLUME WERE A LITTLE HARD TO SEE, SO THIS TIME I'M GONNA SCAN THE DOCS FOR YOU!
WHAT'S THAT? YOU SAY HIGH-RESOLUTION SCANNERS DIDN'T EXIST IN MY TIME? LOOK, DON'T SWEAT THE DETAILS, OKAY?
THESE MUST BE ROUGH SKETCHES OF THE SCHOOL UNIFORM. THE DESIGN OF THAT ONE BOY'S UNIFORM STRIKES ME AS A LITTLE LAZY, BUT MAYBE THAT'S JUST ME?
THESE LOOK LIKE DAMIAN DESIGNS. THE ONE ON THE RIGHT MUST HAVE BEEN THE INITIAL SKETCH. BUT IN MAKING HIM RESEMBLE HIS DAD, HE ENDED UP TOO UGLY AND AN EDITOR MUST HAVE NIXED IT.
GUESS THESE ARE ANYA'S CLASSMATES? LOOKS LIKE THERE USED TO BE ONE WITH GLASSES. MAYBE SHE'LL APPEAR IN A FUTURE CHAPTER? DON'T LOSE HOPE, GLASSES GIRL!
IS THIS THE TEACHING STAFF? KINDA LOOKS LIKE THE CAST FROM THAT SERIES ABOUT MAGIC...
WELL, SEE YA NEXT TIME! (ALTHOUGH I'M GONNA RUN OUT OF STUFF TO SHOW YOU ONE OF THESE DAYS...)

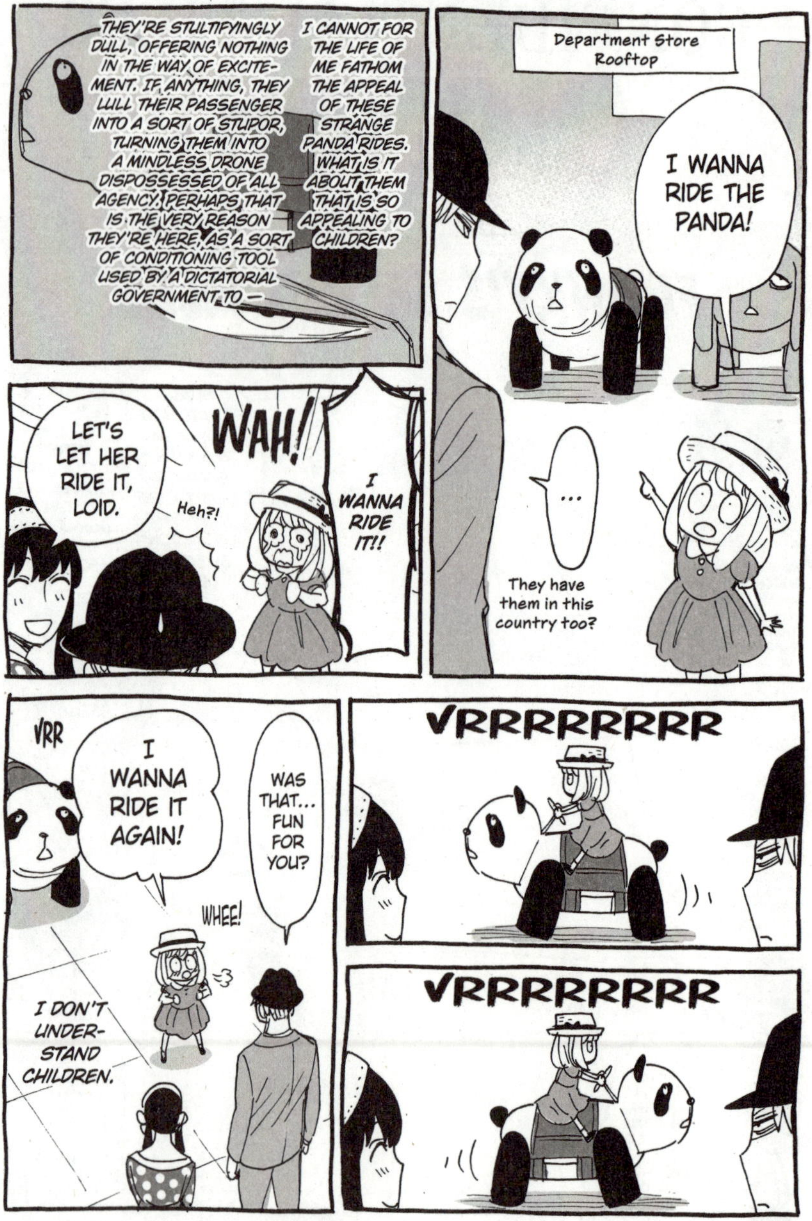
Department Store Rooftop
I WANNA RIDE THE PANDA!
...
They have them in this country too?
I CANNOT FOR THE LIFE OF ME FATHOM THE APPEAL OF THESE STRANGE PANDA RIDES. WHAT IS IT ABOUT THEM THAT IS SO APPEALING TO CHILDREN?
THEY'RE STULTIFYINGLY DULL, OFFERING NOTHING IN THE WAY OF EXCITE-MENT. IF ANYTHING, THEY LULL THEIR PASSENGER INTO A SORT OF STUPOR, TURNING THEM INTO A MINDLESS DRONE DISPOSSESSED OF ALL AGENCY. PERHAPS THAT IS THE VERY REASON THEY'RE HERE, AS A SORT OF CONDITIONING TOOL USED BY A DICTATORIAL GOVERNMENT TO—
I WANNA RIDE IT!!
WAH!
Heh?!
LET'S LET HER RIDE IT, LOID.
VRRRRRRRRR
VRRRRRRRRR
WAS THAT... FUN FOR YOU?
I WANNA RIDE IT AGAIN!
VRR
WHEE!
I DON'T UNDER-STAND CHILDREN.

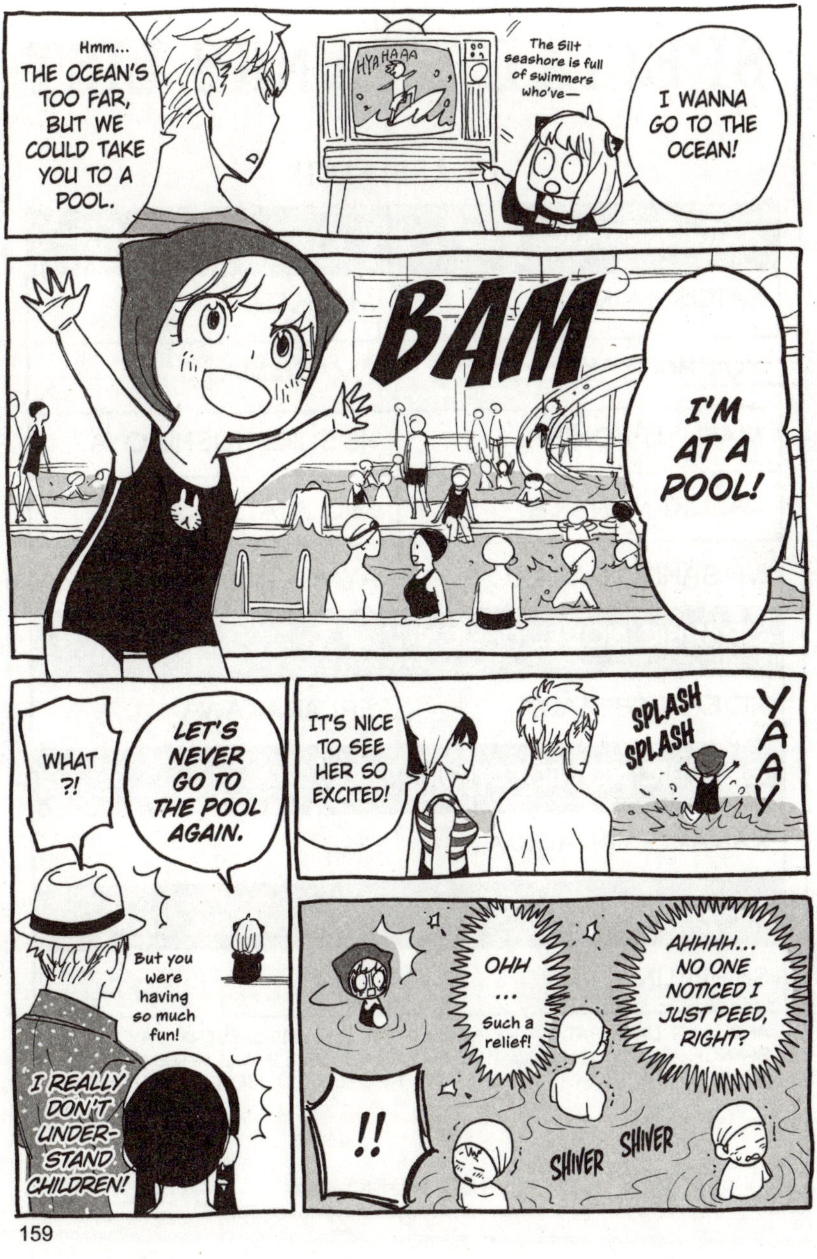

The Silt seashore is full of swimmers who've—
I WANNA GO TO THE OCEAN!
HYAHAAA
Hmm... THE OCEAN'S TOO FAR, BUT WE COULD TAKE YOU TO A POOL.
I'M AT A POOL!
BAM
YAAAY
SPLASH SPLASH
IT'S NICE TO SEE HER SO EXCITED!
AHHHH... NO ONE NOTICED I JUST PEED, RIGHT?
OHH... Such a relief!
!!
SHIVER
SHIVER
LET'S NEVER GO TO THE POOL AGAIN.
WHAT?!
But you were having so much fun!
I REALLY DON'T UNDER-STAND CHILDREN!

SPY×FAMILY VOL. 2
SPECIAL THANKS LIST

·CLASSIFIED·

ART ASSISTANCE	
SATOSHI KIMURA	MAEHATA
YUICHI OZAKI	AMASHIMA
MAFUYU KONISHI	KEISUKE HOSHINOYA
KAZUKI NONAKA	MIO AYATSUKA
MASAHITO SASAKI	AYAKA KATAYAMA
GRAPHIC NOVEL DESIGN	
HIDEAKI SHIMADA	ERI ARAKAWA
GRAPHIC NOVEL EDITOR	
KANAKO YANAGIDA	
MANAGING EDITOR	
SHIHEI LIN	

AND JUST LIKE THAT, WE'RE ALREADY AT VOLUME 2. EVERY DAY I BLANCH AT HOW QUICKLY TIME FLOWS. VOLUME 3 WILL PROBABLY BE HERE BEFORE I KNOW IT TOO, AND I HOPE WE'LL MEET AGAIN THERE.

—TATSUYA ENDO

EYES ONLY　　　　READ & ~~DESTROY~~　　　　EYES ONLY

SPY×FAMILY

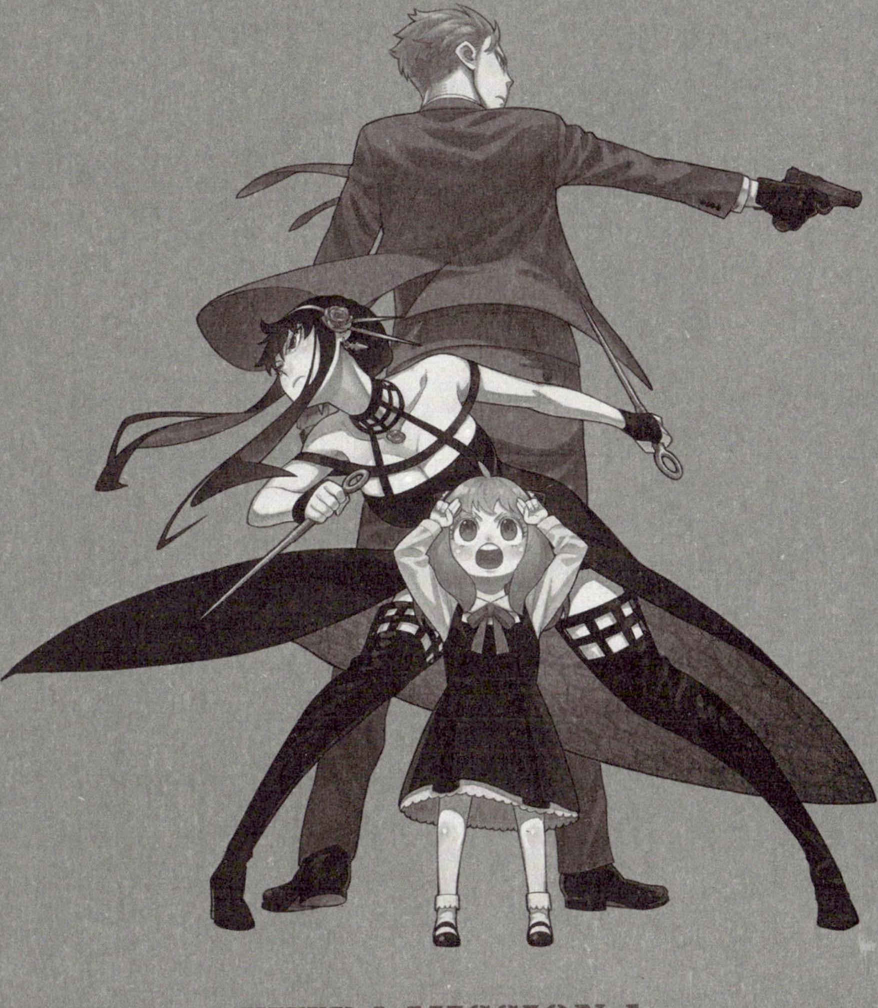

EXTRA MISSION 1

SPY×FAMILY

I WAS FORTUNATE ENOUGH TO HAVE THE
"EXTRA MISSION" THAT FOLLOWS PUBLISHED
AS A ONE-SHOT IN *WEEKLY SHONEN JUMP*.
WE PUT A LOT OF EFFORT INTO IT, SO
I ASKED TO HAVE IT INCLUDED HERE TOO.

THE STORY WAS DESIGNED AS AN
INTRODUCTION TO THE SERIES FOR READERS
WHO WERE NOT FAMILIAR WITH THE MANGA
FROM ITS RUN ON SHONEN JUMP+. IT WAS
PUBLISHED IN JULY, SO WE BASICALLY
IGNORED THE SEASONAL TIME FRAME OF
THE SERIES AND TRIED TO MAKE IT FEEL
A LITTLE MORE SUMMERY.

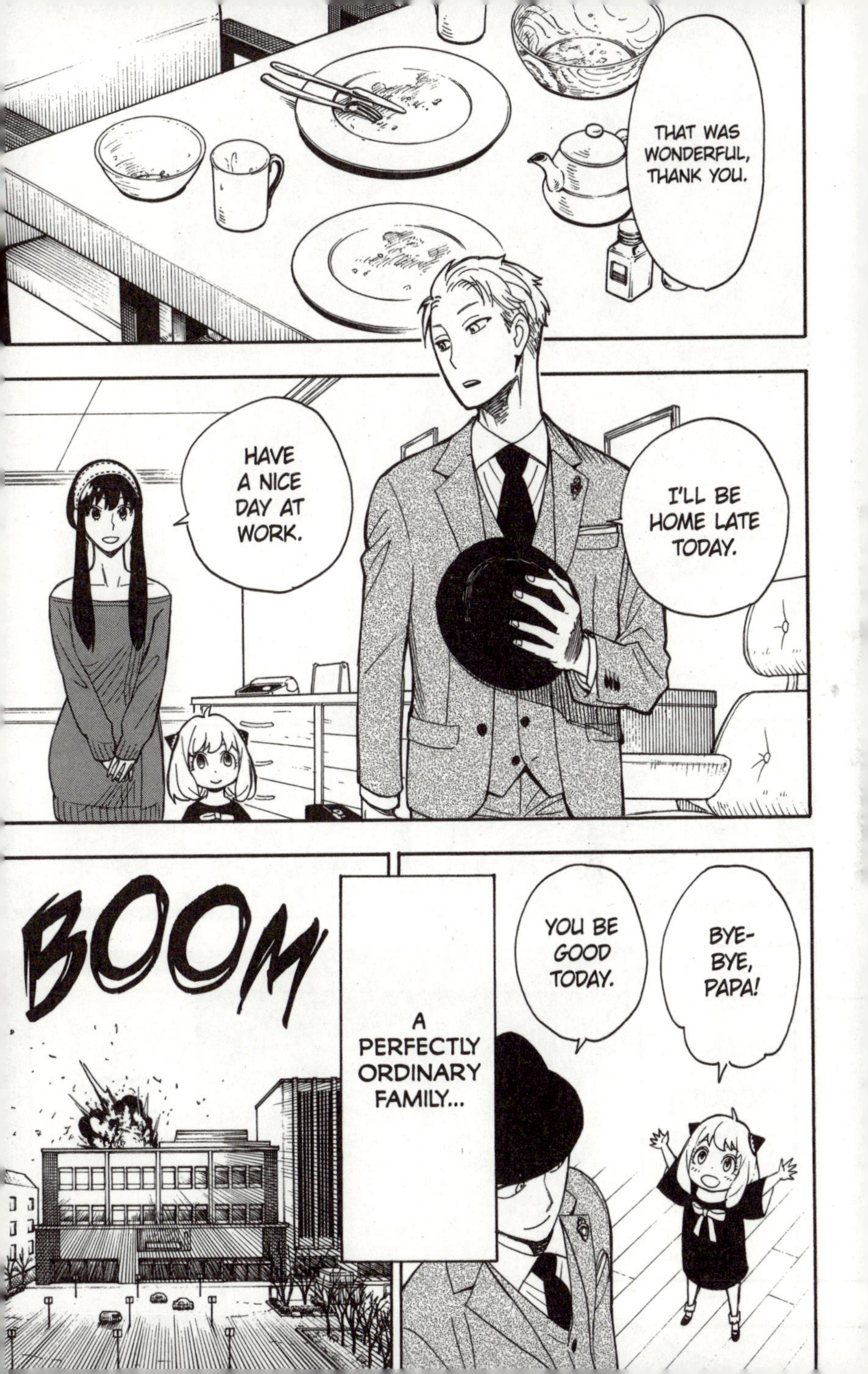
THAT WAS WONDERFUL, THANK YOU.
I'LL BE HOME LATE TODAY.
HAVE A NICE DAY AT WORK.
BYE-BYE, PAPA!
YOU BE GOOD TODAY.
A PERFECTLY ORDINARY FAMILY...
BOOM

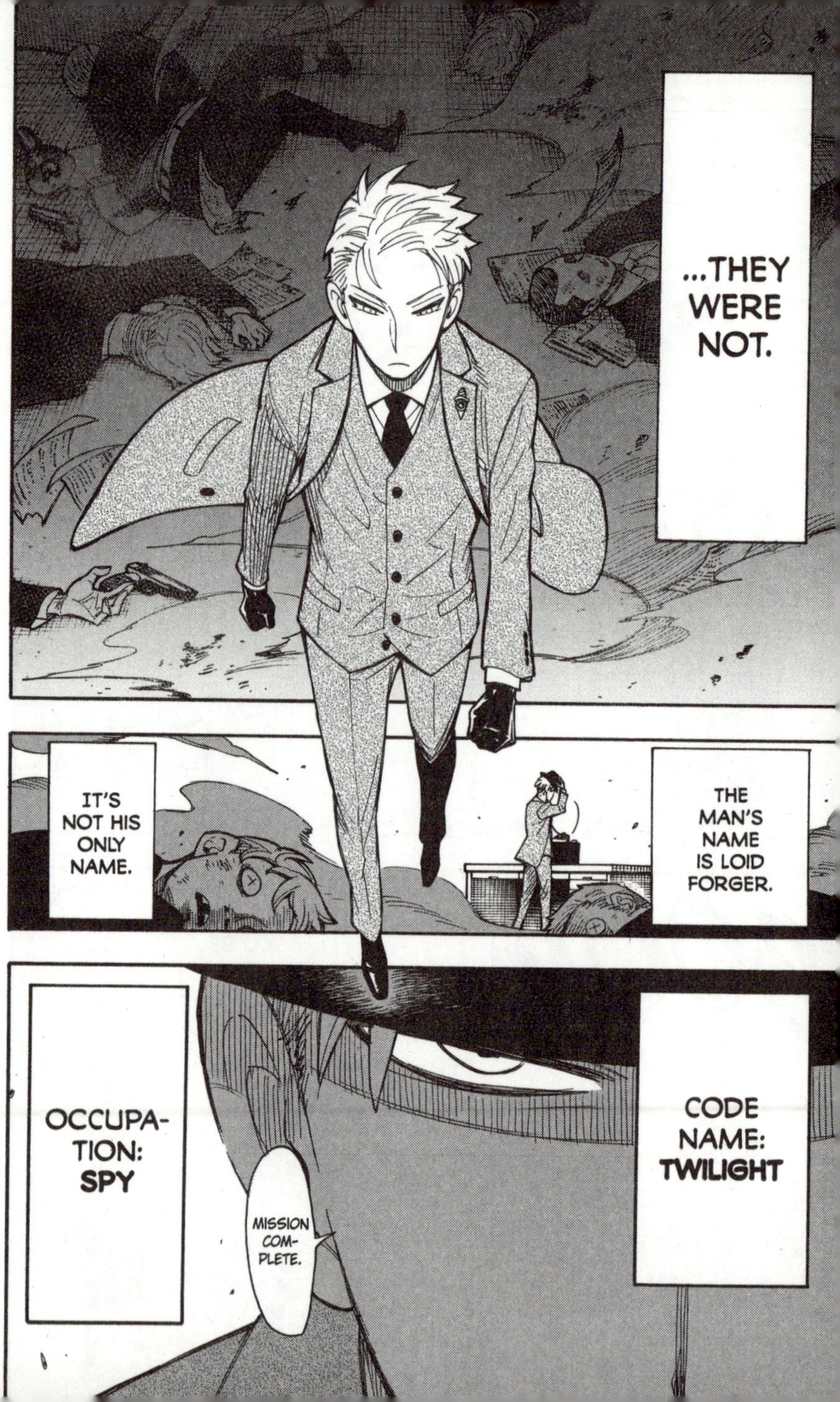
...THEY WERE NOT.
THE MAN'S NAME IS LOID FORGER.
IT'S NOT HIS ONLY NAME.
CODE NAME: **TWILIGHT**
OCCUPATION: **SPY**
MISSION COMPLETE.

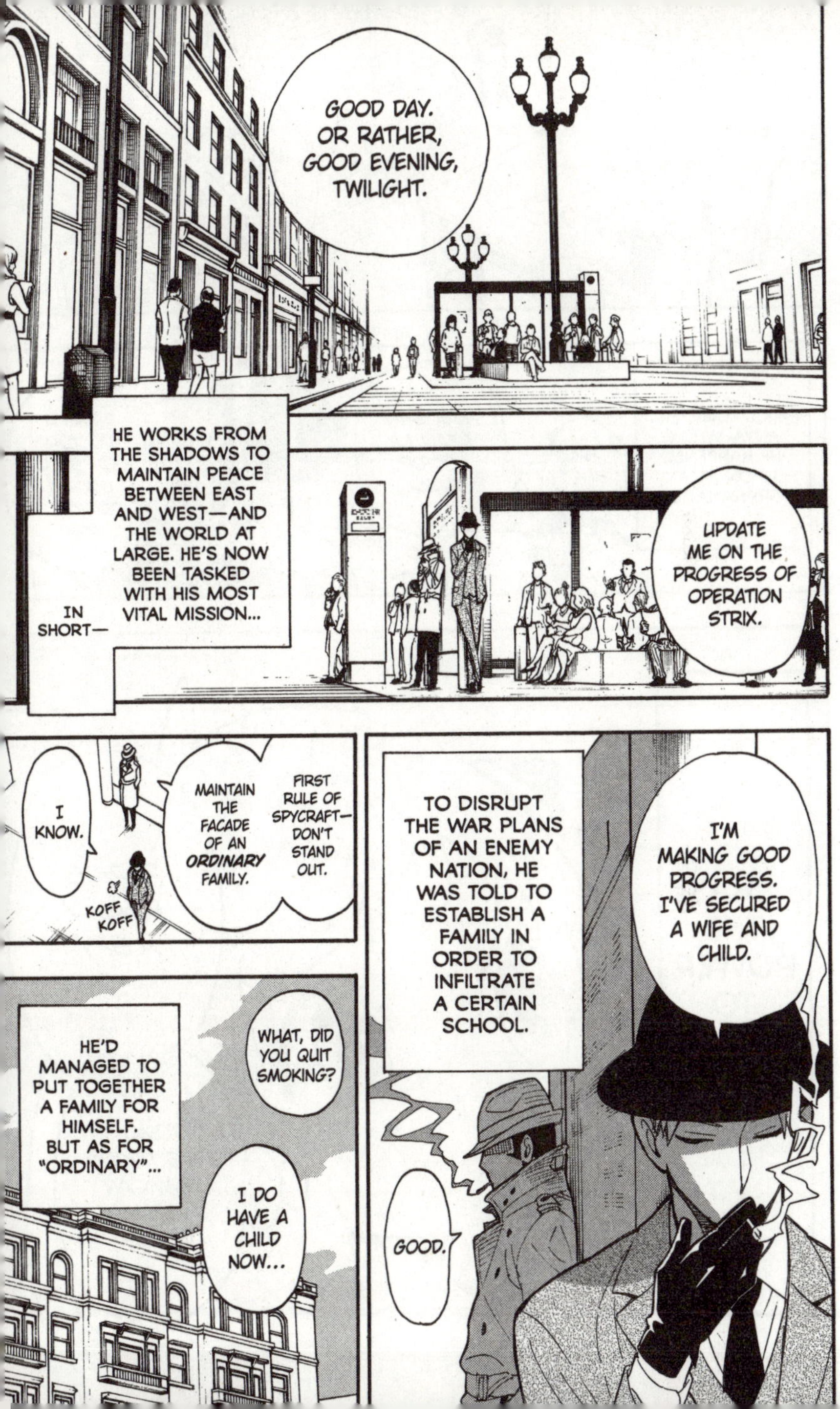
GOOD DAY. OR RATHER, GOOD EVENING, TWILIGHT.
UPDATE ME ON THE PROGRESS OF OPERATION STRIX.
HE WORKS FROM THE SHADOWS TO MAINTAIN PEACE BETWEEN EAST AND WEST—AND THE WORLD AT LARGE. HE'S NOW BEEN TASKED WITH HIS MOST VITAL MISSION...
IN SHORT—
I'M MAKING GOOD PROGRESS. I'VE SECURED A WIFE AND CHILD.
TO DISRUPT THE WAR PLANS OF AN ENEMY NATION, HE WAS TOLD TO ESTABLISH A FAMILY IN ORDER TO INFILTRATE A CERTAIN SCHOOL.
GOOD.
FIRST RULE OF SPYCRAFT—DON'T STAND OUT.
MAINTAIN THE FACADE OF AN *ORDINARY* FAMILY.
I KNOW.
KOFF KOFF
WHAT, DID YOU QUIT SMOKING?
I DO HAVE A CHILD NOW...
HE'D MANAGED TO PUT TOGETHER A FAMILY FOR HIMSELF. BUT AS FOR "ORDINARY"...

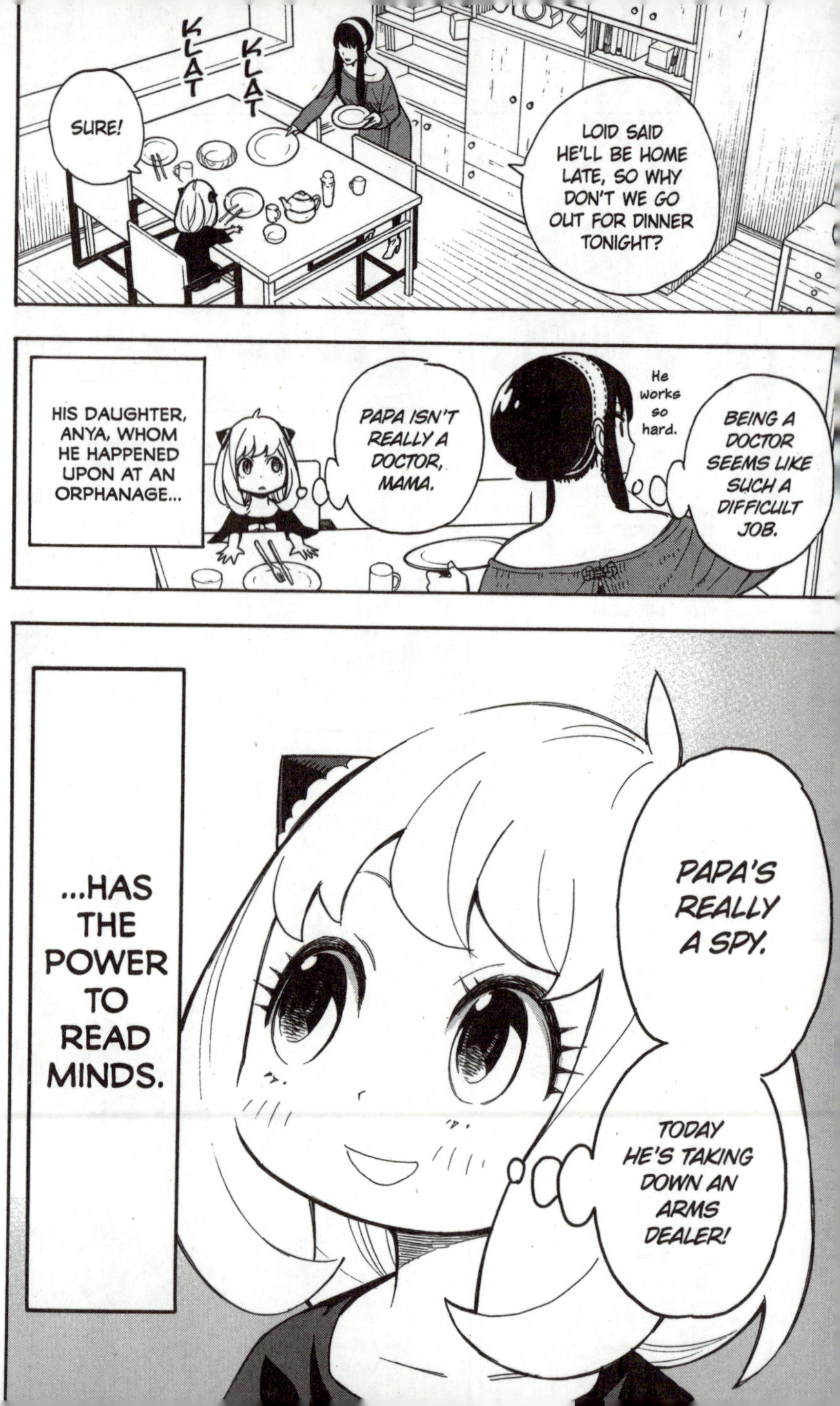
LOID SAID HE'LL BE HOME LATE, SO WHY DON'T WE GO OUT FOR DINNER TONIGHT?
KLAT KLAT
SURE!
BEING A DOCTOR SEEMS LIKE SUCH A DIFFICULT JOB.
He works so hard.
PAPA ISN'T REALLY A DOCTOR, MAMA.
HIS DAUGHTER, ANYA, WHOM HE HAPPENED UPON AT AN ORPHANAGE...
PAPA'S REALLY A SPY.
TODAY HE'S TAKING DOWN AN ARMS DEALER!
...HAS THE POWER TO READ MINDS.

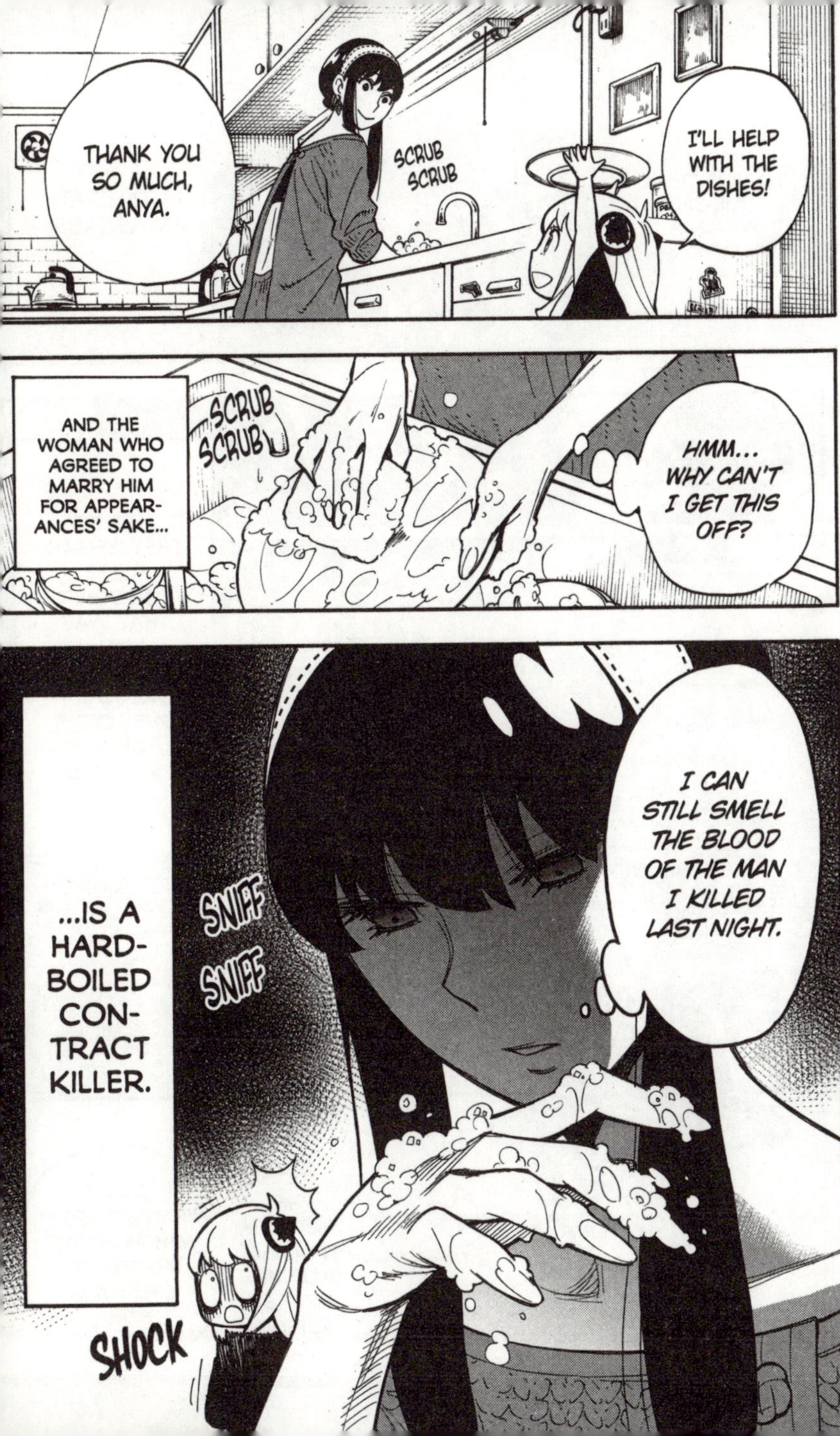
I'LL HELP WITH THE DISHES!
SCRUB SCRUB
THANK YOU SO MUCH, ANYA.
HMM... WHY CAN'T I GET THIS OFF?
SCRUB SCRUB
AND THE WOMAN WHO AGREED TO MARRY HIM FOR APPEARANCES' SAKE...
I CAN STILL SMELL THE BLOOD OF THE MAN I KILLED LAST NIGHT.
SNIFF SNIFF
...IS A HARD-BOILED CONTRACT KILLER.
SHOCK

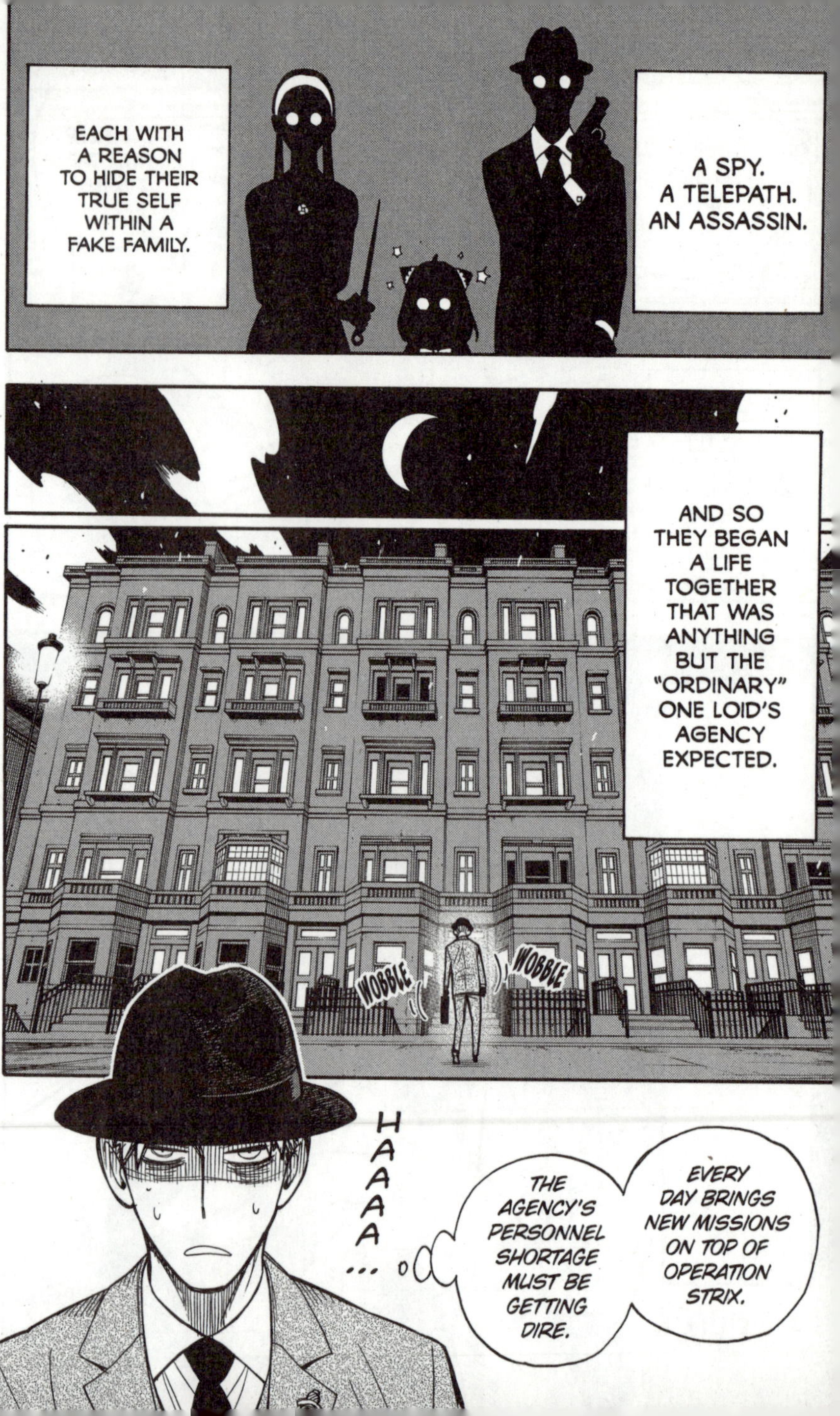
A SPY. A TELEPATH. AN ASSASSIN.
EACH WITH A REASON TO HIDE THEIR TRUE SELF WITHIN A FAKE FAMILY.
AND SO THEY BEGAN A LIFE TOGETHER THAT WAS ANYTHING BUT THE "ORDINARY" ONE LOID'S AGENCY EXPECTED.
WOBBLE
WOBBLE
EVERY DAY BRINGS NEW MISSIONS ON TOP OF OPERATION STRIX.
THE AGENCY'S PERSONNEL SHORTAGE MUST BE GETTING DIRE.
HAAAAA...

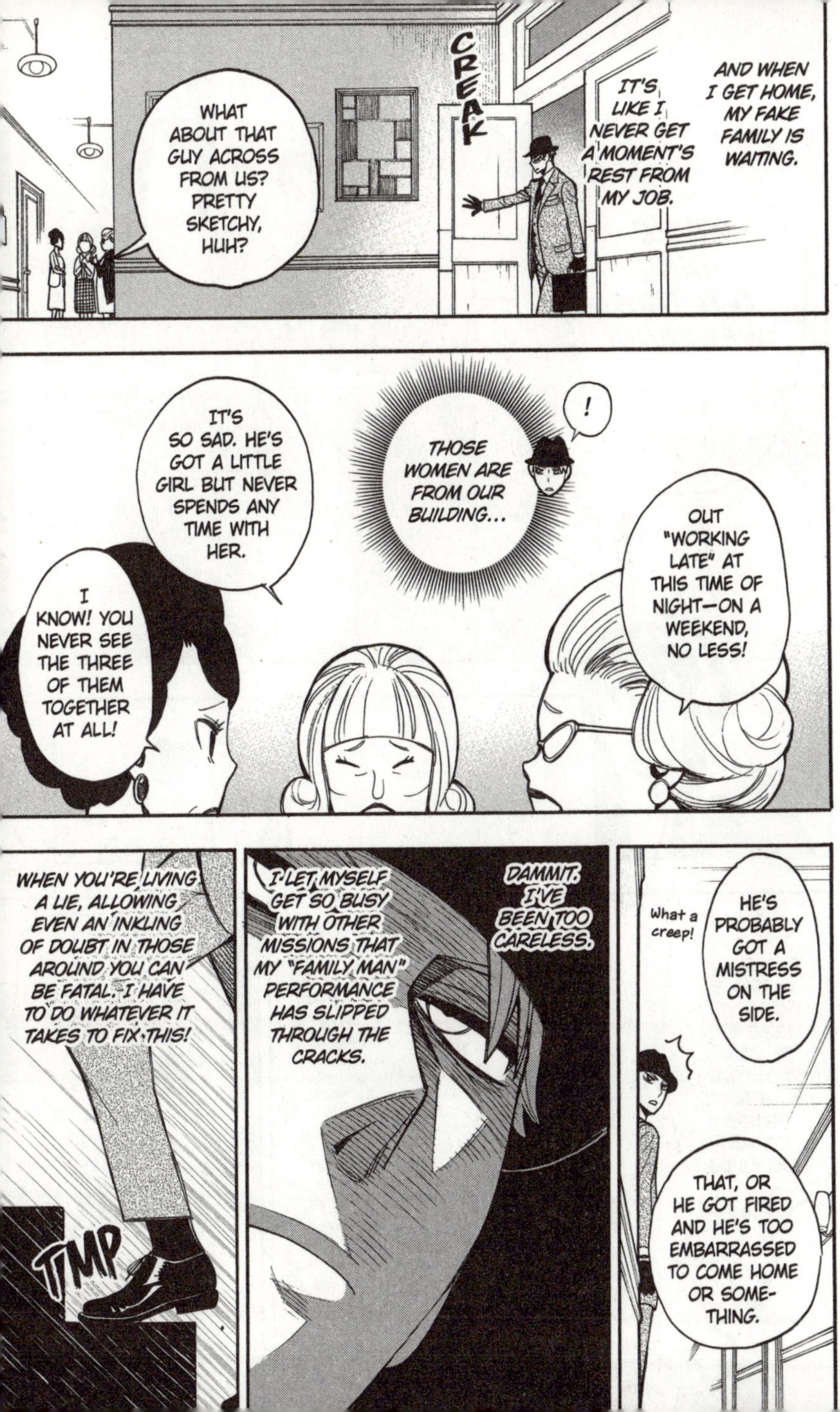
AND WHEN I GET HOME, MY FAKE FAMILY IS WAITING.
IT'S LIKE I NEVER GET A MOMENT'S REST FROM MY JOB.
CREAK
WHAT ABOUT THAT GUY ACROSS FROM US? PRETTY SKETCHY, HUH?
!
THOSE WOMEN ARE FROM OUR BUILDING...
OUT "WORKING LATE" AT THIS TIME OF NIGHT—ON A WEEKEND, NO LESS!
IT'S SO SAD. HE'S GOT A LITTLE GIRL BUT NEVER SPENDS ANY TIME WITH HER.
I KNOW! YOU NEVER SEE THE THREE OF THEM TOGETHER AT ALL!
HE'S PROBABLY GOT A MISTRESS ON THE SIDE.
What a creep!
THAT, OR HE GOT FIRED AND HE'S TOO EMBARRASSED TO COME HOME OR SOME-THING.
DAMMIT. I'VE BEEN TOO CARELESS.
I LET MYSELF GET SO BUSY WITH OTHER MISSIONS THAT MY "FAMILY MAN" PERFORMANCE HAS SLIPPED THROUGH THE CRACKS.
WHEN YOU'RE LIVING A LIE, ALLOWING EVEN AN INKLING OF DOUBT IN THOSE AROUND YOU CAN BE FATAL. I HAVE TO DO WHATEVER IT TAKES TO FIX THIS!
TMP

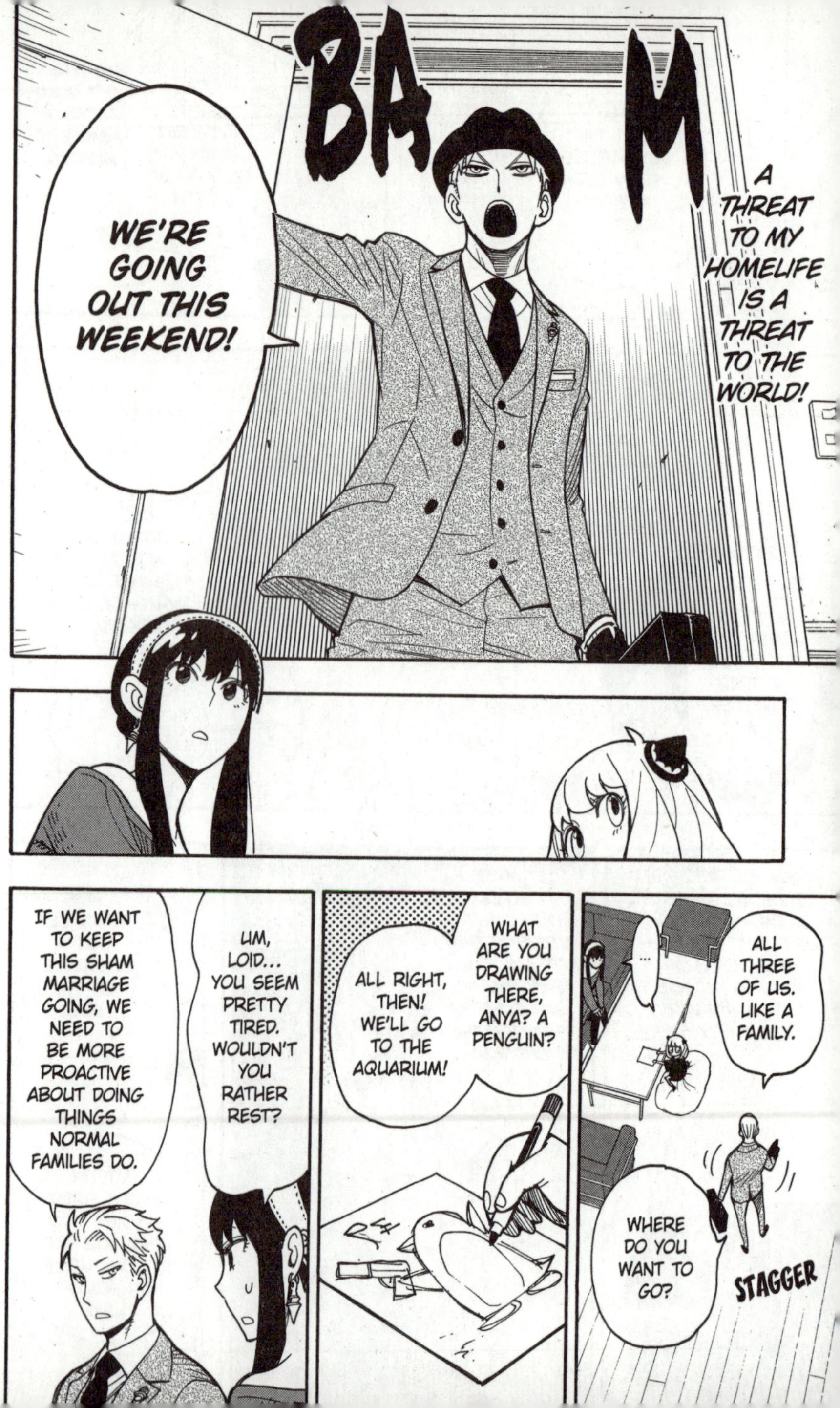
BAM
A THREAT TO MY HOMELIFE IS A THREAT TO THE WORLD!
WE'RE GOING OUT THIS WEEKEND!
ALL THREE OF US. LIKE A FAMILY.
...
WHERE DO YOU WANT TO GO?
STAGGER
WHAT ARE YOU DRAWING THERE, ANYA? A PENGUIN?
ALL RIGHT, THEN! WE'LL GO TO THE AQUARIUM!
UM, LOID... YOU SEEM PRETTY TIRED. WOULDN'T YOU RATHER REST?
IF WE WANT TO KEEP THIS SHAM MARRIAGE GOING, WE NEED TO BE MORE PROACTIVE ABOUT DOING THINGS NORMAL FAMILIES DO.

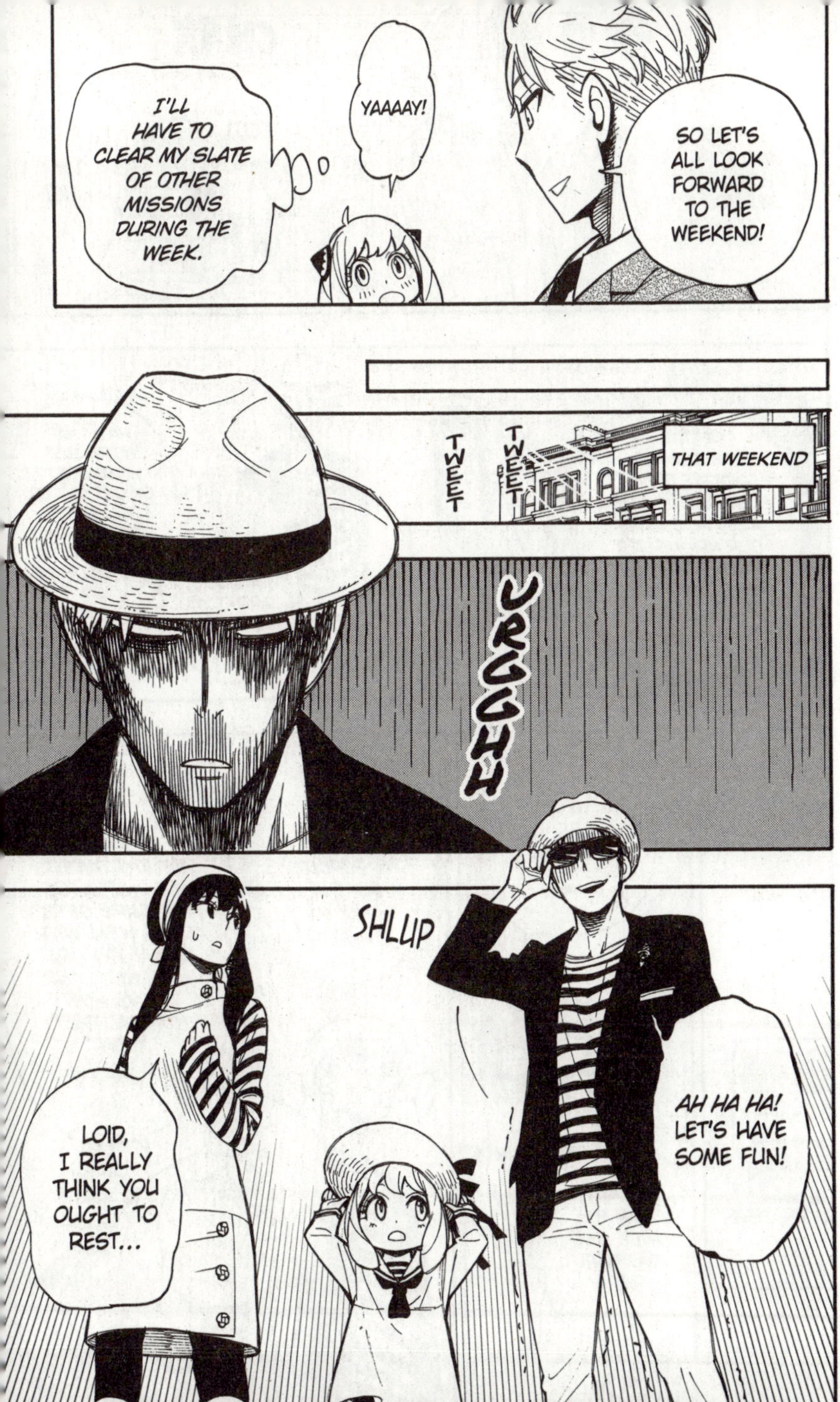
SO LET'S ALL LOOK FORWARD TO THE WEEKEND!
YAAAAY!
I'LL HAVE TO CLEAR MY SLATE OF OTHER MISSIONS DURING THE WEEK.
THAT WEEKEND
TWEET TWEET
URGGHH
SHLUP
AH HA HA! LET'S HAVE SOME FUN!
LOID, I REALLY THINK YOU OUGHT TO REST...

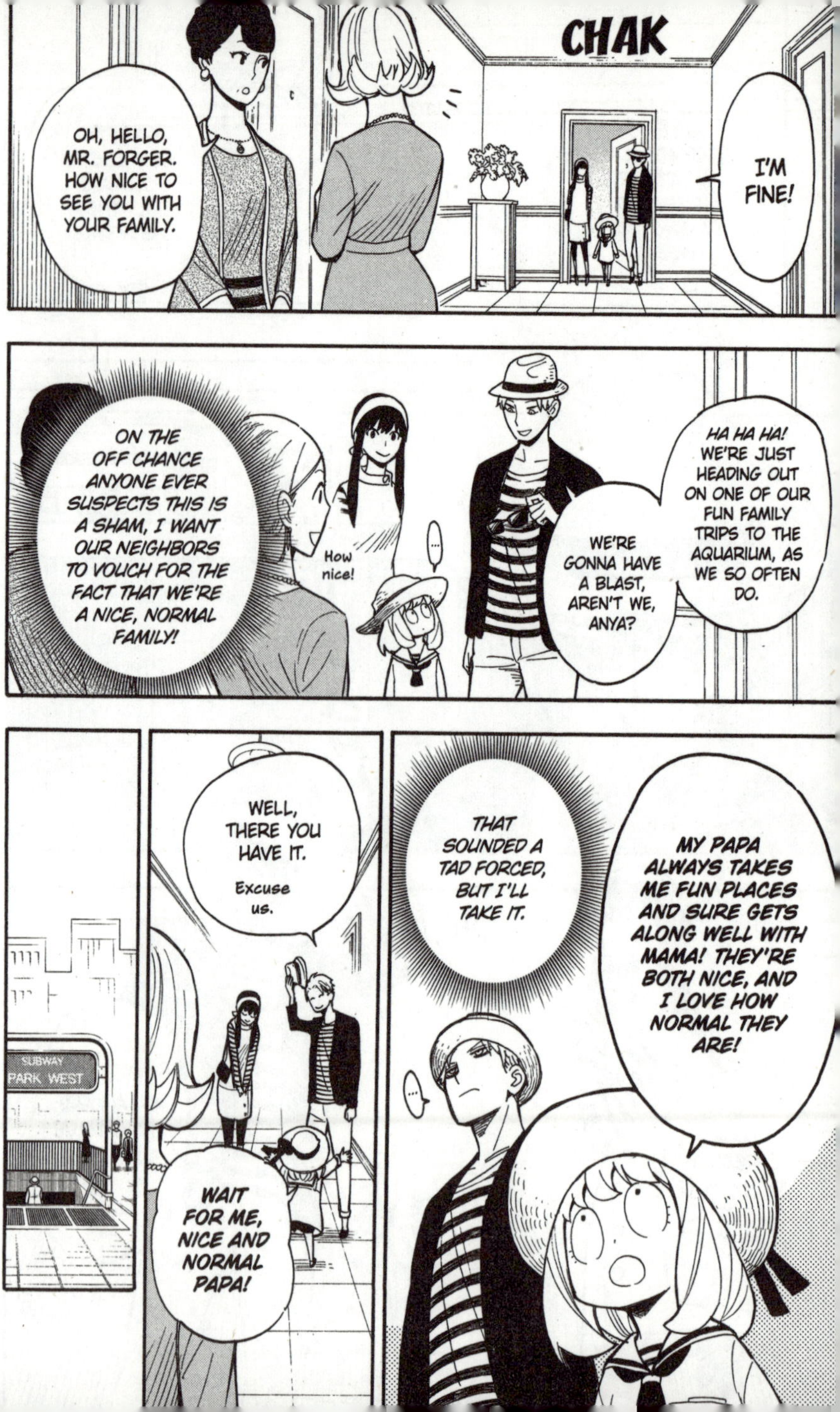
CHAK
I'M FINE!
OH, HELLO, MR. FORGER. HOW NICE TO SEE YOU WITH YOUR FAMILY.
HA HA HA! WE'RE JUST HEADING OUT ON ONE OF OUR FUN FAMILY TRIPS TO THE AQUARIUM, AS WE SO OFTEN DO.
WE'RE GONNA HAVE A BLAST, AREN'T WE, ANYA?
...
How nice!
ON THE OFF CHANCE ANYONE EVER SUSPECTS THIS IS A SHAM, I WANT OUR NEIGHBORS TO VOUCH FOR THE FACT THAT WE'RE A NICE, NORMAL FAMILY!
MY PAPA ALWAYS TAKES ME FUN PLACES AND SURE GETS ALONG WELL WITH MAMA! THEY'RE BOTH NICE, AND I LOVE HOW NORMAL THEY ARE!
THAT SOUNDED A TAD FORCED, BUT I'LL TAKE IT.
...
WELL, THERE YOU HAVE IT.
Excuse us.
WAIT FOR ME, NICE AND NORMAL PAPA!
SUBWAY
PARK WEST

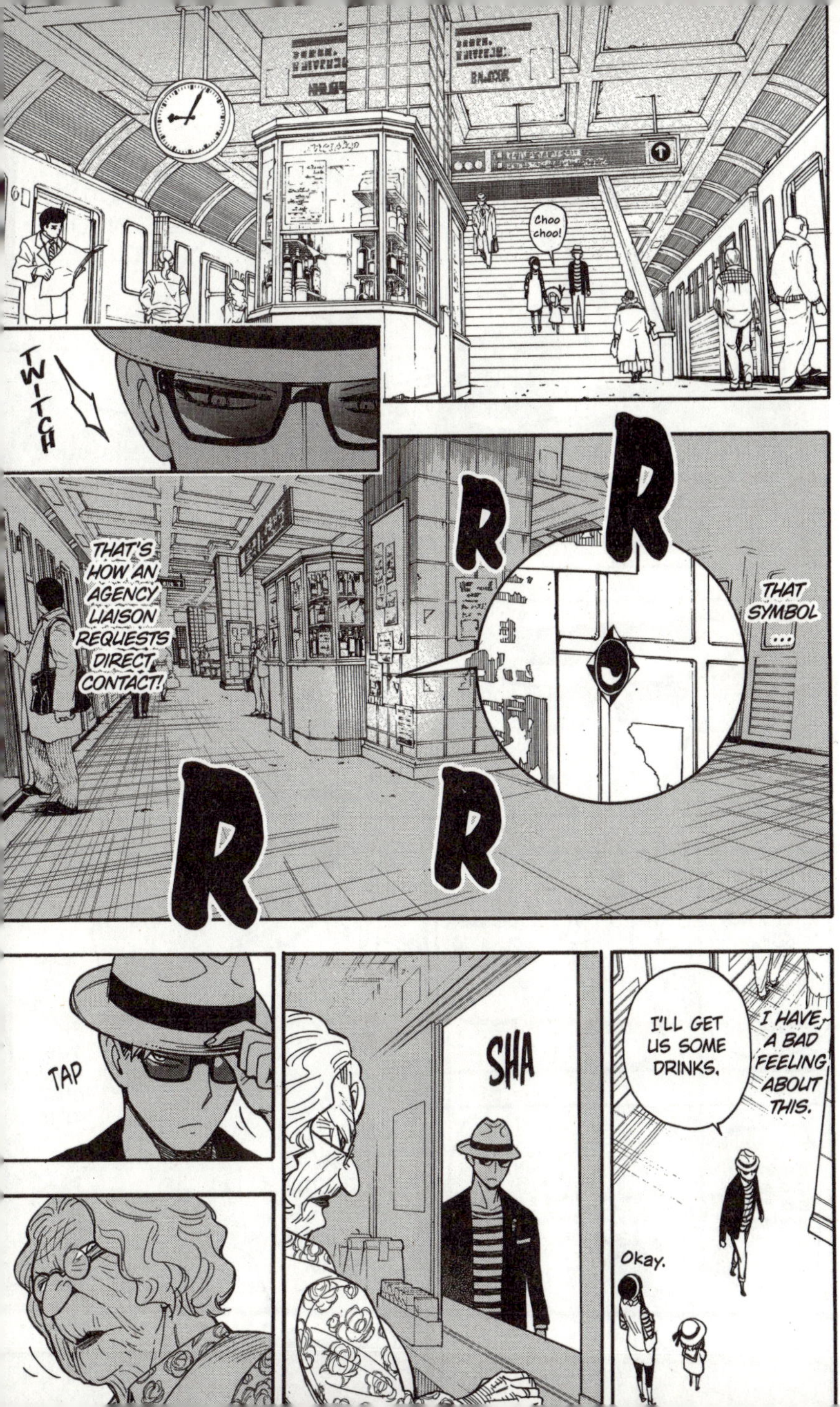
Choo choo!
TWITCH
R R
THAT SYMBOL...
THAT'S HOW AN AGENCY LIAISON REQUESTS DIRECT CONTACT!
R R
I HAVE A BAD FEELING ABOUT THIS.
I'LL GET US SOME DRINKS.
Okay.
SHA
TAP

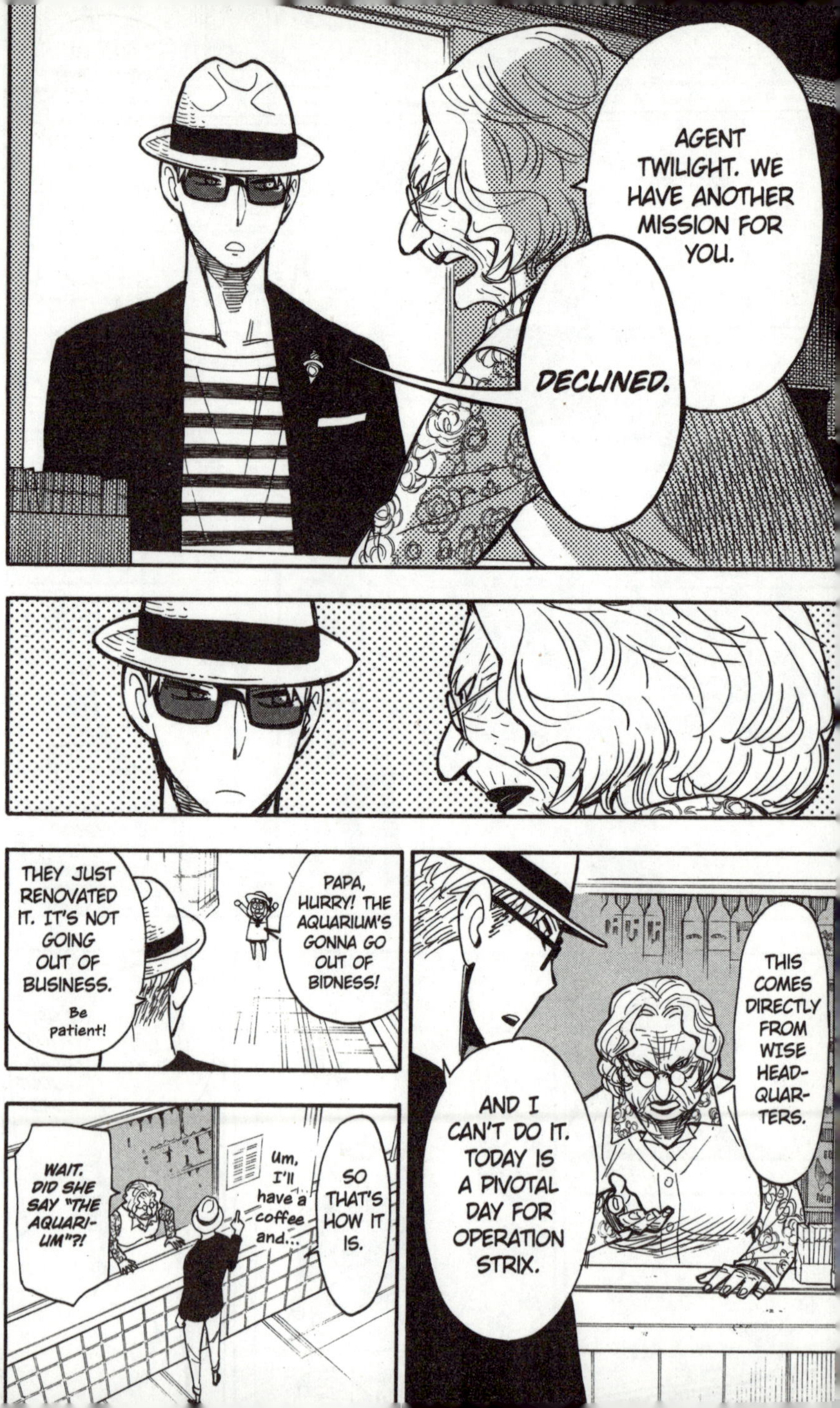
AGENT TWILIGHT. WE HAVE ANOTHER MISSION FOR YOU.
DECLINED.
THIS COMES DIRECTLY FROM WISE HEAD-QUARTERS.
AND I CAN'T DO IT. TODAY IS A PIVOTAL DAY FOR OPERATION STRIX.
PAPA, HURRY! THE AQUARIUM'S GONNA GO OUT OF BIDNESS!
THEY JUST RENOVATED IT. IT'S NOT GOING OUT OF BUSINESS.
Be patient!
SO THAT'S HOW IT IS.
Um, I'll have a coffee and...
WAIT. DID SHE SAY "THE AQUARIUM"?!

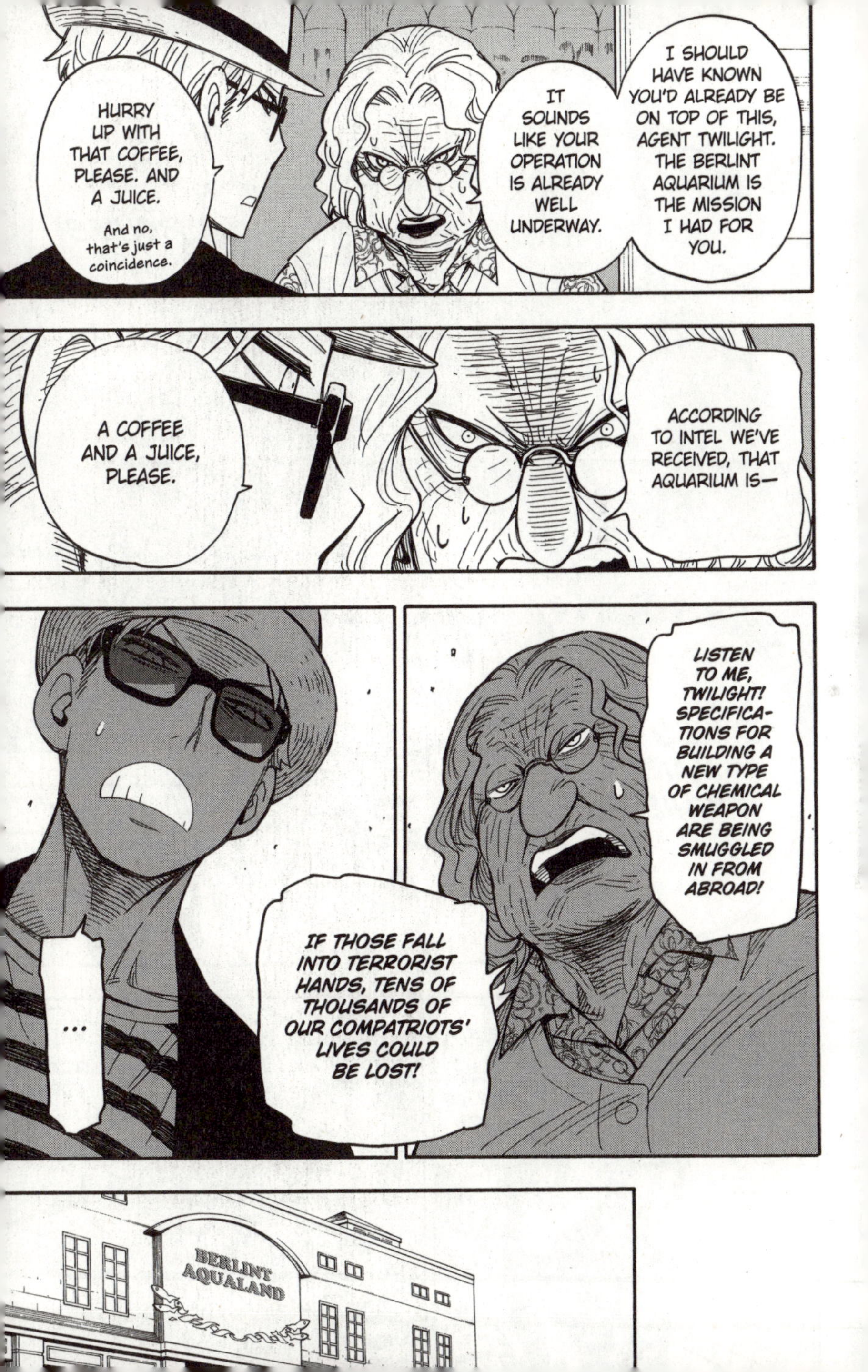
I SHOULD HAVE KNOWN YOU'D ALREADY BE ON TOP OF THIS, AGENT TWILIGHT. THE BERLINT AQUARIUM IS THE MISSION I HAD FOR YOU.
IT SOUNDS LIKE YOUR OPERATION IS ALREADY WELL UNDERWAY.
HURRY UP WITH THAT COFFEE, PLEASE. AND A JUICE.
And no, that's just a coincidence.
ACCORDING TO INTEL WE'VE RECEIVED, THAT AQUARIUM IS—
A COFFEE AND A JUICE, PLEASE.
LISTEN TO ME, TWILIGHT! SPECIFICA-TIONS FOR BUILDING A NEW TYPE OF CHEMICAL WEAPON ARE BEING SMUGGLED IN FROM ABROAD!
IF THOSE FALL INTO TERRORIST HANDS, TENS OF THOUSANDS OF OUR COMPATRIOTS' LIVES COULD BE LOST!
...
BERLINT AQUALAND

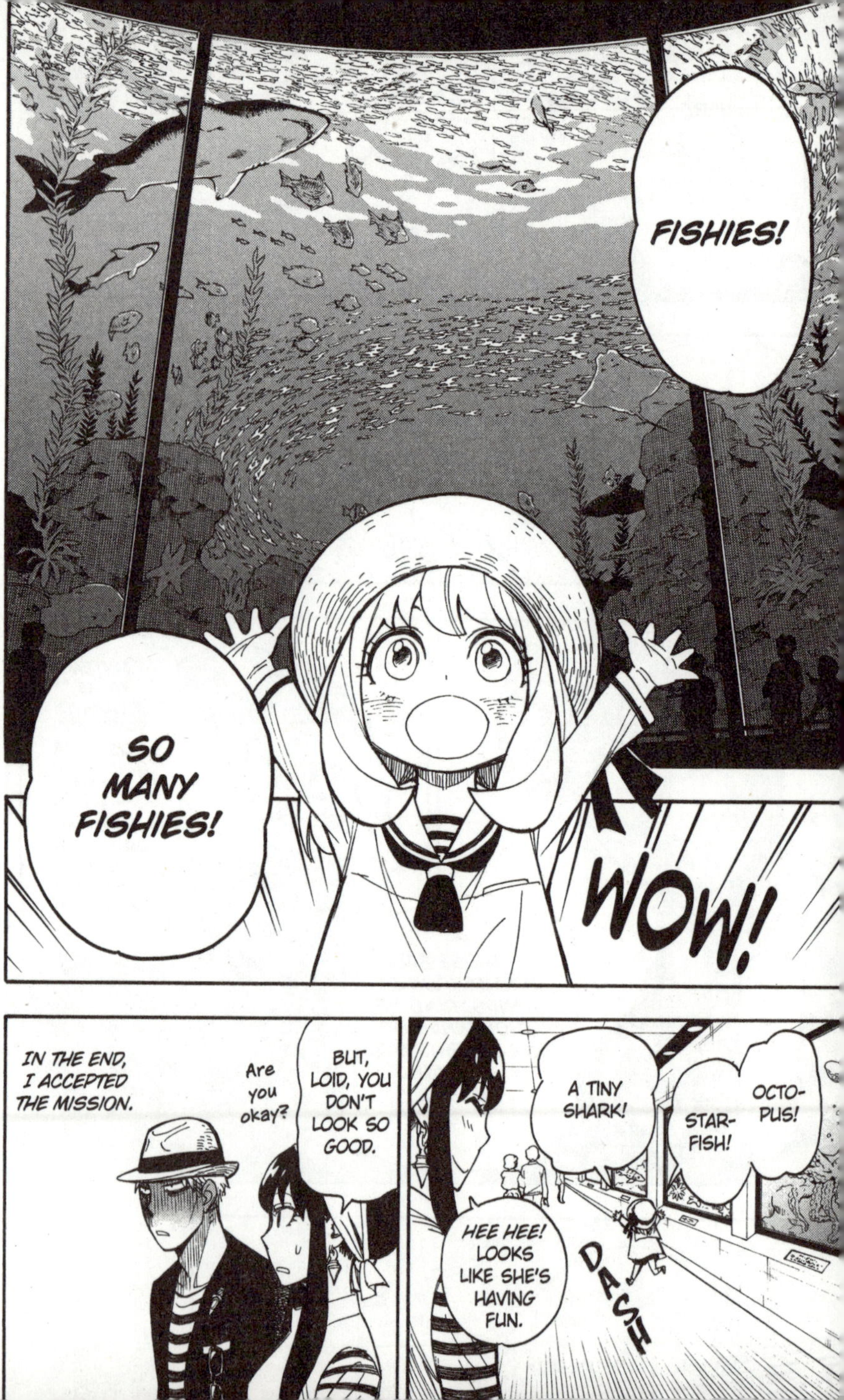
FISHIES!
SO MANY FISHIES!
WOW!
OCTO-PUS!
STAR-FISH!
A TINY SHARK!
DASH
HEE HEE! LOOKS LIKE SHE'S HAVING FUN.
BUT, LOID, YOU DON'T LOOK SO GOOD.
Are you okay?
IN THE END, I ACCEPTED THE MISSION.

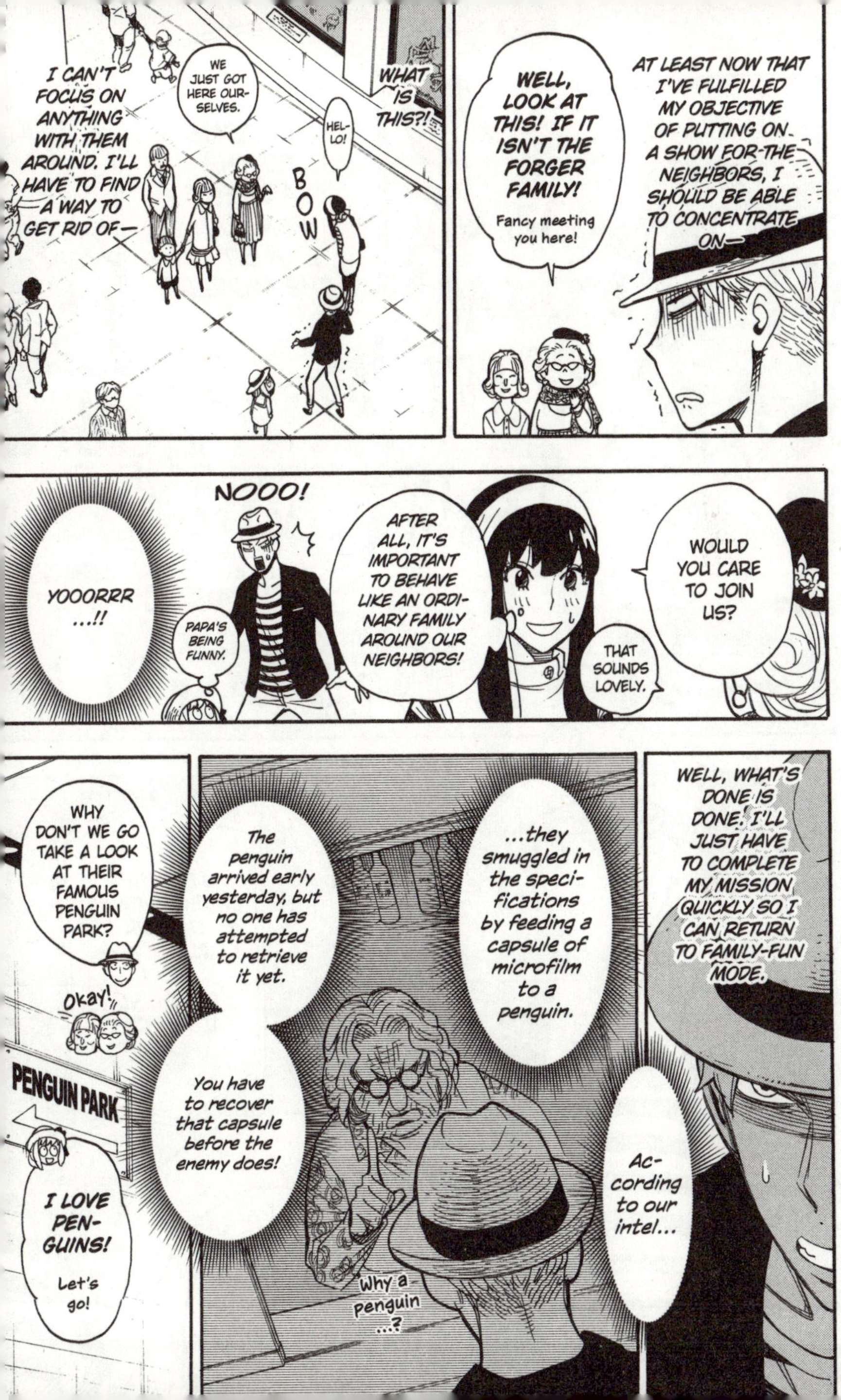
AT LEAST NOW THAT I'VE FULFILLED MY OBJECTIVE OF PUTTING ON A SHOW FOR THE NEIGHBORS, I SHOULD BE ABLE TO CONCENTRATE ON—
WELL, LOOK AT THIS! IF IT ISN'T THE FORGER FAMILY!
Fancy meeting you here!
WHAT IS THIS?!
WE JUST GOT HERE OURSELVES.
HEL-LO!
BOW
I CAN'T FOCUS ON ANYTHING WITH THEM AROUND. I'LL HAVE TO FIND A WAY TO GET RID OF—
WOULD YOU CARE TO JOIN US?
THAT SOUNDS LOVELY.
AFTER ALL, IT'S IMPORTANT TO BEHAVE LIKE AN ORDINARY FAMILY AROUND OUR NEIGHBORS!
NOOO!
PAPA'S BEING FUNNY.
YOOORRR ...!!
WELL, WHAT'S DONE IS DONE. I'LL JUST HAVE TO COMPLETE MY MISSION QUICKLY SO I CAN RETURN TO FAMILY-FUN MODE.
According to our intel...
...they smuggled in the specifications by feeding a capsule of microfilm to a penguin.
The penguin arrived early yesterday, but no one has attempted to retrieve it yet.
You have to recover that capsule before the enemy does!
Why a penguin ...?
WHY DON'T WE GO TAKE A LOOK AT THEIR FAMOUS PENGUIN PARK?
Okay!
PENGUIN PARK
I LOVE PENGUINS!
Let's go!

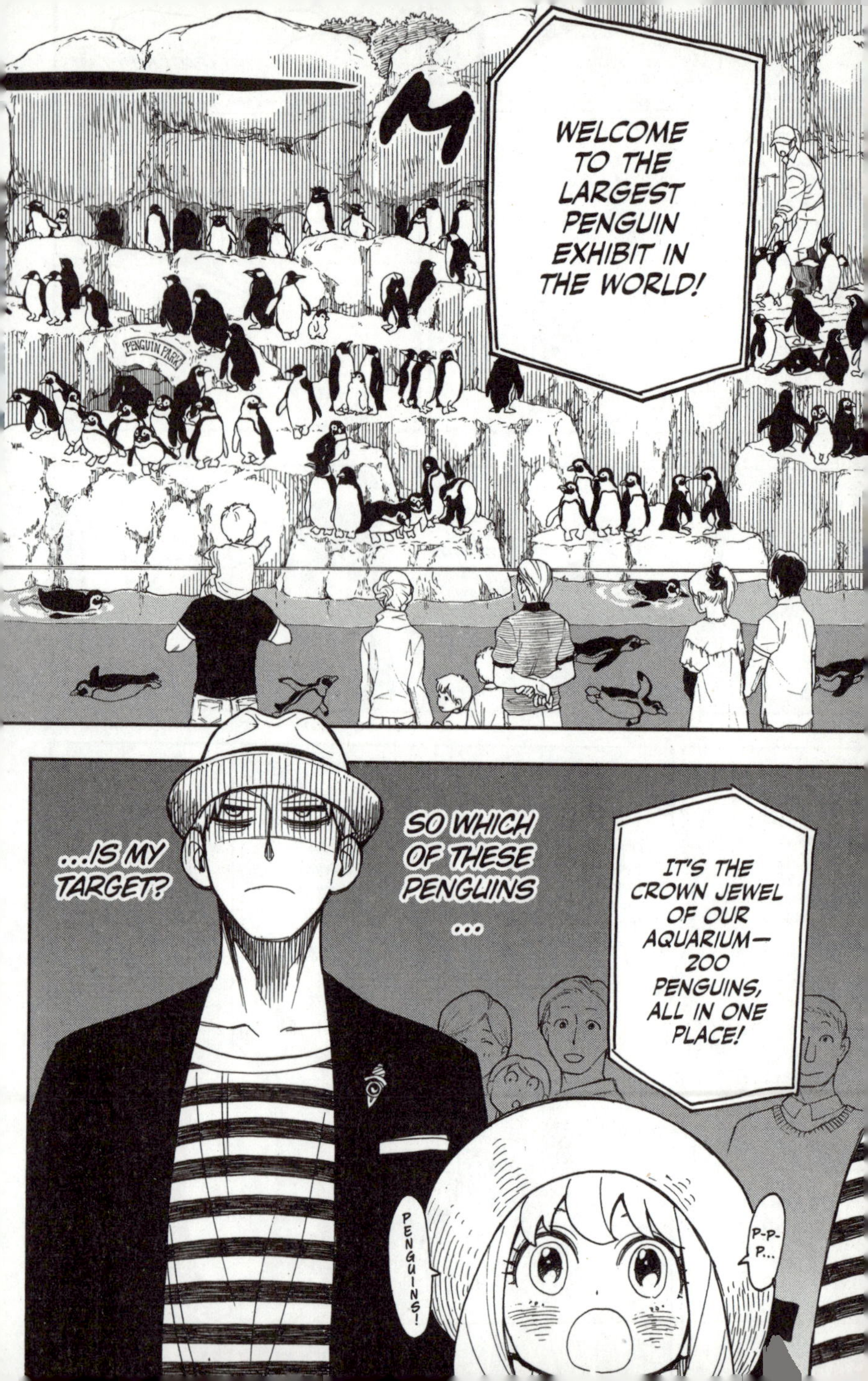
PENGUIN PARK
WELCOME TO THE LARGEST PENGUIN EXHIBIT IN THE WORLD!
IT'S THE CROWN JEWEL OF OUR AQUARIUM-ZOO PENGUINS, ALL IN ONE PLACE!
SO WHICH OF THESE PENGUINS ...
...IS MY TARGET?
P-P-P...
PENGUINS!

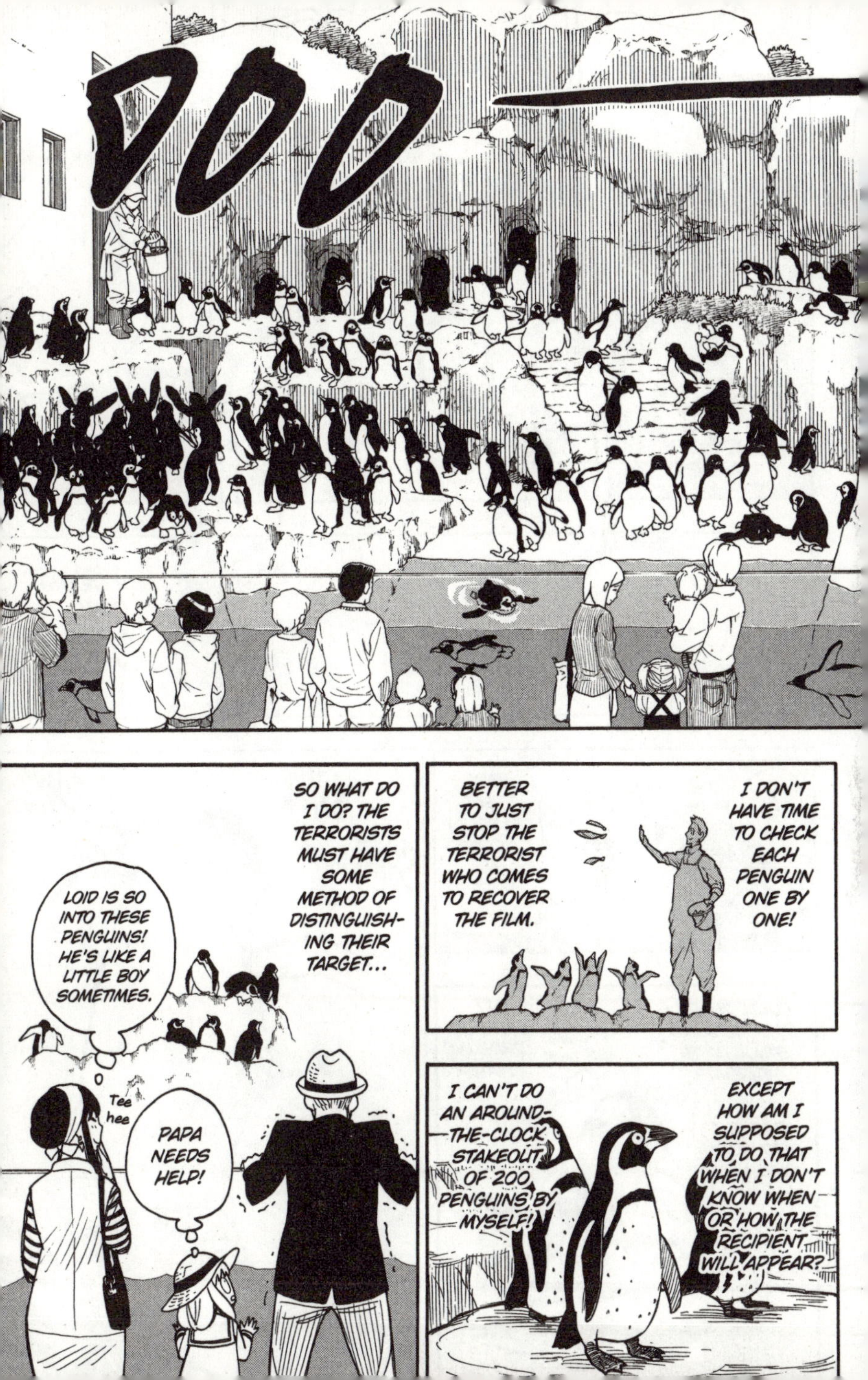
DOOO
I DON'T HAVE TIME TO CHECK EACH PENGUIN ONE BY ONE!
BETTER TO JUST STOP THE TERRORIST WHO COMES TO RECOVER THE FILM.
EXCEPT HOW AM I SUPPOSED TO DO THAT WHEN I DON'T KNOW WHEN OR HOW THE RECIPIENT WILL APPEAR?
I CAN'T DO AN AROUND-THE-CLOCK STAKEOUT OF 200 PENGUINS BY MYSELF!
SO WHAT DO I DO? THE TERRORISTS MUST HAVE SOME METHOD OF DISTINGUISHING THEIR TARGET...
LOID IS SO INTO THESE PENGUINS! HE'S LIKE A LITTLE BOY SOMETIMES.
Tee hee
PAPA NEEDS HELP!

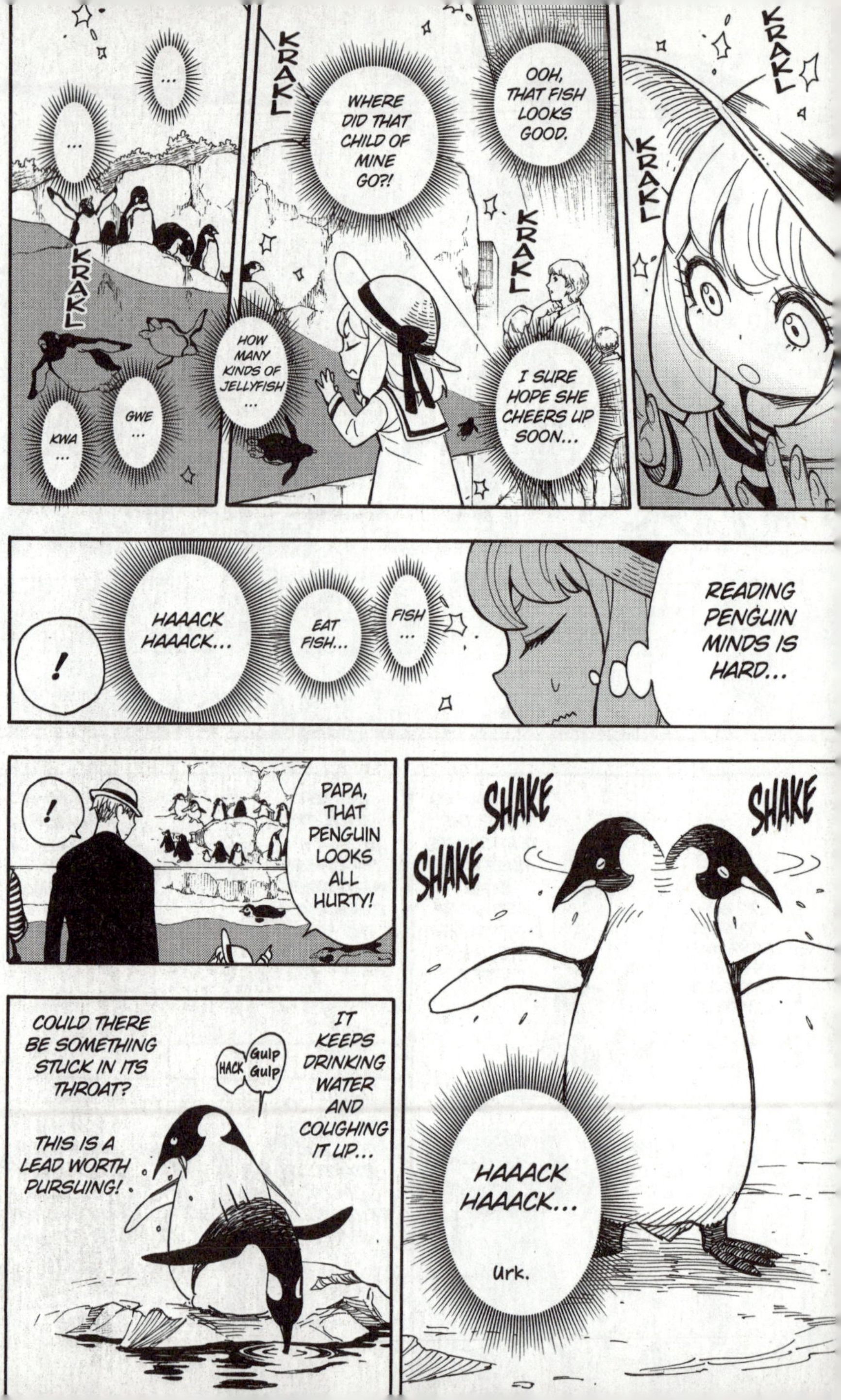
KRAKL
KRAKL
OOH, THAT FISH LOOKS GOOD.
KRAKL
WHERE DID THAT CHILD OF MINE GO?!
KRAKL
I SURE HOPE SHE CHEERS UP SOON...
HOW MANY KINDS OF JELLYFISH...
...
...
KRAKL
GWE...
KWA...
READING PENGUIN MINDS IS HARD...
FISH...
EAT FISH...
HAAACK HAAACK...
!
SHAKE
SHAKE
SHAKE
HAAACK HAAACK...
Urk.
PAPA, THAT PENGUIN LOOKS ALL HURTY!
!
IT KEEPS DRINKING WATER AND COUGHING IT UP...
Gulp Gulp
HACK
COULD THERE BE SOMETHING STUCK IN ITS THROAT?
THIS IS A LEAD WORTH PURSUING!

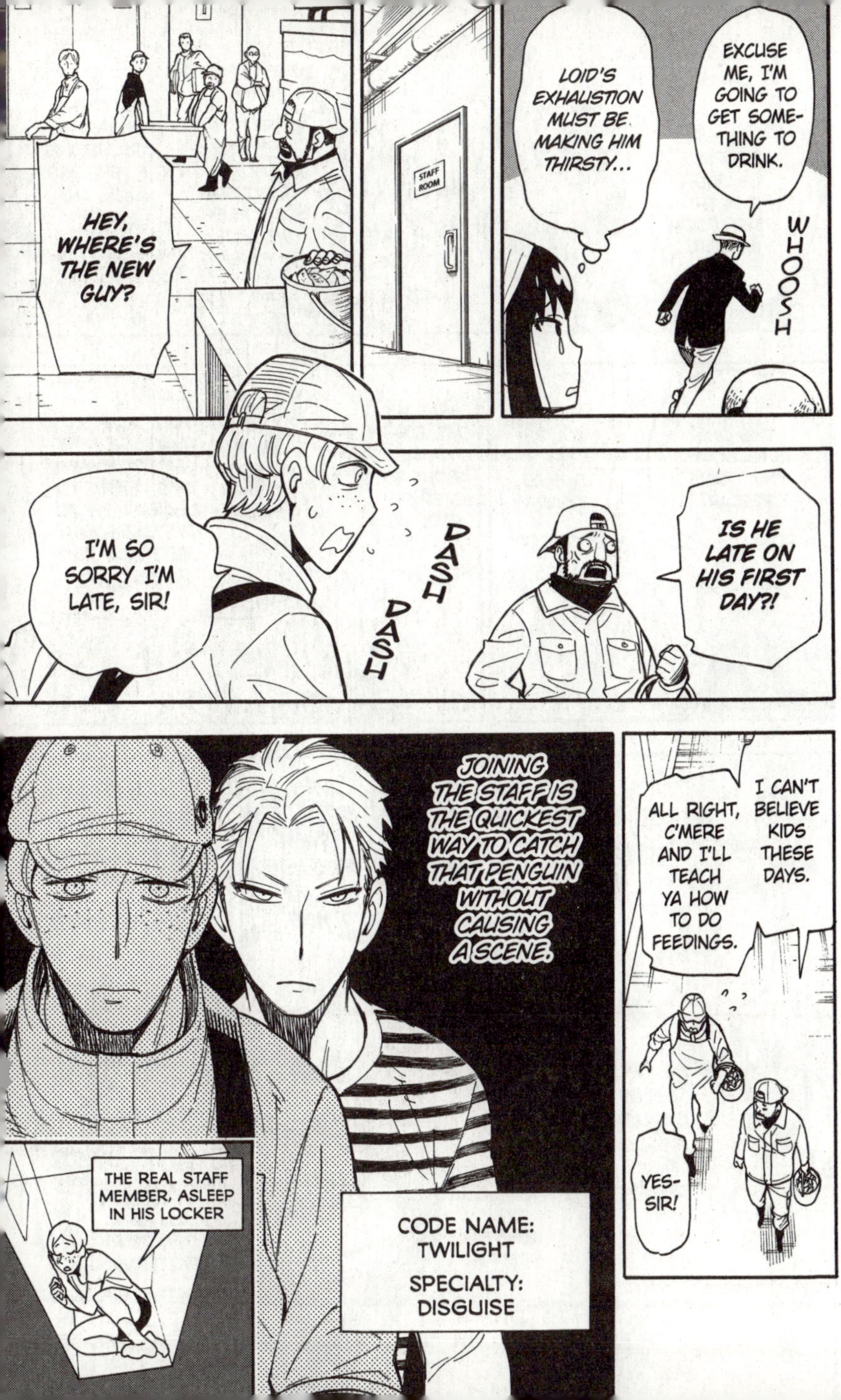
EXCUSE ME, I'M GOING TO GET SOMETHING TO DRINK.
LOID'S EXHAUSTION MUST BE MAKING HIM THIRSTY...
WHOOSH
STAFF ROOM
HEY, WHERE'S THE NEW GUY?
IS HE LATE ON HIS FIRST DAY?!
DASH DASH
I'M SO SORRY I'M LATE, SIR!
I CAN'T BELIEVE KIDS THESE DAYS.
ALL RIGHT, C'MERE AND I'LL TEACH YA HOW TO DO FEEDINGS.
YES-SIR!
JOINING THE STAFF IS THE QUICKEST WAY TO CATCH THAT PENGUIN WITHOUT CAUSING A SCENE.
CODE NAME: TWILIGHT
SPECIALTY: DISGUISE
THE REAL STAFF MEMBER, ASLEEP IN HIS LOCKER

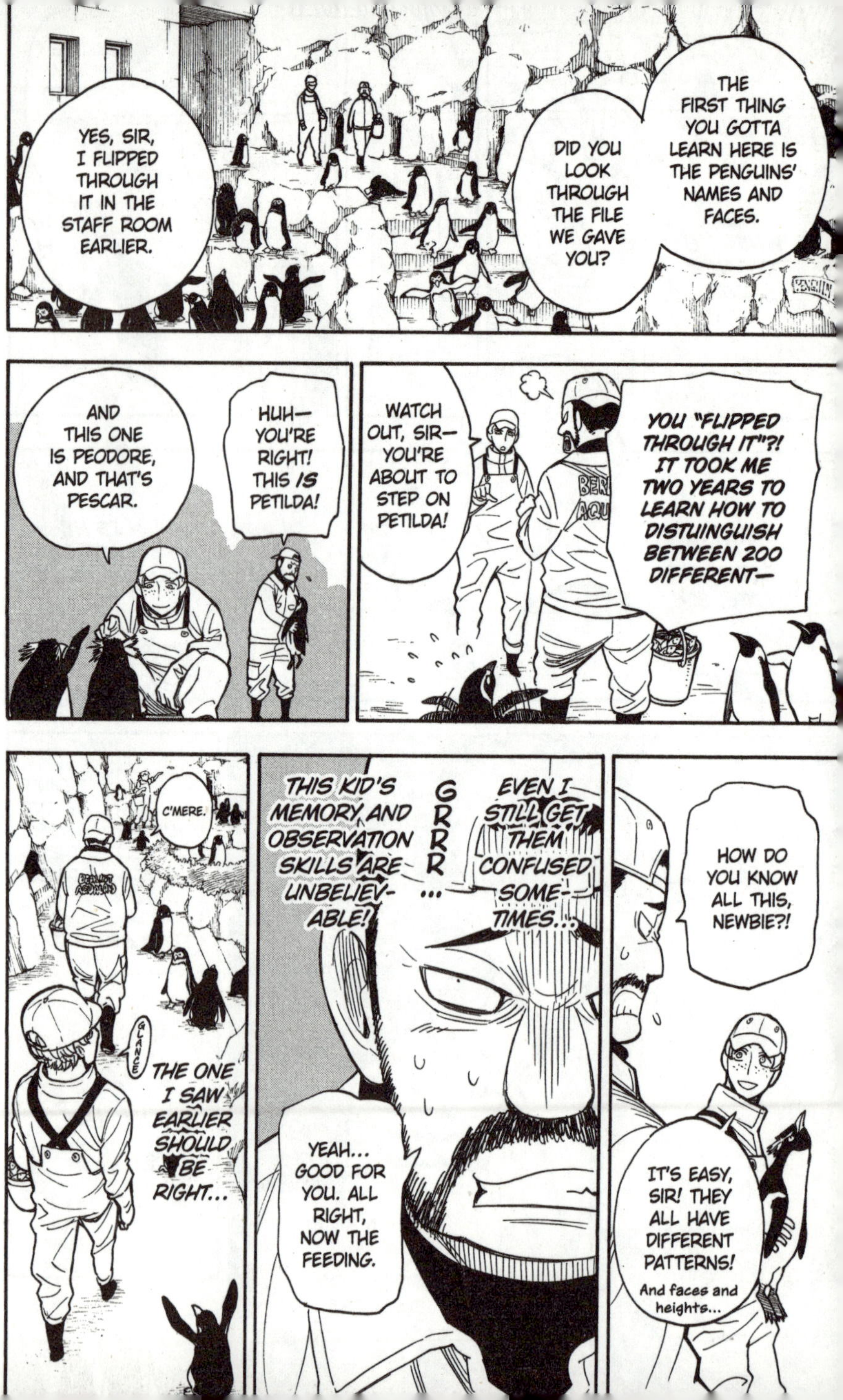
THE FIRST THING YOU GOTTA LEARN HERE IS THE PENGUINS' NAMES AND FACES.
DID YOU LOOK THROUGH THE FILE WE GAVE YOU?
YES, SIR, I FLIPPED THROUGH IT IN THE STAFF ROOM EARLIER.
YOU "FLIPPED THROUGH IT"?! IT TOOK ME TWO YEARS TO LEARN HOW TO DISTUINGUISH BETWEEN 200 DIFFERENT—
WATCH OUT, SIR—YOU'RE ABOUT TO STEP ON PETILDA!
HUH—YOU'RE RIGHT! THIS *IS* PETILDA!
AND THIS ONE IS PEODORE, AND THAT'S PESCAR.
HOW DO YOU KNOW ALL THIS, NEWBIE?!
IT'S EASY, SIR! THEY ALL HAVE DIFFERENT PATTERNS!
And faces and heights...
EVEN I STILL GET THEM CONFUSED SOMETIMES...
GRRR...
THIS KID'S MEMORY AND OBSERVATION SKILLS ARE UNBELIEVABLE!
YEAH... GOOD FOR YOU. ALL RIGHT, NOW THE FEEDING.
C'MERE.
GLANCE
THE ONE I SAW EARLIER SHOULD BE RIGHT...

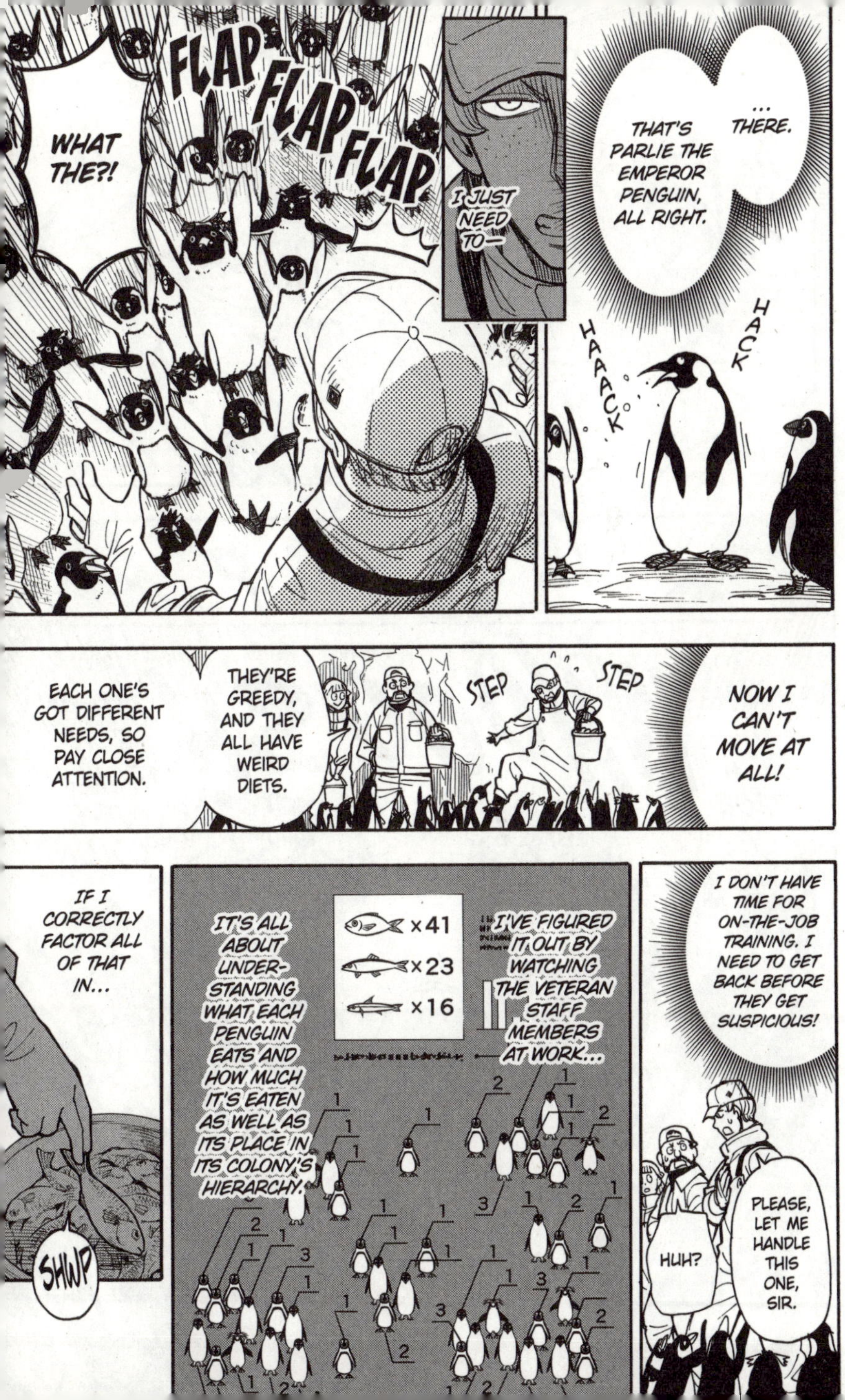
... THERE.
THAT'S PARLIE THE EMPEROR PENGUIN, ALL RIGHT.
HAAAACK
HACK
I JUST NEED TO—
FLAP FLAP FLAP
WHAT THE?!
NOW I CAN'T MOVE AT ALL!
STEP
STEP
THEY'RE GREEDY, AND THEY ALL HAVE WEIRD DIETS.
EACH ONE'S GOT DIFFERENT NEEDS, SO PAY CLOSE ATTENTION.
I DON'T HAVE TIME FOR ON-THE-JOB TRAINING. I NEED TO GET BACK BEFORE THEY GET SUSPICIOUS!
PLEASE, LET ME HANDLE THIS ONE, SIR.
HUH?
I'VE FIGURED IT OUT BY WATCHING THE VETERAN STAFF MEMBERS AT WORK...
×41
×23
×16
IT'S ALL ABOUT UNDERSTANDING WHAT EACH PENGUIN EATS AND HOW MUCH IT'S EATEN AS WELL AS ITS PLACE IN ITS COLONY'S HIERARCHY.
IF I CORRECTLY FACTOR ALL OF THAT IN...
SHWP

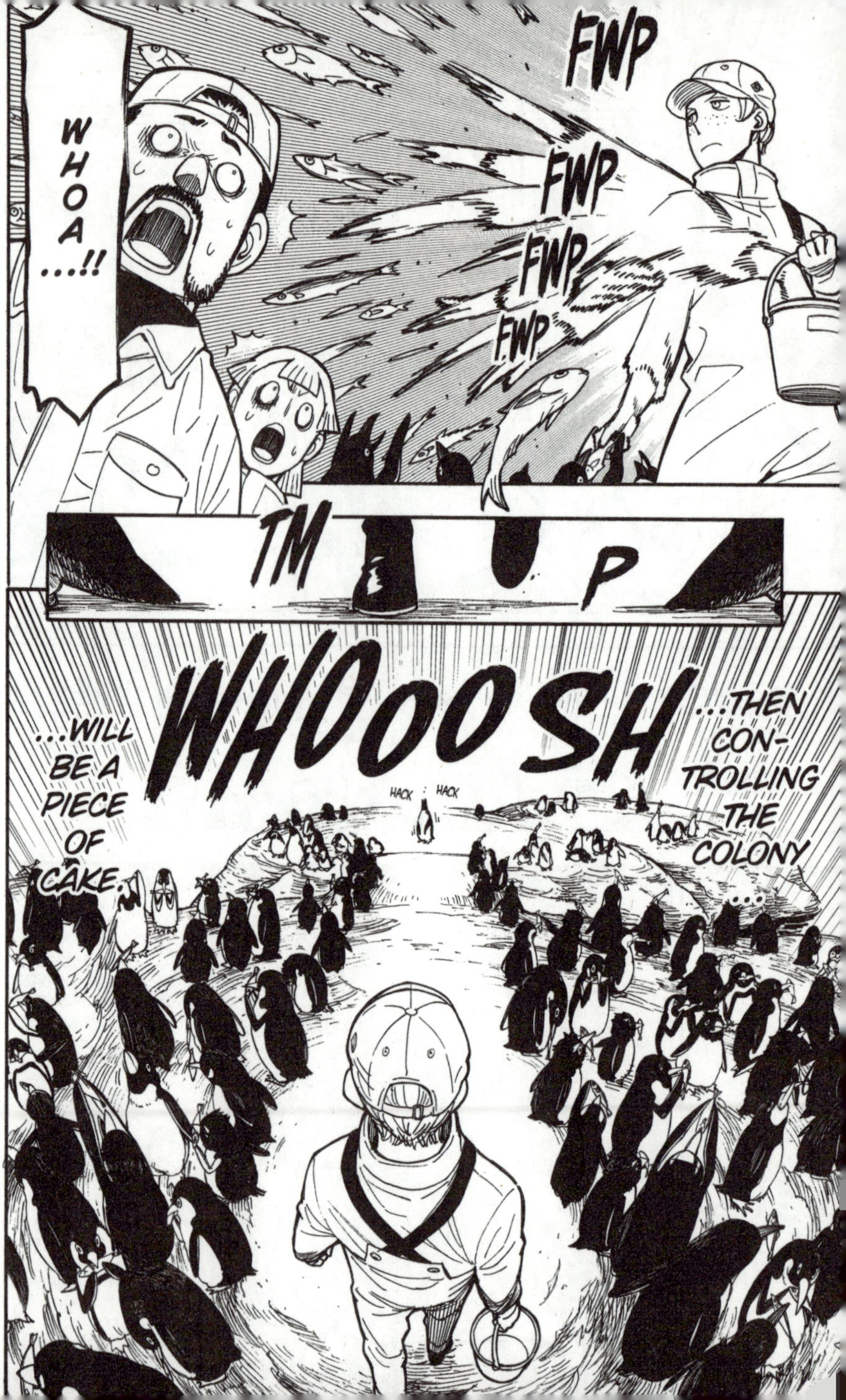
FWP
FWP
FWP
FWP
WHOA...!!
TM
P
...THEN CONTROLLING THE COLONY...
WHOOOSH
HACK
HACK
...WILL BE A PIECE OF CAKE.

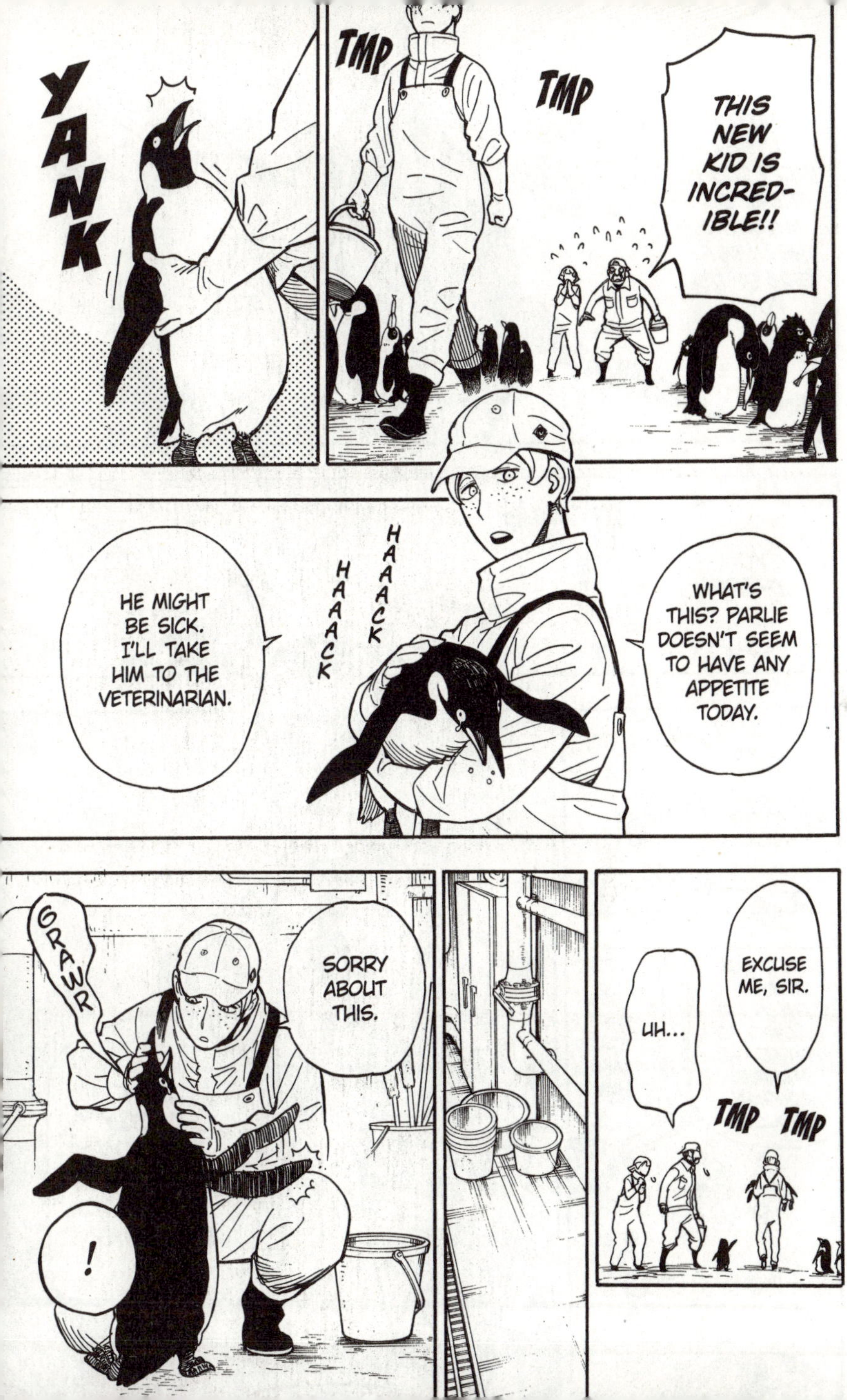
THIS NEW KID IS INCREDIBLE!!
TMP
TMP
YANK
WHAT'S THIS? PARLIE DOESN'T SEEM TO HAVE ANY APPETITE TODAY.
HAAACK
HAAACK
HE MIGHT BE SICK. I'LL TAKE HIM TO THE VETERINARIAN.
EXCUSE ME, SIR.
UH...
TMP
TMP
SORRY ABOUT THIS.
GRAWR
!

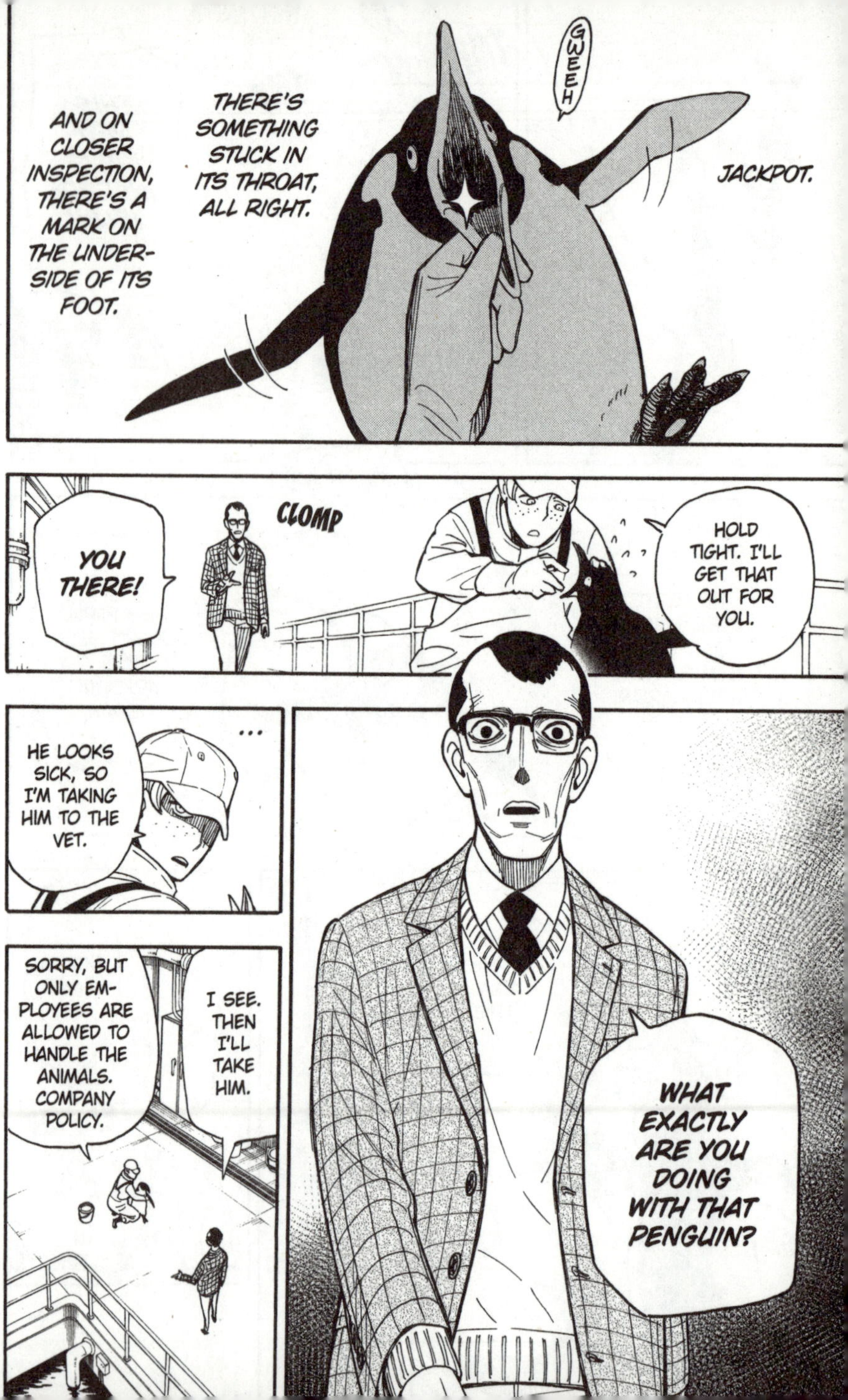
JACKPOT.
GWEEH
THERE'S SOMETHING STUCK IN ITS THROAT, ALL RIGHT.
AND ON CLOSER INSPECTION, THERE'S A MARK ON THE UNDER-SIDE OF ITS FOOT.
HOLD TIGHT. I'LL GET THAT OUT FOR YOU.
CLOMP
YOU THERE!
WHAT EXACTLY ARE YOU DOING WITH THAT PENGUIN?
...
HE LOOKS SICK, SO I'M TAKING HIM TO THE VET.
I SEE. THEN I'LL TAKE HIM.
SORRY, BUT ONLY EM-PLOYEES ARE ALLOWED TO HANDLE THE ANIMALS. COMPANY POLICY.

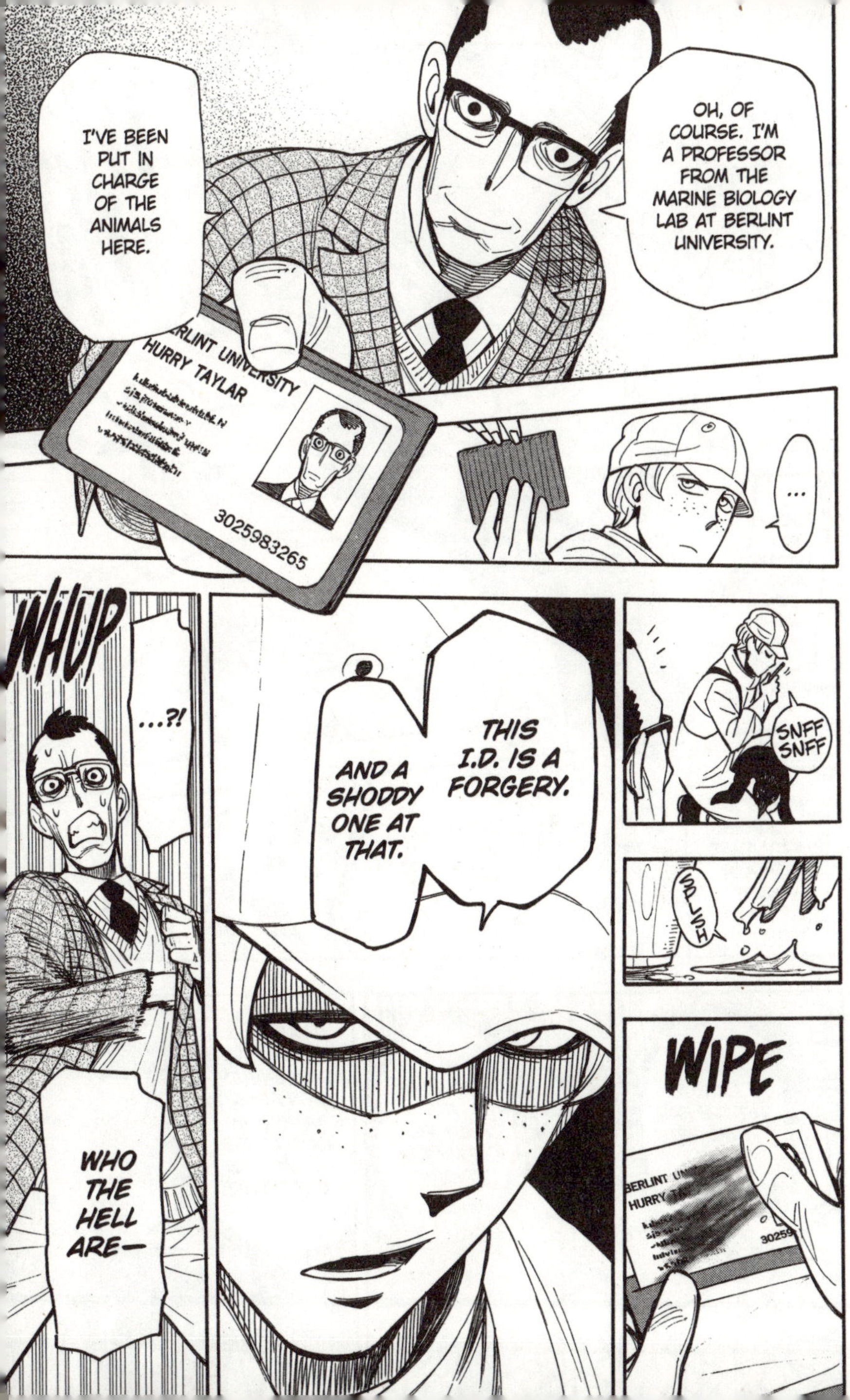
OH, OF COURSE. I'M A PROFESSOR FROM THE MARINE BIOLOGY LAB AT BERLINT UNIVERSITY.
I'VE BEEN PUT IN CHARGE OF THE ANIMALS HERE.
BERLINT UNIVERSITY
HURRY TAYLAR
3025983265
...
SNFF SNFF
SPLSH
WIPE
BERLINT UN
HURRY TA
30259
THIS I.D. IS A FORGERY.
AND A SHODDY ONE AT THAT.
WHUP
...?!
WHO THE HELL ARE—

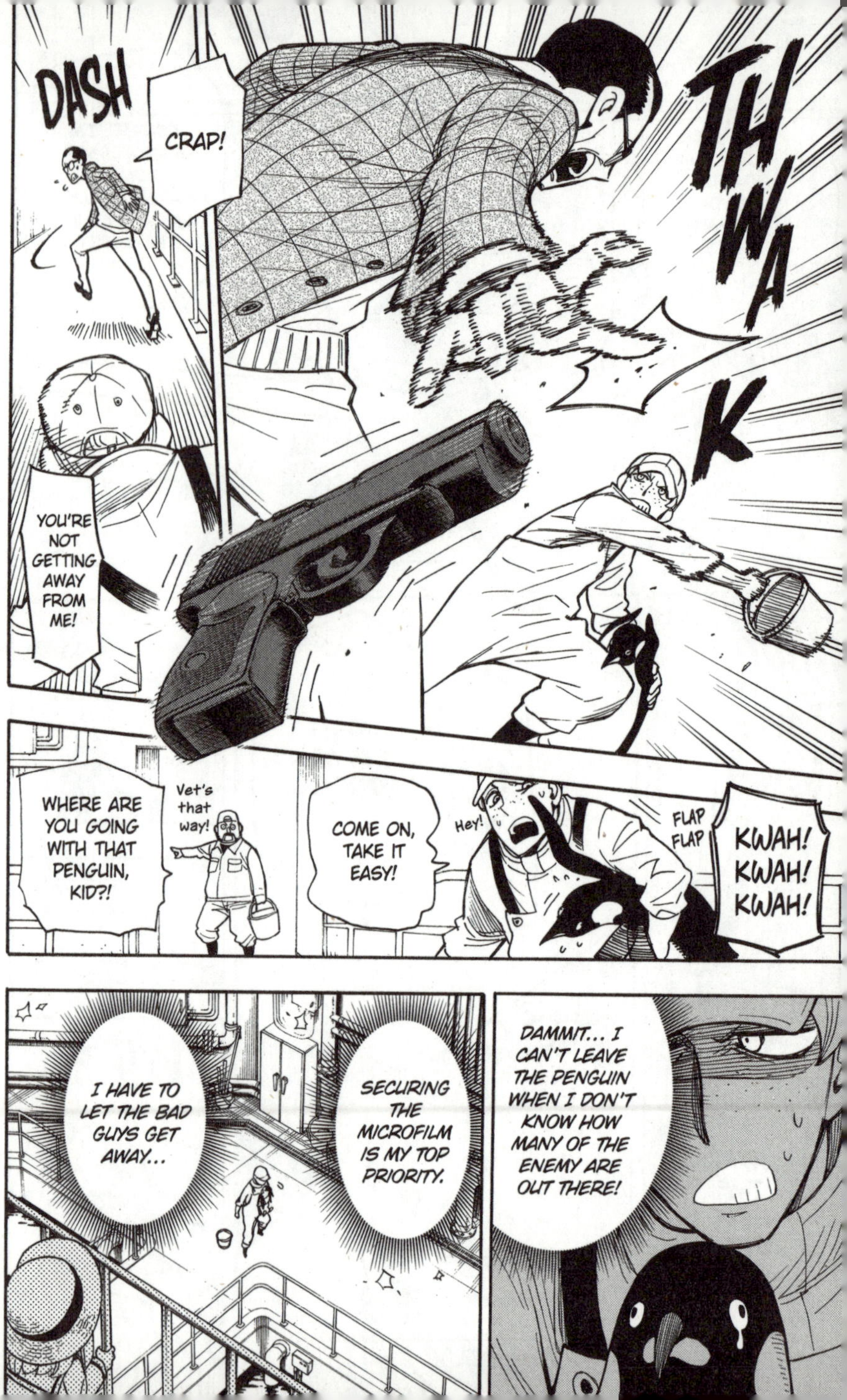
THWAK
DASH
CRAP!
YOU'RE NOT GETTING AWAY FROM ME!
KWAH! KWAH! KWAH!
FLAP FLAP
Hey!
COME ON, TAKE IT EASY!
Vet's that way!
WHERE ARE YOU GOING WITH THAT PENGUIN, KID?!
DAMMIT... I CAN'T LEAVE THE PENGUIN WHEN I DON'T KNOW HOW MANY OF THE ENEMY ARE OUT THERE!
SECURING THE MICROFILM IS MY TOP PRIORITY.
I HAVE TO LET THE BAD GUYS GET AWAY...

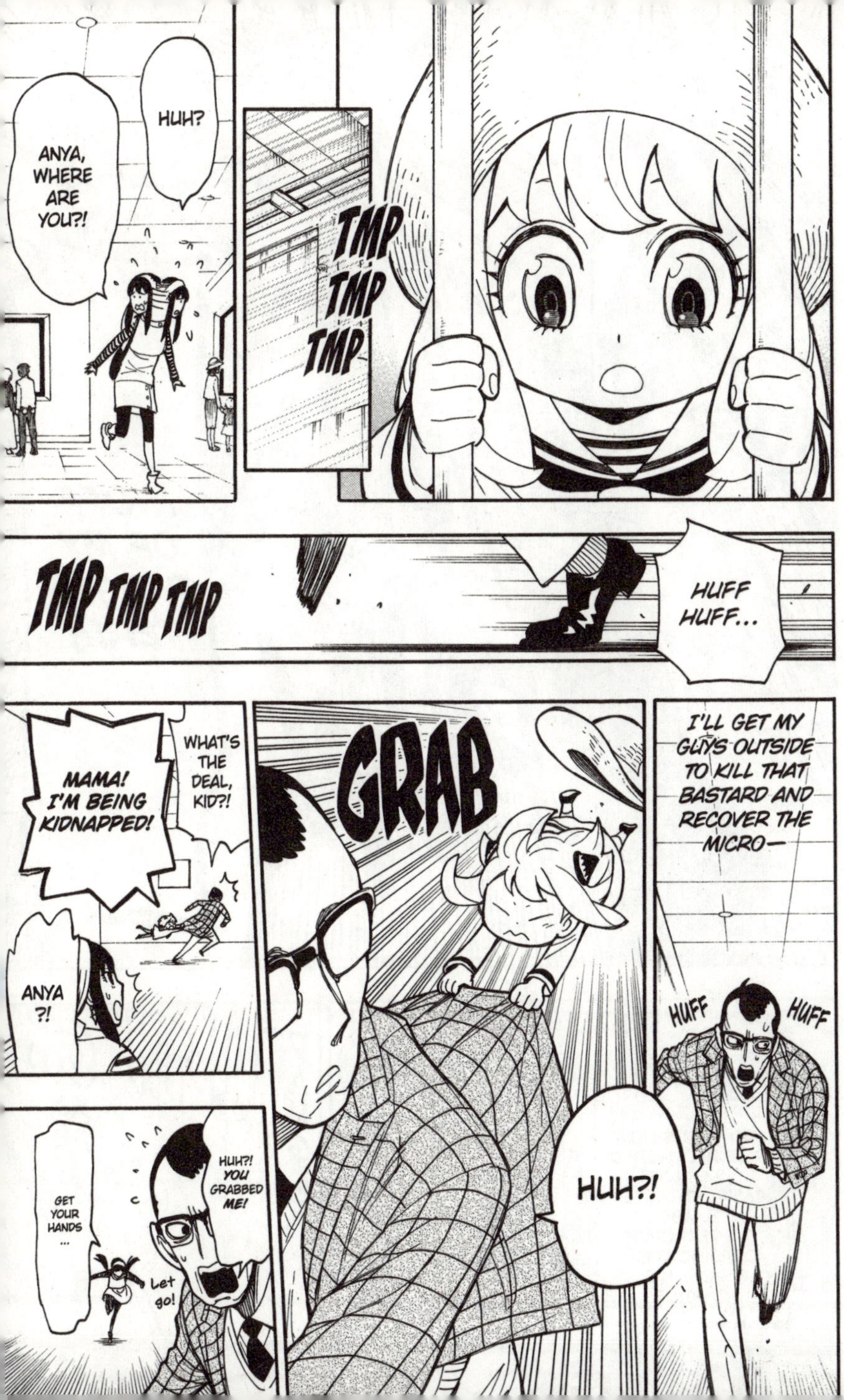
TMP
TMP
TMP
HUH?
ANYA, WHERE ARE YOU?!
HUFF HUFF...
TMP TMP TMP
I'LL GET MY GUYS OUTSIDE TO KILL THAT BASTARD AND RECOVER THE MICRO—
HUFF
HUFF
GRAB
HUH?!
WHAT'S THE DEAL, KID?!
MAMA! I'M BEING KIDNAPPED!
ANYA ?!
HUH?! YOU GRABBED ME!
GET YOUR HANDS ...
Let go!

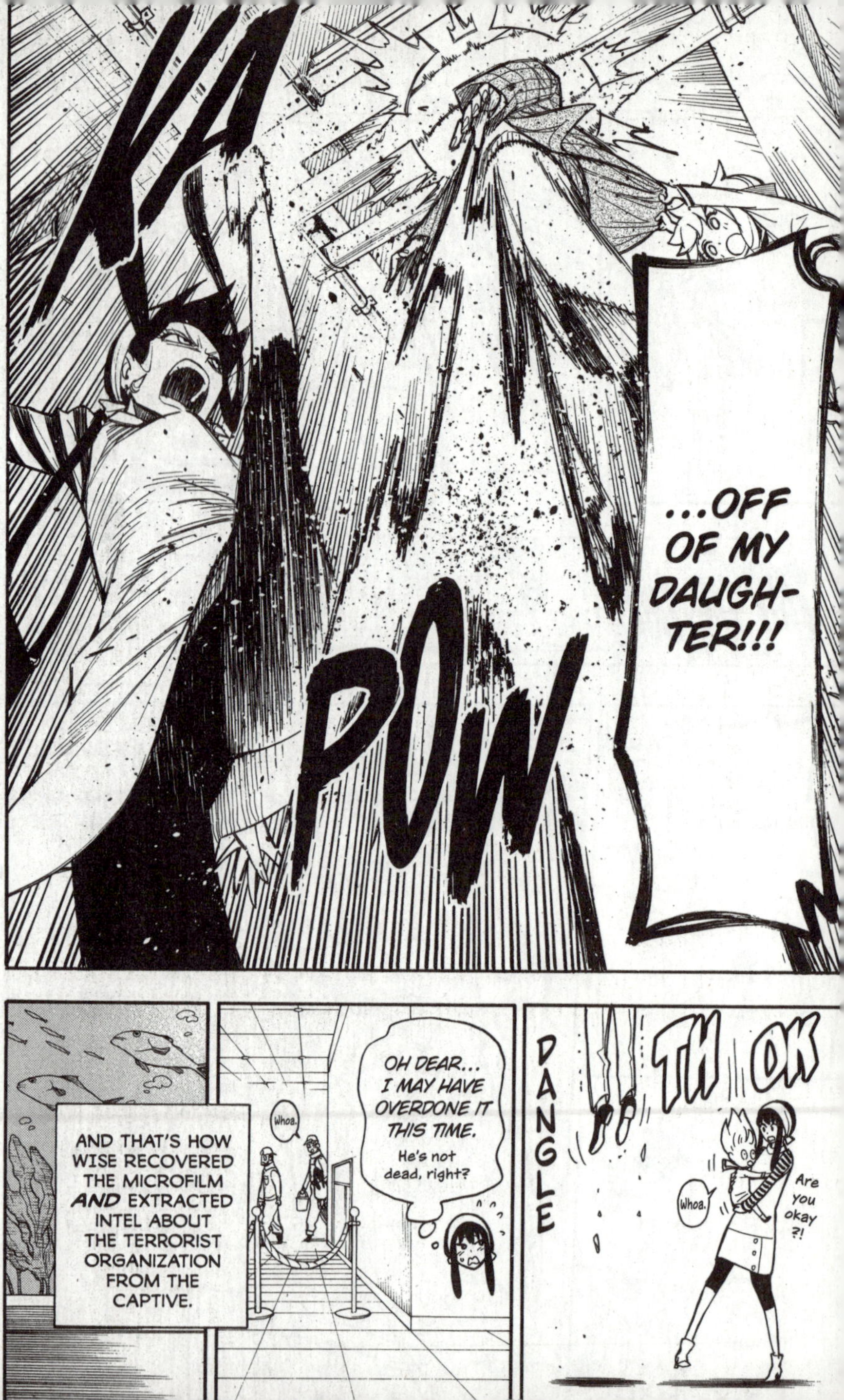
...OFF OF MY DAUGH-TER!!!
POW
DANGLE
TH OK
Whoa.
Are you okay?!
OH DEAR... I MAY HAVE OVERDONE IT THIS TIME.
He's not dead, right?
Whoa.
AND THAT'S HOW WISE RECOVERED THE MICROFILM *AND* EXTRACTED INTEL ABOUT THE TERRORIST ORGANIZATION FROM THE CAPTIVE.

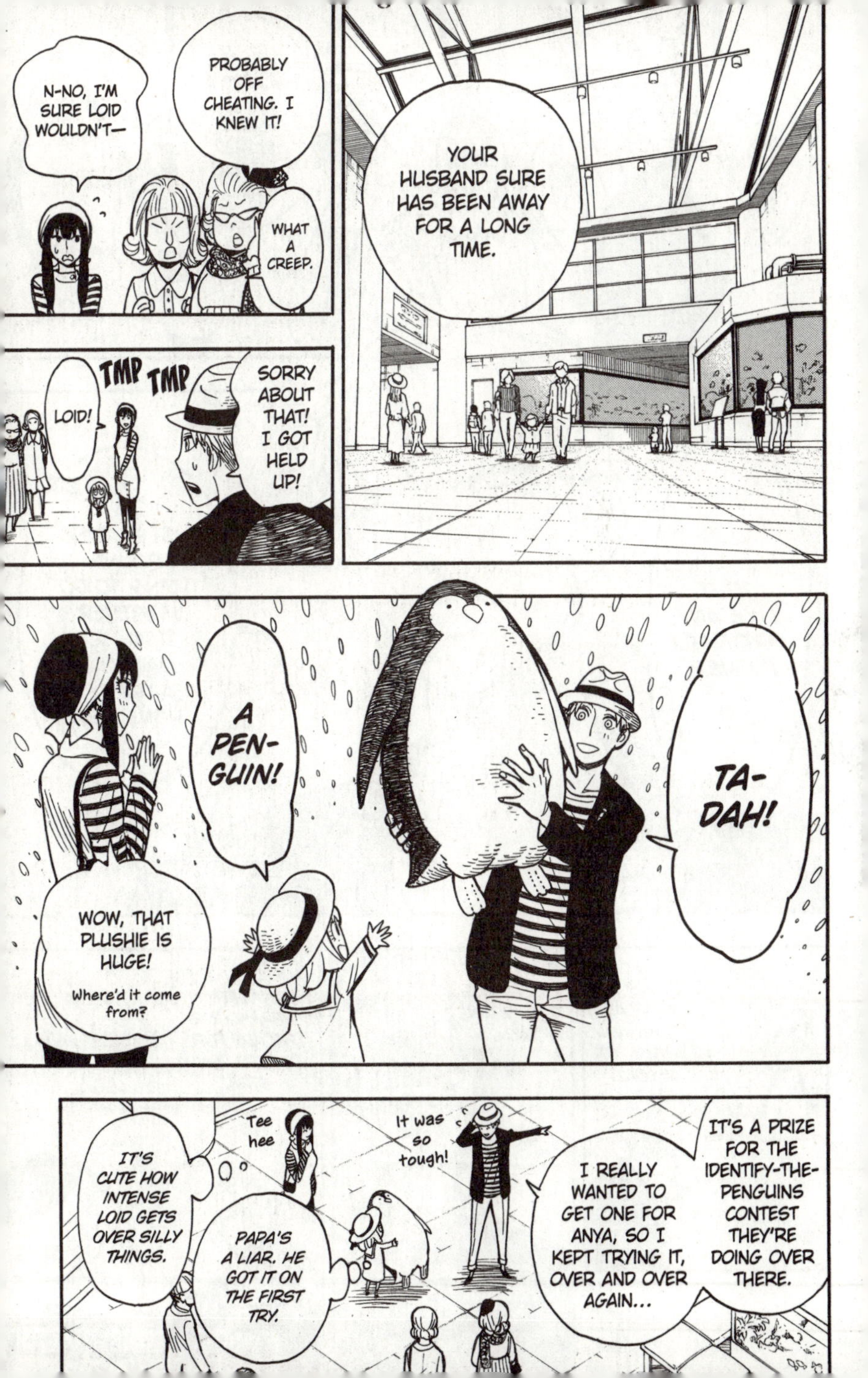

YOUR HUSBAND SURE HAS BEEN AWAY FOR A LONG TIME.
PROBABLY OFF CHEATING. I KNEW IT!
WHAT A CREEP.
N-NO, I'M SURE LOID WOULDN'T—
SORRY ABOUT THAT! I GOT HELD UP!
TMP TMP
LOID!
TA-DAH!
A PEN-GUIN!
WOW, THAT PLUSHIE IS HUGE!
Where'd it come from?
IT'S A PRIZE FOR THE IDENTIFY-THE-PENGUINS CONTEST THEY'RE DOING OVER THERE.
I REALLY WANTED TO GET ONE FOR ANYA, SO I KEPT TRYING IT, OVER AND OVER AGAIN...
It was so tough!
Tee hee
PAPA'S A LIAR. HE GOT IT ON THE FIRST TRY.
IT'S CUTE HOW INTENSE LOID GETS OVER SILLY THINGS.

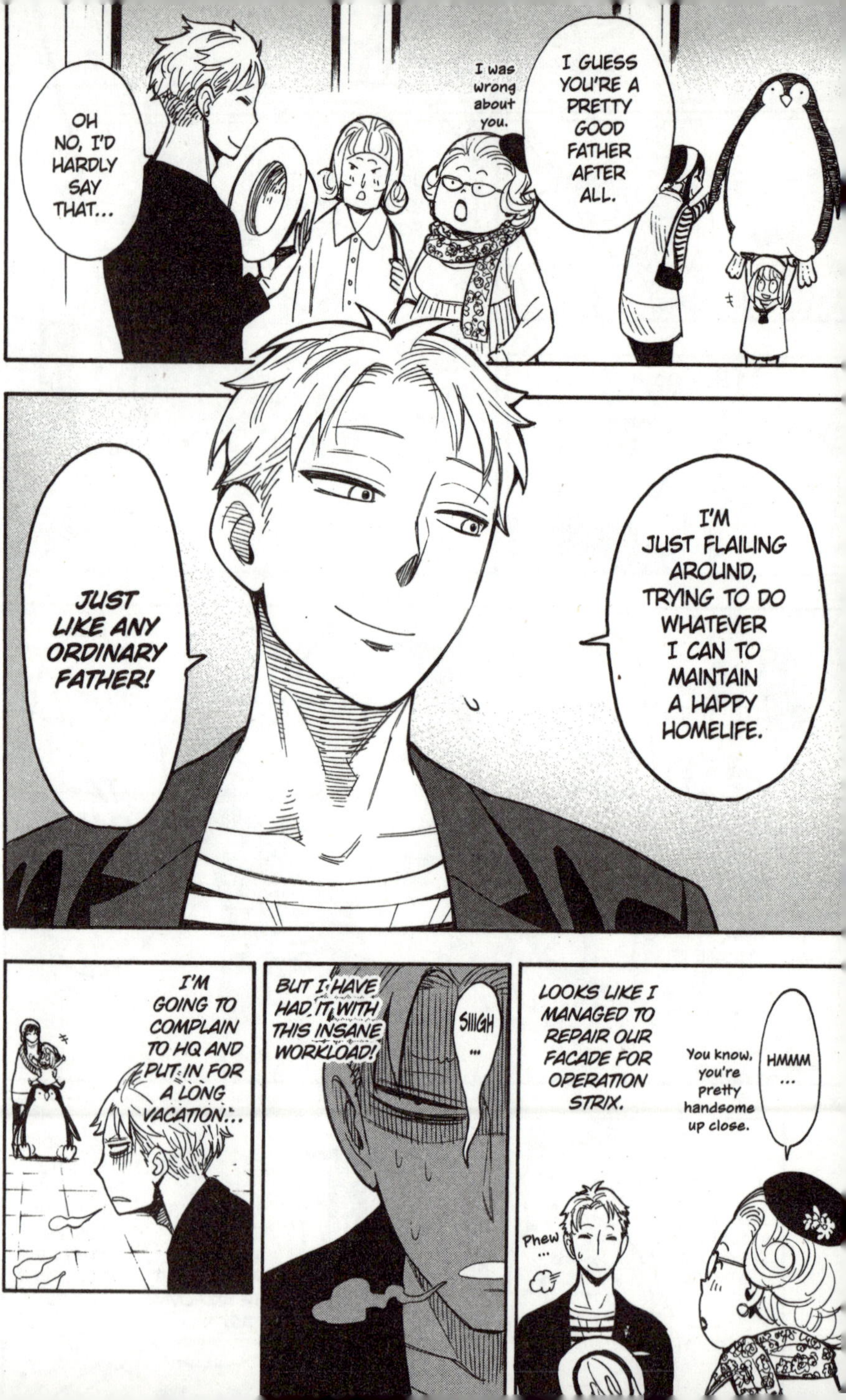
I GUESS YOU'RE A PRETTY GOOD FATHER AFTER ALL.
I was wrong about you.
OH NO, I'D HARDLY SAY THAT...
I'M JUST FLAILING AROUND, TRYING TO DO WHATEVER I CAN TO MAINTAIN A HAPPY HOMELIFE.
JUST LIKE ANY ORDINARY FATHER!
HMMM...
You know, you're pretty handsome up close.
LOOKS LIKE I MANAGED TO REPAIR OUR FACADE FOR OPERATION STRIX.
Phew...
SIIIGH...
BUT I HAVE HAD IT WITH THIS INSANE WORKLOAD!
I'M GOING TO COMPLAIN TO HQ AND PUT IN FOR A LONG VACATION...

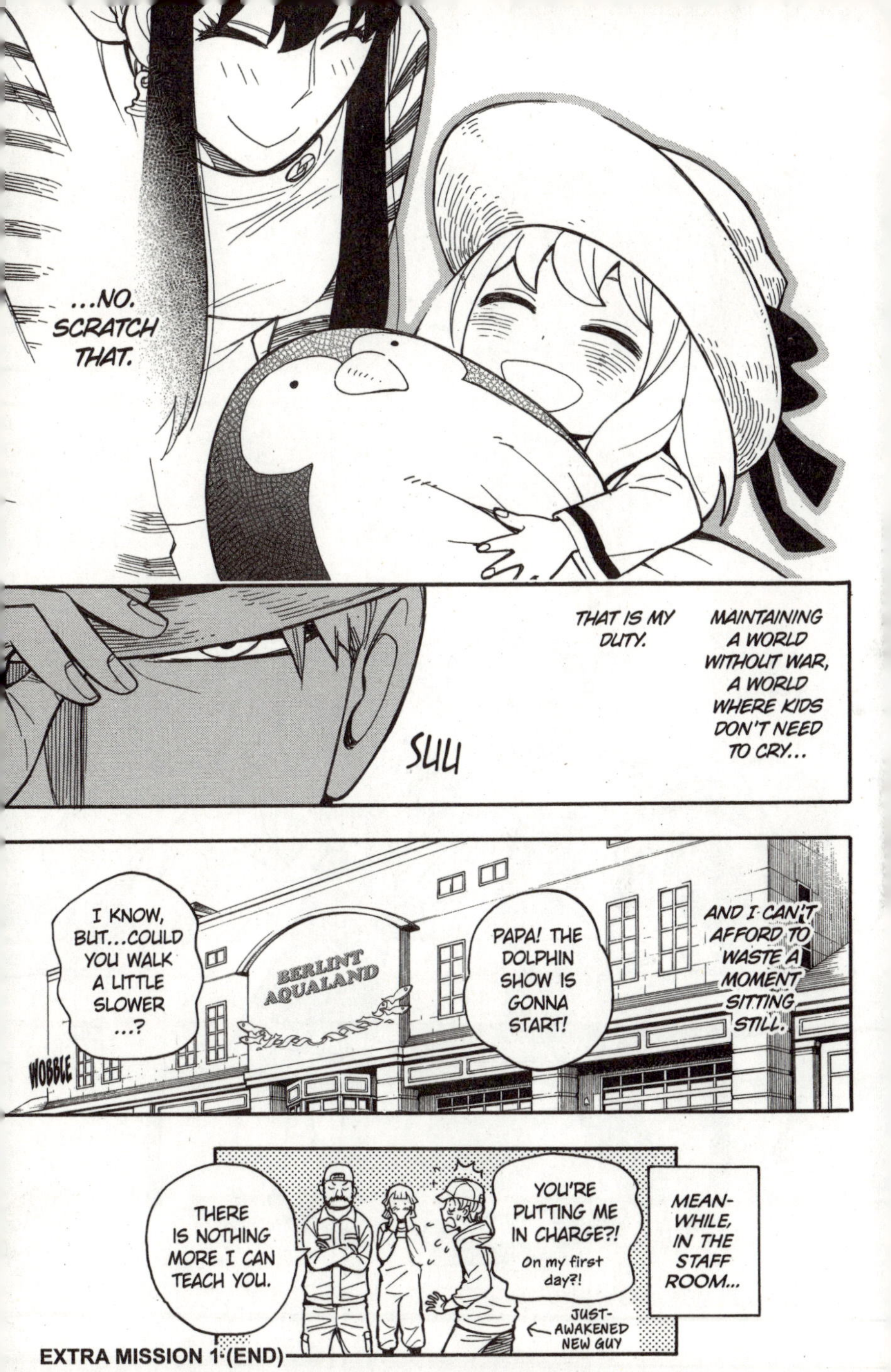
...NO. SCRATCH THAT.
MAINTAINING A WORLD WITHOUT WAR, A WORLD WHERE KIDS DON'T NEED TO CRY...
THAT IS MY DUTY.
SUU
AND I CAN'T AFFORD TO WASTE A MOMENT SITTING STILL.
PAPA! THE DOLPHIN SHOW IS GONNA START!
BERLINT AQUALAND
I KNOW, BUT...COULD YOU WALK A LITTLE SLOWER ...?
WOBBLE
MEAN-WHILE, IN THE STAFF ROOM...
YOU'RE PUTTING ME IN CHARGE?! On my first day?!
JUST-AWAKENED NEW GUY
THERE IS NOTHING MORE I CAN TEACH YOU.

EXTRA MISSION 1 (END)

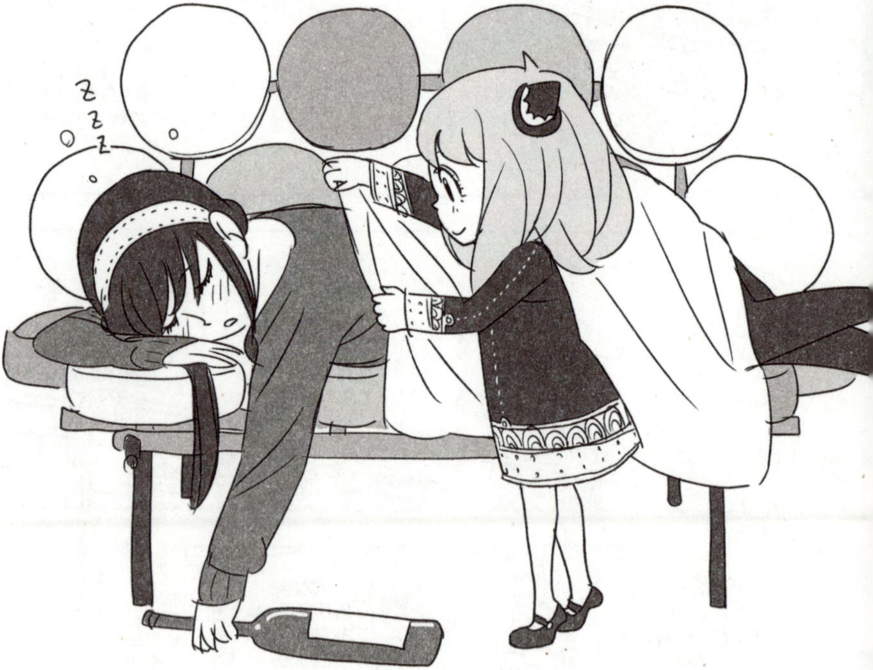
ZZZ

Anya's Favorite Things

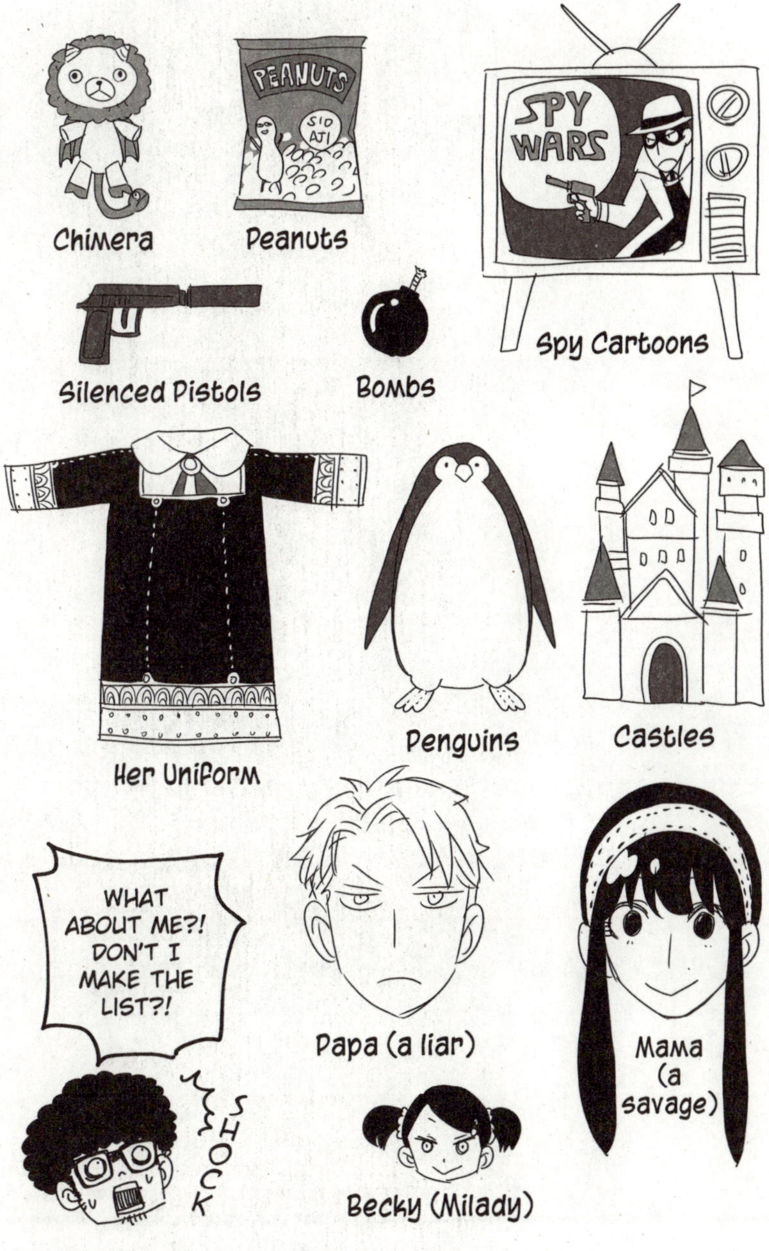
SPY WARS
Spy Cartoons
PEANUTS
SIO AJI
Peanuts
Chimera
Bombs
Silenced Pistols
Castles
Penguins
Her Uniform
Mama (a savage)
Papa (a liar)
WHAT ABOUT ME?! DON'T I MAKE THE LIST?!
Becky (Milady)
SHOCK

It's been suggested that spying is the world's second-oldest profession. As both perpetrators and victims of deception, spies have colored human history with their lies.

I myself spread misinformation on a daily basis, such as when I tell my editor, "I'll get those pages in to you today for sure!"

—TATSUYA ENDO

Tatsuya Endo was born in Ibaraki Prefecture, Japan, on July 23, 1980. He debuted as a manga artist with the one-shot "Seibu Yugi" (Western Game), which ran in the Spring 2000 issue of *Akamaru Jump*. He is the author of *TISTA* and *Gekka Bijin* (Moon Flower Beauty). *Spy x Family* is his first work published in English.

SPY×FAMILY ②

SHONEN JUMP Edition

STORY AND ART BY TATSUYA ENDO

Translation **CASEY LOE**

Touch-Up Art & Lettering **RINA MAPA**

Design **JIMMY PRESLER**

Editor **AMY YU**

SPY x FAMILY © 2019 by Tatsuya Endo
All rights reserved.
First published in Japan in 2019 by SHUEISHA Inc., Tokyo.
English translation rights arranged by SHUEISHA Inc.

The stories, characters and incidents mentioned in this
publication are entirely fictional.

Printed in Italy

Published by VIZ Media, LLC
P.O. Box 77010
San Francisco, CA 94107

10 9 8 7
First printing, September 2020
Seventh printing, April 2022

VIZ MEDIA

viz.com

SHONEN JUMP

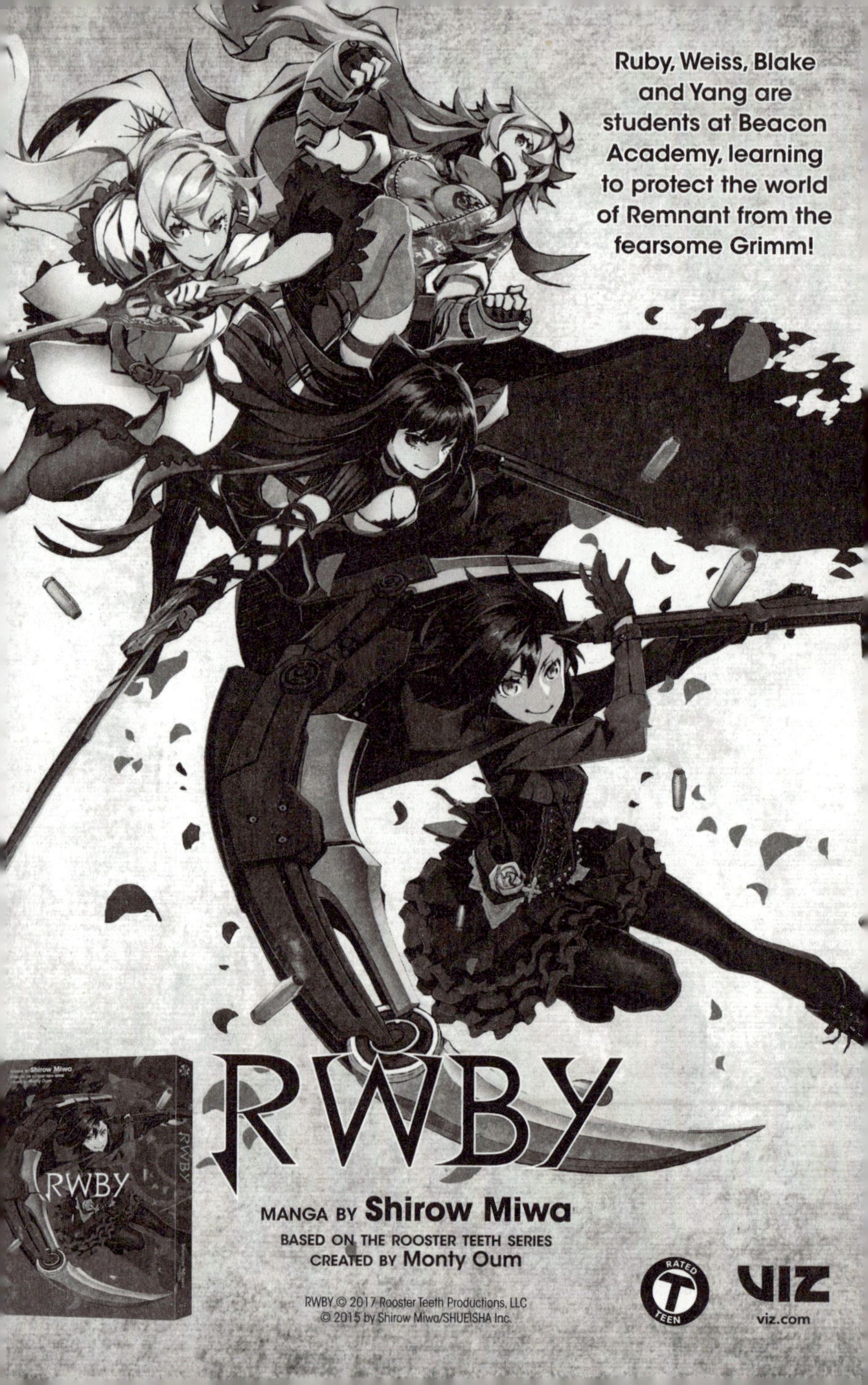
Ruby, Weiss, Blake and Yang are students at Beacon Academy, learning to protect the world of Remnant from the fearsome Grimm!
RWBY
MANGA BY Shirow Miwa
BASED ON THE ROOSTER TEETH SERIES
CREATED BY Monty Oum
RWBY © 2017 Rooster Teeth Productions, LLC
© 2015 by Shirow Miwa/SHUEISHA Inc.
RATED T TEEN
VIZ
viz.com